GLORIA CHUKWUMA

Raising Up the Next Generation for the Church Life

Lessons and Ministry Excerpts
for Those Serving with Children
and Young People

Compiled from the Ministry of
Watchman Nee and Witness Lee

Living Stream Ministry
Anaheim, CA • www.lsm.org

First Edition, May 2011.

ISBN 978-0-7363-4709-9

Published by

Living Stream Ministry
2431 W. La Palma Ave., Anaheim, CA 92801 U.S.A.
P. O. Box 2121, Anaheim, CA 92814 U.S.A.

Printed in the United States of America

11   12   13   14   15   16   /   9   8   7   6   5   4   3   2   1

CONTENTS

FOREWORD

The Lord surely loves and cares for our children and young people, and His good intention for them is that they would become the next generation in His move. Throughout history He has depended on the faithful labor of His saints to raise up the next generation, mainly their own children, for the continuation of His divine economy on the earth. For this reason the Bible offers substantial help to God's people about raising up the next generation. It is no wonder, therefore, that those who have taken the lead in the ministry among us, Brothers Watchman Nee and Witness Lee, paid careful attention to this matter. The materials that compose this book are drawn from the numerous places in their ministry where they offer fellowship about taking care of our children and young people with a view to their becoming the next generation in His glorious move on the earth.

The published ministry of Brother Nee and Brother Lee is prolific, comprising hundreds of titles and tens of thousands of pages. Thus, while the over four hundred pages of this compilation may seem massive, in relation to the whole of their ministry this line in their fellowship is not actually a major one. As will be seen in the pages to follow, most of their help on this topic comes from excerpts scattered throughout their ministry. If the excerpts are examined in their original contexts, it will easily be seen that most often our brothers offer us help on children and young people as supplemental points to their more central lines of fellowship. Of course, there are a few publications in their ministry where they focused on caring for our children and young people (for example, Brother Lee's *How to Lead the Young People*), but it would not be correct to say that this was a focus of their ministry. Rather, viewed in the whole context of their ministry, their fellowship on children and young people falls squarely within that third line of truth from the Bible, what Brother Lee called "the leaves and the branches," bearing less importance than the former two lines, what he called the central line and the line of supplemental points. While both Brother Nee and Brother Lee often shared on "the leaves and the branches," they did so to bring us all into the central line of the divine revelation, and the original contexts of these excerpts will fully bear this out. (For Brother Lee's fellowship on the lines in the divine revelation of the Bible, see *International Training for Elders and Responsible Ones, Spring 2011: The Central Line of the Bible,* Message 1.)

That being the case, it is with some concern and caution that Living Stream Ministry, as publisher of the ministry of Brother Nee and Brother Lee, offers this compilation to the churches and the saints. In making something of "the leaves and the branches" the focus of so substantial a publication as this, we do not wish to distract any of the dear saints or churches from the central line of the Bible. We sincerely hope that no one among us will make the substance of this book his or her central line or even the focus of his or her ministry among the saints. We hope that all the saints and all the churches everywhere will be just as Brother Nee and Brother Lee were, focused on and laboring for the central line among us, especially when they touched "the leaves and the branches." Of course, some have been called to serve primarily among our children and young people, and we know that such a service is of the Lord and to the Lord. But we certainly feel that all of us should conduct our service so as to lead all in our care to apprehend and experience the central line in the Bible. We further hope that no one among us will use the precious fellowship of our brothers in this book to insist on ways to conduct the children's and young people's work among us. As part of "the leaves and the branches," this fellowship is not to be insisted on, even though we firmly believe that it presents the best guidance for raising up the next generation for the church life. But while we have these concerns, we also have the firm conviction that all the saints in the local churches everywhere will exercise the very same caution that is expressed here, and we are certain that the mere mention of these concerns serves as a sufficient reminder of the pure intention of us all to remain faithful to the central line of truth in the Bible.

Finally, it should be noted that because the fellowship in this book comprises many excerpts from numerous publications, there was the need of organizing and summarizing the content. This will be seen in the lesson outlines that precede each group of excerpts. These outlines, which faithfully crystallize the content of their following excerpts, were composed by a group of blended saints who serve among our children and young people. We are sincerely grateful to them for their labor before the Lord and expect that all the readers of this book will be equally so. We thank the Lord for His grace to them in this labor.

May the Lord use the fellowship in this book to indeed raise up the next generations for the church life.

April 25, 2011   The editorial section
                                              Living Stream Ministry

PART ONE:

INTRODUCTION

VESSELS UNTO HONOR
FOR GOD'S ETERNAL ECONOMY

Scripture Reading: Eph. 3:8-11; Gen. 2:7; Psa. 8:3-4; Ezek. 1:5; Rom. 9:21, 23; 2 Cor. 4:6-7; 2 Kings 4:1-6

I. We need a vision of God's New Testament economy—the desire of God's heart to dispense Himself into His chosen people in His trinity for the producing of the church, which is the kingdom of God that will consummate in the New Jerusalem as the eternal expression of the Triune God—Luke 10:42; John 3:5-6, 14-16; Eph. 2:1-10; 3:8-11.

II. The entire economy of God, and especially that in the New Testament age, is a matter of dispensing; God's creation of man is in the view of the divine dispensing according to the divine economy—Gen. 1:26-27; 2:7; Eph. 1:9-10; 3:8-11:

A. God's New Testament economy is a plan made by God according to His good pleasure; God's good pleasure, His longing, His aspiration, is to dispense Himself into His chosen people—1:9-10.

B. Romans 9:21 discloses God's purpose in creating man; we need to be deeply impressed with the fact that we are God's containers and that He is our content—Gen. 2:7; Acts 9:15.

C. God's selection in His sovereign mercy has a goal, and this goal is to have many vessels to contain God and express Him eternally—v. 15; 2 Tim. 2:20-21:

1. He created us in such a way that we are able to take Him into us and contain Him as our life and life supply—Gen. 2:7, 9.

2. He created us so that we may be one with Him

to express what He is and that He may be glorified in us and with us—John 13:31; 2 Thes. 1:12.

  D. It is not a small matter to be a man; we need to see how glorious and how marvelous it is that we are men—Psa. 8:3-4; Ezek. 1:5:

    1. It is absolutely right to say that the Bible is a book full of Christ, yet we can also say that the Bible is a book full of men—even God Himself became a man—John 1:1, 14; Acts 7:56.

    2. Man is the center of God's plan: if the hub, the center, of a bicycle wheel is taken away, the spokes will collapse; likewise, without man as the center, God's plan would collapse—Gen. 1:26-28, 31; Zech. 12:1.

III. "Does not the potter have authority over the clay to make out of the same lump one vessel unto honor and another unto dishonor...in order that He might make known the riches of His glory upon vessels of mercy, which He had before prepared unto glory"—Rom. 9:21, 23; 2 Tim. 2:20-21; 2 Cor. 4:7:

  A. As vessels, we are not instruments or weapons— we are containers; the believers in Christ are vessels of mercy unto honor and glory—Rom. 9:11-13, 16, 20-21, 23; Judg. 9:9; 1 Sam. 2:30.

  B. Mercy, honor, and glory are actually the Triune God—Lam. 3:21-23; Heb. 2:9; Acts 7:2; Eph. 2:4; 1 Cor. 2:8:

    1. In the initial stage of our experience the Triune God is our mercy—Eph. 2:4.

    2. In the progressing stage of our experience the Triune God is our honor—Heb. 2:9.

    3. In the completing stage of our experience the Triune God is our glory—Rom. 5:2.

  C. Romans 9 reveals that the climax of our usefulness to God is that we are vessels to contain Him and express Him; we are His container and His expression, and He is our content and our life; He lives in us that we may live Him.

IV. "If therefore anyone cleanses himself from these, he

will be a vessel unto honor, sanctified, useful to the master, prepared unto every good work"—2 Tim. 2:21:

A. The believers are vessels unto honor with Christ as their treasure through regeneration; they are containers of honor because Christ Himself is honor; He is the treasure within them—2 Cor. 4:6-7.

B. Honor is the preciousness related to Jesus' worth— 1 Pet. 2:7; Heb. 2:9.

C. These four items together would make Timothy a vessel unto honor according to a certain standard— 2 Tim. 2:21:

1. The word *honor* is related to our nature.

2. The word *sanctified* indicates our position.

3. The word *useful* implies the matter of our function.

4. The word *prepared* reveals the matter of our training.

D. A vessel unto honor has to meet a certain standard that it may contain a specific object of honor— 1 Thes. 5:23:

1. Honorable vessels are of both the divine nature (gold) and the redeemed and regenerated human nature (silver); these, like Timothy and other genuine believers, constitute the firm foundation to hold the truth—2 Tim. 2:19-20; 1 Tim. 3:15.

2. Dishonorable vessels are of the fallen human nature (wood and earth); Hymenaeus, Philetus, and other false believers are of these—2 Tim. 2:17; Matt. 13:31-32.

E. To cleanse ourselves is to "depart from unrighteousness," as an outward evidence of the inward divine nature—2 Tim. 2:19, 21.

V. When God bestows grace on the church, He needs vessels; there is the need for more Timothys to be raised up—2 Kings 4:1-6; 2 Tim. 2:2; 3:17:

A. When a potter turns his wheel and molds his vessels, some become damaged before they even reach the fire; they do not even pass the formative stage; this is a loss—Jer. 18:1-6.

B. It is true that we can save men from the world, but
there is a greater need for raising up people from
among Christian families—2 Tim. 3:15a.
C. We have to expect the second generation, men like
Timothy, to come from our own families—1:5.

Excerpts from the Ministry:

The entire economy of God, and especially that in the New
Testament age, is a matter of dispensing...Many matters are
covered in the New Testament, but if we dive into the depth of
the New Testament as the divine revelation, we will see that
God surely has an economy, a household administration, to
carry out His eternal purpose. This economy is just God's universal operation. If you would ask me what God is doing
today, I would answer that God is operating in one thing and
for one thing: He is spending much time to patiently dispense
Himself into all His chosen people. Everything that is mentioned in the New Testament concerning God has to do with
His dispensing for His economy. (*The Economy and Dispensing of God,* p. 70)

* * *

What we have presented in this message concerning God's
creation of man in the view of His divine dispensing according
to His divine economy is what God desires. This is God's good
pleasure, and this is our ministry, burden, and commission.
We do not have any other burden besides this ministry of God's
economy with His divine dispensing into humanity. We must
learn to receive God's dispensing every day. He is dispensing
Himself to us every moment and in every situation, even in the
small things, for our renewal, transformation, and conforma-
tion. Eventually, we will be glorified. Then we will enjoy the
consummation of His divine dispensing according to His divine
economy. (*The Central Line of the Divine Revelation,* p. 76)

A PLAN MADE BY GOD
ACCORDING TO HIS GOOD PLEASURE

God's New Testament economy is a plan made by God
according to His good pleasure. Concerning this, Ephesians

1:9 says, "Making known to us the mystery of His will according to His good pleasure, which He purposed in Himself." God's good pleasure is the desire of His heart. This good pleasure was what God purposed in Himself for a dispensation, for a plan (v. 10). This plan made by God was according to His good pleasure, the desire of His heart.

We have seen that Ephesians 1:9 speaks of God's good pleasure. Everyone desires pleasure. If we desire pleasure, then certainly God does also. Every living thing desires pleasure. In fact, the more living you are, the more pleasure you need. Because God is the most living One, He surely needs the most pleasure. If we, as fallen sinners, require pleasure, then how much more does God, the living One, have a deep need for it?

Unlike the book of Romans, which begins from the perspective of the condition of fallen man, the book of Ephesians was written from the perspective of God's good pleasure, the desire of His heart. What, then, is God's good pleasure? God's good pleasure is to dispense Himself into us. This is the unique desire of God. We may say that God is "dreaming" of dispensing Himself into us. His longing, His aspiration, is to dispense Himself into His chosen people. (*The Conclusion of the New Testament*, pp. 15, 16)

*   *   *

Romans 9:21 discloses God's purpose in creating man. This verse is unique in its revelation of God's purpose in the creation of man. Without this verse it would be difficult for us to realize that God's purpose in creating man was to make him His vessel to contain Him. We need to be deeply impressed with the fact that we are God's containers and that He is our content.

God's selection in His sovereign mercy has a goal, and this goal is to have many vessels to contain God and express Him eternally. God created us in such a way that we are able to take Him into us and contain Him as our life and life supply, to the end that we may be one with Him to express what He is and that He may be glorified in us and with us. This is God's goal in His selection and in His creation of man. (*The Conclusion of the New Testament,* p. 1187)

MAN—THE CENTER OF GOD'S PLAN

Our God, who is full of wisdom, has a plan, and the entire universe was created according to His purpose, His will, His plan. We must know what God's eternal plan is...Man's position, man's place, in God's plan is very central. It is absolutely right to say that the Bible is a book full of Christ, yet we can also say that the Bible is a book full of men. Even God Himself became a man (John 1:1, 14). Jesus is the complete God and the perfect man. Even after His resurrection and ascension, He is still a man. Before Stephen was stoned, he said that he saw "the heavens opened up and the Son of Man standing at the right hand of God" (Acts 7:56). Stephen saw the Lord Jesus as the Son of Man in the heavens. Man is the center of God's plan. A bicycle wheel may have a hub with many spokes. The hub and the spokes subsist in the wheel. If the hub, the center, is taken away, the spokes will collapse. In like manner, without man as the center, God's plan would collapse. (*A Young Man in God's Plan,* p. 7)

BEARING THE APPEARANCE OF A MAN

The main point of Ezekiel 1:5 is that the four living creatures bear the appearance of a man. Verse 26 says that "upon the likeness of the throne was One in appearance like a man, above it." *Man* is a great word in the Bible. God's intention is with man, God's thought is focused on man, and God's heart is set upon man. God's desire is to gain man. The fact that four living creatures bear the appearance of a man and that God on the throne also bears the appearance of a man indicates that God's central thought and His arrangement are related to man.

Many Christians have been influenced by the concept that it is better to be an angel than to be a man. If you had a choice, which would you prefer to be—an angel or a man? Perhaps many of us would prefer to be an angel. However, God has enough angels, but He is short of men. God does not appreciate angels so much. The angels are His servants. God

tells them to go, and they go; He tells them to come, and they
come. The angels are also our servants (Heb. 1:13-14). As
believers we all have our own angel (Acts 12:12-15). We need
to drop the concept that it is better to be an angel than a man.
We need to see how glorious and how marvelous it is that we
are men. (*Life-study of Ezekiel,* pp. 47, 48)

VESSELS OF MERCY UNTO HONOR AND GLORY

The believers in Christ are vessels of mercy unto honor
and glory. Romans 9:21 says, "Does not the potter have authority over the clay to make out of the same lump one vessel unto
honor and another unto dishonor?" Verse 23 goes on to speak
of God's making known "the riches of His glory upon vessels
of mercy, which He had before prepared unto glory." As vessels, we are not instruments or weapons—we are containers.
According to Romans 9, we contain mercy, honor, and glory.
This mercy, honor, and glory are actually the Triune God. In
the initial stage of our experience the Triune God is our
mercy, in the progressing stage He is our honor, and in the
completing stage He is our glory. At present we are enjoying
our God as mercy and somewhat as honor. When the Lord
Jesus comes back, we shall be fully brought into honor and
also into glory. Then we shall be filled with the Triune God
not only as our mercy but also as our honor and glory.

Romans 9 reveals that the climax of our usefulness to God
is that we are vessels to contain Him and express Him. We
are His container and His expression, and He is our content
and our life. He lives in us that we may live Him. Eventually,
He and we, we and He, will be wholly one in life and nature.
This is our destiny as vessels of mercy.

UNTO HONOR WITH CHRIST
AS THEIR TREASURE THROUGH REGENERATION

The believers are vessels unto honor with Christ as their
treasure through regeneration. Romans 9:21 speaks of vessels
of honor. Second Corinthians 4:6 and 7 say, "The God who said,
Out of darkness light shall shine, is the One who shined in our
hearts to illuminate the knowledge of the glory of God in the
face of Jesus Christ. But we have this treasure in earthen

vessels that the excellency of the power may be of God and not out of us." This treasure is the Christ who dwells within us. We are containers of honor because Christ Himself is honor. He is the treasure within us. Although we have this treasure in earthen vessels, this treasure has not yet been manifested. When the Lord Jesus comes back, Christ as our treasure will be manifested. Then others will be able to see that we, as vessels unto honor, are containers of such a treasure. (*The Conclusion of the New Testament,* pp. 1183, 1187)

THE ONE CROWNED WITH GLORY AND HONOR

In ascension Christ is the One who has been crowned with glory and honor. Hebrews 2:9 says, "We see Jesus, who was made a little inferior to the angels because of the suffering of death, crowned with glory and honor." Here glory and honor are considered a crown. Glory is the splendor related to Jesus' person; honor is the preciousness related to Jesus' worth (1 Pet. 2:7). As the ascended One crowned with glory and honor, Christ is in a state of glory and has a rank of honor. (*The Conclusion of the New Testament,* pp. 336-337)

* * *

Second Timothy 2:21 says, "If therefore anyone cleanses himself from these, he will be a vessel unto honor, sanctified, useful to the master, prepared unto every good work." A vessel unto honor has to meet a certain standard that it may contain a specific object of honor. Here the word *honor* is related to our nature, the word *sanctified* indicates our position, the word *useful* implies the matter of function, and the word *prepared* reveals the matter of training. Paul exhorted Timothy to cleanse himself from the vessels of dishonor that he could be trained in these four matters. These four items together would make Timothy a vessel unto honor according to a certain standard. This also involves our character. (*Vessels Useful to the Lord,* p. 149)

* * *

Honorable vessels are of both the divine nature (gold) and the redeemed and regenerated human nature (silver). These, like Timothy and other genuine believers, constitute the firm foundation (2 Tim. 2:19) to hold the truth. Dishonorable vessels are of the fallen human nature (wood and earth). Hymenaeus, Philetus (v. 17), and other false believers are of these. In 2 Timothy 2:21 Paul goes on to say, "If therefore anyone cleanses himself from these, he will be a vessel unto honor, sanctified, useful to the master, prepared unto every good work." To cleanse ourselves is to "depart from unrighteousness" (v. 19), as an outward evidence of the inward divine nature. The word *these* in verse 21 denotes the vessels unto dishonor, including those mentioned in verses 16 through 18. We should not only cleanse ourselves from anything unrighteous but also from the dishonorable vessels. This means that we must stay away from them. Hence, we must cleanse ourselves from the unrighteous things and from the dishonorable vessels of wood and earth. If we cleanse ourselves from these negative things and negative persons, we shall be vessels unto honor, sanctified, useful to the Master, and prepared unto every good work. *Unto honor* is a matter of nature, *sanctified* is a matter of position, *useful* is a matter of practice, and *prepared* is a matter of training. (*The Conclusion of the New Testament,* pp. 1188-1189)

* * *

Brothers and sisters, it takes ten or twenty years of training in God's hand before a man can become somewhat useful to Him. If we want to run a good race and be somewhat mature in the Lord, we need at least ten or twenty years of training. Yet some who do not take proper care of their own health may die before they reach that point. This is most unfortunate. Some do not start running until they have been in the Lord for twenty or thirty years. Then they touch the right way, and their usefulness begins to blossom. The church should not only have children and young men, but fathers as well. All those who desire to serve the Lord should consider it to be a great waste for a brother or a sister to die prematurely after spending many years and much effort to learn his or her lessons! We know that some vessels are broken and damaged halfway through the process. This is a pity. This is like Jeremiah's speaking concerning the vessels in the hand of the potter being spoiled (Jer. 18:4). When a potter turns his wheel and molds his vessels, some become damaged before they even reach the fire. They do not even pass the formative stage. This is a loss. (*The Character of the Lord's Worker,* pp. 159-160)

* * *

I believe if the Lord is gracious to us, we will gain half of our increase from among our own children and the other half from the "sea" (i.e., the world). If all the increase is from the sea and none is from among our own children, we will not have a strong church. Paul's generation could be saved directly from the world, but the generation after Paul, men like Timothy, came in through their families. We cannot expect our increase to always come from the world. We have to expect the second generation, men like Timothy, to come from our own families. God's gospel does save men from the world, but we also need to bring in men like Timothy. Before the church will be rich, there must be grandmothers like Lois and mothers like Eunice who raise, edify, and nurture their children in the discipline of the Lord. If there are no such people, the church will never be rich.

When God bestows grace on the church, He needs vessels. There is the need for more Timothys to be raised up. It is true that we can save men from the world, but there is a greater need for raising up people from among Christian families. (*Messages for Building Up New Believers,* vol. 2, pp. 540-541, 549)

LESSON TWO

THE BODY OF CHRIST—
THE GOAL OF THE DIVINE ECONOMY

Scripture Reading: 1 Tim. 1:4; Eph. 1:6-8, 10, 22-23; 4:4-6; Rev. 1:20

I. God's economy is God becoming a man that man may become God in life and in nature (but not in the Godhead) to produce the organic Body of Christ, which will consummate in the New Jerusalem—Rom. 8:3; 1:3-4; 12:4-5; Rev. 21:2:

A. The center of God's economy is Christ, and the goal of God's economy is the Body of Christ—Col. 1:15-19; 2:9, 19.

B. The divine economy is God's eternal plan to dispense Christ into His chosen people to produce, constitute, and build up the organic Body of Christ—Eph. 1:10; 3:8-10; 1 Tim. 1:4.

C. God's aim in His economy is to have a group of human beings who have His life and nature inwardly and His image and likeness outwardly; this group of people is a corporate entity, the Body of Christ, to be one with Him and live Him for His corporate expression—Gen. 1:26; John 3:14; 2 Pet. 1:4; Eph. 4:16.

D. The main contents of the New Testament are that the Triune God has an eternal economy according to His good pleasure to dispense Himself into His chosen and redeemed people in His life and in His nature, to make all of them the same as He is in life and nature, to make them His duplication that

they may express Him—3:8-10; 1 John 3:2; Rev.
4:3; 21:11.

II. The consummation of the believers' experience of the
grace of God in His economy is the church as the Body
of Christ—Eph. 1:6-8, 22-23:

A. Grace is the manifestation of the Triune God in
His embodiment in three aspects—the Father (the
source), the Son (the element), and the Spirit (the
application)—1 Cor. 15:10; 2 Cor. 8:9; Heb. 10:29.

B. The grace in God's economy is the embodiment of
God for man to receive as his enjoyment and supply;
as a result, we will be full of the organic element in
our inner being and thus become the organism of
God—2 Cor. 13:14; Eph. 4:4-6; Rev. 21:2.

C. What God wants today is that we experience the
grace in His economy so that the Divine Trinity
may have an organism—John 1:16; 15:1.

D. Every part of the organic Body of Christ is an issue
of the grace of God in the economy of God—Rom.
5:21; 12:3-8.

III. The Body of Christ, the church, is four-in-one: the
Father, the Son, the Spirit, and the Body—Eph. 4:4-6:

A. Ephesians 4:4-6 reveals four persons—one Body,
one Spirit, one Lord, and one God and Father—
mingled together as one entity to be the organic
Body of Christ:

1. With the Body of Christ, the Father is the origin,
the Son is the element, and the Spirit is the
essence; these three are mingled with the Body.

2. The Father is embodied in the Son, the Son is
realized as the Spirit, and They are all in us;
therefore, we are a divine-human constitution—
3:16-20.

3. Because the Father, the Son, and the Spirit are
all one with the Body of Christ, the Triune God
and the Body are now four-in-one.

B. The four-in-one organic entity in Ephesians 4:4-6
corresponds with the golden lampstands in Revelation 1:20:

1. In figure, the golden lampstand signifies the church as the embodiment of the Triune God—the Father, the Son, and the Spirit:

   a. The lampstand is of pure gold, signifying the divine, eternal, incorruptible nature of God the Father—Exo. 25:31; 2 Pet. 1:4.

   b. The solid form, the shape, of the lampstand signifies God the Son as the embodiment of God the Father—Exo. 25:31.

   c. The seven lamps signify God the Spirit being the seven Spirits—v. 37; Rev. 4:5.

2. The church is the Triune God completely mingled with His redeemed people as one to become a golden lampstand shining locally to express God Himself—1:20.

IV. The Body of Christ is the fullness of the all-inclusive Christ, the One who fills all in all—Eph. 1:22-23:

A. The church is the Body, and the Body is the fullness; these two levels of "is" are in succession rather than in parallel—vv. 22-23.

B. The Body is the fullness of the Head, and the fullness is the expression of the Head—v. 23.

C. The fullness of Christ issues from the enjoyment of the riches of Christ; the fullness of Christ is Christ experienced by us, assimilated by us, and constituted into our being to become our element—3:8.

D. Christ, as the One who fills all in all, needs the Body to be His fullness; this Body is His church to be His expression—1:23:

   1. Christ, who is the infinite God without any limitation, is so great that He fills all things in all things—v. 23; 3:18-19.

   2. Such a great Christ needs the church, His Body, to be His fullness for His complete expression—1:23.

V. We need to be universal Christians with a universal view of the universal Body of Christ—vv. 17, 23; Acts 10:9-11; Rev. 21:10:

A. "What God is doing today is to obtain the Body of Christ, not merely you as an individual, nor merely the church in a locality, nor merely the church in a country. He wants to obtain the church in the entire universe"—*Words of Training for the New Way,* vol. 1, pp. 54-55.

B. "It is my desire that you see the light, broaden your view, and realize that we are in God's eternal economy, that you would allow God to have the Body of Christ on the earth"—p. 55.

C. "It is not enough for us merely to have a local view, nor is it enough to have an international view. We must have a universal view. We need to see that Christ is after a Body, and God will prepare a Body for Christ"—p. 55.

Excerpts from the Ministry:

God's economy is God becoming a man that man may become God in life and in nature (but not in the Godhead) to produce the organic Body of Christ, which will consummate in the New Jerusalem. (*Life-study of 1 & 2 Chronicles,* p. 75)

GOD BECOMING MAN AND MAN BECOMING GOD

"God becoming man and man becoming God" is the economy of God; it is beyond the comprehension of angels and men...There is a line concerning the economy of God recorded in the Scriptures, showing us how God became man to make man God. The Bible shows us how man can become God to have a God-man living and thus become an organism of God, which is the Body of Christ. (*The High Peak of the Vision and the Reality of the Body of Christ,* p. 27)

* * *

God made His eternal economy in Christ. The Christ revealed in the New Testament is the embodiment of the Triune God and all the processes through which He has passed, including creation, incarnation, human living, crucifixion, resurrection, and ascension. In such a Christ God made His eternal economy. Therefore, Christ is the element, sphere, means, goal, and aim of God's eternal economy. Christ is everything in God's economy. In fact, all the contents of the eternal economy of God are simply Christ. Christ is the center of God's eternal plan. Christ is the element and the sphere in which, with which, and through which God carries out His household administration to have the church as the household of God and the Body of Christ. (*The Conclusion of the New Testament,* p. 2052)

* * *

The Body of Christ is the Triune God's eternal heart's desire and His ultimate purpose. It is also something that the tripartite men can never think of nor hope and ask for. However, this is the Triune God's anticipated multiplication and His expected increase. This multiplication and increase are God and Christ multiplying and increasing within us, the redeemed people. This is something beyond the imagination of all the religionists and philosophers, yet we who have been graced by God can actually taste it and participate in it for eternity. (*The Issue of the Union of the Consummated Spirit of the Triune God and the Regenerated Spirit of the Believers,* p. 55)

THE DIVINE ECONOMY BEING GOD'S ETERNAL PLAN TO DISPENSE CHRIST INTO HIS CHOSEN PEOPLE

The word *economy* is an anglicized form of the Greek word *oikonomia,* which means "household law or household management or household administration and derivatively administrative dispensation, plan, economy." The divine economy is God's eternal plan to dispense Christ into His chosen people to produce, constitute, and build up the organic Body of Christ (Eph. 1:10; 3:8-10; 1 Tim. 1:4). Since Christ is the embodiment of the Triune God, for God to dispense Christ into His chosen people actually means that God dispenses Himself in Christ into His chosen people. In brief, God's economy is to gain a Body for Christ. This Body is the enlargement of the Triune God for His expression that He may be satisfied. (*Life-study of Job,* p. 205)

BECOMING ONE WITH GOD AND
LIVING HIM FOR HIS CORPORATE EXPRESSION

God has an economy, and this economy involves a plan with many arrangements. God's aim in His economy is to have a group of human beings who have His life and nature inwardly and His image and likeness outwardly. This group of people is a corporate entity, the Body of Christ, to be one with Him and live Him for His corporate expression. As God is expressed not only by the Body but also through the Body, He is glorified. When He is glorified, His people are also glorified in His glorification. In this way God and man are one in glory.

In this oneness we, God's people, are not separate from God, but we definitely remain distinct from Him. We are one with God in life, in nature, in element, in essence, and in constitution. We are also one with Him in purpose, goal, image, and likeness. Nevertheless, no matter how much we are one with God, we do not share His Godhead and will never share it. Man remains man, and God remains God. Yes, in the incarnation of Christ, God became a man, but He did not give up His Godhead. Rather, He has reserved and preserved the Godhead for Himself alone. Thus, man is still limited, and God still possesses the unique Godhead.

The group of human beings who are one with God in every way except in the Godhead is symbolized, signified, depicted, and portrayed by a wonderful, holy city—the New Jerusalem. (*Life-study of Jeremiah,* p. 82)

THE MAIN CONTENTS OF THE NEW TESTAMENT

The main contents of the New Testament are that the Triune God has an eternal economy according to His good pleasure to dispense Himself into His chosen and redeemed people in His life and in His nature, to make all of them the same as He is in life and nature, to make them His duplication that they may express Him. This corporate expression will consummate in the New Jerusalem. Thus, the New Jerusalem is simply the enlarged, the increased, incarnation consummated in full, that is, the fullness of the Triune God for Him to express Himself in His divinity mingled with humanity. (*Life-study of Job,* p. 64)

* * *

My intention, my burden, is to show you that the entire Bible speaks of only one thing—grace, which is God, who is the New Jerusalem. Grace is the manifestation of the Triune God in His embodiment in three aspects—the Father, the Son, and the Spirit. Regardless of what subject the Bible touches, it is concerned with the Triune God in His embodiment in three aspects—the Father, the Son, and the Spirit—being manifested as grace consummating in the New Jerusalem. This is the highest and central revelation shown to us in the entire New Testament. Hence, we cannot touch the righteousness of God without touching grace. God's righteousness and God's grace are not two different things. Romans 5:17 refers to both the abundance of grace and the abundance of righteousness. Righteousness always accompanies grace and is its result. (*The Experience of God's Organic Salvation Equaling Reigning in Christ's Life*, p. 56)

* * *

Today the processed and consummated Triune God has become the life-giving Spirit and is all-inclusive. As such a One, He is in us to bring us all into His organism. In this organism is the organic element that God wants. It is not the outward explanation of doctrines. The more we are right in doctrine, the less organic element we have. The more we remain in the "photo," the less we are in the living person. I hope that our eyes will be opened to see where our real need is. We need to be in the processed and consummated Triune God, taking Him as our life and our person. We are on the cross, and yet in His resurrection we have been resurrected, and we have ascended with Him. Here, God and man are mingled to produce an organism. This is accomplished by grace. The grace in God's economy is the embodiment of God for man to receive as his enjoyment and supply. We should learn to receive such an embodied grace that we may have this enjoyment and supply. As a result, we will be full of the organic element in our inner being and thus become the organism of God. (*The Law and Grace of God in His Economy*, p. 43)

* * *

The grace in God's economy is God's embodiment. God became flesh to dwell among us, full of grace, and of His fullness we have all received, and grace upon grace. When God comes, grace comes. God's embodiment is grace to us. When we receive grace, we obtain God.

God's economy is to work out an organism for the Divine Trinity. How does He work this out? It is by His becoming flesh to be a man that His divinity and humanity might be united and mingled to produce a God-man. This God-man is grace. Whomever He meets, He is grace to them; wherever He goes, He is grace. He is simply grace. If we have Him, we have grace. Hence, in the Bible grace is called the grace of Christ. The embodied grace came for us to receive as our enjoyment and supply. However, there are few who see this today, even fewer who preach this, and very few who live this out.

If we experience the grace in God's economy, there will be a consummation—the organic Body of Christ. Christ to us is grace; as such, He comes into us to be our life and person. He not only lives in us but also lives with us. Moreover, He wants us to live along with Him. This is to enjoy grace as our inner supply. Such an enjoyment of grace spontaneously produces a result. This result is not merely that we do good. Rather, it is that Christ lives with us and we with Him. When we live Christ and magnify Christ, we become the living members, organic members, of Christ, and we all are organically joined as an organism, which is the church. This organism grows continually, and ultimately there will be a consummation— the New Jerusalem. (*The Law and Grace of God in His Economy*, pp. 62-63)

EVERY PART OF THE ORGANIC BODY OF CHRIST BEING AN ISSUE OF THE GRACE IN THE ECONOMY OF GOD

Every part of the organic Body of Christ is an issue of the grace in the economy of God. Grace is the enjoyment of the Triune God—the Father, the Son, and the Spirit—as the enjoyment of life, and the life of God is with God the Father as the substance, God the Son as the element, and God the Spirit as the essence.

Christ, the last Adam, after passing through an all-inclusive death, became the life-giving Spirit in resurrection as the essence of the Divine Trinity to come into us to be our life and everything. Day by day we need to be filled with Him, saturated with Him, permeated by Him, infused by Him, and transfused by Him. Hence, as we read the New Testament, we cannot avoid the word *Spirit*. Especially in the Epistles, the emphasis is on the Spirit, and the Spirit is frequently linked with grace. (*The Law and Grace of God in His Economy*, pp. 67, 68)

AS THE SPIRIT OF THE ONENESS OF THE BODY OF CHRIST, BEING THE ESSENCE OF THE BODY

The Spirit is the oneness of the Body of Christ, being the essence of the Body, which is constituted with Christ as the element, out from the origin of God the Father, to consummate the mingling of the Triune God with the Body of Christ through the divine dispensing (Eph. 4:3-6). Christ is the element of the Body, and the Spirit is the essence. This element is out from the origin of God the Father. Thus, with the Body of Christ, the Father is the origin, the Son is the element, and the Spirit is the essence. This is the Triune God—the origin, the element, and the essence. These three are blended and mingled with the Body of Christ.

The Body of Christ, the church, is four-in-one: the Father, the Son, the Spirit, and the Body. Ephesians 4:4-6 speaks of one Body, one Spirit, one Lord, and one God the Father. In the Body the Spirit is the essence. The essence needs the element, which is the Lord Christ. The element must have an origin, a source, which is the Father. The Father is the source, the origin. Out of the Father there is the element, and within the element there is the essence. God is the origin, the Son is the element, the Spirit is the essence, and the Body is the very constitution. These are four-in-one. However, only the first three are worthy of our worship; the fourth, the Body, should not be deified as an object of worship.

The Spirit as the oneness of the Body of Christ is the essence of the Body to consummate the mingling of the Triune God with the Body of Christ through the divine dispensing. Today something is going on to mingle the Father as the origin, the Son as the element, and the Spirit as the essence with the Body. This mingling is continuing today and will be consummated. The Spirit is the essence of the Body to consummate this mingling. (*The Central Line of the Divine Revelation,* pp. 127-128)

THE CHURCH IN REVELATION

Paul was martyred soon after he wrote the book of Ephesians. After approximately twenty-five years, among the apostles of the first generation, only the aged John was still alive. He was the last one to pass away among the twelve apostles. In writing the book of Revelation, he points out at the beginning that the church in each locality is a golden lampstand, that each lampstand bears not one lamp but seven lamps, and that within the lamps there is the shining light. In figure, the golden lampstand signifies the embodiment of the Triune God. First, the nature of the golden lampstand is pure gold, and in typology gold signifies the Father's glorious nature and life. Next, the golden lampstand is not simply a piece of solid gold. Rather, the gold is beaten into the shape of the lampstand. This signifies that Christ as the embodiment of God the Father became a man and passed through sufferings and trials for the expression of God. Moreover, each lampstand bears seven lamps. Revelation tells us clearly that the seven lamps are the seven Spirits of God (4:5). Therefore, in Revelation the golden lampstand signifies the church as the embodiment of the Triune God—the Father, the Son, and the Holy Spirit. That the church is the embodiment of the Triune God corresponds with Ephesians 4. Ephesians 4:4-6 speaks of one Body and one Spirit, one Lord, and one God and Father of all, who is over all and through all and in all. This indicates that the church is the mingling of the Triune God with the Body. This corresponds with the golden lampstands in Revelation. The church is the Triune God completely mingled with His redeemed people as one to become a golden lampstand shining locally to express God Himself. When this expression is manifested, it is the testimony of Jesus (Rev. 1:2, 9).

At the end of Revelation, when the new heaven and the new earth come, their center is a golden mountain, the New Jerusalem. Upon this mountain is the throne of God, on which are God and the Lamb, Christ. God is the light and Christ is the lamp (21:23). Hence, the New Jerusalem is a lampstand. Ultimately, the New Jerusalem is an aggregate lampstand with Christ as the lamp and God as the light shining out from the golden mountain. This is the ultimate consummation of the church. At the beginning of Revelation, the church is expressed as many lampstands in different localities, with one lampstand for each locality. At the consummation of the church in its manifestation in eternity, all the lampstands are gathered together as the unique, universal lampstand, the New Jerusalem. (*The Four Crucial Elements of the Bible—Christ, the Spirit, Life, and the Church,* pp. 140-141)

* * *

Do not forget the word *is* in Ephesians 1:23: "[The church] *is* His Body, the fullness of the One who fills all in all." This means that the church *is* the Body, and the Body *is* the fullness. These two levels of "is" are in succession rather than in parallel. It is not that on the one hand the church is the Body, while on the other hand the church is the fullness. Rather, it is that the church is the Body, and the Body is the fullness. According to doctrine, the fullness equals the Body, and the Body equals the church. But according to reality, a man can be in the church and still not live in the Body. All the brothers and sisters who meet in Hong Kong are in the church, but who is living in the Body? This becomes a big question mark. Strictly speaking, that which can fulfill God's eternal purpose is not the church in name but the Body. The Body is the fullness of Christ. I repeat that if you look from this angle and measure with this yardstick, you will see that today on earth in the churches there is not much of the element of the Body. (*One Body, One Spirit, and One New Man,* p. 36)

THE BODY OF CHRIST

Ephesians 1:22 and 23 reveal that the church is the Body of Christ. "He subjected all things under His feet and gave Him to be Head over all things to the church, which is His Body, the fullness of the One who fills all in all." The church is not an organization but an organic Body constituted of all the believers, who have been regenerated and have God's life, for the expression of the Head. The Body is the fullness of the Head, and the fullness is the expression of the Head. Christ, as the One who fills all in all, needs the Body to be His fullness. This Body is His church to be His expression.

The church is the Body of Christ, and Christ is the Head of the church (Col. 1:18). Hence, the church and Christ are one Body, the mysterious, universal great man, having the same life and nature. Christ is the life and content of the Body, and the Body is the organism and expression of Christ. As the Body, the church receives everything from Christ; everything of Christ, therefore, is expressed through the church. The two, Christ and the church, are mingled and joined as one, with Christ being the inward content and the church, the outward expression. (*The Conclusion of the New Testament*, pp. 2245-2246)

RESULTING IN THE FULLNESS OF CHRIST

The experience of the riches of Christ results in the fullness of Christ, the Body as Christ's expression (Eph. 1:23). The book of Ephesians speaks both of the riches of Christ and of the fullness of Christ. A tall, husky man is the fullness of America because he has enjoyed the riches of American foodstuffs. Throughout the years of his growth and development, he has consumed a great deal of meat, poultry, vegetables, and fruit. Therefore, as a full-grown man, he becomes the fullness of America. The riches of American foodstuffs did not make him this fullness until he ate them, digested them, and assimilated them. By absorbing the riches in this way, the riches became part of him. Likewise all the aspects of the riches of Christ do not become the fullness of Christ until they are eaten, enjoyed, digested, and assimilated by us. By absorbing these riches in such a way, we become the Body of Christ as His fullness to express Him. Thus, the Body of Christ is constituted of the riches of Christ that have been enjoyed and assimilated by us. Therefore, the Body is the result, the issue, of the experience and enjoyment of the riches of Christ. (*Life-study of Ephesians,* pp. 265-266)

* * *

The riches are outside of us and are objective, not yet having passed through our enjoyment and experience. The fullness is within us and is subjective, being the result of what we have enjoyed and experienced of the riches. If the riches of Christ are placed outside of us, they will be merely the riches of Christ and will not constitute the fullness of Christ. In order for His riches to be constituted into the fullness of Christ, they must be enjoyed, experienced, and digested by us and thus be constituted into the element of our entire being. (*One Body, One Spirit, and One New Man,* pp. 39-40)

* * *

This universal Christ, the Christ who fills all things, the Christ who is both in the heavens and on the earth, needs a Body to be His fullness. When He was on earth as Jesus the Nazarene, He could not be in Judea at the same time He was in Galilee, nor could He be in Jerusalem when He was in Samaria. This was because He was a small Jesus. He was limited by His flesh. But what about today? He has risen from the dead and ascended to the heavens, so He fills all things. He can be in the heavens and on the earth simultaneously; He can be in one place in the heavens, and at the same time He can be in millions of places on the earth. He is such a One who fills all things, so He needs a great Body as His fullness. Thus, today we can say that because He has such a great Body on earth, He is in heaven and He is also in Taipei, in Hong Kong, in Manila, in Singapore, in London, in Germany, in the United States, in Africa, in North America, and in South America. His Body is everywhere. What is this Body? It is His fullness, His universal fullness.

Dear brothers and sisters, you should not merely listen to

this word and take it as doctrine. You must see that today the actual church (I am not speaking of the genuine church alone but the practical, present church) is the fullness of Christ in each locality. In other words, the actual church today is a part of Christ...Christ today is not a local Christ but a universal Christ, and this universal Christ has a part of Himself in every locality. (*One Body, One Spirit, and One New Man,* p. 33)

CHRIST BEING THE HEAD
AND CHRIST BEING THE BODY

How then does Christ constitute Himself into us to become His fullness? I can say it in this way: The Lord Jesus in Himself is the Head, and the Lord Jesus constituted into us is the Body. A person is not a head only but a head with a body. If today I am here as a head hanging in the air and speaking to you, I believe you would be scared to death. If there were only a head without a body, this would not be a complete person. A complete person has both a head and a body. In the New Testament, the Lord Jesus in Himself is the Head, but when He gets into all of us and is constituted into us, then He is the Body. Thus, not only is the Head Christ, but also the Body is Christ. First Corinthians 12:12 says, "For even as the body is one and has many members, yet all the members of the body, being many, are one body, so also is the Christ." This verse clearly tells us that the Body is Christ. The Lord Jesus is the Head, and He is also the Body. We cannot say, however, that we are the Body and also the Head. We can be only the Body and cannot be the Head, but the Lord Jesus can be both the Head and the Body. In Himself, He is the Head, and in us collectively, He is the Body. The Head is individual, while the Body is corporate. Both are Christ. (*One Body, One Spirit, and One New Man,* p. 41)

THE BODY OF CHRIST, THE FULLNESS OF THE ONE
WHO FILLS ALL IN ALL, FOR HIS EXPRESSION

The universal church is the Body of Christ. Ephesians 1:22 and 23 reveal that the church as the Body is "the fullness of the One who fills all in all." The Body of Christ is His fullness, that is, His full expression. The Body is the fullness of the Head, and the fullness is the expression of the Head. Christ, who is the infinite God without any limitation, is so great that He fills all things in all things. Such a great Christ needs the church to be His fullness for His complete expression. (*The Conclusion of the New Testament,* p. 2145)

THE BETTER THE MINGLING, THE MORE THE BLESSING

What God is doing today is to obtain the Body of Christ, not merely you as an individual, nor merely the church in a locality, nor merely the church in a country. He wants to obtain the church in the entire universe. Since this is the case, in our church life today we need to be mingled with all the brothers and sisters on the earth. The more successful the mingling, the better it is. Whoever cannot be mingled with others will eventually be disqualified by the age. In today's age, you cannot be an isolated Christian.

I hope that you can understand, receive, and at the same time, broaden your view. I am not exhorting you to be patient, to condescend, to humble yourself, or to love others as yourself. Those things are trite expressions. Rather, it is my desire that you see the light, broaden your view, and realize that we are in God's eternal economy, that you would allow God to have the Body of Christ on the earth. From now on, not only are we who are in Taipei in one accord, but the entire recovery of the Lord in the whole universe is also one. We are the one Body of Christ. Concerning this point, I have had very clear light all along. In the past three years in Taiwan, I also have gained a considerable amount of experience and realization. In these three years, the Lord has definitely done something in our midst that has broadened us. Everyone's view has been broadened. It is not enough for us merely to have a local view, nor is it enough to have an international view. We must have a universal view. We need to see that Christ is after a Body, and God will prepare a Body for Christ. (*Words of Training for the New Way,* vol. 1, pp. 54-55)

LESSON THREE

KEEPING OURSELVES IN
THE ONE FLOW OF THE LORD'S WORK
FOR THE BUILDING UP
OF THE UNIVERSAL BODY OF CHRIST

Scripture Reading: Matt. 16:18; Ezek. 47:1-12; Eph. 2:21-22;
3:17a; Phil. 2:13; Matt. 7:21-24; Rev. 21:2

I. The book of Acts reveals that in the move of the Lord
there is only one divine stream of the Lord's work and
that we need to keep ourselves in this stream:

A. The divine stream, which has been flowing throughout the generations, is uniquely one; since there
is only one divine stream and since the flow is
uniquely one, we need to keep ourselves in this one
flow—1 John 1:3; Rev. 22:1.

B. When we give the Lord the preeminence in our
entire being, making Him our first love, He becomes
the divine stream to us, flowing within us and out
of us as the first works; the first works are works
that are motivated by, issue from, and express the
Lord as our first love; only works that are motivated by the first love are gold, silver, and precious
stones—v. 1; 2:4-5; 1 Cor. 2:9; 3:12.

C. The flowing of the divine life, which started on the
day of Pentecost and has been flowing throughout
all generations to this day, is just one stream for
God's goal to build up the church for His corporate
expression—Matt. 16:18; cf. Ezek. 47:1-12.

D. We must be faithful to the flowing of this stream
of the divine life, of the fellowship of the Body, of
the testimony of the Lord Jesus, and of the work

of God—Gen. 2:10-14; Psa. 36:8-9; 46:4a; John 7:37-39; Rev. 22:1.

II. In the recovery there is a definite work that is for the building up of the local churches unto the building up of the universal Body of Christ—Eph. 2:21-22; 1 Cor. 16:10:

A. All the co-workers should do the same one work universally for the unique Body; the starting point of the work is the oneness of the Body—3:12; 15:58; 16:10; Eph. 4:4, 11-16.

B. Our work is the work of the Lord's recovery for the building of the Body of Christ—vv. 4, 16:

1. The Body is the governing law of the life and work of the children of God today—1:22-23; 1 Cor. 12:4-6, 12-13, 27.

2. The work of the Triune God in us is to produce the Body of Christ, the reality of which is the Spirit, the pneumatic Christ—Eph. 3:16-21; 4:4-6, 12, 16.

3. The work in the Lord's recovery is the work of His economy, the work of the Body of Christ— 1 Cor. 15:58; 16:10; Col. 4:11.

4. According to Song of Songs 7:11, Christ's lover wants to carry out with her Beloved the work that is for the entire world (fields) by sojourning from one place to another (lodging in the villages); this is to keep one work in one Body— Eph. 4:12.

III. We have to see what God's work is, and we have to know what is God's central work in man—3:17a; Phil. 2:13:

A. The main work of God today is to work Himself into man; only when God is worked into man can God's eternal purpose be fulfilled—Gal. 4:19; Eph. 3:17a; 4:16.

B. God's main goal is not the works but to gain persons through the works; if God does not gain a person, He will have no work, and He will have no way—Acts 9:15; 13:1-2:

1. We have to remember all the time that the need today is for God to work Himself into us rather than for us to work for God—Eph. 2:10; Phil. 2:13.
2. It is not that we work for the Lord but that He works on us; we must not be merely His workers but His work—Eph. 2:10.
3. The kind of person we are determines the kind of fruit we produce; if our person is wrong, we may build up something by what we do but tear down more by what we are—Matt. 7:17-18.

IV. According to the entire revelation of the New Testament, the unique goal of the Christian work should be the New Jerusalem, which is the ultimate goal of God's eternal economy—1 Cor. 3:10; Heb. 12:22; Rev. 21:2:

A. The co-workers must see that we should do only one work, which is to make God's chosen people regenerated ones, sanctified ones, renewed ones—the new man—transformed ones, conformed ones—those conformed to the image of the firstborn Son of God—and glorified ones; all those who will be in the New Jerusalem are this kind of people—1 Cor. 14:26; Eph. 4:12.

B. In this way, we go up level by level until we reach the highest point, where we become the same; there is no more flesh, no more natural being; all are in the Spirit; all are the kingdom of the heavens, and all are beings of the New Jerusalem—this is the highest point—Rev. 4:3; 21:19-21; Gal. 5:16.

Excerpts from the Ministry:

THE STREAM OF THE WORK OF GOD

This stream is also the stream of God's work. Where the stream flows, there is the work of God. This is clear in the book of Acts, a book which speaks to us of the work of God. What is that kind of work that is the work of God? It is a work in the stream of living water. Where the stream of living water flows, there is the work of God. God works along the flowing of the stream of the divine life. If you consider the whole record of the book of Acts, you will see the picture quite clearly. On the day of Pentecost this stream of divine life flowed out of God Himself in Christ with ruling power from the throne. It began to flow from Jerusalem. From there it flowed to Antioch, and then from Antioch it turned to the west; it flowed to Asia, and through Asia it flowed to Macedonia, to Europe. Here is a picture of the flowing of the stream of divine life, and with the flowing of this stream is the work of God. By flowing God works; by flowing God preaches His gospel; by flowing God brings people to be saved. There is a stream that we could call the stream, or the current, of the work. Where it flows, there is the work of God.

This stream has flowed back to the Western world as a supply to His Body. We look to the Lord that it will be increasing in this country and even to all parts of the world. May we remember this in our prayers, and may we be ready to go along with the Lord so that this stream may have a free way to flow without any hindrance in us. We must be faithful to the flowing of this stream of the divine life, of the fellowship of the Body, of the testimony of the Lord Jesus, and of the work of God.

THE ONE STREAM

The flowing of the divine life, which started on the day of Pentecost and has been flowing throughout all generations to this very day, is only one stream. Wherever it goes, wherever it flows, it is not many streams; it is only one. Read the book of Acts, and you will see that there is one stream, one current. This stream started from Jerusalem and flowed to Antioch, and from Antioch it turned to Asia and was flowing there. Then one day the Lord wanted the stream to strike forth into Europe, to Macedonia, but the apostle who was working in the flowing of the stream was not clear about it. Eventually, however, he became clear that the flowing was striking forth from Asia to Europe, and he had to go along with it. It is a familiar story. From Macedonia the stream went in its path to Corinth, to Rome, to Spain, and to all parts of Europe. History tells us that from Europe it flowed to the west, to America, and from the west it flowed to the east and to the south. In reading the history of the church we find that this flowing stream has never been stopped, and we notice that everywhere that this stream flowed, it was just one. It was one in Jerusalem, one to Antioch, one to Asia, one to Europe, and one everywhere it has flowed. Please be clear that there have never been two streams. There is only one stream, and you have to keep yourself in this one stream. (*The Divine Stream,* pp. 6-7, 8, 12-13)

THE INTENTION TO DO AN EXTRA WORK IN THE UNIQUE WORK OF THE LORD'S RECOVERY

The present problem among us came out of something that was hidden in the past. One of these hidden things was the intention to do an extra work in the unique work of the Lord's recovery. In the recovery there is a definite work that is for the building up of the local churches unto the building up of the universal Body of Christ. This is the work. But among us, there was a case of someone who wanted to do an extra work within the work. This person would not leave the recovery or give up the church life. Instead, he insisted on having a particular work of his own, by his own effort, within the recovery. This was a divisive factor. (*Elders' Training, Book 10: The Eldership and the God-ordained Way (2),* pp. 18-19)

* * *

All the co-workers in all the regions should do the same one work universally for the unique Body. We should do only one work. There should not be several works in the Lord's recovery. In the past there were several works in the recovery. This is still lingering among us. There is the risk and the danger that these different works will issue in divisions. We have to consider our present situation so that we can eliminate the number of works. The work should be just one. Even Paul and Peter did not carry out two works. Even though they worked in different regions, they had only one work to build up the Body of Christ. (*Elders' Training, Book 11: The Eldership and the God-ordained Way (3),* pp. 118-119)

THE STARTING POINT OF THE WORK BEING
THE ONENESS OF THE BODY

The starting point of the work in Antioch was the sending forth of two or three men. However, if workers are sent out by the work, the question of organization may come in. During our gathering this time, brothers from different localities have come on their own accord. Such a kind of gathering is not a product of organization, teachings, or doctrines. It is a product of the Body's need. There is only one Body. What is manifested in all the places is the same life. This life is the reality of the Body. The work is produced out of this reality. This is the Lord's standard. If we compare our work with the Lord's standard, we will see that we have surely come short. The Lord has shown us today that individual works can never come up to the standard of the Body. If we do not see this, insisting instead on our individual works, we will face a stone wall. All works that are not the issue of the Body life will sooner or later hit a stone wall. The Lord will lead us to the point where we have to take the way of the Body. He will lead us to the point where we will not be able to go on or even to live if we do not take the way of the Body. If a man falls into the river, surely he will cry out for help. In the same way, the Lord will force us to cry out for help to be rescued out of our individual works. This is the starting point of the work. The starting point of the work is the oneness of the Body. (*The Collected Works of Watchman Nee,* vol. 57, pp. 74-75)

DOING ONLY THE WORK OF THE LORD'S RECOVERY

Anyone who has a vision today can be clear at a glance that neither Brother Nee nor I carried out our own personal work; our work is the work of the Lord's recovery for the building of the Body of Christ. I say this with the hope that you will be influenced by me. I was greatly influenced by Brother Nee, and I hope that you will also be influenced by him.

If we all do the work of the Lord's recovery, there will be the one Body. If only three or five people who are of the same mind go out to work in a small region, the outcome is not oneness or one accord; rather, that outcome creates division. This is the very reason for the turmoil in recent years.

If we look back, what did Brother Nee accomplish, and what have I accomplished? All that we have done is left here for the Lord to show grace to His children; the work that we have done is the Lord's recovery. I hope that we all can see this. We must see the Body of Christ and be very clear concerning this vision. This vision must become our governing and controlling vision. We must do the work of the Lord's recovery under this vision. The work of the Lord's recovery is the work of His economy, the work of the Body of Christ. (*The Governing and Controlling Vision in the Bible*, pp. 32, 33)

* * *

The church is the life of the Body in miniature; the ministry is the functioning of the Body in service; the work is the reaching out of the Body in growth. Neither church, ministry, nor work can exist as a thing by itself. Each has to derive its existence from, find its place in, and work for the good of the Body. All three are from the Body, in the Body, and for the Body. If this principle of relatedness to the Body and inter-relatedness among its members is not recognized, there can be no church, no ministry, and no work. The importance of this principle cannot be over-emphasized, for without it everything is man-made, not God-created. The basic principle of the ministry is the Body. The basic principle of the work is the Body. The basic principle of the churches is the Body. The Body is the governing law of the life and work of the children of God today. (*The Normal Christian Church Life*, pp. 187-188)

THE REALITY OF THE BODY OF CHRIST

Now we go on to see the reality of the Body of Christ. The reality of the Body of Christ is the Spirit, and the Spirit is the resurrection. Brother Nee made a statement, saying that "the Holy Spirit is the reality of resurrection; without the Holy Spirit, there is no resurrection." In John 11:25 the Lord Jesus said, "I am the resurrection and the life." He is not only the life but also the resurrection. However, most of us can understand that the Spirit is life, but we cannot comprehend that the Spirit is resurrection. The Lord Jesus said that He is the resurrection. What is this resurrection? This resurrection is the ultimate consummation of the Triune God. The work of the Triune God in us is to produce the Body of Christ, the reality of which is the Spirit, the pneumatic Christ. This Spirit as the consummated Triune God, the resurrection, works in us. When we have the pneumatic Christ, the consummated Triune God, the resurrection, we are practically the Body of Christ. (*The High Peak of the Vision and the Reality of the Body of Christ*, p. 43)

WANTING TO CARRY OUT WITH HER BELOVED THE WORK THAT IS FOR THE ENTIRE WORLD

"Come, my beloved, let us go forth into the fields; / Let us lodge in the villages" (S. S. 7:11). This reveals that she wants to carry out with her Beloved the work that is for the entire world by sojourning from one place to another. This indicates that she is not sectarian. In the Lord's work it is not easy to keep our work open, to not keep our work "in our pocket." We must learn to keep the work open, so that others can come to sojourn there and we can go to sojourn elsewhere. This is to keep one work in one Body. (*Life-study of Song of Songs*, p. 59)

GOD'S CENTRAL WORK

Today we have to see what God's work is, and we have to know what is God's central work in man. We must be led to see the way to receive God's life. After we receive this life, we should know how to live in this life, so that God can have a way among us. This is God's central work...What we need today is not peripheral works but God's central work. (*Messages Given during the Resumption of Watchman Nee's Ministry*, vol. 1, pp. 151-152)

GOD'S CENTRAL WORK— WORKING HIMSELF INTO MAN

Ephesians 3:19 speaks of the fullness of God. This fullness is the content. God's intention is to fill us with this content. Verse 20 shows us how God accomplishes this, that is, how He fills us with His fullness. The main work of God today is to work Himself into man. Unless our living, our walk, and our work are linked up with God's center, they will all pass away. Even the so-called blessings and peace will pass away. The only thing that will remain is God's work within us. I know that many will think that I am saying the wrong thing, and I know that many will misunderstand my words. But if a man loves the Lord with a pure heart, he will see the revelation.

GOD'S WORK IN TIME
BEING TO WORK HIMSELF INTO MAN

Everything that does not belong to God Himself, even if it has been created by Him, will all pass away. The heavens, the earth, and all things, even we ourselves, will all pass away, because the heavens, the earth, and all things, including ourselves, are not God Himself. That is why they will all pass away. No matter how good you are, and how nice and how clean you look, all these things will pass away. Of course, humanly speaking, it is always better to do good than to do evil. But the good and evil that come from the tree of the knowledge of good and evil are the same before God. Everything that is not of God will pass away. The Chinese have a saying: "Humility brings profit, while arrogance brings loss." But both of these things will also pass away. Today we are not evaluating matters from a temporary point of view. Rather, we are evaluating matters from an eternal point of view. Many things may appear to be good in time, but they cannot endure for eternity. Good is something that exists in time; it cannot be brought into eternity. To do good is the goal of those in the world, but a Christian's goal belongs to eternity. In eternity, there are only things that belong to God. Only God's things are eternal. It is true that God's things pass through time, yet they proceed from eternity and extend through eternity. Everything that God accomplishes in time and in the world is for the accomplishment of His eternal purpose, which is to work Himself into man. Only when God is worked into man can God's eternal purpose be fulfilled. God passes through time in order that He can work Himself into man, that is, in order for Him to mingle Himself into man. (*Messages Given during the Resumption of Watchman Nee's Ministry,* vol. 1, pp. 125-126)

GOD CARING FOR THE PERSON
MORE THAN FOR THE THINGS

In the church the most important thing is the person. The importance of the person far exceeds that of any work. In the world it is just the opposite; there, the work is more important than the person. But for us the person is more important. Time stands between the two eternities; both creation and redemption are within the span of time. During the span of time, God does many works. God's main goal, however, is not the works but to gain persons through the works. God does not work for the sake of working, but for the sake of gaining men through His works. God is not here merely to accomplish a work but to use His work to gain some people. Hence, our views have to be changed. (*Messages Given during the Resumption of Watchman Nee's Ministry,* vol. 1, p. 189)

THE PERSON BEING GOD'S METHOD AND WAY

The service of the elders has to do with the person of the elder. It does not depend on the method but on the person. In the New Testament it is very difficult to find out what is the method or way to serve. Some places seem to speak about the method or the way, but actually the emphasis is still the person himself. The person is the way, and the person is the Lord's work. If God does not gain a person, He will have no work, and He will have no way. A way is a course that a person takes. If God does not gain man, He will have no course to take. Man thinks that the most important thing to do is to find a good way. However, God's work does not involve giving us the ways but is a matter of gaining the persons. If God can gain two or three brothers here, He will have a way. Even if I present to you the best way to be an elder, it will be useless if the person is wrong. We, the person, should be gained by God. We have to learn to be the proper person more than to learn to do the proper things. It is meaningless for things to be done properly without the person being a proper one. What you are is what you do. You cannot serve God beyond what you are as a person. Hudson Taylor said in his book *Union and Communion* that what we are is more important than what we do. This word left a deep impression on me. We should know how to help the brothers and sisters properly. (*Messages Given during the Resumption of Watchman Nee's Ministry,* vol. 1, pp. 59-60)

* * *

We have to remember all the time that the need today is for God to work Himself into us rather than for us to work for God. All those who will only work for God without allowing God to work in them will eventually be rejected. Only those who allow God to work in them through various circumstances, people, matters, and events will be blessed by Him. (*Messages Given during the Resumption of Watchman Nee's Ministry,* vol. 1, p. 111)

* * *

To love the Lord Jesus does not mean to work for Him. Working for Him means nothing to the Lord Jesus. If you do not believe this today, some day you will believe it. But that day will be too late. It is not that we work for Him but that He works on us. We must not be merely His workers but His work (Eph. 2:10). We must take in the Lord so that He may perfume us and transform us. Then we will progress from one figure to another and will arrive at the stage of the palanquin and the crown. But we still need to go on to the garden and the city. May the Lord be merciful to us and take us all the way! Life and building are the two main items of the Lord's recovery. This is why we must attain to the garden and the city. (*Life and Building as Portrayed in the Song of Songs,* pp. 85-86)

A GOOD TREE PRODUCING GOOD FRUIT, A CORRUPT TREE PRODUCING EVIL FRUIT

I do not believe that there is anything that is more real than the things in the spiritual realm. A person cannot cheat God. He cannot cheat himself, and he cannot cheat the saints.

In two years' time, you will see the effect of my words today. The kind of person you are determines the kind of children you produce. Those who love the world will produce Christians who love the world. Those brothers and sisters who seek after modern fashions, if they can bring others to salvation at all, will bring in ones who are flippant and shallow. Those who have a hot temper will surely bring in Christians with a bad temper. A good tree produces good fruit, and a corrupt tree produces evil fruit (Matt. 7:17-18). The kind of person we are determines the kind of fruit we produce. (*Messages Given during the Resumption of Watchman Nee's Ministry,* vol. 1, pp. 62-63)

* * *

Brother Watchman Nee used to tell us that some people build up twelve inches by what they do but tear down fourteen inches by what they are. This means that they tear down more than they build up. Hence, it is better for them not to do anything. We may build up a certain amount by our Bible doctrine and knowledge, but we will damage more than we build up because of our shortage of the humanity of Jesus. In the church life we need the humanity of Jesus much more than the gifts, the so-called baptism, or the knowledge of the Bible. (*Christ as the Reality,* p. 108)

THE UNIQUE GOAL OF THE CHRISTIAN WORK

According to the entire revelation of the New Testament, the unique goal of the Christian work should be the New Jerusalem, which is the ultimate goal of God's eternal economy.

THE MAIN CAUSE OF THE CHURCH'S DEGRADATION

The degradation of the church is mainly due to the fact that nearly all the Christian workers are distracted to take many things other than the New Jerusalem as their goal.

OVERCOMING EVERYTHING
THAT REPLACES THE NEW JERUSALEM AS OUR GOAL

Hence, under the degradation of the church, to be an overcomer answering the Lord's call needs us to overcome not only the negative things but even more the positive things that replace the New Jerusalem as the goal.

AN OVERCOMER'S GOAL

An overcomer's goal should be uniquely and ultimately the goal of God's eternal economy, that is, the New Jerusalem. (*The Vital Groups,* p. 131)

BROTHER LEE'S FELLOWSHIP ON APRIL 6, 1997

The following is Brother Lee's fellowship given on April 6, 1997:

The co-workers must see that we should do only one work, which is to make God's chosen people regenerated ones, sanctified ones, renewed ones—the new man—transformed ones, conformed ones—those conformed to the image of the firstborn Son of God—and glorified ones. All those who will be in the New Jerusalem are this kind of people.

Specifically, God proceeds step by step to make a chosen one of God a person who is regenerated, sanctified, renewed, transformed, conformed to the image of the firstborn Son of God, and even glorified by God. In this way, we go up level by level until we reach the highest point, where we become the same. There is no more flesh and no more natural being. All are in the spirit. All are the kingdom of the heavens, and all are beings of the New Jerusalem. This is the highest point. If you understand this, you can explain it to the brothers and sisters, and you can ask them to speak the same. (*The Ministry,* vol. 1, no. 1, October 1997, p. 49)

THE IMPORTANCE OF THE CHILDREN
AND YOUNG PEOPLE'S WORK
FOR THE FUTURE OF THE LORD'S RECOVERY

Scripture Reading: Rev. 22:12, 20; Luke 18:16-17; 2 Tim. 3:15;
1:5; 2:2

I. We all need to know what age we are in, what the
present revelation is from God, where we should be,
what we should do, and what flow we should enter into;
time is short, and the day of the Lord's second coming is approaching—Rev. 22:12, 20; cf. Matt. 24:37-39;
2 Tim. 3:1-3.

II. We cannot continue to work as we have in the past; in
the past we neglected the work with the children and
the young people, and we highly regarded a general
work—Luke 18:16-17:

A. "Your eyes have to be open. Do not be too busy outwardly. You should work on the young people, the
junior highers, and the high schoolers. You should
also work on the children until each week there
are at least ten thousand children being taught by
us. Those who are six or seven years old now will
be high schoolers in ten years. If you are willing to
do this, you can definitely succeed"—*The Ultimate
Significance of the Golden Lampstand*, p. 55.

B. No family will disregard its children; as a priority
a family looks after its children, raises them, and
teaches them; hence, we must serve the many children in God's family—2 Tim. 3:15; 1:5.

C. All the churches must have a children's work; if we

work with these children, they will all be young
brothers and sisters after six to seven years.

   D. The co-workers must lead the church to receive a
burden for the children's work; the church should
concentrate its effort on this work.

III. We must let God open our eyes to see the preciousness
of the young people and their importance in God's
hands—cf. Dan. 1:2, 4; 2 Tim. 2:2; 1 Tim. 4:12:

   A. In whatever a person does, the most important
thing is to have a heart—2 Cor. 6:11; Col. 3:23:

     1. If you want to do this work, you must like the
young people, care for them, and be concerned
about their affairs; this may be considered the
minimum "capital" required for the young people's work—Matt. 19:14.

     2. If you have no interest in the young people and
have no heart for them, doing the young people's
work only out of reluctance, then it is useless—
v. 13.

     3. Some brothers and sisters are doing the young
people's work out of their preference, but it is
not weighty enough to do the young people's work
with such a heart—1 Kings 4:29.

   B. When we see the importance and value of a certain
matter, then spontaneously we have a heart for
it—2 Tim. 2:2; cf. 1 Thes. 3:8.

IV. The future of the church hinges on the young people—
2 Tim. 2:2; cf. Deut. 1:38:

   A. If we read through the Bible carefully, we will discover a fact: it is not easy to find a case showing
that God called an old person to do a new thing or
a thing of great consequence—1 Sam. 3:1, 4; Dan.
1:4, 8; Matt. 4:18-20:

     1. We can say that virtually everyone used by God
to begin a new thing or chosen by God to turn
the age was a young man—Deut. 1:38.

     2. Nearly every work that the young people were
called by God to do was a work that turned the
age; for the carrying out of all these works of

great consequences, God always called young men—1 Sam. 3:1, 4.

B. For usefulness in the Lord's hand, for the spread of the Lord's kingdom, and for the propagation of the Lord's work, the responsibility undoubtedly falls on the shoulders of the young people—cf. Acts 2:14-41.

C. If the Lord delays His coming back for five, ten, fifteen, or twenty years and He wants to accomplish something, the commission will have to be entrusted to the young people—Matt. 24:14; 28:19-20; 2 Tim. 2:2; 4:5:

1. Nevertheless, the conditions today, such as the "greenness of the crops," the desolation of the church, and the scarcity of overcomers, tell us that the Lord cannot come back so soon—1 Tim. 4:1-5; 2 Tim. 3:1-13.

2. Therefore, seeing such a situation, we believe that there may be still a considerable amount of time in which the Lord wants to accomplish something on the earth—2 Pet. 3:9.

3. Twenty years from now those who will be useful to the Lord are those who are in their twenties or younger today—2 Tim. 3:14-15, 17:

   a. There must be a group of young people who are saved to receive proper spiritual help today so that they can gain the experience and be used by the Lord in the future—2:2.

   b. If there are no young people gained by the Lord today, after our departure there will be no one to succeed us; then there will be a gap—cf. Deut. 1:37-38.

4. If there are young brothers and sisters raised up by the Lord, and if we are preserved to give them an absolutely positive leading instead of erroneous limitations, then there is no need to wait until the Lord takes us away; even today they can become useful in the Lord's hands— 2 Tim. 3:10; 1 Cor. 16:10.

D. The future of the work and the usefulness in the

future, no doubt, are with the young people; from the view of the future of the work, we should put our emphasis on the younger ones—cf. Deut. 1:38.

Excerpts from the Ministry:

KNOWING THE AGE WE ARE IN
AND THE PRESENT REVELATION OF GOD

We all need to know what age we are in, what the present revelation is from God, where we should be, what we should do, and what flow we should enter into. Time is short, and the day of the Lord's second coming is approaching. We must no longer be drugged by the religious things. We need to wake up to see where we should be and what we should do. This is a serious matter. The Lord Jesus likened this age to the age of Noah, saying, "Just as the days of Noah were, so will the coming of the Son of Man be. For as they were in those days before the flood, eating and drinking, marrying and giving in marriage...until the flood came and took all away" (Matt. 24:37-39). We must not be here unclear, drugged, and befuddled by the present situation. We must see what the age is, where we should be, and the way we should follow. (*The Testimony of Jesus,* p. 32)

BEING ONE WHO KNOWS THE AGE

We must be those who know the age. If we truly know the Bible, we will be able to see what kind of age we are in according to the prophecies in the Bible and the world situation today. When I was first saved more than sixty years ago, I loved the Bible very much and studied the Bible diligently. At that time some books concerning prophecy had been published in Europe, so I bought some and read them. There are many prophecies related to the world situation, especially prophecies regarding the Jews, the Middle East, and the Persian Gulf nations. These prophecies speak mainly about two matters. The first matter is the restoration of the Jewish nation, and the second matter is the return of Jerusalem into the hands of the Jews. (*Being Up-to-date for the Rebuilding of the Temple,* p. 61)

* * *

We cannot continue to work as we have in the past; we must change our ways. In the past we neglected the work with the children, the young people, and the sisters. We highly regarded a general work, but we paid little attention to the young people's work, and we merely prayed for the children's work. Now we must concentrate our efforts on the children, the young people, and the sisters. Moreover, the messages we give must minister Christ as the Spirit in a simple and direct way. We should focus on these primary matters and nothing else. (*The Collected Works of Witness Lee, 1967,* vol. 1, p. 270)

* * *

When I returned to Taiwan ten years ago, I was very clear, saying, "Your eyes have to be open. Do not be too busy outwardly. You should work on the young people, the junior highers, and the high schoolers. You should also work on the children until each week there are at least ten thousand children being taught by us. Those who are six or seven years old now will be high schoolers in ten years. If you are willing to do this, you can definitely succeed." The brothers told me at that time that there were twenty-three thousand names on the list of the church in Taipei, comprising at least eight thousand homes. If each family has one or two children, there should be twelve thousand children. When they asked me concerning a place for the children to meet, I said, "There is no need to go to the meeting hall, and it is not necessary to meet on the Lord's Day. You can meet on Saturdays or in the evenings. You can simply meet in the homes of the brothers and sisters. Out of the eight thousand families, you can choose three to four hundred homes to be the places for the children's meetings, with each home holding thirty children. If you continue in this work, you will see how much you can accomplish!" Starting from 1966 and 1967 I have been talking about this very matter and have been expecting the church to practice it, because we do have the basic strength to work it out. If we had worked from that time until now, 1977, ten thousand children would have become high schoolers of sixteen to seventeen years of age. Immediately, there would be ten thousand "seeds" in different high schools. At that time, I also said that we had to work on the junior highers, the high schoolers, and the college students to gain several thousand in each category. In this way, the number of children and young people added together would be at least twenty to thirty thousand. Moreover, children increase endlessly. When these ten thousand get into high school, another ten thousand will take their place. It is a pity that you did not practice what I said! (*The Ultimate Significance of the Golden Lampstand,* pp. 55-56)

CHILDREN'S WORK

The first matter for the sisters' service is the children's work. Concerning the children's work, within me there is truly a heavy burden. All the churches must have a children's work. According to statistics, forty-five percent of the population of Taiwan is under fifteen years of age. This is roughly six million people. Many local churches have quite a few families with children. I estimate that there are about ten thousand children in the church in Taipei and about the same number of children in the churches in the rest of Taiwan. If we work with these twenty thousand children, they will all be young brothers and sisters after six to seven years. This is what the sisters should do.

In the past the church in Taipei did not pay adequate attention to this. Of the ten thousand children in Taipei, only about five hundred come to the meeting on the Lord's Day; eight to nine thousand children are without any care. In spite of all the effort we use to preach the gospel in Taipei, we may not be able to bring three or even two thousand people to salvation in a year. If we cultivate our ten thousand children, they will all become young brothers and sisters in six or seven years. This means that we will have an average increase of a thousand people every year. (*The Collected Works of Witness Lee, 1967,* vol. 1, pp. 304-305)

* * *

Some may think that it is easy to care for the children who are between the ages of five and twelve by simply giving them a piece of candy. However, to handle the children in this way will not yield a good result. According to my observation, the most difficult work to do effectively is the children's work. (*The Collected Works of Witness Lee, 1967,* vol. 1, p. 311)

THE WHOLE CHURCH
ENDEAVORING IN THE CHILDREN'S WORK

Whether or not we succeed in the children's work depends partly on the teaching material and partly on the brothers and sisters who take the lead. The responsible brothers and the co-workers in every place must see the importance of the children's work in God's family. How can a family not take care of its children? This should be a great matter to us. No family will disregard its children; as a priority a family looks after its children, raises them, and teaches them. Hence, we must serve the many children in God's family.

From this time onward, the co-workers should give more thought to the way they lead people to know the Lord. They must pay attention to the sisters and the children. The co-workers should not say that they are not gifted for these two aspects of the work and therefore cannot do the work. If they cannot do it, they must learn how to do it; they should always learn. The co-workers do not need to be personally involved in doing the children's work. They can meet with the leading sisters in a locality and entrust the burden for the children's work to them, and they can encourage them. They must lead the church to receive a burden for the children's work. The church should concentrate its effort on this work.

The leading sisters in the churches must receive a burden for the children's work. Under the arrangement of the church and the leading of the elders, they should concentrate on the children's work and lead all the sisters to participate. The elders are too busy to take care of the details. Instead of waiting for the elders, the sisters should pray much and make plans. They can then present their plans for the children's work to the elders for their approval. This is just like a family in which the husband is busy with his job and cannot plan the details for the household. The wife can make plans and carry things out with the consent of the husband. In this way the wife does not do anything independently and will still be able to take care of the details of the household in a timely way. (*The Collected Works of Witness Lee, 1967*, vol. 1, pp. 313-314)

* * *

During these years, among a few churches, often I have emphatically charged the brothers and sisters that they must take care of the young people...The reason I purposely encourage young people is that I clearly realize one thing: if a church cannot raise up the young people, this church has no future...The church needs the second generation. The future of the church hinges on the young people. (*The Elders' Management of the Church,* pp. 108-109)

* * *

The future of the Lord's recovery is very promising. At present, in the United States there are at least seven thousand seeking saints in the Lord's recovery. Over the next ten years, many of our children will become members of the church. When some of them are in their twenties, they will be quite useful to the Lord. Brother Nee, for example, was raised up by the Lord when he was only nineteen. (*Life-study of 1 Peter,* p. 285)

SEEING THE PRECIOUSNESS
OF THE YOUNG PEOPLE

In whatever a person does, the most important thing is to have a heart. Without a heart, a person will not want to do anything, and even if he does something, he will not be enthusiastic in doing it. Of course, this is also true with the young people's work. If you want to do this work, you must like the young people, care for them, and be concerned about their affairs. This may be considered the minimum "capital" required for the young people's work. If you have no interest in the young people and have no heart for them, doing the young people's work only out of reluctance, then it is useless.

Sometimes our heart may arise from our preference. When we like something, naturally we will have a heart to do it. Sometimes the heart we have may come from our knowledge.

When we see the importance and value of a certain matter, we will spontaneously have a heart for it. According to my observation of the real situation among us concerning the young people's work, I see that some brothers and sisters are doing it out of their preference. Because they are naturally inclined to the young people and they enjoy contacting the young people, they come to do the young people's work. We cannot say that this is wrong. We have to admit that no matter how much grace we have received and how great the spirituality we possess, we are still human—we still have the part that is human. But here we have to say that it is not weighty enough to do the young people's work with such a heart. If we truly want to do the young people's work, and do it in a weighty manner, we must let God open our eyes to see the preciousness of the young people and their importance in God's hands. If we see this, we will appreciate this work, and spontaneously we will have a heart within us for it.

THE FUTURE OF THE LORD'S WORK
DEPENDING ALTOGETHER
ON THE YOUNG PEOPLE

If we read through the Bible carefully, we will discover a fact: It is not easy to find a case showing that God called an old person to do a new thing or a thing of great consequence. This may discourage the older brothers and sisters, but it is something undeniable. Indeed, we cannot see that God ever called an old person to do a new thing. Seemingly, Moses received God's call when he was eighty years old, but if we carefully read the Bible, we will see that actually the first time he received God's call was not when he was eighty years old. Rather, when he was still young, God's calling had already begun in him. If you read on, whether it was Joshua, Caleb, Samuel, or David in the Old Testament, or whether it was the twelve disciples called by the Lord Jesus in the New Testament, when they were first gained by the Lord, none of them was an old man. Not only is this true in the Bible, but even in all of church history it is hard to find a strong illustration to show that God called an old man when He had a new and important thing to do. We can say that virtually everyone used by God to begin a new thing or chosen by God to turn the age was a young man.

I would like to give you a testimony. Thirty years ago the Lord's work in China had a new beginning. In that period of time God did not call any old people. All the ones who are around fifty years old and who are standing firmly to serve before the Lord today were still young people who, thirty years ago, were around twenty years old. They were raised up by the Lord in the schools for that new work. Brothers and sisters, if you see this, you will treasure the young people before God.

Furthermore, nearly every work that the young people were called by God to do was a work that turned the age. God called Moses to turn one age, and He called Joshua to turn another age. Obviously, His calling of Samuel turned another age. The prophethood, priesthood, and kingship all hung on this young man Samuel. He was truly one who turned the age. David was also one who turned the age. Furthermore, we can see that Daniel and his three friends were young ones among the people in captivity. Through them God turned that age of captivity. Then in the New Testament, the first to emerge was John the Baptist. We know that he was a young man called by the Lord. God used him to turn the age at his time. We can go on to look at Paul, who was an apostle especially used by God. The Bible says that he was a young man when he was visited by the Lord (Acts 7:58). We all admit that Paul was a man who turned the age. I dare not overstate the case, but my feeling is that the work which the Lord started among us in the East thirty years ago also considerably bore the nature and element of an age-turning work. For the carrying out of all these works of great consequences, God always called young men.

I would like to tell you, brothers and sisters, that because we saw this, we have been paying much attention to the young people's work for nearly twenty years. This is not to say that one young person's soul is worth two older persons' souls. This is not what I mean. What I am saying is that a person has to be gained by the Lord at a young age if he will have some usefulness in God's hands or a future in God's work. This is an obvious fact...

Quite often I have said that for salvation, for the receiving of grace, and for the enjoyment of the Lord's salvation the older ones are absolutely precious. However, for usefulness in the Lord's hand, for the spread of the Lord's kingdom, and for the propagation of the Lord's work, the responsibility undoubtedly falls on the shoulders of the young people. If the Lord delays His coming back for five, ten, fifteen, or twenty years and He wants to accomplish something, the commission will have to be entrusted to the young people. Concerning those of us who are already over fifty, we all hope that we may be alive to see the Lord come back and not have to pass through the Jordan River of death. Nevertheless, we have to admit that the conditions today, such as the "greenness of the crops," the desolation of the church, and the scarcity of overcomers, tell us that the Lord cannot come back so soon. It is not that the Lord does not want to come back. Rather, He desperately wants to come back soon, but our condition does not allow Him. Therefore, seeing such a situation, we believe that there may be still a considerable amount of time in which the Lord wants to accomplish something on the earth.

Of course, we should also believe that the Lord may come back tomorrow. Nearly two thousand years ago He already said, "Behold, I come quickly!" In His estimation a thousand years are like one day; with Him there is no time element. On our side, however, if the Lord delays, I cannot believe that a number of us who are now over fifty will still be alive thirty years later. Some of the brothers and sisters are even older than I am and are in their sixties, and others are in their seventies. In any case, if the Lord delays His coming back, I am afraid we cannot wait that long and will all be gone. May I ask, who then will continue to do the Lord's work? You may be very spiritual, even too spiritual, and say, "The Lord will be responsible for all these matters." Of course, this is true; the Lord will be responsible. There is no denying this. But one thing is clear: Whether He takes direct responsibility or He wants you or me to do something for Him, the way is with the young people. Twenty years from now those who will be useful to the Lord are those who are in their twenties or younger today.

It is a universally accepted fact that a person receives education for twenty-five years, gains experience for another twenty-five years, and then becomes truly useful in the final twenty-five years. Three twenty-five years make a total of seventy-five years. I hope all our young people will live for seventy-five years—twenty-five years to receive spiritual education, another twenty-five years to gain spiritual experience, and the final twenty-five years to be used by God. I also hope that those who are in their fifties now will take good care of their health for the Lord's sake. However, brothers and sisters, please consider: Unless there is a group of young people who are saved to receive proper spiritual help today, how can they gain the experience and be used by the Lord in the future? If there are no young people gained by the Lord today, after our departure there will be no one to succeed us. Then there will be a gap.

Let me give you a testimony. Thirty years ago when the Lord raised us up in China, it was truly a hard time for us. Since there was no one who could help us in our service, we had to strenuously grope around in every matter. At that time we had left Christianity behind; therefore, even in the matter of how to meet we had to feel our way around little by little. Now, after more than thirty years, the young people then have become old people. If the Lord does not have a group of young people today to receive help, after some time, when we pass away, will there not be a gap? This will not only delay the day of the Lord but also diminish the effectiveness of our work. If there are young brothers and sisters raised up by the Lord, and if we are preserved to give them an absolutely positive leading instead of erroneous limitations, then there is no need to wait until the Lord takes us away; even today they can become useful in the Lord's hands.

We already saw this clearly more than twenty years ago. Therefore, from that time on we paid a great deal of attention to gaining the young intellectuals in the universities and hospitals. Thank the Lord, this work had good progress from 1936. The Lord gained a good number of young people from the Union Medical College in Peking, from a certain hospital in Tientsin, from the Ch'i Lu University in Tsinan, from the

College of Nursing in Shanghai, and from some universities in Nanking. Many young medical students, resident physicians, nurses, and even professors became our brothers and sisters. About ten years later, among us nearly all the co-workers and responsible ones in the churches all over the country were the young people gained at that time. Therefore, after the War of Resistance against Japan [1937-1945] was won and the country was restored, then the Lord brought us back to Shanghai where there was a small work of revival again in the regions of Nanking and Shanghai. At that time we concentrated nearly seventy to eighty percent of our efforts on the young people. Within those two to three years all the work among the college students received much blessing from the Lord. Many young ones were gained by Him. By saying this much, I hope that the brothers and sisters can see the importance of the young people's work. This should create a heart in us to appreciate the young brothers and sisters.

I would say to you, brothers and sisters, that I love the older ones. The Lord can testify for me about this. But I also would ask the older ones to forgive me because I would also say that I really appreciate the young people's work. Some spread words about me, saying that Brother Lee only cares for the young people's work and that he has chased all the older ones out to the street. I deny this; I never had that intention. However, for the future of the Lord's work, I would ask the older ones to pray much for the young people. The future of the work and the usefulness in the future, no doubt, are with the young people. From the view of saving souls, we should treat older ones and younger ones equally. From the view of the future of the work, however, we should put our emphasis on the younger ones. If the church or the work fails to gain young people, it will be like a family that has only some childless old people: an old grandfather who is eighty-five years old, a father who is sixty years old, and a son who is nearly forty years old. There are no younger ones under them; there are no crying ones or shouting ones. Rather, everyone is well-behaved. This is abnormal.

Sometimes when someone says to me, "Brother Lee, it seems that our church is in a mess and is not very orderly," I would say, "That is actually a good sign." When you visit a family, if you see some are crying, some are shouting, some are fighting, some are doing somersaults, and some are rolling on the floor, that is a good sign; it indicates that the family is flourishing. If a family has only an eighty-five year old grandfather, a sixty-year-old father, and a forty-year-old son, certainly no one will be rolling on the floor. Even if any of them desires to roll on the floor, he would not have the strength to do it. Therefore, all year round they live in quietness, orderliness, and loneliness. Brothers and sisters, we can be sure that such a family does not have to sell its house; the house will become someone else's house before long. In the same manner, when you visit a church, if you see throngs of young people there, then you should praise the Lord that the church has a future. You do not need to ask whether those young people are good or bad. Just as in a family, it does not matter how naughty the children are; they are still better than none. If there are no children, the family is doomed to hopelessness. Some children who are undesirable today may become desirable tomorrow. There is always hope.

In summary, we need to gain the young people in the church and in the Lord's work. Anyone who works for the Lord with insight needs to pay attention to this matter. If you see this, your heart will be burdened to love the young people regardless of whether they are good or bad. Having a young one who is not very desirable is better than having none at all. May the brothers and sisters as the Lord's lovers all love the young people for the future of the church and for the Lord's work. (*How to Lead the Young People*, pp. 1-15)

GOD'S ORDAINED WAY
BEING TO GAIN HOUSEHOLDS

Scripture Reading: Acts 2:39; Josh. 24:15; Gen. 7:1; Exo. 12:3; 2 Sam. 6:11; Luke 19:9; Acts 16:31; 1 Cor. 7:14; Eph. 1:4-5

I. In considering the exercise and practice of the God-ordained way to preach the gospel, we must include the unit of God's salvation; God's promise of salvation takes the household as a unit, not the individual as a unit—Acts 2:39; 16:31:

   A. Concerning eternal life, the Bible takes an individual, not a household, as the unit; however, concerning salvation, it shows that men are saved household by household—1 John 5:12; Gen. 7:1.

   B. We hope that all the children who are born among us will not need our extra effort in the future to bring them to salvation and to rescue them out of the world; some have already been born into our fleshly family; we should make sure that they are born into our spiritual family also—Psa. 87:5; 2 Tim. 1:5.

   C. Whether or not the church will go on in the next generation depends on whether we can bring our own children to the Lord; if we lose as many as are born to us, our second generation will be gone—Psa. 127:3-5:

      1. If generation after generation all those who are born into our midst stand fast and if we also have some increase from the outside, the church will be strong and its number will increase—2 Tim. 1:5.

  2. We must never give birth to a child only to lose it later; instead, those who are born to us must be regenerated—Psa. 127:3.

II. The basic principle in the Bible is that God saves men household by household:

 A. In the Old Testament:

  1. The whole house entering the ark—Gen. 7:1; 1 Pet. 3:20.

  2. The whole house being circumcised—Gen. 17:12-13.

  3. A passover lamb for each household—Exo. 12:3-7.

  4. The priesthood being for the household—Num. 18:1, 11.

  5. The household salvation of Rahab the harlot—Josh. 2:19; 6:17.

  6. The household being blessed—2 Sam. 6:11.

  7. Rejoicing with the household—Deut. 12:7; 14:26.

 B. In the New Testament:

  1. The household of Zaccheus—Luke 19:9.

  2. The household of a nobleman—John 4:53.

  3. The household of Cornelius—Acts 10:2; 11:14.

  4. The household of Lydia—16:15.

  5. The household of the jailer—v. 31.

  6. The household of Crispus—18:8.

  7. The promise of the Spirit being to you and your children—2:39.

  8. Peace to a house—Luke 10:5-6.

  9. The household of Stephanas—1 Cor. 1:16.

  10. The household of Onesiphorus—2 Tim. 4:19; 1:16.

III. In the Bible the head of a family has the special responsibility before God for bringing his whole household to the Lord and to His service; the head of the household can decide for his entire household—Josh. 24:15:

 A. We should declare with faith that we have decided that our family will be a family that worships God and that our family will be a family that believes in the Lord; if we exercise our authority to take the lead, our children will go along—2 Cor. 4:13; Mark 2:4-5.

B. The household is ours, and we have the power to decide whether this house will serve the Lord; when we take this stand, everyone who is under us will come to the Lord; they will have no other way to take—1 Cor. 11:3.

IV. Household salvation is one of the greatest principles in the Bible; once you are saved, your whole household should be saved; as an individual you must first stand firm for the Lord, and then your household will change—7:14:

A. When we invite people to come to a meeting of the church, many will come by themselves; if we go to visit people in their homes, we will reach their whole household—Luke 19:5-9.

B. One of the greatest failures of the Protestants is that they are too loose with their next generation; they allow their next generation to have the freedom to choose their own faith—Prov. 22:6.

C. We may be selfish even in praying for the salvation of our children; not to pray for our children is wrong, but to be fully occupied with prayer for them in a selfish way is also wrong; the matter of the salvation of our children and their spiritual welfare is also a test to us—11:25.

D. We should raise up our children according to the Lord's teaching; this is our duty and we should do it, but eventually their salvation and seeking of the Lord depend upon God's eternal choosing and predestination—Eph. 1:4-5.

Excerpts from the Ministry:

THE UNIT OF GOD'S SALVATION

In considering the exercise and practice of the God-ordained way to preach the gospel, we must include the unit of God's salvation. Most people, whether Christians or non-Christians, think about God's salvation as involving individuals.

The natural mind thinks of one person as the unit of God's salvation. This kind of thinking is contrary to God's economy, God's plan. God's ordained way is to gain households, not just individuals. (*The Exercise and Practice of the God-ordained Way,* p. 71)

GOD'S PROMISE OF SALVATION
BEING TO THE HOUSEHOLD

Now we come to the subject of the unit of salvation. Everything is measured by units. The unit of salvation is the household.

According to the Bible, in God's dealings and communications with man, He has given man many promises. If we know these promises, we will reap great benefit for ourselves. If we do not know them, we will suffer great loss.

God's promise of salvation takes the household as a unit, not the individual as a unit. If a newly saved person sees this from the very beginning, he will be spared many headaches, and he will gain much benefit for himself. When God saves man, He takes the whole family, rather than an individual, as a unit.

Concerning eternal life, the Bible takes an individual, not a household, as the unit. However, concerning salvation, it shows that men are saved household by household. The unit of salvation is the household. We want to spend a little time to consider several portions of the Word. This will show us clearly that salvation is for the whole household. We can inquire of God according to these words. We can deal with Him not only for ourselves individually but also for our whole family.

We hope that all the children who are born among us will not need our extra effort in the future to bring them to salvation and to rescue them out of the world. Some have already been born into our fleshly family. We should make sure that they are born into our spiritual family also. We cannot afford to lose them year by year and then fight to rescue them back year by year. We cannot just beget them into the world; we still must bring them to the Lord.

If all the brothers and sisters agree that this is the way we should take, we will have at least as many saved ones as the number of children in our midst. The Lord has placed them in our hands. We should not let them go; we must make sure that they are saved. Otherwise, it will take considerable effort to bring them back from the world. All the little fishes born of our big fishes should be on our side; we should not let them go back into the sea and then struggle to catch them again. Whether or not the church will continue with its second generation depends on whether our children belong to the Lord.

I hope that the brothers and sisters will see the importance of this matter. Whether or not the church will go on in the next generation, whether or not those after us will go on, depends on whether we can bring our own children to the Lord. If we lose as many as are born to us, our second generation will be gone. If generation after generation all those who are born into our midst stand fast and if we also have some increase from the outside, the church will be strong and its number will increase. We must never give birth to a child only to lose it later. Instead, those who are born to us must be regenerated.

EXAMPLES FROM THE BIBLE

The Bible reveals the basic principle that God saves men household by household. How can we prove this? Let us examine various portions of the Word.

In the Old Testament

The Whole House Entering the Ark

Genesis 7:1 says, "Then Jehovah said to Noah, Come into the ark, you and all your household," and 1 Peter 3:20 says, "A few, that is, eight souls, were brought safely through by water."

The ark was not for an individual; it was for the whole house. In Genesis 6 we see a man who was righteous before God— Noah. The Bible does not say that the sons and daughters-in-law of Noah were righteous. The Bible only says that Noah was a righteous man before God. However, when God prepared a way of salvation for Noah, He commanded Noah's whole house to enter the ark. Therefore, the household, not an individual, entered the ark.

A new believer should bring every member of his household into the ark. You can say to the Lord, "I have believed in You. You have said that my whole household can enter into the ark. Lord, please bring my whole household into the ark now." God will honor your faith.

The Whole House Being Circumcised

Genesis 17:12-13 says, "Every male throughout your generations, he who is born in the house or bought with money from any foreigner who is not of your seed. He who is born in your house and he who is bought with your money must be circumcised; thus My covenant shall be in your flesh for an everlasting covenant."

God called Abraham and made a covenant with him, saying, "I will establish My covenant between Me and you and your seed after you" (v. 7). The sign of the covenant between God and Abraham was circumcision. All who were circumcised belonged to God, and all who were not circumcised were not of God. God also told Abraham that his whole household needed to be circumcised, including those who were born in his house and those who were bought with his money. Therefore, the promise of circumcision was not given to Abraham alone but to his whole household. Circumcision takes the household as a unit. God's promise came to Abraham's house, not to him alone.

A Passover Lamb for Each Household

Exodus 12:3-7 says, "Speak to all the assembly of Israel, saying, On the tenth of this month each man shall take a lamb according to his fathers' house, a lamb for a household...And they shall take some of the blood and put it on the two doorposts and on the lintel of the houses in which they eat it."

The passover lamb was clearly given to a household, not to an individual. Again we see the importance of a household before God. The passover lamb had to do with a household; it was not an individual matter. A lamb was not prepared for each person, but for each household. The blood struck on the doorposts and the lintel was to protect the whole household. The angel of destruction would pass over a whole household.

It is marvelous to see that the salvation prepared by the Lord Jesus Christ is not for an individual alone but for the whole household, just like the passover lamb. If one man eats the lamb, it means that only he is being saved. But if the whole household eats the lamb, it means that the whole household is being saved. Salvation is for the whole household. The whole household eats the lamb, and similarly the whole household strikes the blood. The whole household enjoys these things together. May God open our eyes to see that salvation is a matter of the whole household, not individuals. (*Messages for Building Up New Believers,* vol. 2, pp. 303-308)

* * *

In Exodus 12, the passover lamb was eaten according to households. If a household was too small for the lamb, they were to share their lamb with a neighboring house (vv. 3-4). Furthermore, the blood of the passover lamb was put on the doorposts and the lintel of the house in which they were instead of upon any individual. To take the Passover as an individual is contrary to God's economy. Jesus Christ, as the Passover lamb, is not only for individuals; He is for a whole house. If we do not take care of the household as the unit of God's salvation, we are violating the principle of God's economy. (*Exercise and Practice of the God-ordained Way,* p. 71)

The Priesthood Being for the Household

God's promise of the priesthood was also for a whole house. It was not for one or two individuals. Numbers 18:1 says, "Then Jehovah said to Aaron, You and your sons and your father's household with you shall bear the iniquity of the sanctuary."

Verse 11 says, "This also is yours, the heave offering of their gift, even all the wave offerings of the children of Israel. I have given them to you and to your sons and to your daughters with you, as a perpetual statute; everyone who is clean in

your house may eat it." God gave all the sacrifices and offerings
to the house of Aaron. The sacrifices were for the house of
Aaron, not for Aaron alone. This is because God accepts the
house as a whole. Please remember that the priesthood was
for Aaron's house, not for Aaron alone. The priesthood took
the household as a unit.

Household Salvation

Joshua 2:19 says, "Anyone who goes forth from the doors
of your house into the street, his blood will be upon his own
head, and we will be innocent. And whoever is with you in the
house, his blood will be upon our heads if a hand should come
upon him." Joshua 6:17 says, "And the city shall be devoted to
Jehovah for destruction, it and all that is in it. Only Rahab
the harlot shall live, she and all who are with her in her
house, because she hid the messengers we sent."

Here we see Rahab the harlot and her household being
saved. What did she do? She received the spies. When she
received the spies, God gave her a sign. She was to tie a line of
scarlet thread in the window. All who were in the house that
had the scarlet thread were spared, while the rest of the
inhabitants of Jericho were killed. The scarlet thread signifies salvation. The scarlet-thread salvation saved Rahab's
household; it did not save just her.

We need to be very clear about the scope of salvation.
Chapter 2 of Joshua gives the promise, and chapter 6 gives
the actual execution. Both the promise in chapter 2 and the
execution in chapter 6 show us that Rahab's whole household
was saved. All who were in the house that had the scarlet
thread were saved. God's salvation is for the whole household,
not for individuals.

The Household Being Blessed

Second Samuel 6:11 says, "And the Ark of Jehovah remained in the house of Obed-edom the Gittite three months;
and Jehovah blessed Obed-edom and all his household."

Jehovah's blessing in the Old Testament was to the household. While the Ark remained in the house of Obed-edom,

Jehovah blessed the whole household. The unit of the blessing is the household, not the individual.

Earlier we spoke of the matter of salvation. We will see that this principle is not just confined to salvation. It governs many matters in both the Old Testament and the New Testament. The house is considered one unit. God's children, especially those who are the head of their house, should realize that God deals with man according to households. If you are ignorant of this fact, you will miss much. If you are the head of a family, you need to lay hold of this fact. You need to say, "Lord, You have told me that You are dealing with my household, not with just myself alone. Therefore, I ask You to save my whole household."

Not only does the head of a household need to lay hold of this fact, but other members of the household also need to inquire of the Lord concerning their father's house. Rahab was not the head of her house; she had a father. But Rahab held to God, and her household was blessed and saved. It is very good if you are the head of your household because you can speak for your household. But even if you are not the head of your household, you can still speak in faith as Rahab, saying, "Lord, turn my household to You to receive Your grace and blessing."

Rejoicing with the Household

Deuteronomy 12:7 says, "There you shall eat before Jehovah your God, and you and your households shall rejoice in all your undertakings, in which Jehovah your God has blessed you." You and your household receive the blessing of God and rejoice therein.

Deuteronomy 14:26 says, "You shall exchange the money for anything that your soul desires, for oxen, for sheep, for wine, for strong drink, or for anything that your soul would like; and you and your household shall eat there before Jehovah your God and rejoice."

Have you seen this? God promised the Israelites that they would eat, drink, and rejoice before God on that day, household by household. In other words, blessing is for the household, not for the individual.

In the New Testament

What about the New Testament? In the Old Testament, God gained men household by household, and the same is true in the New Testament.

The House of Zaccheus

Luke 19:9 says, "Jesus said to him, Today salvation has come to this house." This is wonderful. The New Testament declares the same principle. I am afraid that many people have been preaching for over twenty years about personal salvation only. However, the Lord tells us that "salvation has come to this *house.*"

When you preach the gospel, you must pay attention to household salvation. You must not look merely for individual salvation. If you truly believe and expect this, your work will undergo a great change. This depends entirely on your faith and expectation. If you expect others to come to the Lord one by one, they will come one by one. If you believe that they will come household by household, they will come household by household. The scope of God's salvation is the household. You must not make this scope smaller than it should be.

The Household of a Nobleman

John 4:53 says, "Then the father knew that it was in that hour in which Jesus said to him, Your son lives; and he believed, he and his whole house." Here only one person was healed— the son. However, the Bible says that "he believed, *he and his whole house.*" You can lay hold of this fact before the Lord. Although the son was the one who directly received His grace, the whole household turned and believed. Our hope and expectation is that we would bear fruit in such a prevailing way.

The Household of Cornelius

Acts 10:2 says that Cornelius was "devout and one who feared God with all his household, giving many alms to the people and beseeching God continually," and 11:14 says, "[Peter] will speak words to you by which you shall be saved, you and all your house."

Cornelius's entire household was saved; it was not just one person who was saved. Cornelius invited his relatives and close friends to hear the words of Peter. While Peter was speaking, the Holy Spirit fell upon all those who were in Cornelius's house, and all of them received salvation.

The Household of Lydia

Acts 16:15 says, "She was baptized, as well as her household." The apostle preached the gospel to Lydia's household, and the whole household believed and was baptized.

The Household of the Jailer

Acts 16:31 says, "Believe on the Lord Jesus, and you shall be saved, you and your household." This is one of the most outstanding verses in Christianity. Believe on the Lord Jesus, and you shall be saved, you and your household. God's Word does not say that if you believe on the Lord Jesus, you and your household shall receive eternal life. It says that if you believe on the Lord Jesus, you and your household will be saved.

Throughout the entire Old Testament, God dealt with man by households. Likewise in the New Testament, He deals with man by households. This is the smallest unit; one cannot reduce it to a smaller one. If anyone believes in the Lord Jesus, his whole household shall be saved. This is indeed a wonderful thing. I do not know why this is so, but the Lord's Word says it is so. The Old Testament and the New Testament are consistent; both recognize the same unit.

The church in Philippi started with a jailer. Paul said, "Believe on the Lord Jesus, and you shall be saved, you and your household." Verse 34 says, "And he brought them up into his house and set a table before them; and he exulted because he had believed in God with all his household." Here we see a wonderful picture. In the beginning the promise was given to the jailer; no one else heard it. "Believe on the Lord Jesus, and you shall be saved, you and your household." Later, the jailer brought his household to Paul. After Paul spoke to them, they were baptized. Then the jailer brought them into his house and set a table before them; and he exulted, having believed in God. "Believe on the Lord Jesus, and you shall be saved, you and your household"—this is not something difficult to achieve. The apostle gave the jailer a promise, and his whole household was saved. Everyone listened, everyone was baptized, and everyone exulted.

Suppose the apostle told the jailer, "Believe on the Lord Jesus, and you shall be saved." If this was the case, we would have to wait a few days after a person was saved, teach him something, and hope that he would understand. Then he might gradually testify to his family, and his family might eventually believe and be saved. If this had been the case, how long would it have taken for the jailer's household to be saved? The apostle did not preach the gospel this way. He did not deal with individuals one by one; instead, he addressed the whole household. He said, "You and your household" shall be saved. You need to see this: The salvation of a household is no different and certainly no more difficult than the salvation of one person. You should never forfeit the privilege of saving the whole household. If you bring the whole household along, the whole household will be saved.

I hope that when the church preaches the gospel five or ten years from now, household after household will be turning to the Lord. From now on, the goal of our workers in evangelism should be whole households. If our goal is a household, we will gain a household. If our goal is only an individual, we will gain only an individual. God does things according to our faith.

If we are clear about God's way with men, we will not suffer unnecessary loss. God takes a household as a unit. If God gains a person, He should gain his whole family as well, regardless of how many persons there are in that family. I hope you will tell the brothers to rise up household by household. Those who are the head of a family have the ground to bring their whole household to the Lord, and they should help their families be saved.

Household salvation means household rejoicing. This is a great matter! If we see that God's dealing with man is by households, we will experience much blessing. We must learn to lay hold of this promise of God. (*Messages for Building Up New Believers,* vol. 2, pp. 308-313)

* * *

In Acts 16:31, Paul told the jailer, "Believe on the Lord Jesus, and you shall be saved, you and your household." In this verse we do not see any word concerning bringing a sheep. However, as soon as one believes in the Lord, he will immediately think of his household: his parents, wife, children, brothers, sisters, aunts, uncles, and cousins. All these are one's "household." The scope of this household is extremely broad. Strictly speaking, this whole household is your "kids." You must take them along. (*Key Points on the Home Meetings,* p. 58)

The Household of Crispus

Acts 18:8 says, "Crispus, the ruler of the synagogue, believed in the Lord with his whole household…and were baptized."

In the Bible there are individuals who believed in the Lord and there are households that believed in the Lord. Notice how easy it is for God's grace to come to a household. The whole household of Crispus believed and was baptized.

The Promise of Pentecost
Being Given to You and Your Children

Let us consider the condition at Pentecost. Acts 2:39 says, "For to you is the promise and to your children, and to all who are far off, as many as the Lord our God calls to Himself."

The promise of Pentecost includes the forgiveness of sins and the receiving of the Holy Spirit. It was given "to you" *and* "to your children"; it was not merely given "to you." Those who are heads of the family in particular should lay hold of this promise and say, "Lord, Your promise is for me and also for my children. It cannot be mine without my children also being included. I want it for myself, and I want it also for my children."

Peace to a House

Luke 10:5-6 says, "Into whatever house you enter, first say, Peace to this house. And if a son of peace is there, your peace shall rest upon it; but if not, it shall return upon you."

The Lord says that when a person sets out to preach the

gospel, he should say as he enters into a house, "Peace to this *house.*" This shows that God's peace comes to man by households. It is not just given to individuals, but to households. If anyone is worthy of peace in a house, peace will come to his entire household. This verse is clear enough. God deals with man by households. Thank God, peace comes to man household by household.

The Household of Stephanas

First Corinthians 1:16 says, "I did baptize the household of Stephanas also." Here Paul said that he baptized every member of the household of Stephanas. Like the jailer and the house of Lydia, Stephanas's whole household believed and was baptized.

The Household of Onesiphorus

Second Timothy 4:19 says, "Greet Prisca and Aquila and the house of Onesiphorus," and 1:16 says, "May the Lord grant mercy to the house of Onesiphorus, for he often refreshed me and was not ashamed of my chain." Here was a family that took care of Paul, a household that was not ashamed of his chain. Notice again that it was not an individual matter but something to do with a household.

These numerous cases provide ample proof in both the Old Testament and the New Testament that God deals with man by households. This is particularly true in the case of salvation; God takes the household as a unit. (*Messages for Building Up New Believers,* vol. 2, pp. 313-315)

THE NEED FOR THE HEAD OF THE HOUSEHOLD TO MAKE A DECLARATION

I would like to speak specifically to the heads of households. In the Bible most of those who bore some responsibility were the heads of households. The head of a family has the special responsibility before God for bringing his whole household to the Lord and to His service. You need to take your stand as the head of your family to declare that your household will believe in the Lord and that you will not tolerate anyone who will not believe. The head of the household can decide for his entire household. Even if the little children do not believe, you can still say that your household will believe in the Lord, because this household is yours and not your children's. You are responsible for your household, not your children. You can declare Joshua 24:15 before the Lord and before your whole family: "As for me and my house, we will serve Jehovah." You have to acknowledge that your family is a believer's family. You need to declare this by faith, and you need to put your wife and children on this ground. Always lay hold of this fact: I am the head of my family, and my family will believe in God. My household will not believe in the devil. I have decided that this family will be a family that worships God. I have decided that this family will be a family that believes in the Lord. If you declare this with faith, and if you exercise your authority to take the lead, your children will go along.

I believe the head of every household should make the declaration of Joshua 24:15. You should gather your children and dependents together and tell them, "As for me and my house, we will serve Jehovah." Then as long as you are in the household, your household will serve the Lord. The household is yours, and you have the power to decide whether this house will serve the Lord. When you take this stand, everyone who is under you will come to the Lord; they will have no other way to take. This is marvelous! (*Messages for Building Up New Believers,* vol. 2, pp. 317-318)

THE NEED TO BRING
THE WHOLE HOUSEHOLD TO THE LORD

I hope that the newly saved brothers and sisters will pay attention to this matter. Once you are saved, you should gather your family members together and declare to them, "From this day forward, my household belongs to God." You need to declare this whether or not they belong to the Lord and whether or not they agree. You are the head of the house and you should do this. You should take the matter into your own hands. You should declare that your household will serve the Lord. When you exercise your faith to stand firm this way, you will prevail.

If those who are saved through us are saved household

by household instead of one by one, what a difference it will make! Brothers and sisters, do not be too loose with your children at home. One of the greatest failures of the Protestants is that they are too loose with their next generation; they allow their next generation to have the freedom to choose their own faith. The Catholics do not have to preach the gospel. Their increase through natural birth alone is greater than the increase the Protestants have in a lifetime. Have you seen Catholics preaching the gospel on street corners like the Salvation Army? No. They just propagate through natural birth, generation after generation. Two become four, and four become eight. Every Roman Catholic child automatically becomes a Roman Catholic. The Catholics do not pay much attention to increase from the outside. As long as a person is born into Catholicism, he is dragged into the religion whether or not he eventually becomes a true believer. It is no wonder that the Catholic population exceeds the Protestant population by more than three times. Do not be nonchalant in this matter, and do not allow your own children to drift away.

Let me repeat: A new believer needs to declare right from the start that his household belongs to the Lord. Not only must he be the Lord's individually; he also must declare that his household is the Lord's. Take full control of this matter, and it will be done for you. You have to declare again and again at home, "As for me and my house, we will serve the Lord. All who live in this house should decide to serve the Lord." You should bring your family to the Lord. You should not make any excuse. Do not allow anyone to drift away.

Household salvation is one of the greatest principles in the Bible. Once you are saved, your whole household should be saved. As an individual you must first stand firm for the Lord, and then your household will change. I hope that you will pay attention to this matter. This is a great blessing. If you do this, you will bring more people to the Lord. (*Messages for Building Up New Believers,* vol. 2, pp. 319-320)

*   *   *

When we invite people to come to a meeting of the church, many will come by themselves. If we go to visit people in their homes, we will reach their whole household. From this we can realize that "door-knocking" reaches the household, not only one person. When we knock on people's doors, we are observing the principle of God's economy. It is a shame if we despise the God-ordained way of reaching people with the gospel. We must take this God-ordained way of preaching the gospel, which is according to the biblical revelation. (*Exercise and Practice of the God-ordained Way,* pp. 71-72)

GAINING THE WHOLE FAMILY

When you go out to visit people, do not care for the number, but care for the family. Our goal is not to get only one individual. Our goal is to get one family. When we talk to people, our talk must pave the way to get the whole family. If it is only a couple, we have to have the goal not merely to gain the wife or the husband but to gain both. If the mother is pregnant, we must have the intention that we will gain this child also. We should gain every member of the family.

When you go, always exercise to gain the whole family. If you are preaching the gospel to a seventeen-year-old young man, you have to consider his parents. By baptizing this young man, you may spoil your work on the whole family. You have to exercise your wisdom to decide whether you should baptize him or not. If you do not baptize him, this does not mean that you give him up. Rather, this is a kind of preparation for you to get his parents and to get his whole family. If you go out persistently, you can gain at least two solid families each year. (*Exercise and Practice of the God-ordained Way,* pp. 81-82)

* * *

However, no matter how good an example is set by the parents, how the children develop depends on God's mercy. On the one hand, the parents must keep a high standard, but on the other hand, they need to trust in the Lord. Day by day we should tell Him, "Lord, these children are not mine; they are Your possession placed in my custody for a period of time. Lord, what I am doing with them is simply fulfilling my responsibility. How they will turn out, Lord, depends absolutely on Your mercy."

It is possible for parents to be selfish concerning the spiritual welfare of their children. If their children get saved and become spiritual, they are very happy. However, these parents may not be happy to see the children of other families becoming more spiritual than their children. Most parents in the church hope that their children will become the future apostles, elders, and deacons. Thus, even in this matter, we are selfish.

I once read of a certain woman who prayed desperately for her child to be saved. Although she prayed daily for years, still her child was not saved. One day she inquired of the Lord why He did not answer her prayers and keep His promise. The Lord told her that He would surely keep His promise and answer her prayers. However, she was too selfish. If she would stop praying so much for her child and begin to pray for the children of others, she would see His faithfulness. From that time onward, she began to pray for other children to be saved. After a short while, her child was saved.

This story illustrates the fact that we may be selfish even in praying for the salvation of our children. Not to pray for our children is wrong, but to be fully occupied with prayer for them in a selfish way is also wrong. Hence, the matter of the salvation of our children and their spiritual welfare is also a test to us. (*Life-study of Ephesians,* pp. 521-522)

* * *

Although the Lord promised a child to Abraham, the child did not come for many years. The Lord even put Abraham into a situation in which he was forced to pray for the household of Abimelech so that they could have children (Gen. 20:17). If we were Abraham, we might have found it difficult to pray. We might have said, "I am too pitiful. I have been praying for myself for many years, yet I have not received a child. How can I pray for them?" However, when Abraham prayed, God answered the prayer not only for Abimelech but also for Abraham (21:1-2). If we turn our prayer from ourselves to others, we will receive what we desire (Job 42:10). It is because we are too self-centered in our prayer that the Lord needs to teach us a lesson. If we water others, we will be watered, and if we care for others, we will be cared for. (*The Normal Way of Fruit-bearing and Shepherding for the Building Up of the Church*, p. 39)

* * *

I have seen many devoted Christians. Among them, one was Brother Nee. Not all of Brother Nee's brothers were properly saved. Brother Nee's mother was a sister who loved the Lord very much. It is no wonder that she would weep for her sons. I have seen many others like this. Even among us there are many good sisters who love the Lord very much and pray for their children nearly every day, even though their children do not believe. On the other hand, some parents are not so devoted, yet their children love the Lord. Eventually, I have bowed down before the Lord. The Lord's word is true. We should raise up our children according to the Lord's teaching. This is our duty and we should do it, but eventually their salvation and seeking of the Lord depend upon God's eternal choosing and predestination. If our raising of our children could decide their spiritual future, this would be against God's predestination.

It is difficult to say who is chosen. We simply must do our duty to raise up our children according to the teaching of the Lord. Whether or not they have been chosen is not up to us. Some may say, "Because it is not up to us, we need not do much." However, this also is wrong. (*A Word of Love to the Coworkers, Elders, Lovers, and Seekers of the Lord,* pp. 12-13)

PART TWO:

PARENTS

THE PERSON, LIVING, AND
RESPONSIBILITY OF THE PARENTS

Scripture Reading: 1 Thes. 1:5; 2 Cor. 6:1; John 1:12-13; 1 John
3:2; Phil. 1:19-21a; 3:10; Deut. 6:7; Psa. 78:5-7; Joel 1:3; Acts
2:38-39; Eph. 6:4; 2 Tim. 1:5; 3:15; Gal. 6:7-8

I. God pays more attention to what we are than to what
we do or to what we can do; He cares for the kind of
person we are and for the kind of life we live—1 Thes.
1:5:

A. In the church the most important thing is the person; the person is the way, and the person is the
Lord's work—John 5:19; 6:57; Phil. 1:19-26; Acts
20:18-35; Matt. 7:17-18; 12:33-37.

B. The head of the household manages the family by
his person; it is the person that manages the
family, not a method that does it—2 Cor. 6:1, footnote 1; Rev. 21:16:

1. To do anything, first there is the need of a
person to do it; next comes the method; there is
no need for a good method of administration;
rather, there is the need of a good person for
administration—Exo. 4:10, footnote 1.

2. As soon as we become involved with methods,
we fall into pretense; genuineness denotes a
consistency within and without—cf. 32:19-21.

II. We need to see that we are God-men, born of God and
belonging to God's species; this is the beginning of the
God-man living—John 1:12-13; 1 John 3:2:

A. We are regenerated of God the Spirit to be spirits—
gods (John 3:6b) belonging to the species of God to

see and enter into the kingdom of God—John
1:12-13; 3:3, 5-6; 1 John 3:9:

1. If we realize that, as children of God, we are God
   in life and in nature, we will be radically changed;
   the atmosphere and everything related to us will
   also be changed—John 1:12-13; 1 John 3:2.
2. If all of today's Christians realized that they were
   God in life and in nature, the whole world would
   be different—Acts 17:6.
3. When we think of ourselves as God-men, this
   thinking, this realization, revolutionizes us in our
   daily experience—Eph. 4:22-24.

B. We need to have a God-man living in our married
   life—Phil. 1:19-21a; 3:10:

1. "Do we live Christ at home with our husband or
   wife and with our children? We need a real revival
   to be God-men who live a life of always denying
   ourselves and being crucified to live Christ for
   the expression of God"—*Life-study of 1 & 2 Chronicles,* p. 77.
2. "We need to be careful in every detail. For instance, when we talk to our spouse, we have to
   talk according to the spirit. We need to walk in
   all things according to the spirit (Rom. 8:4). We
   need to be warned and be on the alert that whatever we say, whatever we do, whatever we express,
   our attitude, our spirit, and our intention must
   be purified by the life-giving, compound, all-
   inclusive Spirit"—p. 49.

III. Apart from the book of Proverbs, the Old Testament
does not seem to give us much teaching concerning
parenting, but there are some good examples—Exo.
12:3-7; Deut. 6:7-9, 20-21; 11:18-21; Psa. 78:5-7; Joel
1:3:

A. Adam and Eve were saved, and they passed on the
word of salvation to the following generation; we
also must share these things with our own children, telling them the sad story of man's fall and

proclaiming to them the good news of God's salvation—Gen. 3:21; 4:4.

B. "By faith Abel offered to God a more excellent sacrifice"; since Abel had such faith, exercised this faith, and offered a sacrifice to God in accordance with this faith, he must have heard the preaching of the glad tidings from his parents—Heb. 11:4.

C. Noah inherited all the godly ways of his forefathers: Noah inherited Adam's way of salvation, Abel's way of offering, Enosh's way of calling on the name of the Lord, and also Enoch's way of walking with God—Gen. 3:21; 4:4, 26; 5:22.

D. In the preparation of Moses, God prepared godly parents who infused him with godly thoughts after his birth; through the infusing of his parents, Moses had the godly thought and concept that he needed to rescue the children of Israel—Exo. 2:7-9; Heb. 11:24-25.

E. With the exception of Joshua and Caleb, those who were qualified and ready to take possession of the good land were younger ones, the second generation—Num. 14:29-31, 38; Deut. 1:35-36:

1. The second generation did not pass through as much as the first generation did, but they received the benefit of what the first generation experienced—11:2-7; Josh. 1:1-3.

2. What the older ones experienced was very effective in building up the younger ones; therefore, God was able to prepare from the second generation more than six hundred thousand men with a rich inheritance and strong background who were qualified to be formed into an army to fight with Him and for Him—Deut. 1:10-11.

3. The principle is the same with us in the Lord's recovery today; what the older ones have experienced is being passed on to the younger ones and will be very effective in building them up and preparing them to fight with God and for God—2 Tim. 2:2.

IV. The New Testament pays much attention to teachings for parents and does not pay much attention to teachings about being children; both Ephesians 6 and Colossians 3 put more emphasis on parents than on children—Acts 2:38-39; Eph. 6:4; Col. 3:21; 2 Tim. 1:5; 3:15:

A. In summarizing the words in the Bible concerning parenting, the main thing parents should do is nurture their children in the teaching and admonition of the Lord and not provoke them to anger or discourage them; this means that parents must exercise self-control and must not be loose in any way—Eph. 6:4; 1 Thes. 2:7.

B. Timothy's faith dwelt first in his grandmother Lois and his mother Eunice and was transmitted to him—2 Tim. 1:5; 3:15; Eph. 6:4.

C. Mary's poetic praise is composed of many quotations from the Old Testament, indicating that the Lord Jesus would grow up in a family that would be filled with the knowledge and love of God's holy Word—Luke 1:46-55.

V. We must realize that the Christian life is a life of sowing; everything we do is some kind of sowing, either to the flesh or to the Spirit—Gal. 6:7-8:

A. Everything parents say to their children and do with them is a seed sown into them—cf. 2 Tim. 3:10.

B. In the church life we are constantly sowing tiny seeds; to be careful in our sowing is to be watchful concerning our living—cf. Heb. 13:7.

VI. God's ordained principle is that a father must live a life that is a pattern, an example, to his children; nevertheless, we must realize that the way our children turn out ultimately depends on the Lord's mercy—Rom. 9:10-13; Eph. 6:4:

A. Therefore, we must do our duty to live a proper life as an example to our children, but we should not be discouraged or proud because of how our children turn out; Jacob and Esau were twins, but Romans

9:10-13 shows that their destiny depended on God's selection.

B. The best and most proper way to be a parent is to live as an example to our children and pray for the Lord's mercy.

C. If our living establishes a proper standard, we are not liable if our children behave badly; however, if we do not live as a pattern, our children's bad behavior is our responsibility.

D. In order to be a good example, we must love the Lord and His Word, deal with sins, hate the self, and learn the lessons of the cross; this will be an example not only to our children but also to all the saints.

Excerpts from the Ministry:

WHAT WE ARE AND WHAT WE DO

In [2 Corinthians] 2:12—3:11 Paul covers the ministry of the new covenant, and in 3:12—7:16, the ministers of the new covenant. The section in this Epistle on the ministers of the new covenant is much longer than the section on the ministry of the new covenant. The reason for this is that God cares much more for the ministers than He does for the ministry. In other words, God cares more for what we are than for what we do. This means that what we are is much more important to Him than what we do.

Today both in the Christian world and the secular world more attention is given to what people do than to what they are. Christians mainly pay their attention to work or ministry, yet neglect the being of the person who does the work. They pay attention to the work and the ministry much more than to the worker and the minister. But according to the Bible, God pays more attention to what we are than to what we do or to what we can do. He cares for the kind of person we are and for the kind of life we live. Therefore, in 2 Corinthians Paul first presents the New Testament ministry. Then he goes on to show that this excellent, marvelous ministry needs excellent ministers with an excellent life.

We need to be deeply impressed by the fact that God cares much more for what we are than for what we do. What we do must be measured by what we are. Furthermore, our being must match our work; that is, what we are must match what we do. Our being must match our doing. Thus, our being and our doing go together. If we care only for what we do and not for being the right kind of person, then what we do will not be very weighty. Our doing will be weighty only when it is matched by what we are in our being. (*Life-study of 2 Corinthians,* pp. 339-340)

THE PERSON BEING GOD'S METHOD AND WAY

The service of the elders has to do with the person of the elder. It does not depend on the method but on the person. In the New Testament it is very difficult to find out what is the method or way to serve. Some places seem to speak about the method or the way, but actually the emphasis is still the person himself. The person is the way, and the person is the Lord's work. If God does not gain a person, He will have no work, and He will have no way. A way is a course that a person takes. If God does not gain man, He will have no course to take. Man thinks that the most important thing to do is to find a good way. However, God's work does not involve giving us the ways, but is a matter of gaining the persons. If God can gain two or three brothers here, He will have a way. Even if I present to you the best way to be an elder, it will be useless if the person is wrong. We, the person, should be gained by God. We have to learn to be the proper person more than to learn to do the proper things. It is meaningless for things to be done properly without the person being a proper one. What you are is what you do. You cannot serve God beyond what you are as a person. (*Messages Given during the Resumption of Watchman Nee's Ministry,* pp. 59-60)

THE EXAMPLE OF MARGARET BARBER

Margaret Barber was a great example to Watchman Nee in the one matter of paying more attention to life than to work. He realized that God cares for what we are more than what we do, and his work was according to this principle. He observed how Miss Barber continually stressed the matter of life, paying almost no attention to her work.

From time to time, he and Miss Barber would go together to listen to a Christian speaker. He always admired either the speaker's eloquence, knowledge, zeal, ability, or natural power of persuasion. Then Miss Barber would point out to him that what he admired was neither of life nor of the Spirit. What he admired might be able to stir people up and motivate them to perform certain works, but it could never minister life to people. Through such spiritual diagnosis, he was educated to discern and distinguish the difference between life and work. He began to realize that most of the sermons given by preachers and Christian teachers were not grains of life but flakes of chaff. He also observed that in most Christian work, supposedly carried out for Christ, there is very little life ministered to people. (*Watchman Nee—A Seer of the Divine Revelation in the Present Age,* p. 85)

THE PERSON OF AN ELDER

We all know that to do anything, first there is the need of a person to do it. Next comes the method. The Chinese say that the kind of thing accomplished depends on the kind of person carrying it out. The method may be the same. But for you to do it, it will succeed. For me to do it, it may fail. For you, there may be a good result. For me, the result may not be very good. Hence, the problem is not the method but the person.

I would seriously warn the brothers that to manage affairs in the church, it is dangerous to use any method when the person is not right. What are methods? To put it in terms that are not so nice, methods are crafts. To be crafty is to be political. To administrate a church, you cannot be political. The work of all those who manage the church in a political way will result in vanity. The worldly politicians can play politics, but the elders in the church cannot play politics. The church is not a society; the church is a family. In a family, the head of the household cannot be crafty or play politics. The head of the household manages the family by his person. It is the person that manages the family, not a method that does it. In the same way, the church is the house of God. There is no need for a good method of administration; rather, there is the need of a good person for administration.

I admit that this lesson is difficult to learn. We are all sons of Adam, and it is difficult for our hearts to be broad. We all have a wicked nature. For us to be human is easy, but for us to deal with others honestly is very difficult. Nevertheless, brothers, since we have received the Lord's mercy to be appointed as elders among His people, we should be honest persons. We are not here to learn some methods of being elders. Rather, we are here to be enlightened, to submit to the Lord's hand, and to receive His dealings. It is not a question of picking up some method, but a matter of receiving His dealings. To be an elder is a matter of the person. As soon as we become involved with methods, we fall into pretense.

Brothers, even your politeness and courtesy have to be genuine. For some elders, even their politeness to the brothers and sisters is false. In the world, there may be the need for polite pretense, but in the church, the elders should not have any polite pretense. Furthermore, even your anger has to be genuine. It is true that an elder should restrict his temper, but there should not be any false restriction. False restrictions are but attempts to be human and political. (*The Elders' Management of the Church,* pp. 25-27, 31)

BELONGING TO THE SPECIES OF GOD

We are regenerated of God the Spirit to be spirits—gods (John 3:6b) belonging to the species of God to see and enter into the kingdom of God (vv. 3, 5). John 1 tells us how we received the authority to be the children of God. Then John 3 speaks of regeneration again. Verse 6 says, "That which is born of the flesh is flesh, and that which is born of the Spirit is spirit." We are the flesh and born of the flesh in our natural life. But we were born of God the Spirit to be spirits, gods. That which is born of a cow is a cow. That which is born of a horse is a horse. We are born of the Spirit, and the Spirit is God. John 4:24 tells us clearly that God is Spirit. Because we are born of God the Spirit, we must be gods in life and in nature but not in the Godhead. If we do not believe that we who are born of God are gods, then what are we? That which is born of the Spirit is spirit.

Our second birth caused us to enter into the kingdom of God to become the species of God. The animals and plants have their particular species. We are born of God, so we are gods belonging to the species of God. We should always remember that we are God-men belonging to the species of God. A God-man does not quarrel with others. This is an intrinsic-study of the Word of God.

Regeneration is the first step of Christ's organic salvation. The washing of regeneration purges away all the things of the old nature of our old man (Titus 3:5). This washing is an organic saving. Without regeneration's washing, there would be layers of the old creation in our being. Perhaps some would feel that they are not of the species of God, but of the "species" of the Americans. This species should be washed away. We need to see that regeneration as the first step of Christ's organic saving is to wash away the layers of the old creation of our old nature.

We must not forget that we are God-men belonging to God's species. As God-men born of God and belonging to God's species, we cannot speak to our spouse in a loose way. A husband must be a God-man, living as a God-man. To be merely a good man is far away from God's good pleasure. We need to see that we are God-men, born of God and belonging to God's species. This is the beginning of the God-man living.

God loves you. God has a good pleasure to make you the same as He is. He is God, so you must be God also. A God-man living is God living. This kind of teaching is much higher than the teaching concerning how to be holy or victorious. In my early days as a believer, I saw many books on how to live the Christian life, but these books did not really reveal the way. How can you be holy? You can be holy by living a God-man life. How can you be victorious? It is only by living a God-man life. Never forget that you are a God-man, born of God and belonging to God's species. (*The God-man Living,* pp. 8-9)

REVOLUTIONIZED BY REALIZING
THAT WE ARE GOD-MEN

When we think of ourselves as God-men, this thinking,

this realization, revolutionizes us in our daily experience. For example, a brother may be unhappy with his wife. But he remembers that he is a God-man, and immediately his attitude is changed. Then he will desire to be a God-man husband.

We need to understand that to be a part of mankind is to be something negative. In God's view *mankind* is a negative term referring to fallen man. As believers in Christ and children of God, we are not mankind—we are God-man kind. To realize this is to be changed, even revolutionized. When we realize that we are God-men, we will say, "Lord, You are the first God-man, and we are the many God-men following You. You lived a human life, not by Your human life but by God's divine life to express Him. His attributes became Your virtues. You were here on this earth dying every day. You were crucified to live. Lord, You are my life today and You are my person. You are just me. I therefore must die. I need to be conformed to Your death. I have to be crucified to die every day to live a God-man's life, a human life yet not by my human life but by the divine life, with Your life and Your nature as my constitution to express You in Your divine attributes, which become my human virtues." This makes us not just a Christian or a believer in Christ but a God-man, one kind with God. This is the highest point of God's gospel. (*Life-study of 1 & 2 Chronicles,* pp. 27-28)

REVOLUTIONIZED BY REALIZING WHO WE ARE

Since the ministry began in the United States in 1962, I have actually ministered only one matter—God becoming a man that man may become God in life and in nature. However, it was not until February 1994 that I received such a clear view with a heavy burden to tell God's people that we all are God in life and in nature but not in the Godhead.

To know who we are and to realize who we are revolutionizes us. Suppose a certain brother who has been living like a scorpion realizes that, as a child of God, he is God in life and in nature. Immediately this brother will be radically changed. The atmosphere and everything related to him will also be changed. If all of today's Christians realized that they were God in life and in nature, the whole world would be different.

During the past ten months, I have often checked with myself: "Is a God-man like this? You have spoken that the believers have become God in life and in nature, yet what are you now? Are you God or are you something else?" My answer has been to repent and ask for the Lord's forgiveness because at least some of the things I did were not in Him or according to Him. This realization has revolutionized me. (*Life-study of 1 & 2 Chronicles,* p. 12)

LIVING THE LIFE OF A GOD-MAN
IN OUR MARRIED LIFE AND IN THE CHURCH LIFE

Let us now consider the situation in the recovery. We all are believers. We believe in the Lord Jesus. We have repented and come back to the Lord, and we have been saved, even dynamically saved. Yet in our daily life we may not have the living of a God-man.

We have pointed out that for the children of Israel to keep the law was to live God and express God. However, they did not keep the law, and therefore they did not live God and express God. The situation is the same with us today. For the most part, we do not express God in our daily living.

We need to have a God-man living in our married life. If a married brother would live the life of a God-man in his married life, he would surely be a good husband, for he would be a real God-man in loving his wife. Likewise, if a married sister would live the life of a God-man in her married life, she would be a good wife, submitting herself to her husband.

We also need to have a God-man living in the church life, especially in relation to what we call the vital groups. How can we have a vital group if we ourselves are not vital? This is impossible. Suppose at dinner a brother and his wife are not happy with each other. They even exchange words and argue for quite a long time. Suddenly they remember that later that evening they must attend a meeting of their vital group. But how could this couple be vital in the meeting? Because they are not vital at home in their married life, they have no way to be vital in the meeting.

We have such a Spirit within us, but what do we live and how do we live? Do we live Christ? In the church meetings we may live Christ, but do we live Christ at home with our husband or wife and with our children? We need a real revival to be God-men who live a life of always denying ourselves and being crucified to live Christ for the expression of God. (*Life-study of 1 & 2 Chronicles,* pp. 76-77)

* * *

We need to be careful in every detail. For instance, when we talk to our spouse, we have to talk according to the spirit. We need to walk in all things according to the spirit (Rom. 8:4). We need to be warned and be on the alert that whatever we say, whatever we do, whatever we express, our attitude, our spirit, and our intention must be purified by the life-giving, compound, all-inclusive Spirit. Otherwise, we will lose much in the enjoyment of Christ, today's good land. (*Life-study of 1 & 2 Chronicles,* p. 49)

* * *

When we have problems in our daily life, we do not have to seek advice from others, because we have a spirit in us and the Lord as the Spirit dwelling in our spirit is very near to us. We can ask Him about everything, without any need to use the telephone or the fax machine, for He can talk with us right within us. You can talk with Him and confer with Him in everything. The Lord's Word says, "In nothing be anxious, but in everything, by prayer and petition with thanksgiving, let your requests be made known to God" (Phil. 4:6). Hence, if you have some problem, you just need to tell Him. He is right within you, and He is with you face to face. The Triune God— the Father, the Son, and the Spirit—is in us not to trouble us but to be our Paraclete, Comforter, Supporter. I always pray, "O Lord, now I am going to take a walk. Support me, sustain me, and strengthen me." This is to drink the Lord. In this way I have no anxiety. When anxiety comes, you should say, "O Lord, this anxiety is Yours, not mine; I give it to You because You bear it for me." Thus, you receive the Lord's element into you, and metabolism will work constantly in you. Consequently, what is expressed through you outwardly is Christ. This is to live Christ. Those who do not know this secret consider to live Christ a difficult thing. Actually, you just need to practice speaking with the Lord constantly; then spontaneously you will live Christ. (*The Organic Aspect of God's Salvation,* pp. 54-55)

* * *

Adam and Eve certainly must have preached the gospel to their children, telling Cain and Abel how they had been created by God, how they had been charged by God not to eat of the tree of knowledge, how they had disobeyed God and had eaten of that tree, how they were in fear and trembling as they awaited the sentence of death, and how God came in to preach the gospel by promising them that the seed of the woman would bruise the head of the serpent. Furthermore, Adam and Eve must also have told them how they had stood naked in the presence of God and how God had slain some lambs as sacrifices, using the skins to make robes to cover their nakedness that they could stand before God and have fellowship with Him. I am convinced that Adam and Eve preached this gospel to their children. Evidence of this is found in Hebrews 11:4, which says, "By faith Abel offered to God a more excellent sacrifice than Cain." According to the Bible, faith comes from hearing the word that is preached (Rom. 10:17, 14). Since Abel had such faith, exercised this faith, and offered a sacrifice to God in accordance with this faith, he must have heard the preaching of the glad tidings from his parents. Out of that word he received faith. He did not present his sacrifice according to his own opinion or learning, and his offering was not his own invention. He presented his offering by faith according to the words preached by his parents.

Adam was a good father, taking the lead in believing the gospel. I hope that all the fathers reading this message will be leaders in believing the gospel. Eve, a good wife and mother, was also a believer, following her believing husband and opening the way for her child to believe. Therefore, in Genesis 4 we have a believing father, a believing mother, and a believing child. Look at this family—they all believed in the same gospel. When people have asked me if Adam and Eve were saved, I have said, "Why not? If you are saved, then certainly they were saved as well. In fact, they were saved much earlier than you were." Adam and Eve were pioneers in believing the gospel. Adam cut the way, Eve paved the way, and Abel walked on the way. Now we are followers of Abel. I wish that every father would be an Adam, every mother an Eve, and all the children Abels. The first family on the earth was a gospel family, a family of believers.

Adam and Eve were saved, and they passed on the word of salvation to the following generation. We also must share these things with our own children, telling them the sad story of man's fall and proclaiming to them the good news of God's salvation.

Once again I say that I strongly believe that [Cain's] parents preached the gospel to him and his brother, telling them of their need for coverings made from the skins of the sacrificial lambs. I believe that this accounts for Abel's desire to be a feeder of the sheep. (*Life-study of Genesis,* pp. 289-290, 292, 293)

INHERITING THE GODLY WAYS OF THE FATHERS

[The kind of life that God can use to change the age] always inherits the godly ways of the forefathers. Thank God that Noah, the tenth generation from Adam, had many good forefathers...Noah inherited Adam's way of salvation (Gen. 3:20-21)...Noah also inherited Abel's way of offering (4:4)... The third godly way that Noah inherited was Enosh's way of calling on the name of the Lord to enjoy all that He is (v. 26)...Noah also inherited [all the fathers'] way of living and begetting (5:3-28)...Noah also inherited the fifth way, [Enoch's] way of walking with God (vv. 22, 24). (*Life-study of Genesis,* pp. 390-391)

* * *

Question: Was Moses called after he turned eighty?

Answer: A person's calling has a beginning, course, and completion. If we investigate the time when Moses was called, it was before the foundation of the world. The calling of Moses was not an accidental act or idle whim of God. The name Moses means "drawn out." Long before the foundation of the world, he was drawn out. God also set apart Paul in his mother's womb (Gal. 1:15). Not only did the matter of our calling take place before the foundation of the world; even our salvation occurred before the foundation of the world.

This shows that God took several steps in the preparation of Moses. First, God prepared godly parents who infused him with godly thoughts after his birth (Exo. 2:7-9). Second, God prepared the environment of the palace in Egypt for him so that he could receive the best education of his time to lead the children of Israel (3:10; Acts 7:22). Moses' commission could not have been undertaken by someone who did not have any training. Hence, God allowed him to enter into the palace to be properly regulated and cultivated. Third, through the infusing of his parents, Moses had the godly thought and concept that he needed to rescue the children of Israel (Heb. 11:24-25). To him, this was the beginning of God's calling. Fourth, God prepared the wilderness for him in order to train his character. Although he had godly thoughts and had received a high education, his character was not fully trained, nor had he gone through any human sufferings (Acts 7:23-28). He was very strong. He had no children or any special environment, so God caused him to shepherd a flock in the wilderness for forty years so that he could be refined in a furnace like hard steel (v. 29). When all these environments had been arranged successfully, God came in and called him in a definite way. At this time, God's calling was complete (v. 30).

Hence, it is difficult to determine when God called Moses. If we consider the source, we must say that it was before the foundation of the world, but also it was in the palace, the wilderness, and the training process. Then God came in. The principle is the same with us. If we look back, we can testify that our calling was predestinated by God in eternity past. Then at a certain time, He arranged for us to be in the proper environment and did not let us go; it was at that time that we answered His call. (*Knowing Life and the Church*, pp. 234-235)

* * *

With the exception of Joshua and Caleb, those who were qualified and ready to take possession of the land were younger ones. They were of the second generation. The older ones, those of the first generation, had passed through many things and had learned many lessons. However, they were not qualified to enter into the land. The lessons learned by the first generation surely became part of the heritage passed on to the second generation. Their children certainly inherited from their parents all the lessons they learned during the forty years in the wilderness. By their birth the younger ones were put into a position to inherit the tradition of their family and all that their parents had experienced.

I believe that the fathers spoke to their children about their experiences in Egypt, in the exodus from Egypt, and in the wilderness. No doubt, the fathers spoke about how they were cruelly treated as slaves in Egypt, about how God in His mercy sent Moses to deliver them from bondage, about how they kept the Passover on the fourteenth day of the second month, and about how they marched out of Egypt and crossed the Red Sea. The fathers must have also explained to their children that they entered into the wilderness without food but that God fed them with manna and supplied them with water from the smitten rock. They might have also explained that although they eventually felt that manna was loathsome, they nevertheless appreciated it. The people did not grow any crops, but for forty years they daily received the heavenly supply of manna. Furthermore, the younger ones learned about Moses and about the great help he rendered to the people of Israel. Moses himself was not allowed to enter into the good land, but he contributed many constructive factors to God's people.

The second generation did not pass through as much as the first generation did, but they received the benefit of what the first generation experienced. I believe that the older generation told the younger generation about all they experienced, enjoyed, and suffered. This speaking was part of the raising up, or the building up, of the second generation. What the first generation experienced was not experienced in vain, for it was passed on to the second generation. What the older ones experienced actually was not effective for them, but it was very effective in building up the younger ones. Therefore,

God was able to prepare from the second generation more than six hundred thousand men with a rich inheritance and strong background who were qualified to be formed into an army to fight with Him and for Him.

The principle is the same with us in the Lord's recovery today. The recovery has been in the United States for twenty-seven years and has passed through many things. Do you think that all these things have been in vain? They certainly have not been in vain. These things are being passed on to the younger ones in the Lord's recovery and will be very effective in building them up and preparing them to fight with God and for God. The younger ones in the Lord's recovery have a rich inheritance. Because this inheritance is being passed on to the younger ones and even being constituted into them, I have the full assurance that when a further testing comes, there will be a very positive result. (*Life-study of Numbers,* pp. 368-369)

THE RESPONSIBILITIES OF PARENTS

Apart from the book of Proverbs, the Old Testament does not seem to give us much teaching concerning parenting. In the New Testament, however, Paul wrote something about being parents. Most books in the world teach children how to be children; not many books teach parents how to be parents. Most people pay attention to teachings for children. But the New Testament pays much attention to teachings for parents. It does not pay much attention to teachings about being children. Although it does teach us something about children, the emphasis is not on children. Both Ephesians 6 and Colossians 3 put more emphasis on parents than on children. We should learn to be proper parents because God pays more attention to parents than to children.

If we try to summarize the words in the Bible concerning parenting, the main thing parents should do is nurture their children in the teaching and admonition of the Lord and not provoke them to anger or discourage them. This means that parents must exercise self-control and must not be loose in any way. This is Paul's teaching concerning the subject.

As difficult as it is to be a husband or a wife, I hope you will realize that there is something more difficult—being a parent. Being a husband or a wife involves only two people; being a parent involves more. Being a husband or a wife is a matter of personal happiness; being a parent is something that affects the well-being of the children of the next generation. The responsibility over the future of the children of the next generation is on the shoulders of the parents.

We have to realize how serious this responsibility is. God has placed a person's body, soul, and spirit, even his whole life and future, into our hands. No individual influences another individual's future as much as parents. No one controls a person's future as much as parents. Parents almost have a say in whether their children will go to hell or to heaven. We must learn to be good husbands and good wives, but above all we must learn also to be good parents. I believe that the responsibility of being a parent is more than that of being a husband or a wife. (*Messages for Building Up New Believers,* vol. 2, pp. 519-520)

UNFEIGNED FAITH

Verse 5 of 2 Timothy 1 says, "Having been reminded of the unfeigned faith in you, which dwelt first in your grandmother Lois and your mother Eunice, and I am persuaded dwells also in you." Here Paul reminds Timothy of the unfeigned faith, which is in him. This faith first indwelt Timothy's grandmother and then his mother. Now it dwells in him. (*Life-study of 2 Timothy,* p. 5)

* * *

Mary as a young woman was very familiar with the Old Testament. Mary was the right person, the proper vessel, selected by God to be the channel for the Savior's incarnation. In ancient times, females were not as well educated as males. However, although both Mary and Elizabeth were females, they both had gained a great deal of knowledge from the Old Testament. (*The Practice of Prophesying,* pp. 23-24)

* * *

Mary's poetic praise is composed of many quotations from the Old Testament. This indicates that she was a godly woman, qualified to be a channel for the Savior's incarnation. It also indicates that the Lord Jesus would grow up in a family which would be filled with the knowledge and love of God's holy Word.

Although Mary was a young woman, she was very knowledgeable concerning the Old Testament and could quote verses from it in her praise to God. Actually, her praise was a composition of quotations from the Scriptures. Surely she was the right person for God to use in conceiving the Savior who was to be born.

As we consider Mary's praise, we can see something of the reason she was chosen by God for the conception of the Man-Savior. No doubt Mary also taught the Lord Jesus many portions from the Scriptures as He was growing up. (*Life-study of Luke*, pp. 33, 37)

* * *

Everything we do is some kind of sowing, either to the flesh or to the Spirit. Wherever we may be and whatever we are doing, we are sowing seeds. You sow at work and also at school. The elders sow while they are caring for the church, and those who minister the Word sow as they minister. Husbands and wives are constantly sowing in their married life, and parents are sowing in their family life. Everything parents say to their children and do with them is a seed sown into them. Day by day we all are sowing. The Christian life is a life of sowing. Furthermore, the place where we live and work is our farm. You are sowing even by the way you dress or style your hair. Virtually everything you do is an act of sowing. It is crucial for us to realize that the Christian walk must be a walk by the Spirit and a life of sowing to the Spirit.

In our experience, the flesh should be crucified. As Paul says in Galatians 5:24, "They who are of Christ Jesus have crucified the flesh with its passions and its lusts." We should not continue to walk according to the flesh. We should not be in the flesh in expressing our attitudes. In speaking to their children, parents need to be in the Spirit and according to the Spirit. Otherwise, what they say will be a sowing unto the flesh. We should also be careful of the way we express our attitude. Even the expression of an attitude may be sowing according to the flesh. On the other hand, we may express our attitude by sowing unto the Spirit. We should also be cautious in expressing opinions. Do you have the assurance that the utterance of your opinion is according to the Spirit? If not, be careful, lest you sow unto the flesh. If we all sow unto the Spirit day by day, many problems will be eliminated. The troubles in the church life and in the family life will diminish. Most problems and troubles come from sowing unto the flesh.

Seeds are small. Have you ever seen a farmer sow seed which is a foot in diameter? No, the seeds a farmer sows are tiny. The same is true of our sowing. We may regard certain things as tiny—a little gossiping or a little criticizing—but they are seeds sown into others. Have you ever asked yourself how many seeds you have sown into others, seeds that are not according to the Spirit but according to the flesh? In the church life we are constantly sowing tiny seeds. Even the way one brother looks at another is a seed. We certainly sow to the flesh when we criticize, argue, or condemn. In principle, all that we say or do is a seed sown either to the flesh or to the Spirit.

In 5:25 Paul speaks of walking by the Spirit, and in 6:8, of sowing unto the Spirit. Actually, to walk by the Spirit is to sow unto the Spirit. Whenever we walk by the Spirit, we sow unto the Spirit. Sowing unto the Spirit, we eventually reap life eternal.

The fact that we may sow either to the flesh or to the Spirit and thereby reap either corruption or eternal life should encourage us to be careful in what we say and do. Let us realize that everything in our daily living is a sowing either to the flesh or to the Spirit. (*Life-study of Galatians,* pp. 258-261)

* * *

The word *sowing* is actually equal to living. To be careful in our sowing is to be watchful concerning our living. I repeat, sowing causes a certain result. This was the reason Paul warned us to be careful of our sowing. (*Life-study of Galatians,* p. 311)

* * *

The first kind of relationships in human life is family relationships. First Timothy 3:4 says, "One who manages well his own house, having his children in subjection with all gravity." Managing one's house is a matter of taking the lead, but Paul's concept here is not mainly related to authority. As a husband and father, an overseer should take the lead in his family not merely by ruling but by establishing a good example and pattern. A family is not like a government or an organization, which are led by authority. A father's leadership in his family should not mainly be based on his ruling with authority but should instead be based on the pattern of his daily living. Similarly, to be an elder does not mean to rule the church with authority. This concept is absolutely wrong. A father's management of his family is very different from a supervisor's management of a business. A supervisor may hire and fire employees, but a father cannot hire or fire his children. The basic need in a family is the father's example. As a father, an elder must live properly before his family. This is the proper way to manage one's house. In our home we should not try to exercise our authority as a king, law officer, administrator, or school principal. Paul's concept in this section concerns the overseers' daily living. It does not work to merely discipline our children. God's ordained principle is that a father must live a life that is a pattern, an example, to his children.

As overseers, we must take the lead in our family by presenting a pattern in our living. This is our duty. However, if our children are in subjection with all gravity, we should not think that it is because of our doing; instead, we have to worship the Lord for His mercy. Although the disposition of our children is not under our control, this does not mean we can neglect our duties to live as an example and to spend as much time and energy as we can on our children. Nevertheless, we must realize that the way our children turn out ultimately depends on the Lord's mercy. We know that this is true, because if two children are siblings and are raised by the same parents with the same care, they may still turn out very different. One may have a good character and become a seeking believer, while the other may have a poor character and not even be saved. Therefore, we must do our duty to live a proper life as an example to our children, but we should not be discouraged or proud because of how our children turn out.

Paul's word concerning an overseer's children in verse 4 does not involve salvation or spirituality. We should be a good example to our children, but whether or not they will eventually be saved depends on God's predestination. Jacob and Esau were twins, but Romans 9:10-13 shows that their destiny depended on God's selection. We cannot cause our children or anyone else to be spiritual, but we can establish an example by living a sober, temperate, and orderly life and by seeking the Lord. If two flesh brothers listen to the same gospel message, one may be saved, but the other may not. We have seen cases like this. Therefore, we must be zealous in preaching the gospel and convincing people to receive the Lord, but we must also realize that a person's salvation ultimately depends not on our effort but on God's predestination. We should not think that because it depends on God's predestination, we do not need to preach the gospel. We must do our duty. Similarly, we should not assume that our children will behave well if we are a good example, nor should we neglect our duty. The best and most proper way to be a parent is to live as an example to our children and pray for the Lord's mercy.

If our living establishes a proper standard, we are not liable if our children behave badly. However, if we do not live as a pattern, our children's bad behavior is our responsibility. If they are good, the credit does not go to us, but if they are bad, we receive the "debit." This is the divine accounting. We should not say that God is not fair. Romans 9:20 says, "O man, who are you who answer back to God? Shall the thing molded say to him who molded it, Why did you make me thus?" We cannot argue with God. If our children behave well and are eventually saved and live before the Lord, we must worship the Lord, saying, "Lord, I am nothing. Even my best behavior is like dust; it means nothing. I can only thank You for Your mercy." We should not ascribe anything to our goodness. We have to acknowledge God's predestination, His mercy, and His grace. If our children begin to live sinfully, we must humble ourselves, praying, "Lord, forgive me. I accept the blame because I may have neglected to adequately care for them in some aspect." This must be our attitude.

Paul's concept in 1 Timothy 3:1-7 concerns the overseers'

living. Whether our children behave well is secondary; the primary matter is whether we have a proper living. We must take the lead and manage our family well by having a living that presents a positive pattern to them. This depends on what we are; it is a matter of life. (*Basic Principles concerning the Eldership,* pp. 49-51)

SANCTIFYING OURSELVES
FOR THE SAKE OF THE CHILDREN

Scripture Reading: John 17:19; 4:6-7, 27; Eph. 5:26-27; Num. 6:3-4; 1 Thes. 5:23; 1 Thes. 4:4; Judg. 13:12-14

I. Although the Son is absolutely holy in Himself, He still sanctified Himself in His way of living while He was on earth in order to set an example of sanctification for His disciples—John 17:19; Eph. 5:26-27:

A. There were many things that He could have done that were not contrary to His own holiness; nevertheless, He refrained from doing them because of weakness in the disciples—John 17:19.

B. In many matters the disciples' weakness directed the Lord and restricted His freedom; the Lord could do many things, but He did not do them because He did not want the disciples to misunderstand or be stumbled—4:6-7, 27.

C. In order for us to be holy, we first need to be separated unto God positionally—Matt. 23:17:

1. With respect to our family, neighbors, colleagues, and friends, we need to be separated; many Christians, however, are saved but not separated—Titus 2:14; cf. Neh. 13:23-24, 30.

2. Once a person is saved, he should also be separated; this is the reason a believer is called a saint; to be holy is to be separated unto God—Rom. 1:2, footnote 3.

II. Those who have children should sanctify themselves for the sake of their children; this means that we should refrain from doing many things that we could do for the sake of our children—John 17:17, 19; Num. 6:1-12:

A. Many strong believers would be raised up in our second generation if all the parents of this generation would be good parents; the future of the church depends on the parents—2 Thes. 3:9; Phil. 3:17.

B. A Nazarite had to abstain from wine and anything related to its source, signifying that we must abstain from all kinds of earthly enjoyment and pleasure, which lead to lustful conduct and a lustful intention—Num. 6:3; Judg. 13:2-20; Psa. 104:15; Eccl. 10:19; 2 Tim. 2:22; 3:1-5.

C. We must see that God has committed the children to us; so we must set a standard for ourselves in morality, in conduct, and in all moral judgments regarding right and wrong; we must set a high standard for what is ideal, and we must also set a standard for ourselves in spiritual matters—1 Thes. 5:23:

1. A child may remember or forget what you say, but what he sees surely will remain in him forever; he develops his sense of judgment from you, and he also develops his system of values from you—1 Cor. 9:27.

2. Every parent must remember that his actions will be repeated in his children; his actions will not stop with him; the whole life of Christian children depends on the behavior of their parents—2 Tim. 1:5; 3:15.

3. You must sanctify your words; when your children speak, they should also sanctify their words and be accurate with them; when you say something wrong, you must make a point to admit your mistake; in this manner you will train your children to sanctify their words—1 Tim. 4:12.

D. We must realize that parents need to exercise self-control, sacrificing their own freedom; God has committed a human body, along with his soul, into our hands; if we do not exercise self-control and give up our freedom, we will have a difficult time answering to our God in the future—1 Cor. 9:25; Gal. 5:22-23.

E. We must see that in order for us to bring the children to the Lord in a genuine way, we need to be a person who walks with God; we cannot send our children to the Lord merely by pointing our fingers to heaven; we have to walk in front of them—1 Cor. 9:27; Rom. 2:21:

1. After Enoch begot Methuselah, the Bible says that he walked with God; when the burden of the family was upon him, he felt that his responsibility was too great and that he could not manage it by himself; so he began to walk with God—Gen. 5:21-22.

2. When Samson was in the bosom of his mother, he was sanctified to be a Nazarite; Samson was a Nazarite from his mother's womb for the full course of his life—Judg. 13:7.

3. Hannah prayed desperately not mainly for herself but for God; she promised God that if He gave her a male child, she would return the child to Him by the vow of a Nazarite—1 Sam. 1:11, 22, 28.

4. Lot's children were corrupted by living in the wicked city—Gen. 19:15.

F. We must keep, preserve, safeguard, our vessel clean in sanctification before God; it must be holy, separated, and saturated with God and also kept in honor before man—1 Thes. 4:4; Rom. 13:14.

III. According to both the Old Testament and the New Testament, the first thing we must eliminate for the sake of God's dwelling place is our idols—Gen. 35:1-2; Acts 19:19-20:

A. Jacob charged everyone in his household to purify themselves; we must not only put away the foreign gods but also purify our whole being; our whole

being, manner of life, and expression must be
changed—Gen. 35:2; 2 Cor. 7:1.

B. In addition to putting away the foreign gods and
purifying themselves, Jacob's household changed
their garments; to change garments means to
change our manner of life—Gen. 35:2; Rev. 22:14a.

C. The material used in making the golden calf in
Exodus 32 was the gold of the earrings belonging
to the children of Israel; the record in this chapter
makes clear that self-beautification leads to idolatry—vv. 1-3.

Excerpts from the Ministry:

THE SON SANCTIFYING HIMSELF

John 17:19 says, "And for their sake I sanctify Myself, that
they themselves also may be sanctified in truth." Although
the Son is absolutely holy in Himself, He still sanctified Himself in His way of living while He was on earth in order to set
an example of sanctification for His disciples. Consider the
way He contacted the Samaritan woman (4:5-7). The Lord did
not meet her at night in a private home but during the day in
the open air. As far as the Lord Himself was concerned, He could
have met with the Samaritan woman, who was an immoral
person, at any place and at any time. But as a man a little over
thirty years of age, it would not have been a good example for
His disciples if He had contacted her privately in her home at
night. If He had done that, the disciples might have been con-
fused. But, in order to set a good example for His disciples, He
behaved in a sanctified way. This one example was a great
help to His disciples in the future. It is not right for any young
preacher to contact a woman privately at night because there
is too much temptation there. To do such a thing is not holy;
it is worldly. Look at the example of the Lord Jesus: He talked
with Nicodemus, an elderly gentleman, late at night in a private home (3:1-2), but He talked with the immoral Samaritan
woman during the daytime in the open air. In doing this the
Lord sanctified Himself and set an example for His disciples
to follow. (*Life-study of John,* pp. 483-484)

THE LORD
SANCTIFYING HIMSELF
FOR THE SAKE OF THE DISCIPLES

What does it mean to be sanctified before God? The Lord Jesus said, "For their sake I sanctify Myself" (John 17:19). This does not refer to being holy, but to whether or not one is sanctified. The Lord Jesus is holy and His nature is holy. But for the sake of the disciples, He sanctified Himself. There were many things that He could have done that were not contrary to His own holiness; nevertheless, He refrained from doing them because of weakness in the disciples. In many matters the disciples' weakness directed the Lord and restricted His freedom. The Lord could do many things, but He did not do them because He did not want the disciples to misunderstand or be stumbled. As far as the Lord's nature was concerned, He often could have acted a certain way. But He refrained from doing so for the sake of the disciples.

NOT WALKING IN A LOOSE WAY

Those who have children should sanctify themselves for the sake of their children. This means that we should refrain from doing many things that we could do for the sake of our children. There are many things that we could say, but for the sake of the children we do not say them. From the day we bring our children into our family, we should sanctify ourselves.

If you do not restrict yourself, you will not be able to restrict your children. The looseness of those who do not have children, at the most, results in trouble for themselves. But for those who have children, looseness results in damage to their children as well as to themselves. Once a Christian brings a child into the world, he must sanctify himself. Two eyes, sometimes four, are watching you all the time. They will follow you all your life. Even after you have left this world, they will not forget what they have seen in you; the things you do will remain inside of them.

ACTING ACCORDING TO STANDARDS

The day your son is born is the day you should consecrate yourself. You must set a standard for yourself in morality, in conduct at home, and in all moral judgments regarding right and wrong. You must set a high standard for what is ideal, and you must also set a standard for yourself in spiritual matters. You must act strictly according to these standards. Otherwise, you will have problems for yourself, and you will spoil your children. Many children are ruined by their own parents, not by outsiders. If parents are lacking in ethical, moral, and spiritual standards, they will ruin their children.

A young person makes decisions and judgments in his future life according to the training he received during his early years with his parents. A child may remember or forget what you say, but what he sees surely will remain in him forever. He develops his sense of judgment from you, and he also develops his system of values from you.

Every parent must remember that his actions will be repeated in his children; his actions will not stop with him. When you do not have children, you can do whatever you like when you are happy and give up and forget about everything when you are unhappy. But once you have children, you have to restrict yourself. You have to act according to the highest standard of conduct whether you like it or not. The whole life of Christian children depends on the behavior of their parents.

I remember a brother who said something when his son got into trouble. He said, "He is just a replica of me and I am just he." When a parent sees something in his children, he must realize that he is seeing himself. He must see that they are his very reflection. They are just reflecting him. Through them he can see himself.

This is why every couple should consecrate themselves anew to God as soon as they have a child. They should come to the Lord and consecrate themselves to Him again. From that time forward, the Lord has committed a human being, with his entire spirit, soul, life, and future, into their hands. From that day forward, they have to be faithful to the Lord's commitment. Some people are committed to a work for one or two years when they sign a contract. But this work lasts for their entire life; there is no limit to the term of this commitment.

THE SENSE OF BEING ENTRUSTED

Among believers in China, no failure is greater than the failure of parenting. I think this is due to the influence of paganism. Failure in one's career cannot be compared to failure in parenting. Even failure in being a husband or a wife cannot be compared to failure in parenting. A husband or a wife can protect himself or herself, because both are over twenty years of age. But when a child is placed in your hands, he cannot protect himself. The Lord has entrusted a child to you. You cannot go to Him and say, "You have entrusted five children to me, and I have lost three." You cannot say, "You have entrusted ten to me, and I have lost eight." The church cannot go on if parents do not have a sense of being entrusted. We do not want to see our children being rescued back from the world. Suppose we beget children, lose them to the world, and then try to rescue them back. If we allow this to happen, the gospel will never be preached to the uttermost part of the earth. Our children have been taught many teachings, and we have been taking care of them for years. At least these children should be brought to the Lord. We are wrong if we do not take care of our children. Please remember that it is the parents' responsibility to ensure that their children turn out the right way.

Please give me the liberty to say this word. Throughout church history, the greatest failure among Christians is the failure in parenting. This is something no one cares much about. The children are young; they are in your hands and can do nothing much themselves. If you are loose with yourself, you will also be loose with them. We must realize that parents must exercise self-control, sacrificing their own freedom. God has committed a human body, along with his soul, into our hands. If we do not exercise self-control and give up our freedom, we will have a difficult time answering to our God in the future.

THE NEED TO WALK WITH GOD

Parents must not only realize their responsibility and sanctify themselves for the sake of their children; they must also walk with God.

One sanctifies himself for the sake of his children. But this does not mean that he can be loose and careless when he is by himself. He should not exercise self-control merely for the sake of his children. The Lord Jesus was not short of holiness in Himself. He did not sanctify Himself just for the sake of His disciples. If the Lord Jesus sanctified Himself merely for the sake of His disciples, but was not holy in Himself, He would have been a total failure. In the same way, parents must sanctify themselves for their children, but they themselves must also walk with God.

No matter how much zeal you show in your children's presence, they can easily see through you if you are not genuinely zealous. They are very clear, but you may not be that clear. You may be a very loose person yet act carefully in their presence. In reality you are not the person you pretend to be. Please remember that your children can see through you easily. If you are a careless person and you try to act in a discreet way before your children, they will easily detect your carelessness and pretension. You must not only sanctify yourself before them for their sake, but you must also be genuinely holy in yourself, walking with God as Enoch did.

I would like to draw your attention to the example of Enoch. Genesis 5:21-22 says, "Enoch lived sixty-five years and begot Methuselah. And Enoch walked with God after he had begotten Methuselah three hundred years, and he begot more sons and daughters." Before Enoch was sixty-five years old, we do not know his condition. After he begot Methuselah, we know that he walked with God three hundred years. Then he was taken up by God. This is a special case in the Old Testament. Before Enoch begot children, we do not know anything about his condition. But after Enoch begot Methuselah, the Bible says that he walked with God. When the burden of the family was upon him, he started to feel his weakness. He felt that his responsibility was too great and that he could not manage it by himself. So he began to walk with God. He did not walk with God just in the presence of his son; he walked with God even when he was by himself. He felt that if he did not walk with God, he would not know how to raise his children. Enoch begot not only Methuselah but also many other children; nevertheless, he walked with God for three hundred years. His responsibility as a parent did not hinder him from walking with God; rather, it caused him to walk with God. Eventually, he was raptured. Please remember that the first person who was raptured was a father. The first person to be raptured was one who had many children and yet who still walked with God. The way one bears his responsibility in a family is a reflection of his spiritual condition before God.

We must see that in order for us to bring our children to the Lord in a genuine way, we need to be a person who walks with God. We cannot send our children to heaven merely by pointing our fingers to heaven. We have to walk in front of them. Only then can we ask our children to follow us. Even though Christian parents want their children to be better than they are in the hope that their children will not love the world and will go on in a positive way, there are many bad families because the parents themselves draw back. If this is the case, they will never realize their goal no matter how hard they try. We must remember that the standard of the children cannot be higher than the standard of their parents. This does not mean that we should set a false standard. We should have a standard that is genuine and spiritual. If we have this, our children will come up to our standard.

Please remember that your children will learn to love what you love, and hate what you hate. They will learn to treasure what you treasure, and condemn what you condemn. You must set a moral standard for yourself and your children. Whatever your moral standard is, that will be their standard as well. Your standard of loving the Lord will be their standard of loving the Lord. There can be only one standard in a family, not two.

I hope we can see that God has committed our children to us. There can be only one standard in the family. Whatever we forbid our children to do, we should not do. There must never be two standards in a family, one for the children and another for us. We must keep the same standard for our children's sake. We must sanctify ourselves to maintain a standard. Once the standard is set, we must maintain it. I hope we will all take good care of our children. They are constantly watching us. Whether or not they behave well depends on whether we behave well. They are not merely listening to us; they are watching us as well. They seem to know everything. They know if we are pushing them around, and they know if we are acting in front of them. We should not think that we can deceive our children. No! They cannot be deceived. They know how we feel, and they are clear about the true picture. Whatever we demand of our children, we must take the same position in that matter.

BEING ACCURATE WITH WORDS

Parents' words are very important to children. You must not only be a pattern to your children but also realize that your words are very important to them.

Not Making Empty Promises

Please remember that parents should not say anything to their children that they cannot carry out. You must not make empty promises to your children. Do not promise them something if you do not have the ability to fulfill your promise. Do not make a promise to them if you cannot fulfill it. If your children want you to buy something, you have to consider your financial ability. If you can do it, do it. If not, you must say, "I will do my best. I will do what I can do. But I cannot do what is beyond my ability." Every word of yours must be reliable. You should not think that this is a small matter. You must not allow your children to doubt your words. Not only must they not doubt your words, but they also must have the assurance that your words are accurate. If the children find their parents' words to be unreliable, they will grow up acting carelessly. They will think that since one can be careless with his words, he can be careless with anything. Some expressions can be used only in politics; they are not factual. Parents should not use such expressions. Many parents are apparently too kind to their children. They promise whatever their children ask, but nine out of ten times they cannot fulfill their promises. Such wonderful promises produce only one result in the children—disappointment. You must promise only things that you can do. If you cannot do a certain thing, do not promise it. If you are not sure whether you can do it, tell them so. Your words must be accurate.

Orders Needing to Be Carried Out

Sometimes you are not making a promise, but giving an order. If you open your mouth to ask your children to do something, you must make sure that it is done. You have to make them realize that you mean what you say. Many times you give a proper order, but you forget about it. This is wrong. You should not tell your children that it is all right if they do not carry out your order this time, just as long as they do it the next time. If you excuse them, you are not doing them a favor. You should show your children that once you say something, they must carry it out whether or not you remember it. If you say it once, you can say it a hundred times. If your word counts for one thing, your word should count for a hundred things. You should not nullify your own words. Show them from their youth that words are hallowed, whether they are a promise or an order. For example, if you tell your child to sweep his room every morning, you must first consider whether or not it is within his ability to do it. If he does not do it today, you must make sure that he does it the next day. If he does not do it the next day, you must make sure that he does it the third day. You must uphold your order this year, and you must uphold it next year. You have to show your children that your words are not uttered lightly and that once they are uttered, they have to be carried out. If they find that your words do not count, your words will become ineffective. Hence, every word out of your mouth must be practical and principled.

Correcting Exaggerated Words

Sometimes you exaggerate your words. You must find an opportunity to tell your children that you exaggerated your words on that particular occasion. Your words must be accurate. Sometimes you see only two cows but you say that there are three, or you see five birds but say that there are eight. You must correct yourself immediately. In speaking to your children, you must learn to always correct yourself. You should learn to say, "What I just said was not that accurate. There are two cows, not three." You must show them that words should be sanctified. Everything that happens in the family should be for the building up of Christian character. You must sanctify your words. When your children speak, they should also sanctify their words and be accurate with them. When you say something wrong, you must make a point to admit your mistake. In this manner you will train your children to sanctify their words. Many parents say five when they mean three or three when they mean two. They speak loosely and do not set up good patterns at home. As a result, their children never realize that words are sacred.

All these problems occur because there is a lack of discipline from the Lord. We should experience the Lord's discipline and lead our children to the Lord's discipline. At least we should show them that words are sacred. Every promise should be realized and every order should be carried out. Every word has to be accurate. If we do this, our children will receive proper training.

I cannot tell you how many strong believers would be raised up in our second generation if all the parents of this generation would be good parents. I have always wanted to say this: The future of the church depends on the parents. (*Messages for Building Up New Believers,* vol. 2, pp. 520-522, 523-524, 525, 526, 534-536, 549)

TO BE SEPARATED UNTO GOD POSITIONALLY

In order for us to be holy, we first need to be separated unto God positionally. With respect to our family, neighbors, colleagues, and friends, we need to be separated. Many Christians, however, are saved, but not separated. Normally, once a person is saved, he should also be separated. This is the reason a believer is called a saint. Consider the majority of Christians today. They are virtually the same as the worldly people. With them, there is no separation. Many of their relatives and friends do not even know that they are Christians. But to be holy is to be separated unto God. This, of course, is a matter of position. (*Life-study of Ephesians,* p. 28)

* * *

As parents, we must do our duty with respect to our children. This means that we should not only teach them, but also set up an example for them to follow. Just as the Lord Jesus sanctified Himself for the sake of His disciples (John 17:19), so parents should sanctify themselves for the sake of their children. Those who do not have children may be free to do certain things, such as sleep late in the morning. But those with children do not have the liberty to do these things. For the sake of their children, they must be restricted. Children always imitate their parents. Therefore, it is the parents' responsibility to set up a high standard and a proper pattern and example for their children to follow. (*Life-study of Ephesians*, p. 521)

ABSTAINING FROM WINE
AND FROM ANYTHING RELATED TO ITS SOURCE

"He shall separate himself from wine and strong drink; he shall drink no vinegar of wine or vinegar of strong drink, nor shall he drink any juice of grapes, nor eat fresh or dried grapes. All the days of his separation he shall eat nothing that is produced by the grape vine, from the seeds even to the skins" (Num. 6:3-4). Here we see that a Nazarite had to abstain from wine and anything related to its source. This signifies abstaining from the earthly enjoyment and pleasure (cf. Psa. 104:15; Eccl. 10:19). To abstain from all kinds of wine is to abstain from all kinds of earthly enjoyment and pleasure.

We should be careful of anything earthly that makes us happy. Earthly pleasure leads to lustful conduct and to a lustful intention. Earthly enjoyment and pleasure would defile a Nazarite.

A Nazarite had to abstain from vinegar made from wine, from the juice of grapes, and from grapes fresh or dried. This signifies abstaining from anything that issues in earthly enjoyment or pleasure. Vinegar is classified with wine because the source is the same. Wine, vinegar, and grape juice are all prohibited. From this we see that the one who is absolute for God is altogether separated from anything of earthly pleasures. This shows the absoluteness of the Nazarite. (*Life-study of Numbers*, pp. 57-58)

* * *

The Nazarite's separation was of seven days, signifying a full course of time. Samson was a Nazarite from his mother's womb for the full course of his life (Judg. 16:17). (*Life-study of Numbers,* p. 76)

* * *

[Samson's] birth was a miracle initiated by the appearing of the Angel of Jehovah. When Samson was in the bosom of his mother, he was sanctified to be a Nazarite. As he grew up, he was clean and pure according to God's ordination, and he was empowered by the Spirit of God.

Shortly after I decided to give up my job and serve the Lord, I went to Shanghai to see Brother Nee. He told me that in serving the Lord the brothers must learn the principle of not contacting a female, especially a young one, in private. I was deeply impressed by this, and from that time I have practiced Brother Nee's instructions and have also passed them on to the saints. (*Life-study of Judges,* pp. 45, 46)

* * *

Samuel came out of God's economy. God had His eternal economy, but the carrying out of God's economy had come into question. God had ordained that Aaron's descendants would be the priests for the carrying out of His economy, but that priesthood became stale and waning. God's heart's desire was to gain someone to replace that priesthood.

In order to gain such a person, God brought together in marriage Elkanah and Hannah. Elkanah had two wives. According to God's sovereign arrangement, the second wife, Peninnah, had children, but Hannah had no children. Furthermore, "her rival provoked her bitterly to irritate her, because Jehovah had shut up her womb" (1 Sam. 1:6). This forced Hannah to pray desperately not mainly for herself but for God. She promised God that if He gave her a male child, she would return the child to Him by the vow of a Nazarite. God was pleased with Hannah's prayer and her promise and He opened her womb. Hannah conceived, bore a child, and named him Samuel. From this we see that actually no human being was the origin of Samuel. God was the real origin, who motivated His people sovereignly and secretly.

SAMUEL'S GOD-WORSHIPPING PARENTS

Humanly speaking, Samuel's origin was his God-worshipping parents (vv. 1-8). Elkanah and Hannah remained in this line of life not merely for God's eternal salvation but for His eternal purpose. God's salvation is mainly for our benefit, whereas God's purpose is related to the fulfilling of God's desire.

ESPECIALLY HIS GOD-SEEKING MOTHER WITH HER PRAYER

The origin of Samuel was especially his God-seeking mother with her prayer (vv. 9-18). Her prayer was an echo of the heart's desire of God. Her prayer was a human cooperation with the divine move for the carrying out of God's eternal economy.

God wanted a Samuel, yet He needed Hannah's cooperation to pray to Him, saying, "Lord, I need a son." This prayer was very human, yet it was a cooperation with the divine move for God's economy. (*Life-study of 1 & 2 Samuel,* pp. 9-10, 11)

LOT'S CHILDREN BEING CORRUPTED

Lot's children were corrupted by living in the wicked city. The word of the angels in Genesis 19:12 indicates that Lot might have had sons as well as daughters. In chapter 18 Abraham might have considered that there were at least ten people in Lot's family...Lot had to tell his sons-in-law and his children that God was about to judge that city. But when Lot preached the gospel to them, some would not believe the word from the Lord, thinking that he was joking. Verse 14 of chapter 19 says, "And Lot went out and spoke to his sons-in-law, who were to marry his daughters, and said, Rise up; go forth from this place, for Jehovah will destroy the city. But it seemed to his sons-in-law as though he were joking."

Others of Lot's children had no sense of morality (vv. 30-35). Look at what his daughters did after they escaped from the city! After escaping from Sodom, Lot and his daughters still had wine with them (v. 32). If they had not brought the wine with them, how else could they have had it in the cave where they were dwelling? How drugged they were by the sinful situation in Sodom! When I was visiting some saints in Las Vegas in 1963, they vindicated their living in that city, saying, "It is not wrong for us to stay in this gambling city, because we are here as a testimony for the Lord." I did not argue with them, but deep within myself I said, "If you stay here for some years, your children will have no sense about the wickedness of gambling." Many of the young people today have been drugged. Look at the way they dress: there is no sense of morality or feeling of shame. Many times when I am on the street I have to shut my eyes. For young ladies to be without a sense of shame is to be without protection. Throughout the whole world the sense of shame and morality has been drugged. Because most of the young people were raised in a sinful atmosphere, their senses have been drugged. But if they would come in to the church life and remain in its pure atmosphere for a few months, they would never return to the sinful world. They would be unable to stand its smell.

We live in an evil age and need protection from it. Our family and our children must be protected. We all must escape Sodom and shut our doors to its evil atmosphere. If we do not, our descendants will be drugged. How could Lot and his children have conducted themselves in the way they did after Sodom was destroyed? Because their sense of morality had fallen so low. If we remain in the fresh air, we shall immediately sense the bad smell of immorality. But if we do not discern any bad smell, it means that our sense of morality has been drugged. (*Life-study of Genesis,* pp. 696-697)

* * *

At this point I would like to say a word to the young people. As Christians, we may need to read the newspapers to know the world situation. I read a newspaper nearly every day, but certain pages I would never read, for they are defiling. Once your mind has been defiled by looking at a certain picture, it will be very difficult for you to remove this defiling element. Furthermore, we should not listen to certain kinds of conversations or touch things that are unclean. But most important, we should abstain from fornication. We must keep, preserve, safeguard, our vessel clean in sanctification before God. It must be holy, separated, and saturated with God and also kept in honor before man. (*Life-study of 1 Thessalonians,* p. 196)

PUTTING AWAY THEIR FOREIGN GODS—IDOLS

Jacob told his household and all that were with him to put away the foreign gods that were among them (Gen. 35:2). When Jacob and his household were fleeing from Laban, Rachel took the household images (31:34-35). Prior to chapter 35, Jacob never charged Rachel to put them away. But after God had told him to go up to Bethel, everyone had to abandon their foreign gods, their idols. This is a shadow, a type, that is developed throughout the Bible. According to both the Old Testament and the New Testament, the first thing we must eliminate for the sake of God's dwelling place is our idols.

PURIFYING THEMSELVES

Jacob also charged everyone to purify themselves (35:2). We must not only put away the foreign gods but also purify our whole being. In other words, our whole being, manner of life, and expression must be changed. This is not merely regeneration or a little change in life. Rather, it is a full transformation. Here in Genesis 35, Jacob was transformed.

In the Bible, purifying ourselves means to be purified from every pollution. Our whole being must be cleansed from anything that is pollution in the eyes of God. In 2 Corinthians 7:1 Paul says, "Therefore, since we have these promises, beloved, let us cleanse ourselves from all defilement of flesh and of spirit, perfecting holiness in the fear of God." Paul's concept in 2 Corinthians 6 and 7 was the same as Jacob's in Genesis 35. Because the Corinthians were the temple of God, Paul told them to purify themselves. There can be no agreement between the temple of God and idols (2 Cor. 6:16). Idols are idols, and the temple of God is the temple of God. Which side do you take? If idols, then go to your idols. If the temple of God, then come to the temple without any idols.

CHANGING THEIR GARMENTS

In addition to putting away the foreign gods and purifying themselves, [Jacob's household] changed their garments (Gen. 35:2). According to the Bible, to change garments means to change your manner of life.

BURYING THEIR EARRINGS

Verse 4 says, "So they gave Jacob all the foreign gods which were in their hand and the rings which were in their ears, and Jacob hid them under the oak that was near Shechem." Not only were the idols buried, but also the earrings. Earrings are self-beautifying items. These were dealt with in the same way as the idols. Many people's earrings, ornaments, are equal to idols in the eyes of God. When those in Jacob's household were putting away the foreign gods, they also put away their earrings. This indicates that to their conscience their earrings were as abominable as their foreign gods. After touching the church, many sisters had the same conviction and put off this kind of abominable ornament. This is not something related to morality but to the house of God.

God did not charge Jacob to make such a clearance. Still less did He say, "Jacob, you must tell your household and everyone with you to make a clearance and to purify themselves." Why, then, did Jacob charge everyone in this way? Because the house of God is not an individual matter. It is not only Jacob. The house of God must be the house of Jacob becoming the house of Israel. Eventually, all the descendants of Jacob became the house of God, Bethel. The real Bethel was not the tabernacle; it was the children of Israel. Likewise, we must see that today we are the church. We must be purified not only because we are going to Bethel, but because we are to be Bethel. We must put away all foreign gods and abominable ornaments, purify ourselves, and change our garments. Putting away the foreign gods also means putting away all foreign trusts. We must be cleansed in our whole being, inwardly and outwardly, from every pollution, and we must change our manner of life. This is all for the church life. (*Life-study of Genesis,* pp. 1001-1002, 1003, 1005, 1006-1007)

SELF-BEAUTIFICATION LEADING TO IDOLATRY

Another principle implied in this portion of Exodus concerns what an idol is, or what is the principle of an idol. We see this principle in Exodus 32:1-4a: "And when the people saw that Moses delayed to come down from the mountain, the people gathered against Aaron and said to him, Come, make a god for us who will go before us; for as for this Moses, the man who brought us up out of the land of Egypt, we do not know what has become of him. And Aaron said to them, Tear off the gold rings, which are in the ears of your wives, your sons, and your daughters, and bring them to me. And all the people tore off the golden rings which were in their ears and brought them to Aaron. And he took the gold from their hand and fashioned it with an engraving tool and made it into a molten calf."

Here we see the kind of material that was used to make the idol. An idol, of course, must be made with something material. The material used in making the golden calf in Exodus 32 was the gold of the earrings belonging to the wives, sons, and daughters of the children of Israel. It may be that the only ones without golden earrings were the elderly men. The old men were an exception because they do not care for beautification. I can testify that, as an elderly man, I have no interest in beautifying myself. However, it is common for young men and women and also for older women to beautify themselves. Therefore, in Exodus 32 the gold rings were taken from the ears of the wives, the sons, and the daughters and used to make the idol, the golden calf.

Self-beautification leads to idolatry. This is the reason the Lord in 33:5 and 6 gave the children of Israel a commandment related to ornaments: "Now Jehovah had said to Moses, Say to the children of Israel, You are a stiff-necked people; if I were to go up in your midst for one moment, I would consume you. Now therefore put off your ornaments from you, and I will decide what to do to you. Thus the children of Israel were stripped of their ornaments from Mount Horeb onward." The Lord issued this commandment concerning ornaments because, as the record of chapter 32 makes clear, self-beautification leads to idolatry.

Do you know what many Americans are worshipping today? They are worshipping the idols of self-beautification. For example, before a young woman goes to work, she may spend a great deal of time beautifying herself. She may even spend more money on items for self-beautification than she does for food. My concern here is to point out the fact that self-beautification leads to idolatry. First the children of Israel wore golden earrings for self-beautification. Then these golden earrings were fashioned by Aaron into the idol of the golden calf. (*Life-study of Exodus,* pp. 1837, 1838, 1839)

COOPERATING WITH GOD
FOR HIS MOVE, AS PARENTS ENTRUSTED
WITH THEIR CHILDREN, TO CULTIVATE
AND NURTURE THEM IN THE LORD

Scripture Reading: Matt. 6:33; Eph. 6:4

I. The fulfillment of God's economy requires our cooperation, and to cooperate with God means to be bound together with Christ and to have one living with Him by one life—John 14:19b; 6:57; Gal. 2:20:

A. God's heart is to carry out His economy; God's economy is not merely that we should be good, spiritual, holy, or victorious; He desires neither a good man nor a bad man but a God-man—Eph. 1:9-11; 1 John 3:2.

B. Instead of usurping God by praying for our prosperity, health, or family without any consideration of God's economy, we should pray, live, and be persons according to God's heart and for His economy—1 Sam. 4:3; Hag. 1:2-5; Rev. 4:11; Eph. 1:9-11.

C. All things necessary for our human existence need to be under a divine limitation; anything that exceeds our need becomes worldly, and it frustrates us from the economy of God's purpose; in everything God's economy must be the deciding factor—Matt. 24:38.

D. When God's economy is carried out among His people, they are blessed—1 Sam. 7:1-5:

1. Our welfare, our well-being, is linked to the carrying out of God's economy, and we should not

seek our well-being apart from God's economy—
Matt. 6:33.

2. We should not expect prosperity for ourselves;
rather, we should expect that through us the Lord
will do as much as possible to accomplish His
economy.

II. The church cannot go on if parents do not have a sense
of being entrusted; God has committed a human body,
along with his soul, into our hands; we do not want to
see our children needing to be rescued back from the
world—Gen. 48:9; Psa. 127:3; Isa. 8:18:

A. We are wrong if we do not take care of our children;
please remember that it is the parents' responsibility to ensure that their children turn out the right
way—Psa. 127:3.

B. When the children are young, they are in our hands
and can do nothing much themselves; if we are
loose with ourselves, we will also be loose with them;
we must realize that parents must exercise self-
control, sacrificing their own freedom—cf. John
17:19.

C. After the church preaches the gospel and saves
men, it has to deal with all kinds of family problems associated with these men; but if parents are
responsible for the proper nurturing of their children, and if the children are brought up in the
church, the church will be relieved of half of its
burdens—2 Tim. 3:15; 1:5.

III. We should nurture the children in the discipline and
admonition of the Lord; we should tell them what a
proper Christian is by teaching them the discipline of
the Lord—Eph. 6:4:

A. Parents must help their children to have proper
aspirations; how the parents live affects the aspirations of their children; parents must learn to
channel the ambitions of their children in the
proper direction—cf. 2 Cor. 5:9.

B. Many parents cultivate their children's pride and
encourage them to go after vainglory by heaping

praises upon them in front of other people; we do not need to hurt their self-esteem, but we must point out their pride to them—Prov. 16:18; Phil. 2:3; 1 Pet. 5:5.

C. A Christian needs to know how to appreciate others; it is easy to be victorious, but it is hard to accept defeat; when our children are defeated, we need to teach them to accept their defeat with grace—Phil. 2:3-4.

D. From their youth, we should give our children a chance to make their own choices; we should not make every choice for them before they reach the age of eighteen or twenty, or else it will be impossible for them to make any decisions when they grow up—cf. Deut. 30:19; Jer. 21:8.

E. As Christians, we have to train our children to manage their things properly; we must let them know how things should be handled from their youth—Prov. 22:6.

IV. The way children grow up depends on the atmosphere in the family; they must receive nurturing love as they grow up and must experience love in the family—1 Thes. 2:7-8:

A. Half of the work of the church can be done by good parents; however, this work falls upon our shoulders today because there are few good parents—Psa. 127:3.

B. A family must be filled with an atmosphere of love and tenderness; there must be genuine love—1 Thes. 2:7-8.

C. Parents must learn to be friends to their children; we must never allow our children to distance themselves from us; we must never make ourselves unapproachable; we need to remember that friendship is built upon communication; it does not come by birth—Matt. 19:14.

D. The most helpful thing to children is for their parents to spend time with them; the more time parents spend with them, the better:

1. Sometimes we need to have free talks with them about wide-ranging subjects.
2. We should allow them to join in our daily activities, and we should join them in their activities.

Excerpts from the Ministry:

God's heart is to carry out His economy. His heart is not that we always please Him and make Him happy, nor that we should be good, spiritual, holy, or victorious. He desires neither a good man nor a bad man but a God-man. God created us according to His image and wanted us to take His life, signified by the tree of life. Because we became fallen, God became a man to save us, to redeem us. He died an all-inclusive death for us, and He resurrected to beget us by imparting God's life and nature into us, making us God in life and in nature but not in the Godhead.

We should not regard the Bible as a book that teaches us to be a good man or a spiritual man. The Bible reveals that God wants us to be a "Christ-man." To be a Christian is to be a Christ-man, a man of Christ.

We need to be impressed with the fact that the fulfillment of God's economy requires our cooperation. To cooperate with God means to be bound together with God. We may use a three-legged race as an illustration. The runners in such a race must run in pairs, with each partner having one leg bound to one of his partner's legs. In order for the partners to run, they must cooperate with each other and not move independently. This is a picture of the proper Christian life. To be a Christian is to be bound together with Christ and to have one living with Him by one life.

The birth of Samuel involved Hannah's cooperation with God. The old priesthood had become stale and waning, and God wanted to have another beginning. For Samuel's birth, God initiated things behind the scenes. On the one hand, He shut up Hannah's womb; on the other hand, He prepared a provoker (1 Sam. 1:5-7). This forced Hannah to pray that the Lord would give her a male child. In her prayer she made a vow and said, "O Jehovah of hosts, if You will indeed look upon the affliction of Your female servant and remember me and not forget Your female servant, but give to Your female servant a male child, then I will give him to Jehovah for all the days of his life, and no razor will come upon his head" (v. 11). This prayer was initiated not by Hannah but by God. God chose Hannah because she was willing to cooperate with Him. God answered her prayer and opened her womb, and Hannah conceived and bore a son (v. 20). Then according to her vow, she offered her son to God, placing him in the custody of Eli. From this we see that Hannah, Samuel's mother, was one who cooperated very much with God. Her case shows us the kind of persons God expects to have today. (*Life-study of 1 & 2 Samuel,* pp. 5, 6)

* * *

The Ark was a type of Christ as the embodiment of God. It also signified Christ as the presence of the Triune God to be with His people for the carrying out of His economy to establish His kingdom on earth. To bring out the Ark was just to bring out the presence of God. When the children of Israel began to move with the ark from Mount Sinai, Moses offered a prayer to God, saying, "Rise up, O Jehovah, and let Your enemies be scattered" (Num. 10:35). The Ark took the lead to travel onward. The move of the Ark was a picture of God's move on the earth.

In 1 Samuel 4 the elders of Israel were actually usurping God. At that time, God did not intend to move. The children of Israel had no thought of or concern for God's economy, and their bringing out the Ark indicated that they were usurping God for their safety, peace, rest, and profit. They were usurping God, even forcing Him, to go out with them.

Today many Christians usurp God by praying for their prosperity, health, or family without any consideration of God's economy. When we ask God for His healing, we must be fully related to His economy. If you are ill, you should not pray for healing in the way of usurping God. On the contrary, from the depths of your spirit you should say, "Lord, I am not here on earth for my health, my prosperity, my children, or my work. I am here for Your economy. Do You still want me to live on earth for Your economy? I have seen Your economy, I realize that You need Nazarites, and I have a heart to be a Nazarite for You. As one who has been born of God and who has the life and nature of God, I ask You what is on Your heart concerning me." If God intends that you continue living on earth for His economy, you will be healed, either through a physician or through some other way. The point here is that, instead of usurping God, we must pray, live, and be persons according to God's heart and for His economy. (*Life-study of 1 & 2 Samuel,* pp. 22-23)

*   *   *

For us to live for Christ, we need to exist. Without our human existence we cannot live Christ. But today those in the fallen world care for nothing but their existence; they do not care for the purpose of their existence. To exist is one thing, but to exist for the divine purpose is another thing. The purpose ordained by God for our existence is to live Christ, to live God out, and to have God's testimony. But the people of this world have only their existence; they have no purpose. Eventually they make their existence itself the purpose of their existence. They know nothing but existence. Satan picks up the existence of human beings or of human living and uses this existence to usurp people so that today the whole world cares only for existence, not for God's purpose in existence.

All things necessary for our human existence need to be under a divine limitation. Anything that exceeds our need becomes worldly, "Egyptian," something of Pharaoh, and it frustrates us from the economy of God's purpose. In everything God's economy must be the deciding factor. Our living should not be like that of the "Egyptians," the worldly people. We need a place to live, and we need to keep our house clean. But if we continue with our cleaning when it is time to go to the meeting, our cleaning becomes "Egyptian," something apart from the economy of God's purpose. We are on earth not for cleaning but for a feast unto the Lord. Even how much time we spend with our children should be decided by God's economy. Other Christians may act like the people of the world, but we have to be a holy people, a separated people.

Our living and our existence depend on the provision from the heavenly source, not on the supply from the world. For this we need the vision, and we need the exercise of our faith. Moses was a man of great faith to lead two million people out of Egypt into the wilderness, where there was no earthly supply for their human existence. (*Life-study of Exodus,* p. 156)

* * *

The picture portrayed in 1 Samuel 7:1-5 is very beautiful. Here we have a people returning to God and a man—Samuel— who was one with God on earth. We may say that Samuel was the acting God on earth. At least we may say that Samuel was the representative of the very God in heaven to rule over His people on earth. As such a person, Samuel began to minister.

Samuel was faithful to God to do according to what was in God's heart and mind. His whole being and person, not just his doing, living, and work, were according to God. Samuel's being and God's heart were one. For this reason it is not too much to say that Samuel, a man according to God, was the acting God on earth. God's mind was Samuel's consideration. He had no other thought, consideration, or thinking. His living and working were for the carrying out of whatever was in God's heart. As a consequence, Samuel was one who turned the age.

In this replacing priesthood, Samuel anointed Saul and David to be kings (10:1; 16:1, 13) as God ordained that he should go before His anointed continually (2:35b) to supervise the king, observing what the king was doing. This indicates that Samuel, the acting God on earth, was greater than the king. Samuel could be qualified to such an extent because for many years God had been perfecting him for His economy, not for anything else.

When God's economy is carried out among His people, they are blessed. This means that our welfare, our well-being, is altogether linked to the carrying out of God's economy. We should not seek our well-being apart from God's economy. Because this has been neglected and even lost, it needs to be recovered. I wish to say, especially to the young saints, that we should not expect to have prosperity for ourselves. Rather, as saints in the Lord's recovery, we should expect that through us the Lord will do as much as possible to accomplish His economy. Then we will be blessed. (*Life-study of 1 & 2 Samuel*, pp. 27-30)

* * *

The church cannot go on if parents do not have a sense of being entrusted. We do not want to see our children being rescued back from the world. Suppose we beget children, lose them to the world, and then try to rescue them back. If we allow this to happen, the gospel will never be preached to the uttermost part of the earth. Our children have been taught many teachings, and we have been taking care of them for years. At least these children should be brought to the Lord. We are wrong if we do not take care of our children. Please remember that it is the parents' responsibility to ensure that their children turn out the right way.

Please give me the liberty to say this word. Throughout church history, the greatest failure among Christians is the failure in parenting. This is something no one cares much about. The children are young; they are in your hands and can do nothing much themselves. If you are loose with yourself, you will also be loose with them. We must realize that parents must exercise self-control, sacrificing their own freedom. God has committed a human body, along with his soul, into our hands. If we do not exercise self-control and give up our freedom, we will have a difficult time answering to our God in the future.

NURTURING CHILDREN IN THE DISCIPLINE
AND ADMONITION OF THE LORD

You must nurture your children in the discipline and admonition of the Lord (Eph. 6:4). The discipline of the Lord is telling a person how he should behave himself. You must consider your children as Christians, not Gentiles. The Lord's discipline tells a person how he should behave as a Christian. The Lord intends that all of our children become Christians. He has no intention that any of them be a Gentile or an unsaved person. You should plan on all of them becoming not just Christians, but good Christians. You should tell them what a proper Christian is by teaching them the discipline of the Lord. Here we must briefly cover a number of points.

Helping Children to Have Proper Aspirations

The biggest thing about a child is his aspirations. Every child has an aspiration when he is young. If the government allowed every child to print his business card, I think many children would print "President," "Chairman," or "Queen." Parents must help their children to have proper aspirations. If you love the world, your children will probably want to be the president, a millionaire, or a great academic. How you live affects the aspirations of your child. Parents must learn to channel the ambitions of their children in the proper direction. They should aspire to be lovers of the Lord. They should not aspire to love the world. You should cultivate such an ambition within them while they are young. Show them that it is an honorable thing to die for the Lord, that it is a precious thing to be a martyr for the Lord. You have to be an example to them, and you have to tell them your ambitions. Tell them what you want to be if you are given the opportunity. Tell them what kind of Christian you want to be. In this way, you will channel their ambitions in the proper direction. Their goals will change, and they will know what is noble and what is precious.

Not Encouraging the Pride of Children

Children have another problem: They are not only ambitious and aspiring but also proud of themselves. They may boast about their own cleverness, skill, or eloquence. A child can find many things to boast about. He may think that he is a very special person. Parents should not discourage them, but neither should they cultivate their pride. Many parents cultivate their children's pride and encourage them to go after vainglory by heaping praises upon them in front of other people. We should tell them, "There are many children who are like you in this world." Do not try to encourage their pride. We should enlighten children according to the discipline and admonition of the Lord. They should be able to think, to speak, and to learn all the skills. But you have to tell them that there are many who are like them in this world. Do not destroy their self-esteem, but do not allow them to become proud. You do not need to hurt their self-esteem, but you must point out their pride to them. Many young people leave home only to find out that they have to spend ten or twenty years in the world in order to learn how to do things properly. By then it is too late. Many young people have a wild temper at home. They are so proud that they cannot work properly. We do not want our children to become disheartened, but neither do we want them to be proud or to think that they are somebody.

Teaching Children to Accept Defeat and to Learn Humility

A Christian needs to know how to appreciate others. It is easy to be victorious, but it is hard to accept defeat. We can find champions who are humble, but it is rare to find losers who are not bitter. This is not a Christian attitude. Those who are good in some areas should learn to be humble and not boastful. At the same time, when a person is defeated, he should learn to accept his defeat. Children are very competitive. It is all right for them to be competitive; they want to win at ball games, track meets, and in their school work. You have to show them that it is right for them to study well at school, but they have to learn to be humble. Encourage them to be humble. Tell them that there are many other students who may be better than they are. When they are defeated, you need to teach them to accept their defeat with grace. A child's problem often has to do with these attitudes. After a game the winner is proud, while the loser will complain that the judge was not fair or that he made the wrong judgment because the sun was glaring in his face. You should help them to develop a humble character. They should be under Christian admonition and should develop Christian character. They can win, and when they lose they can also appreciate others. Admitting defeat is a virtue. The Chinese are greatly lacking in this virtue. Most Chinese blame others when they are defeated instead of conceding with grace. You must nurture your children in the discipline and admonition of the Lord.

Many children say that their teacher plays favorites when others do well on tests. When they do not do well themselves, they say their teacher does not like them. Here we see the need for humility. Christians must have the virtue of accepting defeat. If others are good, we have to say promptly that they are good. We also have to accept defeat and concede that others are smarter, more hard working, or better than we are. It is a Christian virtue to accept defeat. When we win, we should not look down upon everyone else. This attitude is unworthy of a Christian. When others are better than we are, we have to appreciate them. Others may be stronger or jump higher than we do. While our children are still living at home with us, we should train them to acknowledge achievement in others. This training will help them understand themselves when they grow up as Christians. We should know ourselves and appreciate those who are better than we are. If our children are this way, it will be easy for them to experience spiritual things.

Teaching Children to Choose

I hope that we will pay attention to this matter. In many aspects we have to teach our children according to the discipline of the Lord. From their youth, we should give them a chance to make their own choices. We should not make every choice for them until they reach the age of eighteen or twenty. If we do, it will be impossible for them to make any decisions when they grow up. We have to always give them the opportunity to make decisions. Give them the chance to choose what they like and what they do not like. We have to show them whether their choices are right. Give them the chance to choose and then show them the right choice. Let them see it for themselves. Some like to wear short dresses. Some prefer one kind of color, while others prefer another kind of color. Let them make the choices by themselves.

Some people do not give their children the opportunity to make choices. As a result, when their children reach their twenties and marry someone, they do not know how to be the head. You can tell them that the husband is the head of the wife, but they will not know how to be the head. You must not allow them to wait until they are married to find out that they do not know how to be the head. If at all possible, give your children plenty of opportunity to make decisions. When they grow up, they will then know what to do. They will know what is wrong and what is right. Give a child opportunities to make choices from the time he is young. I will say a word to all those who have children: "Give them a chance to choose." Otherwise, many Chinese children will be damaged when they grow up. The damage is often manifested when the children are between the ages of eighteen and twenty. They act in irresponsible ways at this age because they have never been called upon to make any choices. We must teach our children according to the discipline of the Lord. We must teach our children to make choices rather than making all the choices for them. We have to let our children know whether they have made the right choices.

Teaching Children to Manage Things

We must also teach our children to manage things. We must give them the opportunity to take care of their personal belongings, to manage their own shoes, socks, and other affairs. Give them a little instruction and then let them try to manage things by themselves. Let them know how things should be handled from their youth. Some children have a bad start because their fathers love them blindly and do not know how to train them. As Christians, we have to train our children to manage their things properly.

I believe if the Lord is gracious to us, we will gain half of our increase from among our own children and the other half from the "sea" (i.e., the world). If all the increase is from the sea and none is from among our own children, we will not have a strong church. Paul's generation could be saved directly from the world, but the generation after Paul, men like Timothy, came in through their families. We cannot expect our increase to always come from the world. We have to expect the second generation, men like Timothy, to come from our own families. God's gospel does save men from the world, but we also need to bring in men like Timothy. Before the church will be rich, there must be grandmothers like Lois and mothers like Eunice who raise, edify, and nurture their children in the discipline of the Lord. If there are no such people, the church will never be rich. We must give our children the opportunity to manage things from their youth. We must give them the chance to learn to arrange things by themselves. Hold family meetings frequently and allow the children to make decisions. If we have to rearrange the furniture, involve them in its rearrangement. If we have to rearrange the cupboard, involve them in its rearrangement. Teach them to manage things. Whether we have daughters or sons, we have to teach them to manage things. Then they will become a good husband or a good wife in the future.

What is our situation today? Girls should be cared for by their mothers. But many mothers do not take care of them, and the burden is turned over to the church. Boys should be cared for by their fathers. But many fathers do not take care of them, and the burden is also passed on to the church. As a consequence, as men are saved and brought into the church, the business burden of the church doubles. This is because those who are parents do not live properly as Christian parents. After the church preaches the gospel and saves men, it has to deal with all kinds of family problems associated with these men. But if parents are responsible for the proper nurturing of their children, and if the children are brought up in the church, the church will be relieved of half of its burdens. In Shanghai I have often felt that the workers should not be handling the many affairs that they handle; those affairs should be handled by the parents. The parents do not teach their children well, and these children drift into the world. As a result, we have to rescue them back from the world and pick up the burden of teaching them ourselves. This creates much work for the church.

THE ATMOSPHERE IN THE FAMILY BEING ONE OF LOVE

The atmosphere in the family should be one of love. Some become psychologically abnormal or withdrawn because they do not have love at home.

The way a child grows up depends on the atmosphere in his family. If a child does not receive any loving nurturing as he grows up, he will become stubborn, individualistic, and rebellious. Many people cannot get along with others in their adult life because they did not experience love in the family as a child. They saw only quarrels, arguments, and fights in the family. Children from such families grow up abnormally. Those who come from such abnormal families surely grow up to be lonely people. They will be antagonistic toward others. Because they feel inferior in their heart, they try to boost their self-image by considering themselves better than others. All those who have an inferiority complex have a tendency to exalt themselves. This is their means of offsetting their own inferiority.

Many bad elements in society such as robbers and rebels come from families that are void of love. Their personality becomes warped, and they turn against their fellow man when they grow up. When they come to the church, they bring their problems with them. I feel that half of the work of the church can be done by good parents. But this work falls upon our shoulders today because there are few good parents. New believers should see that they should treat their children in a proper way. A family must be filled with an atmosphere of love and tenderness. There must be genuine love. Children who grow up from such families will become normal persons.

Parents must learn to be friends to their children. Never allow your children to distance themselves from you. Never make yourself unapproachable. Please remember that friendship is built upon communication; it does not come by birth. You must learn to approach your children. Be happy to help them so that they will tell you when they encounter problems and seek your counsel when they are weak. They should not go to others when they are weak. They should be able to tell you their successes as well as their failures. You should be their good friend, the approachable and helpful one to them. They should look to you when they are weak and fellowship with you when they are successful. We have to be friends to them. When they are weak, they should be able to come to us for help. We should not be a judge on the throne but a help to them. We should be there whenever they need help, and we should be able to sit down with them and discuss problems with them. They should be able to seek counsel from us as from friends. In a family the parents must earn so much trust from their children that they become their friends. If a parent will do this, he or she will have done the right thing.

You have to learn this lesson from the time the children are young. How dear and near your children are to you depends on how you treat them the first twenty years of their lives. If they are not near to you the first twenty years of their lives, they will not be near to you when they are thirty or forty years old. They will drift further and further away from you. Many children do not like to be near their parents. They are not friends to them and there is no sweet relationship between them. They go to their parents when they have problems in a way that resembles a criminal going before a judge. You must work to such an extent that your children will come and seek your advice first when they have problems. They must feel comfortable confiding in you. If you can achieve this, you will find few problems in your family. In fact, all problems will be solved. (*Messages for Building Up New Believers,* vol. 2, pp. 522-523, 536, 537-541, 544-546)

* * *

Question: How can an elder who is a father care for his family and also be always available to help the saints?

Answer: To be an overseer is difficult. The most helpful thing for children is for their parents to spend time with them. To sit with them, observe what they are doing, and instruct them is the best encouragement to them and prevents them from being idle. Sometimes we need to have free talks with them about wide-ranging subjects. If we do, they will be happy. All children like to learn. The need with our children is endless. The more time we spend with them, the better. We should allow them to join in our daily activities, and we should join them in their activities. However, an elder also needs to be available to help the saints. In order to care for both these needs, we must learn to fellowship with the Lord and follow His leading. What I have shared concerning the eldership are principles. We need the Lord's leading for specific situations. (*Basic Principles concerning the Eldership,* pp. 57-58)

PART THREE:

THOSE WHO LABOR
AMONG THE CHILDREN
AND YOUNG PEOPLE

BEING PATTERNS
FOR FOSTERING THE CHILDREN
AND YOUNG PEOPLE

Scripture Reading: 1 Thes. 1:5-8; 2:1-20; 2 Thes. 3:7, 9; 1 Pet. 5:2-4

I. For new believers to live a holy life for the church life, there is the need of the aspect of fostering—1 Thes. 2:7-12; Eph. 5:29, footnote 1:

A. Paul likens the apostles both to a nursing mother and to an exhorting father; the apostles regarded the believers as children under their fostering care; just as parents care for their children, fostering their growth, so the apostles cared for the new believers—1 Thes. 2:6b-7, 11.

B. First Thessalonians is a word to beginners, to new believers; those who are working with young people or with new believers can receive from this book both a direction and an outline to follow—1:3 and footnote 2.

II. Paul fostered the young believers mainly by presenting them a pattern of life, a pattern of a proper living; this pattern was actually Paul himself—v. 5; 2:10; 2 Thes. 3:7-9:

A. The apostles not only preached the gospel but also lived it; their ministering of the gospel was not only by word but also by a life that displayed the power of God, a life in the Holy Spirit and in the assurance of faith—1 Thes. 1:5.

B. The apostle Paul stressed repeatedly the apostles' entrance toward the believers; this shows that their manner of life played a great role in infusing the gospel into the new converts—vv. 5, 9; 2:1:

1. The apostles were struggling and speaking the gospel to the Thessalonians in the boldness of God—v. 2.
2. The apostles were free from deception, uncleanness, and guile—v. 3.
3. The apostles were first tested and approved by God and then were entrusted by Him with the gospel; hence, their speaking, the preaching of the gospel, was not of themselves to please men but of God to please Him—v. 4; Psa. 139:23-24.
4. The apostles were never found with flattering speech nor with a pretext for covetousness— 1 Thes. 2:5.
5. The apostles did not seek glory from men—v. 6a:
   a. To seek glory from men is a real temptation to every Christian worker; many have been devoured and spoiled by this matter—1 Sam. 15:12.
   b. Lucifer became God's adversary, Satan, because of glory-seeking; anyone who seeks glory from men is a follower of Satan—Ezek. 28:13-17; Isa. 14:12-15; Matt. 4:8-10.
   c. How much we will be used by the Lord and how long our usefulness will last depend on whether we seek glory from men—John 7:17-18; 5:39-44; 12:43; 2 Cor. 4:5.
6. The apostles did not stand on their own authority, or dignity, as apostles of Christ—1 Thes. 2:6b.
7. The apostles cherished the believers and yearned over them as a nursing mother would cherish and yearn over her own children—vv. 7-8, cf. v. 17; Gal. 4:19; Isa. 49:14-15; 66:12-13.
8. The apostles imparted not only the gospel of God to the Thessalonians but also imparted their own souls—1 Thes. 2:8; 2 Cor. 12:15.
9. The apostles considered themselves as fathers in exhorting the believers to walk in a manner

worthy of God, to have a walk that will enable them to enter into the kingdom of God and usher them into the glory of God—1 Thes. 2:11-12.

III. To do the work of fostering—to shepherd people and to cherish and nourish them—is to give them a proper pattern; Paul fed his spiritual children with his own living of Christ—vv. 1-12; 2 Cor. 1:23—2:14; 1 Cor. 9:22; Acts 20:28:

A. Parents are patterns, models, for their children; whatever the parents are, the children will be also; imitating is related to growing; children grow by imitating their parents—2 Thes. 3:9; Heb. 13:7.

B. To give the new believers and young ones a lot of teaching is not the proper way to take care of them; the proper way to foster them is to show them a pattern; by showing them a pattern, you water them, supply them, nourish them, and cherish them— 2 Cor. 3:6; 1 Cor. 8:1b; 1 Thes. 2:8.

C. The source, the origin, of the apostles' preaching was God and not themselves; whenever we preach or teach, we must impress others with the fact that what we are saying is not the word of man but is truly the word of God—v. 13; Heb. 4:12.

D. The church in Thessalonica imitated the churches in Judea—1 Thes. 2:14:

1. Reports concerning the churches in Judea reached the believers in Thessalonica; they must have heard about the churches and the saints, and these reports fostered the growth of the Thessalonian believers—v. 14.

2. Nothing can foster a church or a saint as much as a true story about other saints or churches— Acts 27:21, footnote 2; Rom. 16:4, 13.

E. The inoculating word was part of Paul's fostering of the saints; even inoculation is included in fostering; Paul inoculated the believers against the eventual coming of the Judaizers—1 Thes. 2:15.

F. Paul likened the departure of the apostles from the Thessalonians to a bereavement, a loss the apostles suffered from being separated from the new believers and that caused the apostles to miss them; this word implies that the apostles considered the new converts precious and dear to them—vv. 15-17.

IV. Those who work with the Lord in fostering the believers to walk worthily of God will receive a reward; this reward will be the believers we have fostered, becoming our crown, glory, and joy—1 Thes. 2:19-20; 1 Pet. 5:3-4:

A. Because the apostles rendered such a care to the new believers, the apostles will eventually receive a reward from the Lord—1 Thes. 19-20.

B. First Thessalonians 2:20 indicates that since the apostles were the believers' nursing mother and exhorting father, the believers, as their children, were their glory and joy; apart from them, the apostles had no hope, glory, or crown of boasting—vv. 19-20.

C. "When the Chief Shepherd is manifested, you will receive the unfading crown of glory"—1 Pet. 5:4; Matt. 24:45-47.

Excerpts from the Ministry:

THE FOSTERING OF A HOLY LIFE
FOR THE CHURCH LIFE

The first chapter of 1 Thessalonians covers two main points: the structure of a holy life for the church life and the origin of a holy life for the church life. The structure is composed of the work of faith, the labor of love, and the endurance of hope. The origin of such a life is the preaching of the gospel and the acceptance of the word preached, an acceptance resulting in turning to God from idols, serving a living and true God, and waiting for the Son. Now in chapter 2 we come to the third aspect of a holy life for the church life, the aspect of fostering.

Although the word *fostering* cannot be found in 1 Thessalonians 2, the fact of fostering can be seen in this chapter. Here Paul likens the apostles both to a nursing mother and to an exhorting father. This means that the apostles were mothers and fathers to the new believers. They regarded the believers as children under their fostering care. Just as parents care for their children, fostering their growth, so the apostles cared for the new believers. Thus, in 1 Thessalonians 2 we see the fostering of a holy life for the church life. (*Life-study of 1 & 2 Thessalonians,* p. 96)

* * *

We have emphasized the fact that in 1 Thessalonians we have a word to beginners, to new believers. Those who are working with young people or with new believers can receive from this book both a direction and an outline to follow. If they follow this outline and direction, they will lay a good foundation in their work with new believers. (*Life-study of 1 & 2 Thessalonians,* pp. 129-130)

* * *

Do not think that in the recovery we regard work higher than life. No, we need to concentrate on life. The church is a family. The church may also be compared to a farm or a garden. A family is a place where children grow up, and an orchard is a place where trees grow and produce fruit. Paul's concern in chapter 2 is with the growth of his children. He is fostering the young believers so that they may grow. We may also say that he is watering, nourishing, and cherishing the tender young plants so that they may grow in life. This is the reason that instead of giving the believers a great deal of teaching, he presents them a pattern of life. This pattern of a proper living is actually Paul himself. (*Life-study of 1 & 2 Thessalonians,* pp. 108-109)

PREACHING IN POWER, IN THE HOLY SPIRIT, AND IN MUCH ASSURANCE

In 1:5 Paul continues, "For our gospel did not come to you in word only, but also in power and in the Holy Spirit and in much assurance, even as you know what kind of men we were among you for your sake." The apostles not only preached the gospel; they lived it. Their ministering of the gospel was not only by word, but also by a life which displays the power of

God, a life in the Holy Spirit and in the assurance of their faith. They were the model of the glad tidings they spread. (*Life-study of 1 & 2 Thessalonians,* p. 12)

THE APOSTLES' ENTRANCE

First Thessalonians 2:1 says, "For you yourselves know, brothers, our entrance toward you, that it has not been in vain." The apostle stresses repeatedly their entrance to the believers (1:5, 9). This shows that their manner of life played a great role in infusing the gospel into the new converts. It was not only what the apostles said, but also what they were.

The apostles came to the Thessalonians with the gospel in such a way that the Thessalonians were convinced. The apostles' entrance was not in vain. They were a pattern of how to believe in the Lord and follow Him. Because many came to believe in the Lord Jesus through the apostles, a church was raised up in less than a month. This happened not mainly as a result of preaching and teaching, but through the kind of entrance the apostles had among the Thessalonians.

SPEAKING THE GOSPEL IN MUCH STRUGGLE

Verse 2 of chapter 2 continues, "But having suffered previously and having been outrageously treated, even as you know, in Philippi, we were bold in our God to speak to you the gospel of God in much struggle." In the preaching of the gospel, the apostles experienced God. They enjoyed Him as their boldness in the struggle for the gospel. They were bold not in themselves, but in God, even after they had been outrageously treated by the Philippians. Suffering and persecution could not defeat them because they were in the organic union with the Triune God. According to verse 2, they spoke the gospel of God in much struggle. This indicates that while they were preaching, they were fighting, because persecution was still going on. Hence, they were struggling and speaking the gospel to the Thessalonians in the boldness of God.

HONEST AND FAITHFUL

In verse 3 Paul says, "For our exhortation is not out of deception nor out of uncleanness nor in guile." Deception refers to the goal, uncleanness to the motive, and guile to the means. All three are of and by the subtle and deceiving devil. The word *exhortation* includes speaking, preaching, teaching, and instructing. Paul's exhorting was free from deception, uncleanness, and guile. The apostles were not greedy, and they had no intention of making a gain of anyone. Their coming to the Thessalonians with the gospel was altogether honest and faithful.

APPROVED BY GOD

Verse 4 says, "But even as we have been approved by God to be entrusted with the gospel, so we speak, not as pleasing men but God, who proves our hearts." God's entrusting depends on His approval by His testing. The apostles were first tested and approved by God and then were entrusted by Him with the gospel. Hence, their speaking, the preaching of the gospel, was not of themselves to please men, but was of God to please Him. He proves, examines, and tests their hearts all the time (Psa. 26:2; 139:23-24).

The word *approved* in 1 Thessalonians 2:4 implies being tested. God tested the apostles before He approved them. Based upon this approvedness, God entrusted them with the gospel. God did this in a careful way, for He knows our hearts.

According to our opinion, since God already knows everything, it is not necessary for Him to test us. Yes, before we were born, He already knew what kind of person we would be. Why, then, does God test us? God's testing is not mainly for Himself; it is primarily for us. God knows us, but we do not know ourselves. Because we do not know ourselves adequately, we may think that we are upright, honest, and faithful. However, when we are put to the test, we shall see what we really are and discover that in ourselves we are not honest, faithful, or trustworthy. God's testing, therefore, proves us to ourselves. Only after God proves us in this way shall we have approvedness.

I would encourage the young people not to have confidence in themselves, for they have not yet been tested. I have the assurance that God will use the young people. But God's using of them will come after His testing of them. God cannot entrust anything to us until we have the approvedness that comes from His testing. God's entrusting is based on our approvedness. But we cannot approve ourselves. Only after God has tested us will He grant us approvedness. Then He will entrust something to us and begin to use us.

It was in this way that God entrusted the apostles with the gospel. Because the apostles had been entrusted with the gospel, they spoke not as pleasing men, but as pleasing God, who proves our hearts. Their speaking was based on God's entrusting. Because He had entrusted them with the gospel, they spoke as pleasing God.

In verse 4 we see that we must be approved and then have something entrusted to us. Then we need to speak as pleasing God, the One who proves us. This indicates that we need to pass through testing, approving, and entrusting. Then we shall have something to preach and teach.

NO FLATTERY OR PRETEXT

Verse 5 says, "For neither were we found at any time with flattering speech, even as you know, nor with a pretext for covetousness; God is witness." The Greek word rendered "pretext" also means "pretense, cloak." To have any pretext for covetousness is to peddle or adulterate the word of God (2 Cor. 2:17; 4:2). It is also to pretend to be godly for gain (1 Tim. 6:5; Titus 1:11; 2 Pet. 2:3).

According to 1 Thessalonians 2:5, the apostles were never found with flattering speech. We all must avoid flattery, never speaking in a way to flatter others. In this verse Paul also says that the apostles did not have a pretext, a cloak, for covetousness. They did not have an evil motive that was covered in some way. Because they did not have any pretext or pretense, they did not peddle the word of God or adulterate it. To adulterate something is to mix it with an inferior material, for example, to mix gold with copper or wine with water, and then to sell it as if it were pure. Throughout the centuries, many preachers and teachers have adulterated the word of God in this way. They preached under a pretext in order to make gain for themselves.

From verse 5 we learn to avoid flattery and a pretext for covetousness. In our Christian work we must give no place to such unclean things. No servant of the Lord should use flattery or have some kind of pretext for covetousness. May the Lord have mercy on us and purify us from all these things. May we be able to say that God is our witness that we do not speak words of flattery or have any pretext for covetousness.

NOT SEEKING GLORY FROM MEN

In verse 6 Paul goes on to say, "Nor did we seek glory from men, neither from you nor from others, though we could have stood on our authority as apostles of Christ." To seek glory from men is a real temptation to every Christian worker. Many have been devoured and spoiled by this matter.

The Greek words rendered "stood on our authority" also mean "asserted authority." A literal translation would be "been able to be in weight," that is, been burdensome (see v. 9; 1 Cor. 9:4-12). To assert authority, dignity, or right in Christian work also damages it. The Lord Jesus, while on earth, gave up His dignity (John 13:4-5), and the apostle would rather not use his right (1 Cor. 9:12).

Apparently, seeking glory from men is not as evil as covetousness. However, it is more subtle. The fall of the archangel was due to the seeking of glory. He became God's adversary because of his glory-seeking. Even though he was a leading angel with a very high position, he was still seeking glory. That was the cause of his fall. According to the New Testament, anyone who seeks glory from men is a follower of Satan. The seeking of glory is a trap spread by Satan to snare Christian workers. Therefore, it is very important that all Christian workers learn to avoid the snare of glory-seeking. However, not many have escaped this trap.

How much we shall be used by the Lord and how long our usefulness will last depend on whether we seek glory from men. If we seek glory, our usefulness in the hand of the Lord is finished. The seeking of glory for the self always kills one's usefulness. Therefore, may we all, especially the young, be warned never to seek glory in the Lord's work.

NOT STANDING ON THEIR OWN AUTHORITY

First Thessalonians 2:6 indicates clearly that the apostles

did not stand on their authority as apostles of Christ. They did not assume any standing or dignity. They had to forget that they were apostles and serve God's people as slaves. They were not to remind others of the fact that they were apostles of Christ. Instead, they were to keep in mind that they were brothers serving believers. They were not to assume any standing or dignity.

Those who are believers and also those who are not believers may consider the leading ones, the elders, or the apostles as dignitaries. However, in the local churches there are no dignitaries. Instead of being dignitaries, we are slaves serving one another. Nevertheless, I know of certain ones who did not assume anything when they did not have a position or title. But as soon as they were given a position, perhaps in a service group, they began to assume dignity. This is shameful. We should learn of Paul never to stand on our dignity or assert authority.

A sister whose husband is an elder should not assume dignity because she is the wife of an elder. An elder's wife is not the "First Lady." She is simply a little sister serving the church. Furthermore, her husband is not a dignitary; he is a slave. As an elder, he has been appointed to serve the church as a slave. We all should have this attitude.

Paul's statement, "We could have stood on our authority as apostles of Christ," indicates that even in the early days there was the temptation of assuming authority. People were the same in Paul's time as they are today. Then as well as now, there was the temptation to assume some kind of authority or standing. Paul, however, did not stand on his authority as an apostle in order to claim something for himself. By refusing to stand on his dignity or assert authority Paul is a good pattern for us all. If we follow this pattern, we shall kill a deadly disease germ in the Body of Christ, the germ of assuming a position.

CHERISHING THE BELIEVERS

In verse 7 Paul says, "But we were gentle in your midst, as a nursing mother would cherish her own children." The Greek word rendered "nurse," *trophos,* sometimes means a mother;

hence, it may denote a nursing mother (see Gal. 4:19). Cherishing includes nourishing. Therefore, this word not only includes nourishing but also includes tender care.

Even though Paul was a brother, he considered himself a nursing mother. Surely, he had no thought of position, dignity, or authority. The thought of being a nursing mother is very different from the thought of dignity or position. What position does a nursing mother have? What rank, dignity, or authority belongs to her? Her dignity consists in nourishing and cherishing her children, in taking care of them in a tender way.

The word *cherish* is lovely, a word of utmost tenderness. Paul regarded himself as a cherishing one, not merely as one who serves. He certainly did not control the believers. Neither did he merely serve them. Rather, he cherished them. His care for them was full of tenderness.

IMPARTING THEIR OWN SOULS

In 1 Thessalonians 2:8 Paul continues, "Yearning in this way over you, we were well pleased to impart to you not only the gospel of God but also our own souls, because you became beloved to us." The word *yearning* indicates being affectionately fond of, affectionately desirous of, like a nursing mother affectionately interested in her child whom she nourishes and cherishes. This was what the apostles did with the new believers.

The apostles not only imparted the gospel of God to the Thessalonians; they also imparted their own souls. To live a clean and upright life as portrayed in verses 3 through 6 and 10, and to love the new converts, even by giving our own souls to them, as described in verses 7 through 9 and 11, are the prerequisites for infusing others with the salvation conveyed in the gospel we preach.

Paul's word in verse 8 about imparting their own souls to the Thessalonians can be compared to his word in 2 Corinthians 12 about being spent for the sake of the believers. Paul was willing to spend not only what he had, but was willing to spend himself, his very being. The apostles were willing to impart what they were into the believers. This can be compared to a nursing mother giving herself to her child.

THE APOSTLES' CONDUCT

First Thessalonians 2:9 says, "For you remember, brothers, our labor and travail: While working night and day so as not to be burdensome to any of you, we proclaimed to you the gospel of God." The apostles did not want to be a burden on the Thessalonians. Therefore, they labored night and day in order to proclaim to them the gospel of God.

In verse 10 Paul continues, "You are witnesses, as well as God, how in a holy and righteous and blameless manner we conducted ourselves toward you who believe." *Holy* refers to conduct toward God, *righteous* to conduct toward men, and *blameless* to all—God, men, and Satan. In order to conduct himself in this way, Paul had to exercise strict control over himself. Verse 10 reveals that the apostles were those who practiced self-control.

A FATHER EXHORTING HIS CHILDREN

Verse 11 says, "Just as you know how we were to each one of you, as a father to his own children, exhorting you and consoling you and testifying." The apostle was strong in stressing what or how they were (1:5), for what they were opened the way to bring the new converts into God's full salvation.

In verse 11 of chapter 2 Paul likens himself to a father exhorting his children. In cherishing the believers as their own children, the apostles considered themselves as nourishing mothers. In exhorting them, they considered themselves fathers.

In verse 12 Paul exhorts the believers to walk in a manner worthy of God. If he himself had not walked worthily of God, how could he have exhorted others to do so? In this matter also, he set an example for the believers to follow.

Verse 12 indicates that walking worthily of God is related to entering into His kingdom and being ushered into His glory. The thought here, in contrast to that in verses 1 through 11, is quite deep. Here we have a matter often neglected by Christians. Not many believers are taught to have a Christian walk that will enable them to enter into the kingdom of God, a walk that will usher them into God's glory. Many Christians have never heard such a word. Nevertheless, this is included as part of Paul's teaching to young believers. (*Life-study of 1 & 2 Thessalonians,* pp. 97-104)

* * *

We may think that Paul should have given the new believers more doctrine, teaching, and instructions. Instead, Paul emphasizes the apostles' coming, their preaching and teaching of the Word, and how the new believers accepted this word. Paul's emphasis is on the apostles' conduct, on their living and manner of life. The reason for this emphasis is that Paul wanted to nourish the believers, to cherish and foster them. It was not Paul's intention to give them a lot of knowledge. He did not have the burden to teach them so many things. In the twenty verses of chapter 2 there is actually very little teaching. In verse 12 he does say that God has called the believers into His kingdom and glory; however, he does not develop these matters or explain them. Rather, in verse after verse, Paul mentions his manner of life, his way of preaching, and his being a pattern to the believers.

THE WORK OF FOSTERING

What we have in chapter 2 of 1 Thessalonians is the fostering of the young Christian life. In this chapter Paul is nourishing and cherishing the believers. According to his writing, he behaves himself as a nursing mother and an exhorting father. On the one hand, he is a mother cherishing; on the other hand, he is a father exhorting. His main concern is not teaching, but the carrying out of a fostering work to help the young saints to grow.

In 1:6 Paul says to the Thessalonians, "You became imitators of us and of the Lord." Imitating is related to growing. In fact, in many ways to imitate is to grow. In a family children imitate their parents and older brothers and sisters. The little ones do not invent anything; instead, they imitate others. A very good illustration of this is in the use of language. A child learns the language spoken by his parents. He speaks the same language with the same accent. A child learns the language and the accent by imitation. This illustrates the fact that children grow by imitating their parents. Therefore, in a family to imitate actually means to grow. The children imitate their parents in many things—in gestures, in speech, and even in character. Parents are patterns, models, for their children. Whatever the parents are, the children will be also.

PRESENTING A PATTERN

To give the new believers and young ones a lot of teaching is not the proper way to take care of them. The proper way to foster them is to show them a pattern. By showing them a pattern you water them, supply them, nourish them, and cherish them. This is fostering. If you find that your experience is somewhat lacking, point the new believers to different people in the Bible, for example, to ones such as Enoch, Noah, Abraham, and David in the Old Testament and Peter, John, Paul, and Timothy in the New Testament. We can present the lives of Bible characters in such a way as to foster the growth of the young ones.

If we give too much teaching to new ones and young ones, we shall damage them. Every mother knows that one of the most important matters in the raising of children is proper feeding. Caring for children is ninety percent a matter of feeding and ten percent a matter of teaching. This also should be our practice in caring for new believers in the church. We must learn to have ninety percent feeding and ten percent teaching. Feeding involves the presenting of patterns either from the Bible or from church history. By reading the biographies of saints throughout the ages, we nourish ourselves and experience a kind of fostering. The point here is that the best way to feed others and foster them is to give them a proper pattern. If there is no pattern, there can be no fostering. Only by having a pattern can we feed others.

In the book of 1 Thessalonians Paul was not preaching himself. Rather, he was feeding his spiritual children with his own living of Christ. This means that Paul's way of living was used to feed his spiritual children. This was the reason he emphasized his coming to the Thessalonians, his preaching, his way of handling the word of God, and his manner of living.

THE OPERATING WORD OF GOD

In 2:13 Paul says, "And because of this we also thank God unceasingly that when you received the word of God, which you heard from us, you accepted it not as the word of men but even as it truly is, the word of God, which also operates in you who believe." This verse indicates that the source, the origin, of the apostles' preaching was God and not themselves. The Thessalonians received their word not as the word of men, but as the word of God. Here we see a governing principle: whenever we preach or teach, we must impress others with the fact that what we are saying is not the word of man, but is truly the word of God.

In verse 13 Paul says that the word of God operates in those who believe. Because the word of God is living and operative (Heb. 4:12), it operates in the believing ones. Once we receive and accept the word, it operates within us.

IMITATORS OF THE CHURCHES

In 1 Thessalonians 2:14 Paul continues, "For you, brothers, became imitators of the churches of God which are in Judea in Christ Jesus, for you also suffered the same things from your own countrymen, even as they also from the Jews." The apostle taught the same thing in all the churches (1 Cor. 4:17; 7:17; 11:16). This indicates that all the churches should bear the same testimony of Jesus. Hence, they all are lampstands of the same kind (Rev. 1:9, 20).

The church in Thessalonica imitated the churches in Judea. Certainly reports concerning the churches in Judea reached the believers in Thessalonica. How could the Thessalonians have imitated the churches in Judea if they had not heard anything concerning them? They must have heard about the churches and the saints. These reports fostered the growth of the Thessalonian believers. Once again we see that nothing can foster a church or a saint as much as a true story about other saints or churches.

INOCULATION

First Thessalonians 2:15 continues, "Who both killed the

Lord Jesus and the prophets and drove us out; and they are
not pleasing to God and are contrary to all men." Paul was
wise in writing this verse. Here he is inoculating the believers
against the eventual coming of the Judaizers. Paul injected a
healthy warning concerning the Judaizers into the Thessalonian saints. Here Paul seems to be saying, "Brothers, don't
regard Jewish things as marvelous. The Jews are not for God,
and they are not one with God. They killed the Lord Jesus, and
they also drove us out. Be prepared, Thessalonians, for one
day the Judaizers will come to you to undermine what we
have done. Don't take their word, for they are against us. They
are contrary to all men, and they are not pleasing to God."
This surely was an excellent inoculation.

This inoculating word was also part of Paul's fostering
of the saints. Even inoculation is included in fostering. In
caring for their children, parents seek to protect them from
disease. Even in caring for a garden we try to protect the
plants from disease or insects. Otherwise, disease may ruin
the plants, and the insects may devour them, especially the
tender parts. Therefore, in order to protect a garden, we may
spray the plants with insecticide. We may say that in this verse
Paul was giving the believers at Thessalonica a divine germ-
repellent. He warned them not to have any confidence in the
Jews or to give them any credit. On the contrary, the Thessalonians were to reject them.

Paul continues this warning in verse 16, where he says of
the Jews, "In that they forbid us to speak to the Gentiles that
they may be saved, so that they fill up their sins always. But
wrath has come upon them to the uttermost." Paul points out
that the Jews did not want the Thessalonians to hear the
word of the apostles in order to be saved. This word is part of
Paul's inoculation.

BEREAVED OF THE SAINTS

In verse 17 Paul goes on to say, "But we, brothers, having
been bereaved of you for a little while, in presence, not in
heart, were more abundantly eager with great desire to see
your face." This word implies that the apostles considered the
new converts precious and dear to them. Paul likened their

departure from them to a bereavement, a loss they suffered from being separated from them and that caused them to miss them. In this verse we also see the apostles' yearning over the new converts.

In verse 17 Paul seems to be saying, "Brothers, we have been bereaved of you. We wanted to stay with you, and we miss you very much. But although we are bereaved of you in presence, we are not bereaved of you in heart. In our heart we are still with you. We are very eager with much desire to see your face."

Paul's word in verses 15 through 17 is emotional. Because he was emotional, he could touch the emotion of others. When Paul spoke about the Jews negatively, he was emotional. Likewise, when he spoke about the apostles positively, he was also very emotional. Paul's expression of deep emotion caused the believers to love the apostles and to shut out the Judaizers. This too is related to fostering children, to protecting them, to raising them without their being damaged by negative things.

Paul certainly knew how to foster the saints. He spoke about himself in such a way as to foster them and also to inoculate them. In fostering the Thessalonians, Paul pointed out to them that the Jews who opposed and persecuted needed to be shut out, but the Jews who came to them as apostles were lovable.

RECEIVING A REWARD

In verses 19 and 20 Paul indicates that those who work with the Lord in fostering the believers to walk worthily of God will receive a reward. This reward will be the believers we have fostered becoming our crown, glory, and joy. What a glory it would be to any Christian worker for the ones he has fostered to be matured at the Lord's coming back! What a crown and joy this would be to him! But on the contrary what a shame it would be if none of the believers had grown and matured.

Many of us are working with young saints. The result of our work should be the maturing of these believers. If they mature properly, they will be in the kingdom participating in

God's glory. This maturity will then become our crown, joy, and boast before the Lord Jesus at His coming. Suppose, however, that we work continually with new believers, but to no avail. If this is the situation, at the Lord's coming back there will be no result of our work. What a shame that would be! When the Lord Jesus comes, the result of our work will be manifested. That result will also be our reward, our crown, our joy.

We see the same principle in 1 Peter 5:4. Here Peter says that the elders will be rewarded with a crown of glory. However, this reward will depend on the result of their eldership. If as a result of their eldership the saints mature, that maturity will become a crown of glory to the elders. That will then be their reward.

Chapter 2 of 1 Thessalonians is a healthy word for us all. From this chapter we learn how to work with the young ones and the new ones so that they may be fostered to grow into maturity and that there may be a positive result of our work before the Lord at His coming. This result will then be our crown and glory as the reward of our work today. (*Life-study of 1 & 2 Thessalonians,* pp. 107-108, 109-110, 111, 112-113, 115-116)

*   *   *

In verses 1 through 12 we have the care of a nursing mother and an exhorting father, and in verses 13 through 20 we see the reward given to those who foster believers in this way. Because the apostles rendered such a care to the new believers, the apostles will eventually receive a reward from the Lord. (*Life-study of 1 & 2 Thessalonians,* p. 96)

HOPE, JOY, AND CROWN

In verses 19 and 20 Paul concludes, "For what is our hope or joy or crown of boasting before our Lord Jesus at His coming? Are not even you? For you are our glory and joy." The Greek word rendered "coming" in verse 19 is parousia, a word that means "presence." The Lord's coming is His presence with us. In this light these two earlier Epistles were written. Every chapter of the first Epistle ends with the Lord's coming back.

Verse 20 indicates that since the apostles were the believers' nursing mother and exhorting father (vv. 7, 11), the believers, as their children, were their glory and joy. Apart from them, the apostles had no hope, glory, or crown of boasting.

Here Paul seems to be saying, "You are our hope, our joy, and our crown of boasting. Brothers, we are here only for you; we are not here for anything else. If we do not have you, we do not have anything. You are our hope, even as your hope is the Lord's coming back. Without you, at the Lord's coming back we shall be short of joy and glory. We need you! You are our hope, our joy, our crown, and our glory before the Lord Jesus at His coming." Once again Paul expressed deep emotion in caring for his children. He certainly was a father exhorting his children. As such an exhorting father, it seems as if Paul was saying, "Children, we are here only for you. Without you, life is meaningless. If it were not for you, we would not want even to live." Such a word from parents is deeply touching; it touches the heart of the children.

Would you not be touched deeply if your parents wrote such a word to you? Would you not be touched if they said that without you life is meaningless, that they are living on earth only for you? No doubt, when you heard or read such a word, your tears would flow. This kind of speaking fosters children and helps them to grow.

As a good father, Paul knew how to touch the heart of his children. If you are able to touch the heart of others, you will be successful in fostering their growth. The best way to foster others is to touch their heart deeply. (*Life-study of 1 & 2 Thessalonians,* pp. 114-115)

THE UNFADING CROWN OF GLORY

First Peter 5:4 says, "And when the Chief Shepherd is manifested, you will receive the unfading crown of glory." At the apostle's time, crowns were given to victors in athletic games and warfare (1 Cor. 9:25; 2 Tim. 4:8). Those were corruptible crowns, whose glory faded. The crown given by the Lord to the faithful elders will be a reward for their loyal service. The glory of this crown will never fade. It will be a portion of the glory for the overcomers' enjoyment in the manifestation of the kingdom of God and Christ (2 Pet. 1:11). (*Life-study of 1 Peter,* p. 295)

PART FOUR:
CHILDREN'S WORK

LESSON TEN

THE IMPORTANCE OF
THE CHILDREN'S WORK IN THE CHURCH

Scripture Reading: Deut. 6:7-9; Prov. 22:6; 2 Tim. 3:15; Acts
16:31; 1:14; Rom. 12:12

I. In the past we did not focus on the children's work;
however, if children's education is not developed, it
will be difficult to have a healthy society—Deut. 6:7-9;
11:18-20; Prov. 22:6; Eph. 6:4; 2 Tim. 3:15.

II. At the beginning, children's meeting was mainly to
care for the saints who brought their children to the
meeting; it was simply a child-care service; gradually,
the matter of preparing teachers came in, and we
compiled material:

A. From our experience we feel that the children's
work is very important; the children's work should
not simply be babysitting in order for the saints to
come to the meetings.

B. However, the children's work has another function,
that is, to cultivate and nurture our next generation; this is worthy of our careful consideration
and examination.

III. The children's work has an additional function, which
is to gain the families of the children—Acts 16:31; cf.
Exo. 12:3-4; Gen. 7:1:

A. Children like to make friends; it is particularly
easy for children between the ages of six and
twelve to make friends, and they listen to their
friends:

1. It is therefore easy for a child to lead another
child; when the children sing hymns together,

the gospel is operating and spreads from one child to another child.

    2. Our purpose, however, is not focused only on the children, but even more, through the children, we want to reach their parents and siblings.

B. From this we can see the importance of the children's work; the children's work is greatly related to the growth of the church.

IV. There is not a definite way to take care of the children's work; there should not be only one aspect to the children's work:

A. There should be many locations for the children's work, meetings can be held at different times, and we can use different methods to conduct the children's meetings; there should also be many goals, and the teaching material should also cover many aspects:

    1. Having many locations—their meetings must have many locations; every saint should open his home and have a children's meeting in his home.

    2. Having material—we have considered using videotaped material, which some localities use; we want to produce a video that shows children from various countries wearing their traditional dress and singing the hymns.

    3. Having many purposes—we can also contact the children's parents and preach the gospel to them and to their relatives; this is the principle of our gospel work; the more people we contact, the better.

    4. Having many ways—the households with children can take the initiative to open their homes and ask their children to invite other children in the neighborhood; the children can watch the children's videotapes, sing children's songs, or listen to a story; this is the way to have a children's meeting once a week.

    5. Having different times—it is best to have different meeting times for the children's meetings;

the schedule should be flexible; we need to utilize the time when the children are out of school to have children's meetings.
B. The way to carry out the children's work depends on the brothers taking the lead in the children's work:
   1. We should not make any special arrangements to get teachers for the children's meetings in the meeting halls; rather, we should find a number of younger brothers and sisters who meet regularly to be the teachers; this kind of service does not require much manpower.
   2. We need to prepare material for the children's meeting; we should not have children's meetings without preparation:
      a. The brothers taking the lead in the children's work need to write and compile material; but the saints can decide the best way to use it.
      b. If some saints are designated to prepare teaching material, the saints will not need to labor that much; we can give only some principles related to the children's work; it is up to the saints to carry them out.
   3. The children's meetings should be in many locations, at different times, and use different methods; we hope that all the saints will pray concerning this matter and not take it lightly; this requires everyone's cooperation—Acts 1:14; Col. 4:2; Rom. 12:12.

Excerpts from the Ministry:

CONCERNING THE CHILDREN'S WORK

In the past, according to our concept of the church life, we did not focus on the children's work. However, with the development of human society and culture, there has been more social and educational emphasis put on children. If children's education is not developed, it will be difficult to have a healthy society. For this reason, more and more scholars and experts are beginning to pay attention to children.

THE BEGINNING OF THE CHILDREN'S WORK

I entered the church life in 1932, and a church was raised up in my hometown in July of the same year. The following year there was the need for a children's meeting. We did not know anything and were simply groping around. At the time, our purpose in beginning a children's meeting was mainly to care for the saints who brought their children to the meeting. It was simply a child-care service. Later, I moved to Shanghai where the children's meeting was more developed. When we began the work in Taiwan, we also began the children's work because the number of children among us was increasing.

This is also the principle in America. The children's work there is more important than any other work. In America before a child turns twelve years of age, his family has quite an influence on his life. Families there manage children as if managing a machine. A child does whatever his parents say. I have been received by many American families and was never bothered by the children under twelve. For example, one family who offered me hospitality had their children take a nap at one-thirty in the afternoon or simply stay in their bedroom. The children were also sent to their bedrooms at six-thirty in the evening. The children could even jump in their rooms, but they were not allowed to shout. This allowed us to have dinner with the parents without any disturbance. Neither was there any interruption in our fellowship when we returned from the meeting. However, it was entirely different when I stayed with a Chinese family. At ten-thirty at night the children were still running around and very noisy. This often did not allow us to have good fellowship.

Since American society pays much attention to the children, when we began the work in America, we studied extensively the best way for children to participate in the meetings. According to the American custom, when parents go out, they never leave their children alone at home. Therefore, most American parents bring their children to the meeting, and the children even sit next to the parents. When the children squirm a little, the mother stops them. As a result, all the children sit quietly. However, this way of handling the children gives them an unpleasant feeling, and eventually they do not like to attend the meetings when they grow up.

Based on our study, we decided to watch the children for the saints. Children's meetings began with the intention of babysitting the children. Gradually, the matter of preparing teachers came in, and we compiled material. The work progressed like a snowball that grows bigger and bigger as it rolls down a hill. Sometimes the children's work needed more than fifty serving saints to prepare the material, teach the lessons, and care for the children. Many saints joined the children's service.

When I returned to Taipei in 1965, I saw that there were quite a number of children. According to the brothers, from 1966 to 1967 there were about four thousand children in the meetings. However, currently there are not more than five hundred children in the twenty halls in Taipei. This situation can be likened to the sun going down. For this reason, I often reminded the brothers to pay attention to the children's work.

THE IMPORTANCE OF
THE CHILDREN'S WORK

From our experience we feel that the children's work is very important. The children's work should not simply be babysitting in order for the saints to come to the meetings. Due to their circumstances, the saints need to bring their children to the meeting, and there is the need to take care of the children for the saints. However, the children's work has another function, that is, to cultivate and nurture our next generation. This is worthy of our careful consideration and examination.

Today several young brothers are elders in various halls. In 1949 when we began the work in Taiwan, the parents of these brothers were not married. They were brought together by us. Thirty years later, their children have grown and are serving in the church, bearing important responsibilities. Similarly, last November I was in the Philippines and was greatly surprised, because a new generation of serving ones has replaced the older generation; a younger generation has been raised up. The co-workers, elders, and my translators were young brothers who were born after 1950. This situation shows that the children's work is very important.

The Children Becoming the Gospel Seeds in Their Schools

God ordained that man be fruitful, multiply, and fill the earth (Gen. 1:28). Thus, man has multiplied, but how do we raise our children? Many years ago we did not know that children could be a great potential for the gospel. We stressed preaching the gospel but neglected the fact that children could also be the fruit of the gospel. When we realized that children could also be considered fruit of the gospel, I fellowshipped with the brothers, asking them to work with the goal of having ten thousand children in Taipei. If we had carried this out at that time and contacted ten thousand children, a majority of them would be older brothers and sisters today. We cannot guarantee that every child would have been saved, but at least eighty percent of the children would have been saved. This would equal eight thousand children. In addition, the ten thousand children was not a fixed number. Every year new children would have been added to us.

When children are saved, they become our young brothers and sisters. After they graduate from primary school, they become seeds of the gospel in junior high school. When we work in the schools, they become our inside helpers and bring their classmates to us. In this way, it is easier to work in the junior high schools. It is difficult to bring the gospel to a school where there are no saints who are teachers or students. However, young brothers and sisters in a junior high school can be likened to little seeds; they are waiting to sprout by responding to our call and bringing their classmates to salvation. When they enter into high school, they again become seeds of the gospel. During their three years of high school, we could bring three times as many people to salvation. When these young saints finish high school and enter college, they are seeds of the gospel in their college. In this way the number of people saved is continually multiplied. This is truly a great thing.

Receiving Spiritual Cultivation in the Church

Suppose these children begin to be cultivated in the children's meetings at the age of six and are saved. They will continue to be cultivated through three years of junior high school, three years of high school, and four years of college. In all, they will receive a total of sixteen years of spiritual education and cultivation. While they will receive sixteen years of secular education, they will also receive sixteen years of spiritual cultivation in the church. How valuable this is! After graduating from college, this group of young brothers and sisters should not hurry to look for a job. Instead, they should stay in the church and receive two years of fulltime training. During the training, they will spend half their time learning the truth and pursuing the growth of life and the other half of their time learning to serve in coordination in the church. After two years they will know whether the Lord is leading them to serve full time for the rest of their lives. It may be that one-tenth of them will continue and serve full time, and the rest will get a job. No matter what they do, these saints will have received sixteen years of spiritual education together with two years of full-time training. When they enter society, they will be different from other people. Such a cultivation is valuable. It is not only a great help to the Lord's work but also beneficial to society, people, and the country.

Families Being Brought In through the Children

Furthermore, the children's work has an additional function, which is to gain the families of the children. Children like to make friends. It is particularly easy for children between the ages of six and twelve to make friends, and they listen to their friends. It is therefore easy for a child to lead another child. When the children sing hymns together, the gospel is operating and spreads from one child to another child. Our purpose, however, is not focused only on the children, but even more, through the children, we want to reach their parents and siblings.

The first thing that the Western missionaries who preached the gospel in China did was to establish schools. Since the people were ignorant and illiterate, the Western missionaries had to educate them before the gospel could be preached widely. There was no school system established in China, and many towns and villages still had the traditional private tutoring. Many people did not like to hear the gospel, but because they wanted their children to be educated, they sent their children to Christian schools. The Chinese have a saying: "He who is near vermilion becomes red, and he who is near ink becomes black." It was impossible for the children who studied in the Christian schools not to hear the gospel, because the schools stipulated that everyone participate in the service on the Lord's Day. On the surface this did not seem to have any effect, but no one can say for certain that there was no effect. Everything depends on the Lord's mercy.

A brother once testified that he believed into Jesus because a person who did not believe in Jesus said, "It is very good to believe in Jesus." This proves that our Lord is real and living. As long as God's name is mentioned and His gospel is preached, someone will be saved. Hence, we should not despise what the Western missionaries did in China. Although not many were saved through the schools, some were saved. It is likely that some did not get saved while they were in school, but after leaving school, they recalled the gospel that they heard while they were in school and were saved. The Western missionaries put much effort into establishing schools not only to educate people but ultimately to preach the gospel to them. Our children's meetings should have the same function; they should gain many unbelieving families.

The Catholic approach is very effective. A Catholic must obtain the approval of a priest to marry a non-Catholic. The priest then gives his approval with the condition that the couple gives their children to the Catholic Church. Hence, before the children are even born, they are members of the Catholic Church. This method is effective. Sometimes we do not care about people. We think that one or two persons do not make a difference. However, there is the saying that many buckets of water make a river. We should know this principle. If we do not care about any drop of water, eventually, no river will be formed. Therefore, we should care for the children. Then as the children grow, they will learn to lead others to salvation, and they will become seeds of the gospel. From this we can see the importance of the children's work. The children's work is greatly related to the growth of the church. May we not take this matter lightly.

THE CHILDREN'S WORK HAVING MANY ASPECTS

There is not a definite way to take care of the children's work. There should not be only one aspect to the children's work. There should be many locations for the children's work, meetings can be held at different times, and we can use different methods to conduct the children's meetings. There should also be many goals. The teaching material should also cover many aspects.

Having Many Locations

Having a children's meeting only in the meeting hall will be a great hindrance to its further development. The children may not all be able to travel to the meeting hall, and the meeting hall may not have sufficient space for the meeting. In the church in Anaheim there are more than ten rooms for children's meetings, but the space is still not enough. Furthermore, the rooms are used only for a few hours every week and have no other use. This is not cost efficient. Even if we have many rooms, it will not be easy for all the children to come to the meeting hall for a scheduled meeting. Their meetings must have many locations.

According to our study, the most effective way is similar to the way we propagate the gospel. Every saint should open his home and have a children's meeting in his home. If a home has no children, then it is up to the individual saint to decide whether he would open his home. Nevertheless, it is best to have the burden to open one's home for the children. Most of the older sisters are burdened for the children. If their children are abroad or married and their circumstances allow them, they should open their home for a children's meeting. They can invite five or six children from the neighborhood to have a children's meeting. They do not have to worry about how to have the meeting, because the church will prepare material for them.

Having Material

We have considered using videotaped material, which some localities use. In Texas some of the children's meetings watch videotapes prepared for the children. We want to produce a video that shows children from various countries wearing their traditional dress and singing the hymns. There would be Japanese children wearing the kimono, Korean children wearing the hanbok, Chinese children wearing Chinese quilted jackets, and Indonesian children wearing the sarong. The children would enjoy watching such a video. After watching the video, we can help the children identify the different nationalities and then say something concerning God's creation.

Having Many Purposes

We can open our homes once or twice a week, even on Saturday afternoons and during vacation time, to invite children to our homes to have a children's meeting. We can also contact the children's parents and preach the gospel to them and to their relatives. This is the principle of our gospel work. The more people we contact, the better. In this way, over a period of time there will spontaneously be an effect. We believe that out of every ten children we care for, three or four will be saved. They might not get saved at this time, but at a later time in their life they will remember something and return to the church. It will be easier for these ones to be saved.

Having Many Ways

The households with children can take the initiative to open their homes and ask their children to invite other children in the neighborhood. The children can watch the children's videotapes, sing children's songs, or listen to a story. This is the way to have a children's meeting once a week.

We have about five hundred fifty children among us. The children between the ages of six and twelve come from roughly four hundred families. If each of the four hundred families opened their home for a children's meeting with ten children, there would be four thousand children meeting in four hundred homes. If we include the homes of the saints who do not have children but are willing to open their homes, it will be easy to reach a total of ten thousand children. This is one of the many ways we can use to preach the gospel. This is also the way to gain something long-term. We hope that the whole church will hear this fellowship and take action.

The meeting hall also has its use, but that might mainly be to babysit children. We will not be able to separate the children into smaller groups, because of a lack of rooms and teachers. When the saints come to a meeting, their children can watch a videotape, sing, and be spiritually cultivated.

Having Different Meeting Times

Furthermore, it is best to have different meeting times for the children's meetings. The schedule should be flexible. The meetings do not have to be on the Lord's Day. Saturday afternoon is also a good time. We need to utilize the time when the children are out of school to have children's meetings.

CRUCIAL MATTERS

The way to carry out the children's work depends on the brothers taking the lead in the children's work. They should determine how to contact the opened homes and how to lead the saints to receive a burden and be faithful. If every home can open to invite children, we will have enough meeting places and manpower. Furthermore, if some saints are designated to prepare teaching material, the saints will not need to labor that much. We can give only some principles related to the children's work. It is up to the saints to carry them out. We also need the elders to promote this matter. If we are diligent, we will gain many people year after year. The children's work will become one source of increase. It is worthwhile for the elders to promote the children's work.

We should not make any special arrangements to get teachers for the children's meetings in the meeting halls. Rather, we should find a number of younger brothers and sisters who meet regularly to be the teachers. Children of various ages can be gathered into one room, and two or three younger saints can tell them stories, sing songs with them, or let them watch a video. This kind of service does not require much man-power. The saints who are between the ages of twenty and thirty can take care of the children. In order to reach the goal of having a large number of children, we need to mobilize the entire church. All the saints need to function for this to prosper.

We need to prepare material for the children's meeting. We should not have children's meetings without preparation. The brothers taking the lead in the children's work need to write and compile material. They need much prayer and fellowship to know the content and write lesson plans. We need to prepare material, but the saints can decide the best way to use it. The meetings should not be monotonous; they can be conducted in many ways.

NEEDING THE PRAYER AND
COORDINATION OF THE SAINTS

The children's meetings should be in many locations, at different times, and use different methods. Moreover, the teachers must have a goal. We should be open. We are taking this way to nourish our children and gain many more children so that the gospel can be preached to their unbelieving families. There are many benefits. We hope that all the saints will pray concerning this matter and not take it lightly. We especially hope that the older sisters can open their homes and gather some children to have children's meetings once a week. It should not be too difficult. There will be results. This requires everyone's cooperation.

The saints who serve either full time or part time and are under thirty years old should not excuse themselves from teaching in the children's meeting. As long as there is no conflict in their schedule, they have an obligation to serve as teachers. This is in addition to their gospel work in the schools. The serving saints who are over thirty years of age need to strengthen the small groups. There are saints who are assigned to work with the small groups, but also everyone should participate and become pillars in the small groups to strengthen the meetings. (*Crucial Words of Leading in the Lord's Recovery, Book 5: Concerning Various Aspects of Church Service,* pp. 81-90)

HAVING THE INCREASE OF THE CHURCH ALSO THROUGH CHILDREN'S WORK

Scripture Reading: Acts 1:8; 2:38-39; 1 Cor. 3:8; Luke 1:77; Matt. 13:3; Rom. 1:16

I. Many years ago we did not know that children could be a great potential for the gospel; we stressed preaching the gospel but neglected the fact that children could also be the fruit of the gospel—Acts 2:38-39; Matt. 28:19-20:

A. We may be doing our best to preach the gospel, but if we pay proper attention to the children's work, in time many more brothers and sisters will be properly brought up in the church:

1. Even if only half of the children came into the church life, we would have thousands of more saints meeting with us.

2. This is a much more effective way to gain the increase than preaching the gospel; moreover, those who are gained in this way will have a good foundation.

B. When children are saved, they become our young brothers and sisters; after they graduate from primary school, they become seeds of the gospel in junior high school—Matt. 13:3; John 12:24:

1. When we work in the schools, the young brothers and sisters become our inside helpers and bring their classmates to us; in this way, it is easier to work in the junior high schools.

2. The young brothers and sisters in a junior high school can be likened to little seeds; they are

waiting to sprout by responding to our call and bringing their classmates to salvation.

C. When they enter into high school, they again become seeds of the gospel; during their three years of high school, we could bring three times as many people to salvation.

D. When these young saints finish high school and enter college, they are seeds of the gospel in their college; in this way the number of people saved is continually multiplied.

E. Suppose these children begin to be cultivated in the children's meetings at the age of six and are saved, and they continue to be cultivated through three years of junior high school, three years of high school, and four years of college; in all, they will receive a total of sixteen years of spiritual education and cultivation.

F. We should not do a work merely among the children in the church; our work must include the children outside the church; this is the children's gospel work—cf. Rom. 9:24:

    1. Every children's home meeting should frequently preach the gospel and invite their relatives and the children of their neighbors; even though some parents will not come, they will allow their children to come.

    2. We believe that many people will be brought in through the children's gospel work; the children's meetings will open up a way to gain people, especially the parents of the other children.

    3. We should not limit our work to the children of the saints who are in our meetings; we also need to invite the children of our neighbors and friends; furthermore, we hope that every home will be open for the gospel.

G. If we continue the children's work, we will be unable to estimate the long-term results; if we labor on the children, our numbers will continually grow— Acts 2:47.

H. We must realize that the children's work is a crucial burden; every locality must be aggressive in the children's work, because there is a greater future in the children's work than in the campus work:

1. When we preach the gospel, we frequently have to go out to gain people; we even go to the campuses to gain people; these people are along the roads and hedges—Luke 14:23.

2. There is only one group of people who are not along the roads: the children in our own homes.

3. The people along the roads might come today or tomorrow, but the people in our own homes will always be there; furthermore, our children can bring other children.

II. Our work for the Lord should have a long-term view; six years go by very quickly; soon the children in first grade will be young brothers and sisters; when they enter junior high school, we can preach the gospel to their classmates in junior high—Acts 1:8; 1 Cor. 3:8; 15:58:

A. While in junior high, they will bring some classmates to salvation—Luke 1:77; Matt. 13:3.

B. After graduation, they will proceed to high school and become the gospel seed in high school; in their three years of high school they will bring three times as many students to the Lord.

C. After these brothers and sisters graduate, they will go on to college and become the gospel seed in college; this kind of multiplying is incredible—cf. John 12:24.

D. These children would be gospel seeds in junior high school, they would be gospel seeds in high school, and they would be gospel seeds in college; they would be seeds the entire time that they are in school—Rom. 1:16.

Excerpts from the Ministry:

Our work for the Lord should have a long-term view. Six years go by very quickly; soon the children in first grade will be young brothers and sisters. When they enter junior high school, we can preach the gospel to their classmates in junior high. When they enter high school, we can lead many of their classmates to be saved. When they enter college, they will be gospel seeds. In this way the young people will multiply year after year. The benefit from this will be very great. Hence, I am pleading with the elders and the co-workers to promote the children's work, to lead all the sisters to take part, and to select and train some young sisters to be teachers. (*The Collected Works of Witness Lee, 1967,* vol. 1, p. 315)

THE CHILDREN BECOMING THE GOSPEL SEEDS IN THEIR SCHOOLS

God ordained that man be fruitful, multiply, and fill the earth (Gen. 1:28). Thus, man has multiplied, but how do we raise our children? Many years ago we did not know that children could be a great potential for the gospel. We stressed preaching the gospel but neglected the fact that children could also be the fruit of the gospel. When we realized that children could also be considered fruit of the gospel, I fellowshipped with the brothers, asking them to work with the goal of having ten thousand children in Taipei. If we had carried this out at that time and contacted ten thousand children, a majority of them would be older brothers and sisters today. We cannot guarantee that every child would have been saved, but at least eighty percent of the children would have been saved. This would equal eight thousand children. In addition, the ten thousand children was not a fixed number. Every year new children would have been added to us.

When children are saved, they become our young brothers and sisters. After they graduate from primary school, they become seeds of the gospel in junior high school. When we work in the schools, they become our inside helpers and bring their classmates to us. In this way, it is easier to work in the junior high schools. It is difficult to bring the gospel to a school where there are no saints who are teachers or students. However, young brothers and sisters in a junior high school can be likened to little seeds; they are waiting to sprout by responding to our call and bringing their classmates to salvation.

When they enter into high school, they again become seeds of the gospel. During their three years of high school, we could bring three times as many people to salvation. When these young saints finish high school and enter college, they are seeds of the gospel in their college. In this way, the number of people saved is continually multiplied. This is truly a great thing. (*Crucial Words of Leading in the Lord's Recovery, Book 5: Concerning Various Aspects of Church Service,* pp. 83-84)

THE CHILDREN'S WORK

When I returned to Taiwan in 1966 and in 1967, there were four thousand children in the children's meetings, and I told the brothers to set a goal of having ten thousand children in the meetings. I also asked the brothers to perfect the junior high and high school brothers and sisters to assist in teaching the children. These children would be gospel seeds in junior high school, they would be gospel seeds in high school, and they would be gospel seeds in college. They would be seeds the entire time that they are in school.

Suppose the youngest child in the children's work was six years old in 1967. He would now be twenty-three. If we had had ten thousand children in the children's work, there would be at least five thousand saints in the church life today. These calculations show that our "business" has failed; we have wasted much time and effort. Even though we have been busy in the church life, there are not more than three thousand five hundred saints in the meetings of the church in Taipei. If we had continued the children's work from 1967 until now, the children who were six years old in 1967 would now be twenty-three, and the ones who were twelve would be twenty-nine. Even if only half of the children came into the church life, we would have four to five thousand saints meeting with us. (*Crucial Words of Leading in the Lord's Recovery, Book 3: The Future of the Lord's Recovery and the Building Up of the Organic Service,* p. 36)

* * *

We fellowshipped concerning the children's work in 1966; that was eighteen years ago. A child who was twelve years old at that time would be thirty now. In other words, the children whom we cared for in 1966 are at least thirty years old now. If we had worked with ten thousand children in 1966, we would have ten thousand young brothers and sisters today. Some may say that our present situation is according to God's will; otherwise, there might be false believers among us. However, we must have quantity before we can have quality. Of course, not all the children would have remained, but at least sixty percent would have remained; out of ten thousand children at least six thousand would be in the church life today. Now we are busy doing our best to preach the gospel, but the number of people we have saved still has not reached six thousand. Beginning in 1966, if the church in Taipei had focused on only the children's work, there would be at least six thousand brothers and sisters who were properly brought up in the church. We must give this careful consideration. (*Crucial Words of Leading in the Lord's Recovery, Book 3: The Future of the Lord's Recovery and the Building Up of the Organic Service,* p. 19)

*   *   *

For such a work we need a group of sisters to give themselves to take care of the children on the Lord's Day. If one sister takes care of ten children, three hundred sisters can take care of three thousand children. The church can send out a formal announcement to notify the saints so that they can coordinate together. Then on the Lord's Day morning numerous sisters can coordinate together; some can pick up the children, some can take care of the little children, and some can teach the older children. If the sisters are willing to labor faithfully in this matter, when the children who are five or six years old are eleven or twelve years old, they will be saved and baptized. There will be ten thousand young saints. This is a much more effective way to gain the increase than preaching the gospel. Moreover, those who are gained in this way will have a good foundation. After they are saved, they will enter junior high school and be gospel seeds; they can initiate preaching the gospel in their schools. In this way we will multiply endlessly. What a precious work that will be! (*The Collected Works of Witness Lee, 1967,* vol. 1, p. 297)

* * *

Among the saints in Taipei there are at least several thousand household units, and all of these households have children. When we say children, we are referring to young people between the ages of six and twelve, that is, elementary school students from first through sixth grade. We believe that there are more than two thousand children of this age group among us. There are also many children in the households of our neighbors, friends, relatives, colleagues, and classmates. We should not do a work merely among the children in the church. Our work must include the children outside the church. This is the children's gospel work. The inhabitants of this island would be happy for their children to know the Lord's truth and gain genuine benefits. This is a great matter, and we must do our best to promote it. By next summer, or at the latest by the end of next year, the church in Taipei can have at least five thousand children who are under the teaching of the brothers and sisters and who are listening to the truth every week.

We might have only one thousand children, but we hope that after one year or less we can have five thousand children. The children who are presently six years old will graduate from college in sixteen years, and the children who are twelve years old will graduate from college in ten years. If we continue the children's work, we will be unable to estimate the long-term results. After the children are saved and graduate from elementary school, they will be gospel seeds in junior high school; after they graduate from junior high school, they will be gospel seeds in high school; and after they graduate from high school, they will be gospel seeds in college. If we labor on the children, our numbers will continually grow. We believe that if we start with five thousand children and continue this work for fifteen or sixteen years, more than ten or twenty thousand young people will be brought in as a result of the children's work. That is a significant number. (*Crucial Words of Leading in the Lord's Recovery, Book 3: The Future of the Lord's Recovery and the Building Up of the Organic Service,* pp. 194-195)

THE CHILDREN'S GOSPEL WORK

Another item is the children's gospel work. We should assign at least ten full-time serving ones to concentrate on the children. It would be best for most of them to be sisters. At present, no more than five hundred children come to the meetings. We hope that we can increase this number to one thousand. The children's meetings should be carried out in the homes. There should not be more than twelve children in a class, and they can have three high school sisters or brothers as their teachers. The full-time co-workers should promote this work, prepare the teaching materials, and take care of all the other matters.

Every children's home meeting should frequently preach the gospel and invite their relatives and the children of their neighbors. Even though some parents will not come, they will allow their children to come. We believe that many people will be brought in through the children's gospel work. I hope that we will have two thousand children by next spring, three thousand by the summer, and four thousand by next fall. There is a great future in this work. If we take this way, there will be ten thousand children in the church in Taipei within two to three years. At least two to three thousand children out of the ten thousand will not be the children of the saints. The children's meetings will open up a way to gain people, especially the parents of the other children. (*Crucial Words of Leading in the Lord's Recovery, Book 3: The Future of the Lord's Recovery and the Building Up of the Organic Service,* pp. 148-149)

* * *

In the future the full-time co-workers will encourage preaching the gospel on the campuses, in the homes, to the children, and in the community. Full-timers are needed for the gospel on the campuses and in the schools; otherwise, it will be difficult to maintain the gospel work. With regard to the children's work, even though the junior high and high school students can teach in the children's meetings, the children's work will be carried forward by the full-timers, because they will prepare teaching materials and make a schedule. The number of children in the church in Taipei has dropped to five hundred because there is a lack of co-workers to carry the work forward. If the children's work is to spread, we must preach the gospel. We should not limit our work to the children of the saints who are in our meetings; we also need to invite the children of our neighbors and friends. Furthermore, we hope that every home will be open for the gospel. This requires that the co-workers visit the saints in order to encourage them to open their homes and that the co-workers help the saints who are willing to open their homes to speak. Initially, the co-workers will have to take the lead in the homes, but after a few gospel times, the saints will be able to take care of the meeting. We need to be flexible in our practice. On the one hand, the co-workers need to go out and encourage the saints, and on the other hand, the saints should not depend on the elders and co-workers; they must learn to do things themselves. (*Crucial Words of Leading in the Lord's Recovery, Book 3: The Future of the Lord's Recovery and the Building Up of the Organic Service,* p. 160)

* * *

We must realize that the children's work is a crucial burden. Every locality must be aggressive in the children's work, because there is a greater future in the children's work than in the campus work. Generally speaking, it is easier to bring in children, and once they come in, they usually remain. Our history confirms this fact. The church in Manila is an example. Most of the saints in the church in Manila were gained by the children's work. Ninety percent of the churches in the Philippines are maintained by saints in their thirties, and most of these saints grew up in the church and attended the children's meeting.

When we preach the gospel, we frequently have to go out to gain people; we even go to the campuses to gain people. These people are along the roads and hedges (Luke 14:23). There is only one group of people who are not along the roads: the children in our own homes. Why do we not work on our own children? The people along the roads might come today or tomorrow, but the people in our own homes will always be there. Furthermore, our children can bring other children. Therefore, they should be a crucial focus of our work. This work is long-lasting and remaining. A child who is six years old today will be thirteen in seven years. That is a good age to enter the church life. When they enter the church life, they are our young brothers and sisters. When they enter junior high school, they will be gospel seeds. Through them, it will be easier for us to work in the junior high schools. (*Crucial Words of Leading in the Lord's Recovery, Book 3: The Future of the Lord's Recovery and the Building Up of the Organic Service,* pp. 218-219)

* * *

Even in our neighborhood there must be a children's meeting that should not be considered as the children's meeting of the church. This is a children's meeting work in the saints' neighborhood. It is easy for us to set up two children's meetings. Every week one sister can take care of two children's meetings with four helpers. On one day, two sisters can assist this one to take care of twenty children. Maybe on another afternoon two more sisters may help to take care of another children's meeting of fifteen to twenty children. We can collect a number of children out of our neighborhood into our home. We can ask the children to sit down on the carpet. We do not even need a piano. There is no need for materials or textbooks, but one living person. She can even sing a song to the children. Within two months we can build up two children's meetings. Then after six months we will have six children's meetings. One sister will not need to take care of all the meetings directly because other sisters will follow her example and have their own meetings. There may be ten children's meetings under the direction of one sister. This would expand to over a thousand children. All of these children are linked to their parents. So through the children many homes will be opened for the church to evangelize. This is the community work. These are the *warm doors* and the parents will welcome us. Although people today are occupied by many things and it seems as if they are not open to the gospel, the best way to overcome this is to have a children's meeting in our own home. The responsibility for this community work lies with the elders. (*Talks concerning the Church Services, Part 2,* pp. 39-40)

PREACHING THE GOSPEL TO THE CHILDREN

The third way of gospel preaching is to preach the gospel to the children. This requires the sisters to pick up the burden. It is not necessary to use the meeting hall as the place for the gospel meeting. Rather, it is best to meet at the saints' homes. Use the weekends to gather the children from your neighborhood and to invite the children of your relatives and friends to your home. Many times parents are saved through their children, so do not overlook the children's work. If, starting from now, we use our effort to work on the gospel for children whose ages range from six to twelve, then after ten or twelve years, they will be those who will rise up to bear the responsibility of the church service. This way may seem slow, but it is actually very fast. This way is also profitable. (*Truth, Life, the Church, and the Gospel—The Four Great Pillars of the Lord's Recovery,* p. 130)

* * *

In the past the children's meeting was always held in the meeting hall and was mostly led by the young people. Now the gospel work on the college campuses and at the junior high and high schools is very active, and the young people all have specific services in this work. Thus, they cannot take care of the children anymore. Hence, we need to rely on the elderly saints to spend the time and effort to teach the children...The elderly saints may use their homes. After the children get off from school, the elderly saints may open their homes and prepare some snacks to welcome them. Then they may sing with the children, tell them stories, and lead them to know God.

Every one of us should be able to do these three things— pray every day, join the small group meetings, and go door-knocking and have home meetings every week. The fourth matter is taking care of the children. I hope that more people will receive the burden to open their homes to take care of the children. Twenty years ago I said that we should have ten thousand children in Taipei, and then ten years later we would have ten thousand young brothers and sisters. If the saints had taken this word and practiced it, we would have twenty to thirty thousand young people today. Moreover, gaining people in this way is very safe, because they are taught by us and receive the gospel from us from their youth. Thus, they should be very solid. If this were the case, many young saints would not need to put aside their gospel work at school to do the children's work. I hope that from now on the elderly saints would pick up the burden and take the lead to do this in their homes. The effect will be very promising in the long run. (*Being Up-to-date for the Rebuilding of the Temple,* pp. 46-47)

LESSON TWELVE

THE CHILDREN'S WORK BEING TO BUILD CHILDREN UP IN THEIR HUMANITY TO BE PROPER HUMAN BEINGS

Scripture Reading: 1 Tim. 3:7; Matt. 19:19; Prov. 22:6; 2 Tim. 3:15; Eph. 6:1-2, 4; Rom. 9:21, 23; 13:1; 2 Tim. 2:20-21; Gal. 3:24; 1 Tim. 3:15; 1 Cor. 3:2

I. Today, many young people have been damaged with respect to their character; it is because of this that we have a children's work for the children; we need to build up their character—1 Tim. 3:7; Acts 6:3; Prov. 28:20a:

A. The children must be built up as proper human beings; this is a matter of character, that is, behavior and habit—Matt. 5:16.

B. From their youth they must learn to honor their parents, love their brothers and sisters, and respect others—19:19.

C. We do not need to give the young ones too much knowledge of the Bible; we should rather build them up with the proper ethics and morality that will constitute a proper character—Prov. 22:6.

II. Character has very much to do with the Lord's service; consider those persons in the Bible whom God used; they were used by God because they possessed a character that was fit for His use—Rom. 12:1; Phil. 2:17; 2 Tim. 2:21; 4:11:

A. Since Abraham, Moses, and Paul all had an excellent character, God greatly used them; the destiny of our usefulness to the Lord hinges on our character—Acts 15:40; Luke 24:27; Matt. 1:2.

B. Character is a serious matter; the measure of grace we receive of the Lord and the degree to which the function of that grace is manifested are determined by the kind of character that we have—Eph. 4:7; 1 Pet. 4:10.

III. To build up a proper humanity is the way to prepare the children to be the best material to receive God's grace— Rom. 9:21, 23; 2 Tim. 2:20-21; 1 Pet. 2:5; Matt. 16:18:

A. It is best to help the children grow up in their humanity by helping them know what a proper human being is, how to honor their parents, and how to be a proper child—Eph. 6:1-2; Col. 1:10; Prov. 22:6.

B. Since our families are part of the fallen race, we parents must exercise God's ordination to restrict our children by ethical teachings, regulations, and discipline.

C. For proper human living in your home, you must teach your children to behave properly by honoring their parents, caring for their brothers and sisters, respecting their neighbors, and not stealing—v. 6; Eph. 6:4.

D. Because children are too young to behave according to Christ, they must be taught to behave according to culture; children are preserved by culture while they are growing up—Rom. 13:1; Gal. 3:23.

E. In caring for their children, Christian parents need to preach the law to them; we should not first preach grace to the children; if we give them regulations according to the law, the law will keep them in custody for Christ—2 Tim. 3:15; Rom. 13:1; Gal. 3:24.

IV. To compile material for the teachers, we need a number of brothers who know the truth and are also skilled in writing—1 Tim. 3:15; 2:4; Titus 1:1:

A. We should give the five- and six-year-olds one thing and the seven- and eight-year-olds something else; we need some brothers and sisters who understand this principle to prepare the lessons—1 John 2:12-13.

B. This requires the careful work of the brothers who compile the teaching material so that the children do not receive premature knowledge—1 Tim. 1:4; Mark 4:8, 11:

1. The most important matter is to build up the humanity and character of the children; this is neglected by many parents today.

2. There is the need for some brothers and sisters to spend the time to prepare lessons and instructions on how to use them—Rom. 12:7; cf. 2 Tim. 2:22; 1 John 2:27.

3. We should not prepare uniform printed lessons to be read in each class; perhaps half a page of points, illustrations, and instructions is adequate; it should be easy to prepare lessons in this way.

V. When many of us were young, we received too much knowledge that only damaged us; we were given many stories, but we were not given the proper verses in a practical way—1 Cor. 3:2; Titus 3:9; 1 Cor. 8:2-3:

A. After hearing all the teachings and stories from the Bible, young ones become "slippery" so that nothing sticks to them; we must not spoil the young ones in this way.

B. Those who have never heard the stories before are easily inspired by them; this is why we should withhold certain stories and simply help the children to know the things of humanity and of God in a practical way—Phil. 4:9.

C. Then when they are saved and begin to attend the church meetings, what they hear will be new to them.

D. We have to beware of two things: first, there is the possibility of premature spiritual knowledge; second, we can give away biblical truths too cheaply:

1. Some teachers are too spiritual; they tell children teachings that are too high and too spiritual; this gives the children premature spiritual knowledge—1 Cor. 3:2.

2. Other teachers treat spiritual things too lightly in an attempt to make the children understand; their speaking does not do justice to the spiritual weight of their subject; this gives away the truth too cheaply—John 5:39; 1 Tim. 6:19.

Excerpts from the Ministry:

BEING BUILT UP IN OUR CHARACTER

We must be built up as proper human beings. This is a matter of our character, that is, our behavior and habit. A person who has been properly built up is a right person with a right character. Today, many young people have been damaged with respect to their character. It is because of this that we have a children's work for the children. We need to build up our children's character. From their youth they must learn to honor their parents, love their brothers and sisters, and respect others. We do not need to give the young ones too much knowledge of the Bible. We should rather build them up with the proper ethics and morality that will constitute a proper character. Many people today are short of such a proper training. (*The Exercise and Practice of the God-ordained Way,* pp. 295-296)

THE IMPORTANCE OF CHARACTER

Whereas our words represent our person, our character is our very person. A person's usefulness, the things that can be entrusted to him, the responsibilities he can bear, and the things he is able to accomplish altogether depend on his character. A carpenter determines the use of a piece of wood based on its quality. Laziness ruins one's usefulness. Accordingly, character has very much to do with the Lord's service. Consider those persons in the Bible whom God used. They were used by God because they possessed a character that was fit for His use. Their character was simply their person. They became persons useful to God because their character could be used by Him. Since Abraham, Moses, and Paul all had an excellent character, God greatly used them. The destiny of our usefulness to the Lord hinges on our character. Whether we are useful before God depends upon the suitability of our human character. (*Character,* p. 17)

THE BUILDING UP OF OUR CHARACTER

In 1953 while I was holding a training, I used an illustration to explain the matter of character. Almost all textile products, whether cotton or silk, must be put into dyeing tubs to be dyed. The dye, when used on the coarsest and worst fabric, does not appear beautiful, but when the same dye is used on the best Chinese silk, the outcome is beautiful and shiny. There is no difference in the dye. Rather, the result or manifestation of the dyeing is altogether related to the quality of the fabric. Today the Spirit is like the dye. We all have been put into the Spirit, yet our manifestations are different. These differences are not due to the Holy Spirit whom we have received, because we all have the same Holy Spirit. Rather, the differences are due to us who are being dyed. This is related to the matter of our character.

The reason the apostle Paul could enjoy the Spirit of God as much as he did was because he had a good character and was diligent in all things. The brother in 1 Corinthians who had committed fornication undoubtedly had less enjoyment of the Holy Spirit because he had a poor character and was indifferent toward everything. The difference between these two people was not due to a difference in the Holy Spirit they had received but due to a difference in their character. The reason a person commits a fallen act is somewhat related to his character. Hence, those who truly love and pursue the Lord, not to mention those who serve and work for the Lord full time, must pay attention to the matter of character if they desire to live the Body life.

Many of the teachings of the Lord Jesus and of the apostles in the New Testament, beginning with Matthew, reveal the matter of our character, even though the word *character* is not used. You cannot inspire a piece of stone or motivate a piece of wood because neither has a living character. Character is a serious matter. The measure of grace we receive of the Lord and the degree to which the function of that grace is manifested are determined by the kind of character that we have. (*Vessels Useful to the Lord,* pp. 153-154)

* * *

As a new Christian and the mother of four children, I would like to know how much scriptural teaching I should impose on them and how much I should insist on their behaving properly.

This is a very practical matter. As human beings, we fell and need the Lord's salvation. After the fall, God came in to restrict man. For example, God imposed restriction on the woman because the fall had come in through her (Gen. 3:16); this restriction was actually a protection. In human society today, chaos would prevail were it not for the restraints of ethical teachings, the police, and the law courts. These have been ordained by God to limit the fallen race. Since our families are part of the fallen race, we as parents must exercise God's ordination to restrict our children by ethical teachings, regulations, and discipline. For proper human living in your home, you must teach your children to behave properly by honoring their parents, caring for their brothers and sisters, respecting their neighbors, and not stealing.

Do not say that ethical teachings are apart from Christ and therefore worthless. The necessities of our human existence are one thing; the experiences of Christ, another. For our human living we must buy groceries, do laundry, lock our doors to prevent burglaries, be careful about fire, open and close windows, and cook and eat. Besides taking care of these earthly matters, we are also learning to experience Christ. These are two different areas; both are needed. (*Life Messages,* vol. 1, pp. 91-92)

THE PROPER USE OF CULTURE

If, after reading these messages on Christ versus culture, Christian parents tell their children that they no longer need culture, this will be a serious mistake. Without culture, children would act like animals. Children must be raised according to the standards of culture. Before they are of a proper age to receive Christ, the children must be built up in culture. The more the children are trained according to culture, the better it will be for them. The children must be trained to honor their parents, to love their brothers and sisters, to behave properly toward their neighbors, to be good students in school, to obey all laws, and to respect their teachers and other adults. Because children are too young to behave according to Christ, they must be taught to behave according to culture. If we did not have culture, we would be barbarians.

Culture should be used to keep the children until they are able to receive Christ and live according to Christ. Children need to be preserved by culture while they are growing up.

As Moses gave the commandments to God's chosen people, parents must give commandments to their children. But when the children are able to realize their need for Christ and repent, we should minister the rich Christ to them and help them to receive Him. We should tell our children that the culture we gave them was only good for a certain time and that now they need to receive Christ. Hence, culture is used by God through parents to keep their children in custody until the time comes for them to receive the Lord. It is important to see this proper use of culture. (*Life-study of Colossians,* pp. 425, 426)

*　*　*

In caring for their children, Christian parents need to preach the law to them. We should not first preach grace to the children. If we give them regulations according to the law, the law will keep them in custody for Christ. Thus, we should first give them the law in a strong way. The law will expose them, guard them, and keep them, serving as a custodian to keep them for Christ. (*Life-study of Galatians,* p. 165)

*　*　*

We must not give [children] anything in a premature way. Rather, we should prepare the lessons according to their age. We should give the five- and six-year-olds one thing and the seven- and eight-year-olds something else. Premature knowledge damages children. We need some brothers and sisters who understand this principle to prepare the lessons. (*The Collected Works of Witness Lee, 1967,* vol. 1, p. 504)

COMPILING TEACHING MATERIAL

What material should we use to teach the children? We should begin by teaching the children how to be a proper human being. We should show them that man is different from the animals and different from the trees, plants, and flowers. After this we should speak of man's character and conduct. We should teach the children to honor their parents and be loving, pure, obedient, honest, and proper in their conduct. We must be careful not to give them a religious thought or concept.

When we speak of the difference between man and the animals, we can mention that man was created by God and also that the heavens and the earth were created by God. We can also say a little about how man was created in God's image. We do not need to say more than this. I do not agree with explaining all of Genesis 1 and 2 to the children. Even if we touch man's fall in Genesis 3, we should speak briefly and should not tell the entire story of the fall. When we speak to children, we should tell them experiential stories; we should not give them too much doctrine. It is not necessarily a benefit for the children to know too much.

We need to train the teachers for the children's meeting in such a way that they can find illustrations by themselves from practical situations. For instance, they can ask the children, "Are you being honest if you steal candy from your older brother?" or "Suppose your mother saves a bigger piece of candy for your younger sister, and this makes you unhappy and jealous. Do you still love your mother and your sister?" When we speak to the children, we must use practical examples.

To compile material for the teachers, we need a number of brothers who know the truth and are also skilled in writing. The material does not need to be in five or six levels. We need only three levels—elementary, intermediate, and advanced. Each level can be used for two years.

The material for the elementary level should be entirely from a child's perspective. When we speak of man, we should ask the children whether man is the same as a dog, a cat, or a tiger. We should tell them that man is not the same as the animals and explain to them why man is different. That is good enough. We should not present a doctrinal explanation but should use only practical examples.

Gradually, as we proceed to the intermediate level, we can give the children a little more Bible knowledge. We can convey to them a deep impression that there is a God in the universe, that man fell and committed sin, and that the Lord Jesus is our Savior. We do not have to give too much doctrine, but we should impress them with the facts in the Bible. Then when the children proceed to an advanced level, they will almost be ready to follow the messages in the big meetings. The children do not need too much doctrine; they only need a general knowledge of the truth. This requires the careful work of the brothers who compile the teaching material so that the children do not receive premature knowledge. (*The Collected Works of Witness Lee, 1967,* vol. 1, pp. 312-313)

* * *

When many of us were young, we received too much knowledge that only damaged us. We were given many stories, but we were not given the proper verses in a practical way. Because of this, no one could speak to us, for example, about the prodigal son. We may have said, "There is no need to talk about that. I already know what the father, the son, the robe, and the calf are. I can tell you the story." After hearing all the teachings and stories from the Bible, young ones become "slippery" so that nothing sticks to them. We must not spoil the young ones in this way. Those who have never heard the stories before are easily inspired by them. This is why we should withhold certain stories and simply help the children to know the things of humanity and of God in a practical way. Then when they are saved and begin to attend the church meetings, what they hear will be new to them.

When the children are young, we should simply tell them about God, His creation, and other simple things. At least by the time they are eight years old, we should help them to realize something concerning the Lord's salvation, and gradually after that, we can help them to know that Christ is life. We should not pass on matters such as pray-reading until they are at least ten or eleven, at which time they should know something concerning how to fellowship with the Lord. For the younger ones, illustrations and demonstrations are more helpful. If we conduct the meetings with the children in a proper way, a two-hour meeting will not be too long. On the contrary, though, to merely tell them story after story will tire them.

The most important matter is to build up the humanity and character of the children. This is neglected by many parents today. Having a good human character will not hinder the children in any way. The teachings of Confucius and Chinese ethics build up character according to the self with self-pride and self-confidence. The kind of character building we practice is absolutely different. We should build up the children in the way of realizing that they can do nothing in themselves, because they are fallen and need a higher life.

There is the need for some brothers and sisters to spend the time to prepare lessons and instructions on how to use them. There is no need to compose the lessons in full; we can simply give some guidelines, such as which week to speak concerning honoring our parents and some hints on how to illustrate this lesson. After being trained, each teacher can choose the particular illustrations he will use. We should not prepare uniform printed lessons to be read in each class. Perhaps half a page of points, illustrations, and instructions is adequate. It should be easy to prepare lessons in this way. (*The Collected Works of Witness Lee, 1967,* vol. 1, pp. 505-507)

*   *   *

We should tell the children Bible stories. Use Bible stories to show them the proper standard of human life. But we have to beware of two things. First, there is the possibility of premature spiritual knowledge. Second, we can give away biblical truths too cheaply. Some teachers are too spiritual. They tell children teachings that are too high and too spiritual. For example, they may teach the children to pray, "Help us, Lord, to deal with our flesh. May Your cross work on us." This gives the children premature spiritual knowledge. It will not help them. Other teachers treat spiritual things too lightly in an attempt to make the children understand. Their speaking does not do justice to the spiritual weight of their subject. This is also wrong. This gives away the truth too cheaply. We have to use the stories in the Bible to teach the children some lessons they can apply in their daily life. We have to teach them to live a normal human life. Of course, we cannot tell too many Bible stories. Otherwise, they will only go home with a bag of stories. Before children are old enough, we should never give them things that are too high or too spiritual for them. (*The Collected Works of Watchman Nee,* vol. 62, pp. 409-410)

LESSON THIRTEEN

THE CHILDREN'S WORK IN THE HOMES
AND IN THE NEIGHBORHOODS

Scripture Reading: Acts 2:46; 5:42; 20:20; 1 Cor. 16:19; Acts
12:12; 1 Cor. 14:12; 1:2

I. The scriptural basis for the small groups and the home
   meetings is the expression *from house to house* in Acts
   2:46 and 5:42; on the day of Pentecost, as soon as the
   church was raised up on the earth, it began to meet
   from house to house—2:41, 46; 5:42; 20:20; 1 Cor.
   16:19:
   A. To gain the increase, we need to have the home
      meetings; we need to have meetings in the new
      believers' homes, in the homes of the ones we gain
      through our preaching of the gospel.
   B. To bring the meetings to the homes is the very
      heart of the God-ordained way; it is a great failure
      in the Lord's recovery if we cannot bring the meet-
      ings to the homes.
   C. To meet in the homes is organic; if we only have a
      meeting hall with a definite, regular schedule, this
      will bring the entire church into the "box" of orga-
      nization and causes us to lose the organic ability—
      Rom. 16:5; 1 Cor. 16:19; Col. 4:15; Philem. 2.
   D. Meeting in the believers' homes is for all the mem-
      bers of Christ to function; in any big meeting it is
      hard for the saints to function, but in a small meet-
      ing with four or five, or two or three, even a small
      boy or girl could function—Acts 2:21, 46; 5:42; 12:12;
      Matt. 18:20.
   E. We have to realize that the way the Lord is taking

is to build up His church in the believers' homes;
once the church is built up in the homes, the homes
will be transformed—1 Cor. 16:19; 14:12; 1:2:

1. The children will be preserved from drifting along
the current of the age; in the end, the family will
become proper and normal.

2. We can invite our relatives to the home meetings,
and they will see the situation in our homes and
will be touched to receive the Lord's salvation.

II. In a family the focus is not on teaching the children
but is on raising them by cherishing, nourishing, and
fostering them so that they may grow—1 Thes. 2:7;
Col. 1:5-6; Eph. 4:15; cf. 2 Pet. 3:18:

A. Their growth is not mainly in knowledge: it is primarily a growth in life; as children grow in life,
they spontaneously receive more education—Col.
1:9; Eph. 4:13.

B. Concerning this matter, we in the Lord's recovery
must have a change in our concept; do not think
that in the recovery we regard work higher than
life; no, we need to concentrate on life—John 17:3;
1 John 5:20.

C. To nurture children means to bring them up, to
raise them, by nourishing them; raising children
requires that the parents give them the needed
instruction related to human life, family life, and
social life—Eph. 6:1-3; 1 Tim. 5:4.

D. For proper human living in your home, you must
teach your children to behave properly; do not say
that ethical teachings are apart from Christ and
therefore worthless—v. 4; Col. 1:28.

III. We need to open up our home; we do not need to meet
with others first; we can initiate our home meeting
by meeting with our family members—Acts 5:42; 2:46;
12:12:

A. To set up a meeting will stir up our heart and will
fan the flame in our heart and in our spirit; first of
all, we will be burned, and then our family will be

burned; to set up a home meeting will keep out many evil things from our homes—2 Tim. 1:6a; Psa. 84:11.

B. The meetings in the believers' homes can be a fruitful testimony to the neighbors around, and they provide an opportunity for witness and gospel preaching—John 19:35; 3 John 12; Acts 5:42:

1. Many who are not willing to go to a "church" will be glad to go to a private house—v. 42.

2. The influence is most helpful for the families of the Christians; from early days the children will be surrounded by a spiritual atmosphere, and will have constant opportunity to see the reality of eternal things—John 14:17.

IV. In our neighborhood there must be a children's meeting that should not be considered as the children's meeting of the church; this is a children's meeting work in the saints' neighborhood:

A. Through the children many homes will be opened for the church to evangelize; this is the community work; these are the warm doors, and the parents will welcome us—Rom. 16:10-11; 1 Cor. 16:15:

1. Although people today are occupied by many things and it seems as if they are not open to the gospel, the best way to overcome this is to have a children's meeting in our own home.

2. Many times parents are saved through their children, so do not overlook the children's work.

B. Every household should preach the gospel; it is very meaningful when the whole family rises up and preaches the gospel.

C. After the children get home from school, the elderly saints may open their home and prepare some snacks to welcome them; then they can sing with the children, tell them stories, and lead them to know God—2 Kings 4:42-44.

D. Gaining people in this way is very safe, because they are taught by us and receive the gospel from us from their youth; thus, they should be very solid—1 Tim. 4:12; Luke 18:21.

Excerpts from the Ministry:

THE FIRST CRUCIAL ELEMENT IN THE CHANGE—
BUILDING UP THE HOME MEETINGS

Building up the home meetings in every believer's home is the first and foremost thing in our new beginning. This is not a matter of choice. As long as a person is a believer, he is our brother in the Lord, even if he is the weakest, coldest, and most indifferent, backslidden person. Therefore, we must make every effort to build up a meeting in his home. I said from the beginning that the small group is the foundation for the building up of the church and that such a small group must be built upon the foundation of the home meetings.

The scriptural basis for the small groups and the home meetings is the expression *from house to house* in Acts 2:46 and 5:42. One and a half years ago I pointed out emphatically that on the day of Pentecost, as soon as the church was raised up on the earth, it began to meet from house to house. That was an unprecedented move; it was something that Judaism had never done before. It was not an idea that Peter inherited from the Jewish religion. Rather, it was a brand new thing, a creative act of God, and something that He ordained. Based on this, we were bold to say that we must have the small meetings, the group meetings, not only the big meetings. Eventually, the group meetings brought in the home meetings. (*Crucial Words of Leading in the Lord's Recovery, Book 1: The Vision and Definite Steps for the Practice of the New Way*, pp. 318-319)

HAVING HOME MEETINGS

The practice of the saints in the early church was to meet in their homes (2:46; 5:42; 20:20). To gain the increase, we need to have the home meetings. The church has been dead, passive, and low in the rate of increase because we do not have the crucial way to gain people through the home meetings. We need to have meetings in the new believers' homes, in the homes of the ones we gain through our preaching of the gospel. If we can only gain people without setting up meetings in their homes, this will be a failure. The most successful way is to gain people's homes for home meetings. Meetings in the homes will work to the uttermost. (*Elders' Training, Book 9: The Eldership and the God-ordained Way (1)*, p. 10)

BRINGING THE MEETINGS
TO THE HOMES

To bring the meetings to the homes is the very heart of the God-ordained way. It will be a great failure in the Lord's recovery if we cannot bring the meetings to the homes. For the past twenty years in the Lord's recovery, we have been bringing people to the meeting halls. The more we work in this way, the fewer people we have, and the worse the condition of the homes becomes. More and more our meetings have become a kind of Sunday morning service. In Christianity many people "go to church" to listen to the singing of hymns and to attend the "service," but their homes are deplorable; their tables may still be scattered with mah-jongg game pieces. In the morning the family attends the service, but in the afternoon the mah-jongg game goes on in the homes. In order to overturn this degraded situation, we must bring the meetings to the homes. (*Crucial Words of Leading in the Lord's Recovery, Book 1: The Vision and Definite Steps for the Practice of the New Way*, p. 216)

* * *

Acts tells us that the early churches met in the homes of the saints. The Epistles tell us of four different homes in which the churches met (Rom. 16:5; 1 Cor. 16:19; Col. 4:15; Philem. 2). To meet in the homes is organic. If we only have a meeting hall with a definite, regular schedule, this will bring the entire church into the "box" of organization and causes us to lose the organic ability. If we take the way revealed in Acts, whatever we do will be organic, not organizational. (*The Excelling Gift for the Building Up of the Church*, p. 52)

* * *

Meeting in the believers' homes is for all the members of Christ to function. In any big meeting it is hard for the saints to function. But in a small meeting with four or five, or two or three, even a small boy or girl could function. He or she could say, "The Lord Jesus loves me, and it is so good that I love Him." This is a small function, but do not despise it. The new believers will function in a small way at first, but from that point, they will continue to progress in life and in function. By the functioning of all the members, the small home meetings will grow and be built up. When a new couple brings forth a little infant, they have the faith that their family will be built up. The same applies to the home meetings. We should exercise our faith and practice the home meetings with much expectation. (*The God-ordained Way to Practice the New Testament Economy*, p. 53)

THE BENEFITS OF BUILDING UP
THE CHURCH IN THE HOMES

We need to realize that the way the Lord is taking is to build up His church in the believers' homes. Once the church is built up in the homes, the homes will be transformed. The husbands and the wives might have been arguing couples, but once they have meetings in their homes, they will stop their arguing. The children will also be preserved from drifting with the current of the age. As a result, the family will become proper and normal. If possible, we should compile some material to teach the brothers and sisters how they should build up their own homes. For example, we should have something to teach them how to behave as parents, children, husbands, and wives. This is scriptural. A book as spiritual as Ephesians contains teachings on being proper husbands, wives, children, parents, slaves, and masters. In the past we were somewhat negligent in this matter. All the brothers and sisters devoted their attention to the big meetings and neglected the building up of the homes. In the coming days we hope that we can compile some messages on the building up of the homes so that every saint's home would be a proper home. Once that happens, we can invite our relatives to the home meetings, and they will see the situation in our homes and will be touched to receive the Lord's salvation. (*Crucial Words of Leading in the Lord's Recovery, Book 1: The Vision and Definite Steps for the Practice of the New Way*, p. 245)

*   *   *

Most Christian workers lack the concept that their work should not mainly be a work of teaching but should be a work of fostering. Paul's concept concerning his work was one of helping believers to grow. For this reason, in 1 Corinthians 3 he says that he planted and Apollos watered, and then God gave the growth. This indicates that Paul's concept of Christian work is that it is a work of life. It is not work in a school; on the contrary, it is work on a farm, in an orchard, in a garden. Hence, it is not mainly a work of teaching others or educating them. But today the work of most Christians is mainly for education and somewhat for edification. This edification, however, is not directly related to life. Instead, it is related to ethics, morality, or the improvement of character. But with Paul the concept of Christian work was altogether different.

According to what he says in 1 Thessalonians 2, Paul regards the believers as members of a large family. Of course, in a family there is the need for some amount of teaching. Both a mother and a father teach their children. However, in a family the focus is not on teaching the children but is on raising them by cherishing, nourishing, and fostering them so that they may grow. Their growth is not mainly in knowledge: it is primarily a growth in life. As children grow in life, they spontaneously receive more education. The knowledge they acquire always goes along with their growth in life. They should not be given knowledge prematurely. This means that their knowledge should not exceed their growth of life. This is the proper concept of Christian work.

Concerning this matter, we in the Lord's recovery must have a change in our concept. Do not think that in the recovery we regard work higher than life. No, we need to concentrate on life. The church is a family. The church may also be compared to a farm or a garden. A family is a place where children grow up, and an orchard is a place where trees grow and produce fruit. Paul's concern in chapter 2 is with the growth of his children. He is fostering the young believers so that they may grow. We may also say that he is watering, nourishing, and cherishing the tender young plants so that they may grow in life. This is the reason that instead of giving the believers a great deal of teaching, he presents them a pattern of life. This pattern of a proper living is actually Paul himself. (*Life-study of 1 Thessalonians*, pp. 108-109)

* * *

To nurture children means to bring them up, to raise them, by nourishing them. Raising children requires that the parents give them the needed instruction related to human life, family life, and social life. The word *admonition* here includes instruction. Paul was probably referring to the Old Testament requirement that parents instruct their children with the word of God (Deut. 6:7). This means that we are to teach our children with the Bible. Along with this instruction, we sometimes must discipline them, chastise them. It is crucial that parents learn to nurture the children in the discipline and admonition of the Lord. (*Life-study of Ephesians*, pp. 520-521)

* * *

As a new Christian and the mother of four children, I would like to know how much scriptural teaching I should impose on them and how much I should insist on their behaving properly.

This is a very practical matter. As human beings, we fell and need the Lord's salvation. After the fall, God came in to restrict man. For example, God imposed restrictions on the woman because the fall had come in through her (Gen. 3:16); this restriction was actually a protection. In human society today, chaos would prevail were it not for the restraints of ethical teachings, the police, and the law courts. These have been ordained by God to limit the fallen race. Since our families are part of the fallen race, we as parents must exercise God's ordination to restrict our children by ethical teachings, regulations, and discipline. For proper human living in your home, you must teach your children to behave properly by honoring their parents, caring for their brothers and sisters, respecting their neighbors, and not stealing.

Do not say that ethical teachings are apart from Christ and therefore worthless. The necessities of our human existence are one thing; the experiences of Christ, another. For our human living we must buy groceries, do laundry, lock our doors to prevent burglaries, be careful about fire, open and close windows, and cook and eat. Besides taking care of these earthly matters, we are also learning to experience Christ. These are two different areas; both are needed. (*Life Messages,* vol. 1, pp. 91-92)

*   *   *

The Greek phrase [*from house to house*] in Acts 5:42 indicates that not one house was missed. They met from house to house. We should not take the way of selecting some promising homes and then having the meetings in those promising homes. This is wrong. Every home of the believers is promising. We need to open up our home. First we can meet with our folks. We do not need to meet with others first. We can initiate our home meeting by meeting with our family members. We who have wives and children all can have a home meeting. We just meet with our folks, with our wife, and with our little children. To set up a meeting will stir up our heart and will fan the flame in our heart and in our spirit. First of all, we will be burned, and then our family will be burned. To set up a home meeting will keep out many evil things from our homes. (*The Home Meetings—The Unique Way for the Increase and the Building Up of the Church,* pp. 19-20)

*   *   *

The meetings in believers' homes can be a fruitful testimony to the neighbors around, and they provide an opportunity for witness and gospel preaching. Many who are not willing to go to a "church" will be glad to go to a private house. And the influence is most helpful for the families of the Christians. From early days the children will be surrounded by a spiritual atmosphere, and will have constant opportunity to see the reality of eternal things. (*The Normal Christian Church Life,* p. 170)

* * *

Even in our neighborhood there must be a children's meeting that should not be considered as the children's meeting of the church. This is a children's meeting work in the saints' neighborhood. It is easy for us to set up two children's meetings. Every week one sister can take care of two children's meetings with four helpers. On one day, two sisters can assist this one to take care of twenty children. Maybe on another afternoon two more sisters may help to take care of another children's meeting of fifteen to twenty children. We can collect a number of children out of our neighborhood into our home. We can ask the children to sit down on the carpet. We do not even need a piano. There is no need for materials or textbooks, but one living person. She can even sing a song to the children. Within two months we can build up two children's meetings. Then after six months we will have six children's meetings. One sister will not need to take care of all the meetings directly because other sisters will follow her example and have their own meetings. There may be ten children's meetings under the direction of one sister. This would expand to over a thousand children. All of these children are linked to their parents. So through the children many homes will be opened for the church to evangelize. This is the community work. These are the *warm doors* and the parents will welcome us. Although people today are occupied by many things and it seems as if they are not open to the gospel, the best way to overcome this is to have a children's meeting in our own home. The responsibility for this community work lies with the elders. (*Talks concerning Church Services, Part 2,* pp. 39-40)

PREACHING THE GOSPEL TO THE CHILDREN

The third way of gospel preaching is to preach the gospel to the children. This requires the sisters to pick up the burden. It is not necessary to use the meeting hall as the place for the gospel meeting. Rather, it is best to meet at the saints' homes. Use the weekends to gather the children from your neighborhood and to invite the children of your relatives and friends to your home. Many times parents are saved through their children, so do not overlook the children's work. If, starting from now, we use our effort to work on the gospel for children whose ages range from six to twelve, then after ten or twelve years, they will be those who will rise up to bear the responsibility of the church service. This way may seem slow, but it is actually very fast. This way is also profitable. (*Truth, Life, the Church, and the Gospel—The Four Great Pillars of the Lord's Recovery*, p. 130)

SMALL GROUP GATHERINGS
AND PREACHING THE GOSPEL IN THE HOMES

A small group should gather once a week in the homes, and we also need to preach the gospel in our homes. Strictly speaking, every brother and sister, whether strong or weak, progressing or backsliding, should preach the gospel in their home. We should keep the principle of preaching the gospel in our own homes and not ask others to preach for us. We all know that the best tasting rice is the rice that we have cooked for ourselves. Even if we do not know how to "cook," it only takes a little practice. Therefore, we encourage the brothers and sisters to open their homes. Every household should preach the gospel. Sometimes the wife can preach the gospel, the husband can give a testimony, and the children can strengthen the words of their parents. Sometimes the children can preach the gospel, the mother can give a testimony, and the father can strengthen the words of the children and the mother. It is very meaningful when the whole family rises up and preaches the gospel. Some recently recovered saints, who used to be unwilling to meet, are taking the lead in this kind of family gospel meeting. In addition to the aforementioned meetings, we suggest having a small group gathering every other week and a family gospel meeting in the intervening weeks. (*Crucial Words of Leading in the Lord's Recovery, Book 4: The Increase and Spread of the Church*, p. 153)

* * *

In the past the children's meeting was always held in the meeting hall and was mostly led by the young people. Now the gospel work on the college campuses and at the junior high and high schools is very active, and the young people all have specific services in this work. Thus, they cannot take care of the children anymore. Hence, we need to rely on the elderly saints to spend the time and effort to teach the children...The elderly saints may use their homes. After the children get off from school, the elderly saints may open their homes and prepare some snacks to welcome them. Then they may sing with the children, tell them stories, and lead them to know God.

Every one of us should be able to do these three things—pray every day, join the small group meetings, and go door-knocking and have home meetings every week. The fourth matter is taking care of the children. I hope that more people will receive the burden to open their homes to take care of the children. Twenty years ago, I said that we should have ten thousand children in Taipei, and then ten years later we would have ten thousand young brothers and sisters. If the saints had taken this word and practiced it, we would have twenty to thirty thousand young people today. Moreover, gaining people in this way is very safe, because they are taught by us and receive the gospel from us from their youth. Thus, they should be very solid. If this were the case, many young saints would not need to put aside their gospel work at school to do the children's work. I hope that from now on the elderly saints would pick up the burden and take the lead to do this in their homes. The effect will be very promising in the long run. (*Being Up-to-date for the Rebuilding of the Temple,* pp. 46-47)

BUILDING UP A PREVAILING CHILDREN'S WORK IN THE CHURCH

Scripture Reading: Psa. 127:3; Heb. 11:7; 2 Tim. 3:15; Eph. 4:7-16; Rom. 16:1, 12-13; 1 Tim. 4:12; Judg. 5:15-16; Dan. 11:32; 1 Cor. 12:14-22

I. We expect the children's work among us to be very prevailing; therefore, we need to have a proper realization and preparation for this work—Gen. 1:28; Psa. 127:3:

A. When we speak of the children's work, we are referring to children who have not graduated from elementary school but are more than five years old; these are the target of our children's work.

B. The saints can open their homes for children's meetings; we need many brothers and sisters to open their homes; how beautiful this service will be, and how much the Lord's work will be propagated!—Acts 2:46; 6:7a.

II. The responsible brothers and the co-workers in every place must see the importance of the children's work in God's family; this should be a great matter to us— Heb. 11:7; Psa. 127:3; Gen. 33:5b; Dan. 1:3-4; Matt. 24:45; 25:16; Rom. 9:23; 2 Tim. 3:15; 1 Tim. 3:4-5; Acts 16:31-32; Eph. 4:12-16; 1 Tim. 4:12:

A. No family will disregard its children; as a priority a family looks after its children, raises them, and teaches them; hence, we must serve the many children in God's family—Psa. 127:3; Eph. 6:4; Matt. 19:13-14.

B. The co-workers do not need to be personally involved in doing the children's work; they can meet with the leading sisters in a locality and entrust the burden for the children's work to them, and they can encourage them—Phil. 1:1c; Rom. 16:1, 12-13.

C. The elders must lead the church to receive a burden for the children's work; the church should concentrate its effort on this work—1 Tim. 2:1-4; Gal. 1:4; 1 Thes. 2:7-11; Rom. 10:17; Acts 16:31-32.

D. All the churches must have a children's work; if we work with these children, they will all be young brothers and sisters after six to seven years—Eph. 4:12-16; Zech. 4:10; cf. Matt. 25:16.

E. We cannot continue to work as we have in the past; we must change our ways; in the past we neglected the work with the children.

III. In carrying out this work, first, a number of sisters should rise up to lead the children's work; the elders should also appoint some sisters to take up this responsibility—Rom. 16:1, 6, 12-13; Mark 15:41:

A. A number of older sisters must receive this burden; over ninety percent of the children's work requires the sisters' participation; otherwise, there is no way for the children's work to succeed—1 Tim. 5:2a; cf. Col. 4:17.

B. The sisters in every church should be persistent to promote the burden for the children—cf. Luke 18:1-8; 1 Sam. 1:11:

1. On the one hand, they should not give the brothers any peace, and on the other hand, they should learn not to assume the leadership but to be full of patience, knowing when to proceed and when to wait—1 Cor. 11:3; John 7:6; Matt. 15:21-28.

2. The sisters should be persistent to develop the children's work in the church; furthermore, according to the leading of the Lord, they should fellowship with other sisters who are serving— 1 Cor. 15:10a; 1 John 1:3, 7; 1 Cor. 12:21-22.

C. The sisters should also bring the children to the

meeting; every week the sisters should consider how to bring the children to the meeting.

D. We must use the young sisters to lead the children's meetings; the church should train the teachers so that the young sisters learn to teach and lead the children—2 Tim. 2:2.

E. Many of the sisters love the Lord, but they need to find the way to do something for the Lord; if we bear the little ones as fruit, the Lord will add them to our account—Matt. 25:14-30; 2 Pet. 1:8; 1 Thes. 2:19:

1. Only eternity will reveal the result of this; perhaps out of a group of children for whom we are caring, some will become apostles—2 Tim. 3:15; 1:2; 1 Cor. 4:17.

2. Therefore, I encourage the sisters to do this good work; all the housewives can bring children to the meetings, and the younger sisters can be trained to cooperate with them to bear these little ones as fruit.

IV. We also need the help of the young people in the children's work; this matter must be developed—1 Tim. 4:12:

A. There is quite a large number of children in every locality; as soon as we begin the children's work, the young people will begin to function; they can all take part in serving the children:

1. We can ask the brothers in the church to perfect the junior high and high school brothers and sisters to assist in teaching the children.

2. With regard to the children's work, even though the junior high and high school students can teach in the children's meetings, the children's work will be carried forward by the full-timers, because they will prepare teaching materials and make a schedule.

B. The young people need to give themselves to this work, and this will give everyone an opportunity to practice speaking.

V. The elderly saints may use their homes; after the children get off from school, the elderly saints may open their homes and prepare some snacks to welcome them:

A. They may sing with the children, tell them stories, and lead them to know God.

B. Gaining people in this way is very safe, because they are taught by us and receive the gospel from us from their youth; thus, they should be very solid.

C. I hope that from now on the elderly saints would pick up the burden and take the lead to do this in their homes; the effect will be very promising in the long run.

VI. When the entire church is mobilized in this way, all the brothers and sisters will have an opportunity to serve; some can open their homes, others can bring the children to the meetings, and still others can teach the children; when all the saints endeavor in one accord for the Lord's heart's desire, the profit will be immeasurable—Judg. 5:15-16; Dan. 11:32; 1 Cor. 12:14-22; Eph. 4:7-16:

A. We should take action immediately; all the churches should encourage the saints in this matter, and we should pray for this matter—Judg. 5:15-16; Dan. 11:32; 1 Tim. 2:1.

B. All the saints want their children to receive spiritual help; even dormant saints want their children to receive spiritual guidance.

Excerpts from the Ministry:

THE CHILDREN'S WORK

We expect the children's work among us to be very prevailing. Therefore, we need to have a proper realization and preparation for this work. When we speak of the children's work, we are referring to children who have not graduated from elementary school but are more than five years old. These are the target of our children's work. If we are unable to take care of the children who are younger than this age group, we will leave them to the care of their parents. In order to give a message to young people or college students, we know that we must be well prepared. Some may think that it is easy to care for the children who are between the ages of five and twelve by simply giving them a piece of candy. However, to handle the children in this way will not yield a good result. According to my observation, the most difficult work to do effectively is the children's work. (*The Collected Works of Witness Lee, 1967,* vol. 1, p. 311)

OPENING THE HOMES FOR CHILDREN'S MEETINGS

The saints should open their homes for children's meetings. When the children's work is carried out in a good way, I estimate that there will be about three hundred groups with twenty-five to thirty children in a group. This is close to ten thousand children. This means that we will need several hundred places for the children's meetings. Of course, we can use the meeting halls, but the number of meeting halls we have will not meet this need. We need many brothers and sisters to open their homes. It would be good to have three hundred meeting places for the children every Lord's Day. How beautiful this service will be! And how much the Lord's work will be propagated! (*The Collected Works of Witness Lee, 1967,* vol. 1, pp. 305-306)

THE WHOLE CHURCH
ENDEAVORING IN THE CHILDREN'S WORK

Whether or not we succeed in the children's work depends partly on the teaching material and partly on the brothers and sisters who take the lead. The responsible brothers and the co-workers in every place must see the importance of the children's work in God's family. How can a family not take care of its children? This should be a great matter to us. No family will disregard its children; as a priority a family looks after its children, raises them, and teaches them. Hence, we must serve the many children in God's family.

From this time onward, the co-workers should give more thought to the way they lead people to know the Lord. They must pay attention to the sisters and the children. The co-workers should not say that they are not gifted for these two aspects of the work and therefore cannot do the work. If they cannot do it, they must learn how to do it; they should always learn. The co-workers do not need to be personally involved in doing the children's work. They can meet with the leading sisters in a locality and entrust the burden for the children's work to them, and they can encourage them. They must lead the church to receive a burden for the children's work. The church should concentrate its effort on this work. (*The Collected Works of Witness Lee, 1967,* vol. 1, p. 314)

* * *

The first matter for the sisters' service is the children's work. Concerning the children's work, within me there is truly a heavy burden. All the churches must have a children's work. According to statistics, forty-five percent of the population of Taiwan is under fifteen years of age. This is roughly six million people. Many local churches have quite a few families with children. I estimate that there are about ten thousand children in the church in Taipei and about the same number of children in the churches in the rest of Taiwan. If we work with these twenty thousand children, they will all be young brothers and sisters after six to seven years. This is what the sisters should do.

In the past the church in Taipei did not pay adequate attention to this. Of the ten thousand children in Taipei, only about five hundred come to the meeting on the Lord's Day; eight to nine thousand children are without any care. In spite of all the effort we use to preach the gospel in Taipei, we may not be able to bring three or even two thousand people to salvation in a year. If we cultivate our ten thousand children, they will all become young brothers and sisters in six or seven years. This means that we will have an average increase of a thousand people every year. (*The Collected Works of Witness Lee, 1967,* vol. 1, pp. 304-305)

* * *

We cannot continue to work as we have in the past; we must change our ways. In the past we neglected the work with the children, the young people, and the sisters. We highly regarded a general work, but we paid little attention to the young people's work, and we merely prayed for the children's work. Now we must concentrate our efforts on the children, the young people, and the sisters. Moreover, the messages we give must minister Christ as the Spirit in a simple and direct way. We should focus on these primary matters and nothing else. (*The Collected Works of Witness Lee, 1967,* vol. 1, p. 270)

* * *

The leading sisters in the churches must receive a burden for the children's work. Under the arrangement of the church and the leading of the elders, they should concentrate on the children's work and lead all the sisters to participate. The elders are too busy to take care of the details. Instead of waiting for the elders, the sisters should pray much and make plans. They can then present their plans for the children's work to the elders for their approval. This is just like a family in which the husband is busy with his job and cannot plan the details for the household. The wife can make plans and carry things out with the consent of the husband. In this way the wife does not do anything independently and will still be able to take care of the details of the household in a timely way. (*The Collected Works of Witness Lee, 1967,* vol. 1, p. 314)

APPOINTING A FEW SERVING SISTERS
TO TAKE THE LEAD

In carrying out this work, we need to pay attention to a few principles. First, a number of sisters should rise up to lead the children's work. A number of older sisters must receive this burden. The elders should also appoint three to six sisters to take up this responsibility. (*The Collected Works of Witness Lee, 1967,* vol. 1, p. 305)

* * *

Furthermore, the sisters should receive a burden to serve in the church; the brothers should not be the only ones who serve. The brothers should have a change in their concept. They should not think that since the sisters should not assume the headship, they cannot participate in the church services.

We should highly regard the service of the sisters. The sisters should have their head covered and not assume the headship, and they should also serve in the church. The sisters should care for two-thirds of the church service, and the brothers should care for one-third. This is a proper proportion. Therefore, the sisters must receive a burden. Without the help of the sisters, the children's work cannot be properly carried out. The same applies to the young people's work. If we want the young people's work to be done to perfection, the sisters must be brought into the work. Over ninety percent of the children's work requires the sisters' participation. Otherwise, there is no way for the children's work to succeed. (*The Collected Works of Witness Lee, 1967*, vol. 1, pp. 269-270)

BEING PERSISTENT IN THE BURDEN
FOR THE CHILDREN

My burden in this chapter is to kindle a fire within the sisters. The sisters in every church should be persistent to promote the burden for the children. On the one hand, they should not give the brothers any peace, and on the other hand, they should learn not to assume the leadership but to be full of patience, knowing when to proceed and when to wait. The sisters should be persistent to develop the children's work in the church. Furthermore, according to the leading of the Lord, they should fellowship with other sisters who are serving. As the sisters fellowship more and more, the burden for the children will increase more and more, and the number of sisters who are burdened will grow as well. Through fellowship, more and more people will be burdened for the children.

The sisters should fellowship about the way to carry out the children's work. For example, they can determine how many sisters are available to be with the children, how many young sisters can teach the children, how many children can come and even bring other children to the meetings, and even how many cannot come. Once they have a general idea of the situation, the sisters should meet with the elders and let them know of the needs in the children's work. This will surely activate the work among the children. Although the sisters should not assume to lead or head up anything, they should be persistent so that the brothers who take the lead can promote this matter. All the sisters' service, including the children's work, should be done in this way.

The sisters who have a burden for the children should stand in the position of sisters with their heads absolutely covered. They should not take the lead or head up anything but only actively promote things. They can speak to the elders so that the elders who do not have a burden will become burdened over time. However, they should not depend on the elders for everything, because the elders will not be able to consider all the details. Instead, the sisters should pray over every matter, have a thorough fellowship among themselves, and then ask the elders to give the word to proceed. The sisters should not expect the elders to make all the arrangements or plan everything for them. The sisters can make plans and arrangements, but before implementing anything, they should bring their plans and considerations to the elders and ask the elders to examine and approve them. If the elders do not approve of a certain aspect of the arrangement, it should be dropped. The sisters should not do anything that has not been approved by the elders. This kind of fellowship and coordination will result in the elders becoming more burdened for the children's work. (*The Collected Works of Witness Lee, 1967,* vol. 1, pp. 341-342)

THE SISTERS BRINGING
THE CHILDREN TO THE MEETING

The sisters should also bring the children to the meeting. If a sister cannot bring ten children, she should be able to bring five. Every week the sisters should consider how to bring the children to the meeting. If the meeting place is inadequate, they can open their homes. The sisters are like nursing mothers who care for the children and pray for them. After the meeting, the sisters need to take the children home. All the sisters should give themselves to this service.

TRAINING THE YOUNG SISTERS TO BE TEACHERS

We must use the young sisters to lead the children's meetings. Two or three other sisters can assist them in teaching the children to sing. The church should train the teachers so that the young sisters learn to teach and lead the children. Some brothers also need to collect and write material for the children's meetings. They should prepare material for the youngest group of children, for the children in the middle grades, and for the older children. (*The Collected Works of Witness Lee, 1967,* vol. 1, p. 305)

* * *

Many of the sisters love the Lord, but they need to find the way to do something for the Lord, not by themselves but by abiding in the vine to impart life into others. If we bear the little ones as fruit, the Lord will add them to our account. Only eternity will reveal the result of this. Perhaps out of a group of children for whom we are caring, some will become apostles. Therefore, I encourage the sisters to do this good work. All the housewives can bring children to the meetings, and the younger sisters can be trained to cooperate with them to bear these little ones as fruit. (*The Collected Works of Witness Lee, 1967,* vol. 1, p. 550)

MOTHERS IN THE CHURCH LIFE

To have the practical church life to the uttermost, in the local church there should be some real sisters and some real mothers. In an earlier message it was my burden to share with you that you need to be a serving sister, but now I am burdened to share with you that you need to be a mother. As long as there is a shortage of sisters like Phoebe among us, the church life is not practical. Yet the serving of that sister is at the beginning of Romans 16, in the first verse. When the church life in practicality reaches a peak, in every church there should be some real mothers. (*Loving Mothers in the Church Life,* pp. 7-8)

USING THE YOUNG PEOPLE
TO STRENGTHEN THE CHILDREN'S WORK

We also need the help of the young people in the children's work. This matter must be developed. There are twenty to thirty thousand children between five and twelve years of age in the homes of the saints in Taiwan. If we can care for these children, in six years they will become gospel seeds. If the children's work progresses well, even dormant saints will send their children to us, and we will be able to regain the dormant ones. I believe that there is quite a large number of children in every locality. As soon as we begin the children's work, the young people will begin to function. They can all take part in serving the children. For a class of twenty children, we will need two teachers. If there are two thousand children in Taipei, we should have one hundred classes, and we will need two hundred young people to coordinate and serve. The young people need to give themselves to this work, and this will give everyone an opportunity to practice speaking. (*The Collected Works of Witness Lee, 1967*, vol. 1, p. 326)

* * *

When I returned to Taiwan in 1966 and in 1967, there were four thousand children in the children's meetings, and I told the brothers to set a goal of having ten thousand children in the meetings. I also asked the brothers to perfect the junior high and high school brothers and sisters to assist in teaching the children. These children would be gospel seeds in junior high school, they would be gospel seeds in high school, and they would be gospel seeds in college. They would be seeds the entire time that they are in school. (*Crucial Words of Leading in the Lord's Recovery, Book 3: The Future of the Lord's Recovery and the Building Up of the Organic Service*, p. 36)

* * *

In the future the full-time co-workers will encourage preaching the gospel on the campuses, in the homes, to the children, and in the community. Full-timers are needed for the gospel on the campuses and in the schools; otherwise, it will be difficult to maintain the gospel work. With regard to the children's work, even though the junior high and high school students can teach in the children's meetings, the children's work will be carried forward by the full-timers, because they will prepare teaching materials and make a schedule. (*Crucial Words of Leading in the Lord's Recovery, Book 3: The*

Future of the Lord's Recovery and the Building Up of the Organic Service, p. 160)

*   *   *

In the past the children's meeting was always held in the meeting hall and was mostly led by the young people. Now the gospel work on the college campuses and at the junior high and high schools is very active, and the young people all have specific services in this work. Thus, they cannot take care of the children anymore. Hence, we need to rely on the elderly saints to spend the time and effort to teach the children...The elderly saints may use their homes. After the children get off from school, the elderly saints may open their homes and prepare some snacks to welcome them. Then they may sing with the children, tell them stories, and lead them to know God.

Every one of us should be able to do these three things—pray every day, join the small group meetings, and go door-knocking and have home meetings every week. The fourth matter is taking care of the children. I hope that more people will receive the burden to open their homes to take care of the children. Twenty years ago I said that we should have ten thousand children in Taipei, and then ten years later we would have ten thousand young brothers and sisters. If the saints had taken this word and practiced it, we would have twenty to thirty thousand young people today. Moreover, gaining people in this way is very safe, because they are taught by us and receive the gospel from us from their youth. Thus, they should be very solid. If this were the case, many young saints would not need to put aside their gospel work at school to do the children's work. I hope that from now on the elderly saints would pick up the burden and take the lead to do this in their homes. The effect will be very promising in the long run. (*Being Up-to-date for the Rebuilding of the Temple,* pp. 46-47)

*   *   *

When the entire church is mobilized in this way, all the brothers and sisters will have an opportunity to serve. Some can open their homes, others can bring the children to the meetings, and still others can teach the children. When all the saints endeavor in one accord for the Lord's heart's desire, the profit will be immeasurable. This will impress the children that we are all for the Lord and are caring for them without compensation. Those who open their homes do not ask for money, those who teach do not ask for money, and those who transport the children do not ask for money. Instead of asking for money, the saints spend their own money to pay the expenses of carrying out the children's service. As a result, everyone will be full of joy. Our conducting children's meetings in this way will deeply impress the children from their youth. They will see people who live for Christ and who sacrifice for Christ, not caring for themselves. This is the ultimate benefit. Furthermore, the impact will unconsciously influence the relatives of the children in such a way that it will be easy to invite them to a gospel meeting. Hence, the children's work is a major service. (*The Collected Works of Witness Lee, 1967,* vol. 1, p. 306)

* * *

We should take action immediately. All the churches should encourage the saints in this matter, and we should pray for this matter. All the saints want their children to receive spiritual help. Even dormant saints want their children to receive spiritual guidance. Once we begin this work, the saints will respond. This will result in multiple benefits; the profit cannot be underestimated. (*The Collected Works of Witness Lee, 1967,* vol. 1, p. 327)

COMPILING CHILDREN'S LESSONS
THAT BUILD UP A PROPER HUMANITY
AND LEAD THE CHILDREN
INTO A PROPER ENJOYMENT
(1)

Scripture Reading: Luke 2:40, 51-52

I. When we speak of the children's work, we are referring to children who have not graduated from elementary school but are more than five years old; these are the target of our children's work:

A. In Christianity, doing the children's work is considered to be like operating a school; hence, it is called Sunday school:

1. In the Sunday school classes they may use textbooks; we do not agree with this method; we feel that our children's meeting should not have the flavor of a Sunday school—Rev. 18:4; Heb. 13:13.

2. From our experience we feel that if we regard the children's work as a school and teach our children from textbooks, it will be of more harm than benefit to them:

a. This method educates the children with premature knowledge; later, when the children grow up, they will not be very open to listen to the truth.

b. The children hear too many Bible stories in Sunday school, and their hearing becomes dull; when they grow up, they will not be moved by what they hear—cf. Heb. 5:11.

c. Hence, the material that we prepare for the

children's work should not be influenced by
the material used in the Sunday schools in
Christianity; not only should we not use their
material; we should not even reference it.

B. We should begin by teaching the children how to
be a proper human being; we should show them
that man is different from the animals and different from the trees, plants, and flowers:

1. After this we should speak of man's character
and conduct; we should teach the children to
honor their parents and be loving, pure, obedient, honest, and proper in their conduct; we
must be careful not to give them a religious
thought or concept.

2. When we speak of the difference between man
and the animals, we can mention that man was
created by God and also that the heavens and
the earth were created by God; we can also say a
little about how man was created in God's image;
we do not need to say more than this.

C. In caring for young children, we must be careful
not to make them religious, not to pass on mere
religious knowledge, and not to tell them too many
Bible stories; furthermore, we should not force them
to pray; if we practice these matters, we will be
successful—Matt. 9:16-17; 2 Cor. 3:6; John 5:39-40;
16:12-13; cf. Matt. 2:4-6.

D. The first thing we should do with elementary age
children is to help them to know how to be persons
with a proper humanity; we must help them to know
what a proper humanity is and how to behave as
human beings—Luke 2:40, 51-52; Prov. 1:1-4; 2
Tim. 2:21:

1. At first we should simply help them to grow up
as proper persons with the full understanding
and realization of what a proper humanity is.

2. To this end, we can have many lessons and use
demonstrations and illustrations; we can bring

a small animal or some flowers and talk about the difference between man and these things.

3. We must also help them to know how to honor their parents, love others, and know the proper elements of human morality, such as humility, patience, and kindness—Exo. 20:12; Eph. 6:1-2; 4:32; cf. 2 Tim. 3:2.

4. In this way we can build them up as proper materials for the Lord's use; to receive the Lord and enjoy Him requires us to have a proper humanity as good material.

5. Within the six years of the elementary age, there are about three hundred Lord's Days to build up the children in their human character; it is very helpful for us to do this.

II. To compile material for the teachers, we need a number of brothers who know the truth and are also skilled in writing; the material does not need to be in five or six levels; we need only three levels—elementary, intermediate, and advanced—cf. Titus 2:1-8; 1 Cor. 3:1-2:

A. The material for the elementary level should be entirely from a child's perspective; we should tell them that man is not the same as the animals and explain to them why man is different—cf. Gen. 1:1—2:7.

B. Gradually, as we proceed to the intermediate level, we can give the children a little more Bible knowledge:

1. We can convey to them a deep impression that there is a God in the universe, that man fell and committed sin, and that the Lord Jesus is our Savior.

2. We do not have to give too much doctrine, but we should impress them with the facts in the Bible.

C. Then when the children proceed to an advanced level, they will almost be ready to follow the messages in the big meetings:

1. The children do not need too much doctrine; they only need a general knowledge of the truth.

2. This requires the careful work of the brothers who compile the teaching material so that the children do not receive premature knowledge.

D. There is the need for some brothers and sisters to spend the time to prepare lessons and instructions on how to use them:

1. There is no need to compose the lessons in full; we can simply give some guidelines, such as which week to speak concerning honoring our parents and some hints on how to illustrate this lesson.

2. After being trained, each teacher can choose the particular illustrations he will use; we should not prepare uniform printed lessons to be read in each class.

3. Perhaps half a page of points, illustrations, and instructions is adequate; it should be easy to prepare lessons in this way.

Excerpts from the Ministry:

THE CHILDREN'S WORK

We expect the children's work among us to be very prevailing. Therefore, we need to have a proper realization and preparation for this work. When we speak of the children's work, we are referring to children who have not graduated from elementary school but are more than five years old. These are the target of our children's work. If we are unable to take care of the children who are younger than this age group, we will leave them to the care of their parents. In order to give a message to young people or college students, we know that we must be well prepared. Some may think that it is easy to care for the children who are between the ages of five and twelve by simply giving them a piece of candy. However, to handle the children in this way will not yield a good result. According to my observation, the most difficult work to do effectively is the children's work.

AVOIDING THE WAY OF SUNDAY SCHOOLS

In Christianity, doing the children's work is considered to

be like operating a school; hence, it is called Sunday school. In Western countries there is a Sunday school for every age: for elderly people, for younger adults, for college age, for teenagers, and for children. The denominations have Sunday school classes, and afterward everyone comes together for the Sunday church service. In the Sunday school classes they may use textbooks. We do not agree with this method. We feel that our children's meeting should not have the flavor of a Sunday school. From our experience we feel that if we regard the children's work as a school and teach our children from textbooks, it will be of more harm than benefit to them. This method educates the children with premature knowledge. Later, when the children grow up, they will not be very open to listen to the truth. The children hear too many Bible stories in Sunday school, and their hearing becomes dull. When they grow up, they will not be moved by what they hear. This is a problem.

Hence, the material that we prepare for the children's work should not be influenced by the material used in the Sunday schools in Christianity. Not only should we not use their material; we should not even reference it. We must drop the way of Sunday school in Christianity. We must never consult their material. Their material will not help us in the children's work; on the contrary, it will cause our work to deviate.

COMPILING TEACHING MATERIAL

What material should we use to teach the children? We should begin by teaching the children how to be a proper human being. We should show them that man is different from the animals and different from the trees, plants, and flowers. After this we should speak of man's character and conduct. We should teach the children to honor their parents and be loving, pure, obedient, honest, and proper in their conduct. We must be careful not to give them a religious thought or concept.

When we speak of the difference between man and the animals, we can mention that man was created by God and also that the heavens and the earth were created by God. We can also say a little about how man was created in God's image. We do not need to say more than this. I do not agree with explaining all of Genesis 1 and 2 to the children. Even if we touch man's fall in Genesis 3, we should speak briefly and should not tell the entire story of the fall. When we speak to children, we should tell them experiential stories; we should not give them too much doctrine. It is not necessarily a benefit for the children to know too much.

We need to train the teachers for the children's meeting in such a way that they can find illustrations by themselves from practical situations. For instance, they can ask the children, "Are you being honest if you steal candy from your older brother?" or "Suppose your mother saves a bigger piece of candy for your younger sister, and this makes you unhappy and jealous. Do you still love your mother and your sister?" When we speak to the children, we must use practical examples. (*The Collected Works of Witness Lee, 1967,* vol. 1, pp. 311-312)

IN CARING FOR CHILDREN, NOT PASSING ON RELIGIOUS KNOWLEDGE BUT BUILDING UP THEIR PROPER HUMANITY

In caring for young children, we must be careful not to make them religious. We must not pass on mere religious knowledge from the Bible, and we should not tell them too many Bible stories. Rather, we should keep back some portions until later. Furthermore, we should not force them to pray. If we will practice these matters, we will be able to be successful. On the positive side, the first thing we should do with elementary age children is to help them to know how to be persons with a proper humanity. We must help them to know what a proper humanity is and how to behave as human beings. To this end, we can have many lessons and use demonstrations and illustrations. We can bring a small animal or some flowers and talk about the difference between man and these things. Then we can tell them how to behave themselves as persons who are altogether different from the lower creatures.

We must also help them to know how to honor their parents, love others, and know the proper elements of human morality, such as humility, patience, and kindness. In this way we can build them up as proper materials for the Lord's use.

To receive the Lord and enjoy Him requires us to have a proper humanity as good material. Within the six years of the elementary age, there are about three hundred Lord's Days to build up the children in their human character. It is very helpful for us to do this.

The mistake made by Christianity in their so-called Sunday schools is that they try to make the children religious by giving them too much knowledge and too many Bible stories. Eventually, this makes it difficult to help them. After they grow up and we refer them to the story of the fall of Adam, they may say, "Since I was five years old, I already knew how Eve took the fruit and gave it to Adam, and man became fallen. There is no need to tell me this again." Because of this, they will not be able to receive inspiration from the Word. That is why we should withhold from them certain stories from the Bible and keep them until a later time. At first we should simply help them to grow up as proper persons with the full understanding and realization of what a proper humanity is. (*The Collected Works of Witness Lee, 1967,* vol. 1, pp. 503-504)

* * *

To compile material for the teachers, we need a number of brothers who know the truth and are also skilled in writing. The material does not need to be in five or six levels. We need only three levels—elementary, intermediate, and advanced. Each level can be used for two years.

The material for the elementary level should be entirely from a child's perspective. When we speak of man, we should ask the children whether man is the same as a dog, a cat, or a tiger. We should tell them that man is not the same as the animals and explain to them why man is different. That is good enough. We should not present a doctrinal explanation but should use only practical examples.

Gradually, as we proceed to the intermediate level, we can give the children a little more Bible knowledge. We can convey to them a deep impression that there is a God in the universe, that man fell and committed sin, and that the Lord Jesus is our Savior. We do not have to give too much doctrine, but we should impress them with the facts in the Bible. Then when the children proceed to an advanced level, they will almost be ready to follow the messages in the big meetings. The children do not need too much doctrine; they only need a general knowledge of the truth. This requires the careful work of the brothers who compile the teaching material so that the children do not receive premature knowledge. (*The Collected Works of Witness Lee, 1967,* vol. 1, pp. 312-313)

PREPARING THE PROPER LESSONS
FOR EACH AGE LEVEL

We should not put all the ages together. We should rather classify the children according to their age. The five- and six-year-olds can be one grade, followed by the seven- and eight-year-olds, the nine- and ten-year-olds, and the eleven- and twelve-year-olds. We should have at least three grades for the six elementary years. At first, we may use a series of meetings to train the teachers of these grades according to the way we have fellowshipped in this chapter. There is the need for some brothers and sisters to spend the time to prepare lessons and instructions on how to use them. There is no need to compose the lessons in full; we can simply give some guidelines, such as which week to speak concerning honoring our parents and some hints on how to illustrate this lesson. After being trained, each teacher can choose the particular illustrations he will use. We should not prepare uniform printed lessons to be read in each class. Perhaps half a page of points, illustrations, and instructions is adequate. It should be easy to prepare lessons in this way. (*The Collected Works of Witness Lee, 1967,* vol. 1, pp. 506-507)

COMPILING CHILDREN'S LESSONS
THAT BUILD UP A PROPER HUMANITY
AND LEAD THE CHILDREN
INTO A PROPER ENJOYMENT
(2)

Scripture Reading: 2 Tim. 2:2; 3:15

III. In order to do the children's work well, we need to pay
attention to these three aspects: the teaching material,
the training of the teachers, and the leading of the
elders; after brothers are designated to compile material, the leading of the elders and the training of the
teachers should follow—2 Tim. 2:2; Eph. 4:12-16; Heb.
13:17.

IV. At the end of each lesson that we give the children, we
can impress them with a short verse from the Bible;
by ministering the lesson, we will lay a good foundation for them to receive something brief from the word
of God—2 Tim. 3:15:

A. We may tell them that as children they need to be
proper human beings who behave in a good way to
honor their parents; we can even use illustrations
from nature; this will interest them very much—cf.
Rom. 1:20a.

B. Then at the end we can read them, "Honor your
father and your mother" (Exo. 20:12), explaining
that this is the word of God in the Bible; we can
ask them to keep it in mind, recite it, and explain
to us what it means.

C. The next time they come together, we can have
them tell us what they heard the previous week

and whether they put it into practice; we may ask
them in what way they honored their parents in
the past week.

D. We must not give them anything in a premature
way; rather, we should prepare the lessons according to their age:

1. We should give the five- and six-year-olds one
thing and the seven- and eight-year-olds something else.

2. Premature knowledge damages children; we need
some brothers and sisters who understand this
principle to prepare the lessons.

V. Gradually, we can help the children to know who God
is, not in a religious way but in a very practical way;
we can lead them to the point that they realize there
is an almighty One, who is God—Exo. 3:6; 20:2:

A. Following this, we can help them to know God's
creation and even the fall of man; for this purpose
we should not merely tell stories; instead, we should
present these matters in a very practical way, using
many illustrations:

1. The best time to present the fall of man is after
we have helped them to know what a proper
humanity is.

2. We can tell them that we are all fallen creatures
and that there is sin within us that weakens us;
to speak concerning the fall in this way is very
realistic—Rom. 7:18.

3. In the same principle, we can tell them how the
Lord Jesus came to accomplish redemption; we
should not speak this as a mere story.

4. We can use the lessons concerning proper humanity and the proper way to behave.

B. Then we can point out to them that the Son of God
has died for us, and we can tell them about the
cross, the death of Christ, and redemption without
passing on mere religious knowledge—1 Cor. 15:3-4;
Eph. 1:7.

C. After the children reach a certain age, we can go on

to tell them that Christ is life, not as a mere story but based on their failures and desires—John 11:25; 14:6; Col. 3:4.

D. Without giving them too much knowledge, we can help them in a practical way to realize what God, creation, humanity, the fall, redemption, and Christ are, and eventually we can help them to receive the Lord and be saved in a definite way.

VI. Perhaps there are brothers and sisters among us who are especially experienced and burdened for the children and who are preparing songs for the children:

A. The poetry must be composed for the young ones in a very skillful way; it is better not to have songs if the songs that we have are of a low standard.

B. The brothers and sisters should also prepare songs for the children's meetings; we should not treat the little ones like the older saints and have them sing the same songs that we do.

VII. Parents like to hear their children sing:

A. The parents may be unhappy if you persuade them to believe in Jesus; but they will pay attention to their children's singing; when they hear the songs, they will be touched.

B. In the home meetings, we need to help even the children to call, speak, or sing a hymn and to quote or speak the word of the Bible.

C. Everyone, both young and old, likes singing; singing is very sweet; you must be like a nursing mother, making your little ones feel pleasant by giving them something sweet.

Excerpts from the Ministry:

In order to do the children's work well, we need to pay attention to these three aspects: the teaching material, the training of the teachers, and the leading of the elders. After brothers are designated to compile material, the leading of the elders and the training of the teachers should follow. We must promote the children's work in every locality. The brothers should promote this work, and the sisters should carry it out. If all the saints are willing to receive this burden and not miss the opportunity, there will be a glorious result. (*The Collected Works of Witness Lee, 1967,* vol. 1, pp. 314-315)

USING PRACTICAL LESSONS TO BUILD UP THE CHILDREN AS PROPER HUMAN BEINGS

At the end of each lesson that we give them, we can impress them with a short verse from the Bible. By ministering the lesson, we will lay a good foundation for them to receive something brief from the word of God. We may tell them, for example, that as children they need to be proper human beings who behave in a good way to honor their parents. We can even use illustrations from nature; this will interest them very much. Then at the end we can read them Exodus 20:12, which says, "Honor your father and your mother," explaining that this is the word of God in the Bible. We can ask them to keep it in mind, recite it, and explain to us what it means. In this way we will impress them with this word. Finally, at this point we can help them to pray with this verse in a very simple way. The next time they come together, we can have them tell us what they heard the previous week and whether they put it into practice. We may ask them in what way they honored their parents in the past week. If we take an adequate time to do this, they will be very interested in what we say. We must not give them anything in a premature way. Rather, we should prepare the lessons according to their age. We should give the five- and six-year-olds one thing and the seven- and eight-year-olds something else. Premature knowledge damages children. We need some brothers and sisters who understand this principle to prepare the lessons.

HELPING THEM TO KNOW GOD, REDEMPTION, AND LIFE IN A PRACTICAL WAY

Gradually, we can help them to know who God is, not in a religious way but in a very practical way. We can lead them to the point that they realize there is an almighty One, who is God. By choosing the best verses concerning God—such as

Exodus 3:6, which says, "I am the God of your father," or 20:2, which says, "I am Jehovah your God"—we can impress them in a brief and simple way that there is an almighty One in the universe, who is our God. Following this, we can help them to know God's creation and even the fall of man. For this purpose we should not merely tell stories. Instead, we should present these matters in a very practical way, using many illustrations. The best time to present the fall of man is after we have helped them to know what a proper humanity is. We may ask them one by one, "Can you practice what you have heard? Have you honored your parents? Have you loved your brothers?" Many of them will admit that they cannot, and some may even shed tears. Then we should ask, "Why have you failed? Why can you not do this?" At this point we can tell them that we are all fallen creatures and that there is sin within us that weakens us. To speak concerning the fall in this way is very realistic.

In the same principle, we can tell them how the Lord Jesus came to accomplish redemption. Again, we should not speak this as a mere story. Rather, we can use the lessons concerning proper humanity and the proper way to behave. We can say, "We know that God commanded us to honor our parents, but we have failed. In the Bible this failure is called sin. How can this problem be solved?" This is the way to speak concerning sin and the problem of sins. Then we can point out to them that the Son of God has died for us, and we can tell them about the cross, the death of Christ, and redemption without passing on mere religious knowledge. After they reach a certain age, we can go on to tell them that Christ is life, not as a mere story but based on their failures and desires. We can ask, "Do you want to have the strength to behave yourself in this wonderful way? You must realize that you yourself do not have this strength. You need Christ to be your life and power." This is the best way to help them. Without giving them too much knowledge, we can help them in a practical way to realize what God, creation, humanity, the fall, redemption, and Christ are, and eventually we can help them to receive the Lord and be saved in a definite way.

When many of us were young, we received too much knowledge that only damaged us. We were given many stories, but we were not given the proper verses in a practical way. Because of this, no one could speak to us, for example, about the prodigal son. We may have said, "There is no need to talk about that. I already know what the father, the son, the robe, and the calf are. I can tell you the story." After hearing all the teachings and stories from the Bible, young ones become "slippery" so that nothing sticks to them. We must not spoil the young ones in this way. Those who have never heard the stories before are easily inspired by them. This is why we should withhold certain stories and simply help the children to know the things of humanity and of God in a practical way. Then when they are saved and begin to attend the church meetings, what they hear will be new to them.

When the children are young, we should simply tell them about God, His creation, and other simple things. At least by the time they are eight years old, we should help them to realize something concerning the Lord's salvation, and gradually after that, we can help them to know that Christ is life. We should not pass on matters such as pray-reading until they are at least ten or eleven, at which time they should know something concerning how to fellowship with the Lord. For the younger ones, illustrations and demonstrations are more helpful. If we conduct the meetings with the children in a proper way, a two-hour meeting will not be too long. On the contrary, though, to merely tell them story after story will tire them.

The most important matter is to build up the humanity and character of the children. This is neglected by many parents today. Having a good human character will not hinder the children in any way. The teachings of Confucius and Chinese ethics build up character according to the self with self-pride and self-confidence. The kind of character building we practice is absolutely different. We should build up the children in the way of realizing that they can do nothing in themselves, because they are fallen and need a higher life. (*The Collected Works of Witness Lee, 1967*, vol. 1, pp. 504-506)

* * *

We may divide the children into two or three levels. Some saints will need to work on the lesson materials, and some need to tell the stories. Children ages four through six may be on the first level. With these ones you only need to sing hymns with them and tell them stories. Children ages seven through nine may be on the second level. With these ones you need to teach them something, which may require some lesson materials. Children ages ten through twelve may be on the third level. With them you need lesson materials to help teach them something deeper. (*Being Up-to-date for the Rebuilding of the Temple,* pp. 46-47)

* * *

Perhaps there are brothers and sisters among us who are especially experienced with and burdened for the children. They should come forth and give us some materials so that the children in various localities may receive the benefit. They should come forth and give us some materials that the children in various localities may receive the benefit. Perhaps there are already some brothers who are preparing songs for the children.

If the children's meeting is carried out properly, it will also provide a good opportunity for some people to believe in the Lord. This meeting indeed needs to be strong. In the future I hope that there will be a few brothers and sisters who will come forth to prepare some materials for the brothers to take care of the children. (*Church Affairs,* pp. 96-97)

* * *

Question: We have been trying to write children's songs using the Scriptures to help the children memorize the Word. It is almost impossible to rhyme these songs since their content is the Scriptures themselves. How do you feel about this point?

To write songs for children is a difficult task, but in principle, I do not agree with writing songs for them with verses from the Scripture. If we want to help the children remember some verses from the Bible, we can simply instruct them to read and recite the verses. We should not try to make the verses singable for the children. I do not mean that we should not do this at all, but this is difficult to do. To write songs for children requires a great amount of skill. Poetry must be composed for the young ones in a very skillful way. I saw a number of songs for the children that were all below standard according to my feeling. It is better not to have songs if the songs that we have are of such a low standard. (*Speaking Christ for the Building Up of the Body of Christ,* pp. 82-83)

PREPARING THE PROPER SONGS FOR THE CHILDREN

The brothers and sisters should also prepare songs for the children's meetings. We should not treat the little ones like the older saints and have them sing the same songs that we do. *Hymns,* #1017, for example, says, "Christ has put on human nature and become a man like me, / He has died upon the cross that I from Adam might be free, / He has risen and as Spirit He has come to live in me / That He might be my life." This hymn does not match the six-year-olds. They may be able to pick up the tune, but they will not understand the words. To prepare the proper children's songs is not easy; it requires much work. We can adopt the melodies of certain hymns, but if possible, we can also compose new melodies. (*The Collected Works of Witness Lee, 1967,* vol. 1, p. 508)

* * *

When we were in northern China, the sisters who taught the children used content from the adults' meeting. At that time the adults met upstairs, and the children met downstairs. When we spoke concerning vanity, they spoke to the children concerning vanity. When we spoke concerning dealing with the flesh, they also spoke concerning the flesh. After I found out about this, I told the serving ones that this would not work. I realized that after the children were baptized, they would not be able to listen to any messages, because before they were saved, they would have already heard messages for the edification of new believers. We should never do the children's work in this way.

Let us consider another example. One morning I was in the meeting hall, and I heard the children singing the hymn "Rock of Ages Cleft for Me." This hymn is too deep for the children. Hence, some of the saints should receive a burden to write songs for the children. The songs should be simple and interesting. They do not need to be religious. We can sing about flowers and birds with a lively tune. Eventually, we can teach the children songs related to God. The children's songs should be of three levels, and each level should include at least fifty songs. (*The Collected Works of Witness Lee, 1967,* vol. 1, p. 313)

* * *

Parents like to hear their children sing. When you visit your relatives, you may first give their children some candy and then teach them to sing a simple hymn. Their parents may be unhappy if you persuade them to believe in Jesus. But they will pay attention to their children's singing. When they hear the songs, they will be touched. (*Key Points on the Home Meetings,* p. 55)

HELPING EVEN THE CHILDREN
TO CALL, SPEAK, OR SING A HYMN AND
TO QUOTE OR SPEAK THE WORD OF THE BIBLE

In the home meetings, we need to help even the children to call, speak, or sing a hymn and to quote or speak the word of the Bible. Suppose that you have baptized a couple, and they have a nine-year-old boy and a three-year-old girl. If you go to help them have a home meeting, you must train even the three-year-old girl. You can tell her that it is easy for her to call a hymn in the meeting and that it is even easier to sing a hymn. You may say, "You know when you are going to have a home meeting and that some brothers will come to help you. Before we come, you can sing a hymn." If you tell the little girl this, she may be singing when you enter the home. Take her song as the start of the meeting. All the little ones like to sing. You may not need to help the little girl sing a whole verse or stanza of a song. If you can help her to sing one line, she may be happy. The little ones can be a very good help to the home meetings. You also can help them to pray. They can pray a simple prayer such as, "Lord Jesus, You are so good. I love You and I know that You are with me." You can instruct the nine-year-old boy to speak some verses, to read some portion of the Word. In this way all the members of the family participate in the meeting. If we do this week after week with this family, they will accumulate many divine riches. (*Speaking Christ for the Building Up of the Body of Christ,* pp. 128-129)

* * *

Everyone, both young and old, likes singing. Do not explain that much to them; explaining is often sour, not sweet. Singing is very sweet. You must be like a nursing mother, making your little ones feel pleasant by giving them something sweet. (*The Exercise and Practice of the God-Ordained Way,* p. 192)

PART FIVE:

YOUNG PEOPLE'S WORK

LESSON SEVENTEEN

THE VISION AND IMPORTANCE
OF THE NEXT GENERATION
IN THE LORD'S RECOVERY

Scripture Reading: Luke 18:16-17; Acts 26:13-19; Num. 14:29-31

I. We must see the preciousness of the second generation and their value in God's hands—Luke 18:16-17:

A. If we truly want to do the young people's work, and
do it in a weighty manner, we must let God open
our eyes to see the preciousness of the young
people and their importance in His hands; if we see
this, we will appreciate this work, and spontaneously we will have a heart within us for it:

1. Everyone who serves the Lord must be a person
with vision—Prov. 29:18; Acts 26:13-19.

2. The governing vision of the Bible is the Triune
God working Himself into His chosen and redeemed people in order to saturate their entire
being with the Divine Trinity for the producing
and building up of the Body of Christ consummating in the New Jerusalem—Eph. 4:4-6; Rev.
21:2, 9-10.

B. Every time God wants to make a dispensational
move, an age-turning move, He must obtain His
dispensational instrument; we must be those who
have dispensational value to God in the last days
to turn the age—12:5-11; 1:20; Dan. 12:3; 9:23;
10:11, 19.

C. God's work in turning the age is always done
through men; before a new age is ushered in, there
are always men in the previous age who are used

by God particularly to turn the age; in every age-turning work, God purposely uses young people:

1. Because men used by God in one age often become fallen and fail to reach His goal, God is forced to turn the age, to have a new start so that He can do what He wants to do in a new age.

2. God's most important dispensational move is to end this age and bring in the age of the kingdom; to do this He must have His dispensational instrument; this is what God wants to do today.

II. The future of the Lord's move and the spreading of the recovery is altogether dependent on the next generation; the Lord needs children and young people for the future of His recovery:

A. We can say that virtually everyone used by God to begin a new thing, or chosen by God to turn the age, was a young man; if we see this, we will treasure the young people before God.

B. With the exception of Joshua and Caleb, those who were qualified and ready to take possession of the good land were younger ones, the second generation—Deut. 1:35-36; 11:2-7; Num. 14:29-31:

1. The second generation did not pass through as much as the first generation did, but they received the benefit of what the first generation experienced.

2. What the older ones experienced was very effective in building up the younger ones; therefore, God could prepare from the second generation more than six hundred thousand men with a rich inheritance and strong background who were qualified to be formed into an army to fight for God's kingdom.

3. The principle is the same with us in the Lord's recovery today; what the older ones have experienced is being passed on to the younger ones and will be very effective in building them up

and preparing them to fight with God and for God.

4. If a brother is left to himself, he may have to stumble for ten years before he can come up with something; but now through the Body he may acquire the same thing in one evening; if such a brother will take the judgment of the Body, he will save a lot of time; the use of authority in the church is for the purpose of cutting down mistakes and shortening the journeys.

C. There must be a group of young people who are saved to receive proper spiritual help today, so they can gain the experience and be used by the Lord in the future; if there are no young people gained by the Lord today, after our departure there will be no one to succeed us and there will be a gap.

D. If you see this, your heart will be burdened to love the young people regardless of whether they are good or bad; may the brothers and sisters as the Lord's lovers all love the young people for the future of the church and for the Lord's work.

III. The Lord's recovery is spreading, and will spread at a good pace; there will be churches in all the major cities and in all the leading countries on earth; if during the coming years many young people are perfected, the Lord's recovery will spread at a rapid speed:

A. We must pursue and grow in our spiritual life, earnestly maintaining a living fellowship with the Lord, fully consecrating ourselves to Him and having proper dealings with Him; to be the Lord's overcomers, we must love the Lord and grasp the opportunity to love Him—Matt. 26:6-13.

B. The next generation must be equipped in the truth; they need to read and get the word into them and get themselves into the word so that they may be mingled with the word—Col. 3:16; Psa. 119:11.

C. The next generation needs to build up a good character; they need to exercise themselves to build up a character that is useful to the Lord—Phil. 4:8, 13.

D. The next generation needs to receive a higher
education; all the young people must get a college
degree, study more diligently than the secular students, get the highest grades, and go on for advanced
degrees:
1. There is a need in the Lord's recovery today for
those with the highest education; the young people must endeavor to gain the best education.
2. If the young people expend their energy in this
way, by the time they are thirty they will be able
to begin their ministry like the Lord Jesus did; if
many take this way, we shall have no shortage.

Excerpts from the Ministry:

SEEING THE PRECIOUSNESS
OF THE YOUNG PEOPLE

In whatever a person does, the most important thing is to
have a heart. Without a heart, a person will not want to do
anything, and even if he does something, he will not be enthusiastic in doing it. Of course, this is also true with the young
people's work. If you want to do this work, you must like the
young people, care for them, and be concerned about their
affairs. This may be considered the minimum "capital"
required for the young people's work. If you have no interest
in the young people and have no heart for them, doing the
young people's work only out of reluctance, then it is useless.

Sometimes our heart may arise from our preference. When
we like something, naturally we will have a heart to do it.
Sometimes the heart we have may come from our knowledge.
When we see the importance and value of a certain matter,
we will spontaneously have a heart for it. According to my
observation of the real situation among us concerning the
young people's work, I see that some brothers and sisters are
doing it out of their preference. Because they are naturally
inclined to the young people and they enjoy contacting the
young people, they come to do the young people's work. We
cannot say that this is wrong. We have to admit that no
matter how much grace we have received and how great the

spirituality we possess, we are still human—we still have the part that is human. But here we have to say that it is not weighty enough to do the young people's work with such a heart. If we truly want to do the young people's work, and do it in a weighty manner, we must let God open our eyes to see the preciousness of the young people and their importance in God's hands. If we see this, we will appreciate this work, and spontaneously we will have a heart within us for it. (*How to Lead the Young People*, pp. 1-3)

GOD'S DISPENSATIONAL MOVE—"NOW" (REV. 12:10)

When God changes His attitude toward a certain matter, He makes a dispensational move. Every dispensational move brings in God's new way. His most important dispensational move is in Revelation 12. He wants to end this age and bring in the age of the kingdom. His purpose is not general and ordinary. How can He bring this age to a close and bring in another? He must have His dispensational instrument. This is what God wants to do today.

THE NEED OF THE MAN-CHILD

The rapture of the man-child brings an end to the church age and introduces the kingdom age. The man-child enables God to move. If there is not a man-child and a rapture, God cannot make a dispensational move. We should never forget that God can be limited. He waits for man in all of His moves. God's binding in heaven is based on our binding on earth; God's loosing in heaven is based on our loosing on earth. Everything depends on the church.

It is God's desire that created beings would deal with fallen created beings. According to His purpose, the whole church should deal with Satan; however, the church has failed. Therefore, there is the need for the overcomers to rise up. God's purpose is fulfilled in the overcomers because they work with Him. We can see the principle of the overcomers throughout the Word of God. God always lays hold of a group of overcomers to make a dispensational move.

Are we at the end of the age? If we are, the kingdom will soon begin. If a dispensational move is near, then God needs an instrument. General work is no longer adequate. The children of God lack a vision; they do not see the seriousness and intensity of the situation. *Now* [in Revelation 12:10] is a matter of dispensation. Just being a good servant of the Lord is no longer good enough; this is not of great use to God. Please note that we are not saying that it is of no use. What are we doing to close this dispensation? What are we doing to bring in the next age? This is a special time, so there is the need of special Christians to do a special work.

Today God is waiting for the man-child. Only the rapture can precipitate the events in Revelation 12:10. God has an order, and He works according to that order. His eyes have left the church; they are now on the kingdom. An overcomer works according to the principle of the Body. The principle of the Body annuls sectarianism and individualism.

After the rapture the woman will be persecuted three and a half years. Many other of her children will go through the tribulation, but God will keep them. Being an overcomer is not primarily for escaping the tribulation. We need to see of what value the rapture is to the Lord, not to ourselves.

Of all the dispensational moves, the man-child is the greatest because it removes man's power and the devil's power, and it brings in the kingdom. We live in the most privileged time; we can do the most for God. *Light will show us the way, but strength and power will enable us to walk the road. A great price must be paid in order to be used now. (The Glorious Church,* pp. 153-154, 156-157)

GOD PURPOSELY USING YOUNG PEOPLE
TO TURN THE AGE

We need to realize that many times God does things on earth to turn an age. When God works on earth, He does so age by age. The reason that God has many age-turning moves is that men used by Him in one age often become fallen and fail to reach His goal. This forces God to turn the age, that is, to have a new start so that He can do what He wants to do in a new age.

We can see many cases like this in the Old Testament. God would bring in a new age by doing something through some people during a particular time. However, due to man's degradation, that age would soon become fallen and degraded. It would become so degraded that God could not have a way with men on earth and could not do anything anymore. As a result, God would have to bring in a new age. Only by bringing in a new age could God do any work again. Unfortunately, the next age did not continue for long before it fell again. God once more could not do any work. Consequently, He had to bring in another age. When one reads the Old Testament, he can see that one age came after another had degraded. One age rose only to see it wane again. Another age rose and then also failed again.

I would like you to realize that God's work in turning the age is always done through men. Before a new age is ushered in, there are always men in the previous age who are used by God particularly to turn the age. And in every age-turning work, God purposely uses young people. The two most obvious examples are Samuel and Daniel. (*Men Who Turn the Age,* pp. 5-6)

* * *

During these years, among a few churches, often I have emphatically charged the brothers and sisters that they must take care of the young people. Because I emphasize this point, it makes the older ones feel very uncomfortable. Sometimes some of them say, "Brother Lee is simply causing the young people to rebel!" Today I speak this before the Lord. The reason I purposely encourage young people is that I clearly realize one thing: if a church cannot raise up the young people, this church has no future. If a local church that has been meeting for many years is not able to raise up the new ones to serve the Lord, it will be like a couple who have been married for many years without children. When this couple have grown old, what would happen to the family? This is why I conclude that a church must have young people at all costs. The church needs the second generation. The future of the church hinges on the young people. (*The Elders' Management of the Church,* pp. 108-109)

* * *

For the future of the Lord's work, I would ask the older ones to pray much for the young people. The future of the work and the usefulness in the future, no doubt, are with the young people. From the view of saving souls, we should treat older ones and younger ones equally. From the view of the future of the work, however, we should put our emphasis on the younger ones. If the church or the work fails to gain young people, it will be like a family that has only some childless old people: an old grandfather who is eighty-five years old, a father who is sixty years old, and a son who is nearly forty years old. There are no younger ones under them; there are no crying ones or shouting ones. Rather, everyone is well-behaved. This is abnormal.

If a family has only an eighty-five-year old grandfather, a sixty-year-old father, and a forty-year-old son, certainly no one will be rolling on the floor. Even if any of them desires to roll on the floor, he would not have the strength to do it. Therefore, all year round they live in quietness, orderliness, and loneliness. Brothers and sisters, we can be sure that such a family does not have to sell its house; the house will become someone else's house before long. In the same manner, when you visit a church, if you see throngs of young people there, then you should praise the Lord that the church has a future. You do not need to ask whether those young people are good or bad. Just as in a family, it does not matter how naughty the children are; they are still better than none. If there are no children, the family is doomed to hopelessness. Some children who are undesirable today may become desirable tomorrow. There is always hope. (*How to Lead the Young People,* pp. 13, 14)

* * *

The future of the Lord's recovery is very promising. At present, in the United States there are at least seven thousand seeking saints in the Lord's recovery. Over the next ten years, many of our children will become members of the church. When some of them are in their twenties, they will be quite useful to the Lord. Brother Nee, for example, was raised up by the Lord when he was only nineteen. (*Life-study of 1 Peter,* p. 285)

GOING TO THE YOUNG PEOPLE

Now we come to the matter of gaining the young people. Every church must go to the young people. In any field the future is with the young people. If an industry or a school does not gain young people, that industry or school has no future. This generation is the generation of the young people. However, this does not mean that we do not appreciate the older ones. (*The Spirit and the Body,* p. 106)

* * *

I realize that more and more the going on of the Lord in His recovery will be with the young people. No doubt the spread of the recovery in this country and elsewhere will be mainly with them. (*Life-study of Ephesians,* p. 586)

* * *

Furthermore, we must also do the children's work in a serious way because the children are the future of the church. You may want to consider preaching the gospel to the children first. (*Truth, Life, the Church, and the Gospel—The Four Great Pillars in the Lord's Recovery,* p. 97)

* * *

If, starting from now, we use our effort to work on the gospel for children whose ages range from six to twelve, then after ten or twelve years, they will be those who will rise up to bear the responsibility of the church service. This way may seem slow, but it is actually very fast. This way is also profitable. (*Truth, Life, the Church, and the Gospel—The Four Great Pillars in the Lord's Recovery,* p. 130)

* * *

Today several young brothers are elders in various halls. In 1949 when we began the work in Taiwan, the parents of these brothers were not married. They were brought together by us. Thirty years later, their children have grown and are serving in the church, bearing important responsibilities. Similarly, last November I was in the Philippines and was greatly surprised, because a new generation of serving ones has replaced the older generation; a younger generation has been raised up. The co-workers, elders, and my translators were young brothers who were born after 1950. This situation shows that the children's work is very important. (*Crucial Words of Leading in the Lord's Recovery, Book 5: Concerning Various Aspects of Church Service,* p. 83)

* * *

For the future of the Lord's recovery, our burden is still for the students. Since nearly all the full-timers will come from the college campuses, we should bring in the students. The more students we bring in, the better. (*Vessels Useful to the Lord,* p. 50)

* * *

The urgent need in the Lord's work today is that we would do the campus work to gain the young people for the Lord's recovery so that we may have a promising future. (*Vessels Useful to the Lord,* p. 72)

THE FUTURE OF THE LORD'S WORK DEPENDING ALTOGETHER ON THE YOUNG PEOPLE

If we read through the Bible carefully, we will discover a fact: It is not easy to find a case showing that God called an old person to do a new thing or a thing of great consequence. This may discourage the older brothers and sisters, but it is something undeniable. Indeed, we cannot see that God ever called an old person to do a new thing. Seemingly, Moses received God's call when he was eighty years old, but if we carefully read the Bible, we will see that actually the first time he received God's call was not when he was eighty years old. Rather, when he was still young, God's calling had already begun in him. If you read on, whether it was Joshua, Caleb, Samuel, or David in the Old Testament, or whether it was the twelve disciples called by the Lord Jesus in the New Testament, when they were first gained by the Lord, none of them was an old man. Not only is this true in the Bible, but even in all of church history it is hard to find a strong illustration to show that God called an old man when He had a new and important thing to do. We can say that virtually everyone used by God to begin a new thing or chosen by God to turn the age was a young man.

Furthermore, nearly every work that the young people were called by God to do was a work that turned the age. God called Moses to turn one age, and He called Joshua to turn another age. Obviously, His calling of Samuel turned another age. The prophethood, priesthood, and kingship all hung on this young man Samuel. He was truly one who turned the age. David was also one who turned the age. Furthermore, we can see that Daniel and his three friends were young ones among the people in captivity. Through them God turned that age of captivity. Then in the New Testament, the first to emerge was John the Baptist. We know that he was a young man called by the Lord. God used him to turn the age at his time. We can go on to look at Paul, who was an apostle especially used by God. The Bible says that he was a young man when he was visited by the Lord (Acts 7:58). We all admit that Paul was a man who turned the age. (*How to Lead the Young People,* pp. 3-4, 5)

* * *

All those who were in the initial stage of the Lord's recovery of the proper church life over fifty years ago were young people in their twenties. Very few were over twenty-five. Most were either in high school or in college. (*Fellowship with the Young People,* p. 8)

* * *

I dare not overstate the case, but my feeling is that the work that the Lord started among us in the East thirty years ago also considerably bore the nature and element of an age-turning work. For the carrying out of all these works of great consequences, God always called young men.

We already saw this clearly more than twenty years ago. Therefore, from that time on we paid a great deal of attention to gaining the young intellectuals in the universities and hospitals. Thank the Lord, this work had good progress from 1936. The Lord gained a good number of young people from the Union Medical College in Peking, from a certain hospital in Tientsin, from the Ch'i Lu University in Tsinan, from the College of Nursing in Shanghai, and from some universities in Nanking. Many young medical students, resident physicians, nurses, and even professors became our brothers and sisters. About ten years later, among us nearly all the co-workers and responsible ones in the churches all over the country were the young people gained at that time. Therefore, after the War of Resistance against Japan [1937-1945] was won and the country was restored, the Lord brought us back to Shanghai where there was a small work of revival again in the regions of Nanking and Shanghai. At that time we concentrated nearly seventy to eighty percent of our efforts on the young people. Within those two to three years all the work among the college students received much blessing from the Lord. Many young ones were gained by Him. By saying this much, I hope that the brothers and sisters can see the importance of the young people's work. This should create a heart in us to appreciate the young brothers and sisters. (*How to Lead the Young People,* pp. 5-6, 11-12)

HELPING THE YOUNG BELIEVERS

We should pay particular attention to the young people in our work in each locality. Today Satan's organizations and philosophies pay particular attention to young people. Can we not infer that God is paying attention to young people as well? This does not mean that the souls of older people are not precious in God's eyes, but it does mean that for the sake of God's work and for the future of the gospel, there is more hope with the young people. Our gospel work should place special emphasis on high school and college students. We should spend and pour out our all to save, cultivate, edify, and lead these young ones. (*The Collected Works of Watchman Nee,* vol. 55, p. 49)

* * *

With the exception of Joshua and Caleb, those who were

qualified and ready to take possession of the land were younger ones. They were of the second generation. The older ones, those of the first generation, had passed through many things and had learned many lessons. However, they were not qualified to enter into the land. The lessons learned by the first generation surely became part of the heritage passed on to the second generation. Their children certainly inherited from their parents all the lessons they learned during the forty years in the wilderness. By their birth the younger ones were put into a position to inherit the tradition of their family and all that their parents had experienced.

I believe that the fathers spoke to their children about their experiences in Egypt, in the exodus from Egypt, and in the wilderness. No doubt, the fathers spoke about how they were cruelly treated as slaves in Egypt, about how God in His mercy sent Moses to deliver them from bondage, about how they kept the Passover on the fourteenth day of the second month, and about how they marched out of Egypt and crossed the Red Sea. The fathers must have also explained to their children that they entered into the wilderness without food but that God fed them with manna and supplied them with water from the smitten rock. They might have also explained that although they eventually felt that manna was loathsome, they nevertheless appreciated it. The people did not grow any crops, but for forty years they daily received the heavenly supply of manna. Furthermore, the younger ones learned about Moses and about the great help he rendered to the people of Israel. Moses himself was not allowed to enter into the good land, but he contributed many constructive factors to God's people.

The second generation did not pass through as much as the first generation did, but they received the benefit of what the first generation experienced. I believe that the older generation told the younger generation about all they experienced, enjoyed, and suffered. This speaking was part of the raising up, or the building up, of the second generation. What the first generation experienced was not experienced in vain, for it was passed on to the second generation. What the older ones experienced actually was not effective for them, but it was very effective in building up the younger ones. Therefore, God was able to prepare from the second generation more than six hundred thousand men with a rich inheritance and strong background who were qualified to be formed into an army to fight with Him and for Him.

The principle is the same with us in the Lord's recovery today. The recovery has been in the United States for twenty-seven years and has passed through many things. Do you think that all these things have been in vain? They certainly have not been in vain. These things are being passed on to the younger ones in the Lord's recovery and will be very effective in building them up and preparing them to fight with God and for God. The younger ones in the Lord's recovery have a rich inheritance. Because this inheritance is being passed on to the younger ones and even being constituted into them, I have the full assurance that when a further testing comes, there will be a very positive result. (*Life-study of Numbers,* pp. 368-369)

THE LEADING IN THE BODY CUTTING SHORT AN INDIVIDUAL'S JOURNEY

There is a strong relationship between a person's spiritual journey and the leading of the Holy Spirit. Why is there the need of the leading of the Body? It is because with the leading of the Body one can somewhat cut short an individual's spiritual journey. If a brother is left to himself, he may have to stumble for ten years before he can come up with something. But now through the Body he may acquire the same thing in one evening. If such a brother will take the judgment of the Body, he will save a lot of time. The use of authority in the church is for the purpose of cutting down mistakes and shortening the journeys. (*Messages Given during the Resumption of Watchman Nee's Ministry,* vol. 2, p. 334)

* * *

Unless there is a group of young people who are saved to receive proper spiritual help today, how can they gain the experience and be used by the Lord in the future? If there are no young people gained by the Lord today, after our departure there will be no one to succeed us. Then there will be a gap. We need to gain the young people in the church and in the Lord's work. Anyone who works for the Lord with insight needs to pay attention to this matter. If you see this, your heart will be burdened to love the young people regardless of whether they are good or bad. Having a young one who is not very desirable is better than having none at all. May the brothers and sisters as the Lord's lovers all love the young people for the future of the church and for the Lord's work. (*How to Lead the Young People*, pp. 10, 14-15)

* * *

Young people, this is a word from my heart. The Lord's recovery is spreading, and I have the assurance that it will spread at a good pace. But the rate of the expansion of the Lord's recovery depends upon the pillars. I believe there will be churches in all the major cities of this country and in all the leading countries on earth. For this, there is the need of the pillars. I hope that you young people will see this. If you see it, you will say, "Lord, I cannot deny that You have appointed me to Your way and that I have heard Your up-to-date word. I realize that I must experience Christ in a subjective way and that I must be perfected in the church life in Bethel. Lord, have mercy on me and grant me the grace I need."

Young people, my burden is that you realize that your responsibility is tremendous. If during the coming years many of you will be perfected, the Lord's recovery will spread at a rapid speed. How much the Lord has done through those who have been perfected to be pillars! What do you think the Lord could do if He had a hundred more?

My burden is not simply to release a message. It is to help you see that today we all have the golden opportunity to be perfected and to be made pillars...I believe that after a few years many of you will become pillars. (*Life-study of Genesis*, pp. 1060-1061)

PREPARING OURSELVES IN SEVERAL MATTERS

Now we need to prepare ourselves in several matters. First,

we must pursue and grow in the spiritual life, earnestly maintaining a living fellowship with the Lord, fully consecrating ourselves to Him and having proper dealings before Him. We are contacting not merely a religious object but a living person. He is the living Spirit who dwells in our spirit. Therefore, we can fellowship with Him and receive His shining, guidance, and supply, allowing Him to regulate us in great or small matters so that we may have genuine growth in life.

Second, we must be equipped in the truth. People read the Bible in black and white according to their own understanding, barely scratching the surface. In particular, the Chinese are filled in their mind with things such as filial piety, honor, humility, patience, and forgiveness. For this reason, when they read the passages in the Bible that talk about honoring the parents, loving the wives, and submitting to the husbands, they feel that these things are very good, because they are similar to the virtues taught by the ancient Chinese sages. Actually, the Bible is full of the light of truth and the revelation of Christ. We need to read, get the Lord's word into us, and get ourselves into His word so that we may be mingled with the word.

The Recovery Version of the New Testament can be called the crystallization of the understanding of the divine revelation, which the saints everywhere have attained to in the past two thousand years. Therefore, now we can simply open the Recovery Version, and regardless of which book or chapter we read, there are some footnotes and explanations that enable us to fully understand it at a glance and immediately see clearly as the veils in heaven open before us. We need to labor on these revelations and this light by studying and pray-reading them again and again, thereby equipping ourselves with the truth.

Third, we need to build up a good character. We have to admit that although we have a God-created character in us, our fallen and corrupted character is loose, lazy, careless, and sloppy. In 1953 when I held a training in Taipei, I put together a small book on thirty character traits—being genuine, exact, strict, diligent, broad, fine, and others—hoping that we could exercise to cultivate them little by little. We should not merely read them and quickly forget about them, like many Chinese who read the books written by Confucius and Mencius. We need to exercise ourselves in these thirty items to build up a character that is useful to the Lord. We need to pray to the Lord, because although we do not have the strength to do this, the Lord is the bountiful supply within us. In Philippians 4 Paul says, "What things are true, what things are dignified, what things are righteous, what things are pure, what things are lovely, what things are well spoken of...take account of these things" (v. 8). These things are all related to character. Then Paul goes on to say, "I am able to do all things in Him who empowers me" (v. 13). Therefore, we can all build up a good character in Him who empowers us.

Fourth, we must receive a higher education. In the process of receiving our education we should learn some languages, especially English, the international language with which we must become proficient. In addition, we should learn at least one other foreign language, be it Spanish, German, French, Japanese, or Korean. These are all major languages that are commonly used in the world today. In brief, we need to be familiarized with two other languages besides Chinese. Not only so, we also need to study and get into the depths of the Bible. For this purpose, it is best that we learn some Greek. The more we learn of literature and languages, the better it is. We must attain to some depth in the study of languages.

Fifth, we need to know history, recognize the situation and the tide of the world, and be aware of the condition on the earth today. We need to pay attention to these five items: life, truth, character, language, and common knowledge. We need to endeavor to practice these things while paying attention to our living. The Lord is living; to be sure, He can bear all our responsibility. Moreover, today the Lord's recovery on the earth is widespread. In this widespread recovery, we mutually care for and supply the needs of each other, which is a great help. Therefore, you should not be anxious; rather, you should diligently equip yourselves by laboring on these matters—life, truth, character, language, and a knowledge concerning world culture, history, current events, and present trends. In this way, we will be able to advance toward the goal to gospelize

Taiwan, Japan, Europe, Australia, and New Zealand. May the Lord bless us with His presence.

If Taiwan is to produce five hundred thousand brothers and sisters for the spread of the gospel overseas, then we need to have five million saints in Taiwan so that one out of every ten saints can go out. The people from Taiwan gospelizing the entire world, and the brothers and sisters from Taiwan trekking all over the earth—what a wonderful prospect that would be! Where will you go—to Africa, South America, Central America, North America, Eastern Europe, or Western Europe? We can pray to the Lord, "O Lord, where should I go? O Lord, where do You want me to go?" May we all answer the Lord, "O Lord, here am I; send me." (*A Blessed Human Life,* pp. 55-57, 58)

* * *

I encourage all the young people to get a college degree. Do not make spirituality an excuse for not studying. Rather, study more diligently than the secular students, get the highest grades, and go on for advanced degrees. Do not stop with one Ph.D., but get two or three Ph.D.'s. Also learn to speak a number of other languages. Gain the "Tyrian" skills and the "Egyptian" knowledge. Become a doctor in biology, medicine, or nuclear physics.

There is a need in the Lord's recovery today for those with the highest education. Young people, you must endeavor to gain the best education. Arrange your daily schedule in this way: seven and a half hours for sleep, one and a half hours for eating, one hour for exercise, eight hours for study, and six hours for spiritual things. If you expend your energy in this way, by the time you are thirty you will be able to begin your ministry like the Lord Jesus did (Luke 3:23). Continue your studies until you are thirty. If many take this way, we shall have no shortage of pillar makers.

Do not get married too soon. I do not like to see the brothers getting married before the age of twenty-five. Do not be burdened down too soon with marriage and children. Rather, use your time and energy for studying. The age of twenty-six is soon enough for brothers to begin having children. Furthermore, I do not like to see the sisters getting married before the age of twenty-two. If the sisters marry too early and have children too soon, they may be overburdened and even spoiled. Follow the schedule I recommend until you are twenty-five years old and see what will be the issue. This surely is good for God's recovery.

Do not stop your schooling too soon. You should get a master's degree, or preferably a Ph.D. All the church people must be learned ones. We are neither ignorant nor undereducated. Rather, we would have the highest education. We would acquire all the wisdom of the "Egyptians," but we would not work for the "Egyptians"—we would work for the holy tabernacle. We should be able to say, "I know medicine and nuclear science, but I am not working for that. I am working for the building up of the church. I have learned a trade, but I am not occupied with this. I am building the pillars for the temple of my God"...Be a person full of learning, but do not use your learning for secular business. Use it fully for the Lord's building work. Your life and your being must not only be transformed but also transferred. (*Life-study of Genesis,* pp. 1100, 1101-1102)

BRINGING THE YOUNG PEOPLE
INTO THE CHURCH LIFE
THROUGH THE HOMES

Scripture Reading: Acts 2:46-47; Rom. 16:5a; Acts 20:20; Heb. 10:25

I. We see clearly that the building of the church is based on home meetings; the home meeting is God's unique way to build His church and reach His goal—Acts 2:46-47; Rom. 16:5a:

A. In the early days of the church life, the apostles built up the church very quickly, and the way of building was the small groups and home meetings—Acts 9:31.

B. The home meetings are the top way, the super way, and eventually the unique way to meet—Rom. 16:5a and footnote 1.

C. At the very beginning the way created by the Holy Spirit and ordained by God was to meet in two ways, in the congregational way and in the home way—Acts 20:20.

D. The home meetings are the unique way for the increase and building up of the church.

II. We should endeavor to bring the young people into the practice of the church life through the homes; the small group becomes our practical church life:

A. We need to be in a definite local church that we can say is our local church; those who are not in the church life are orphans without a home; the day we came into the church life, we knew that we had come home.

B. To bring the meetings to the homes is the very
heart of the God-ordained way; it is a great failure
in the Lord's recovery if we cannot bring the meetings to the homes:
   1. The influence of the home meetings is most helpful for the families of the saints; from early days
   the children will be surrounded by a spiritual
   atmosphere, and will have constant opportunity
   to see the reality of eternal things—2 Tim. 3:15.
   2. The children in the home meetings will be preserved from drifting with the current of the age;
   in the end, the family will become proper and
   normal.
C. According to today's situation, you should not consider that to recover someone, you must bring that
person to the big meetings in order to be successful; as long as he can come to the home meetings
every week, that will be very good—Acts 2:47; John
15:16:
   1. The big meetings cannot keep them, but the meetings from house to house bring people into the
   foundation of the church; once a person joins the
   home meetings, he is kept; this is God's wisdom.
   2. To bring the young people in is easy, but to keep
   them is not so easy; begin by keeping them
   through their junior high years; then you have
   to keep them through their high school years;
   finally, labor to keep them through college; after
   that, they will be safe and secure.
D. We need the young people to go to the campuses,
especially those who are eighteen and nineteen
years old; all the young people in the church life
are useful; this is why we have to work with our
high schoolers:
   1. The gospel must go out from the homes; even
   the campus work can go out from the homes; for
   a church to be strong, the home meetings must
   be built up.
   2. The young people in the church can invite others

to the homes of the middle-aged ones and of the young couples; all these homes need to be open and ready to receive the young people.

E. Actually, the church life will be carried out practically in the group meeting; the most important thing today is to have our own group meeting, which can be considered as our own assembly—Heb. 10:25.

F. We need to lead the young people to come together to break bread and teach them to understand what the breaking of bread is and what its significance is; this is part of their church life.

Excerpts from the Ministry:

THE UNIQUE WAY TO MEET

When the day of Pentecost came, the church began with one hundred twenty as the initiation. Then that initiation brought in on the very first day of the church life three thousand, then on another day five thousand. They began to meet not according to the Jewish congregational way of the Old Testament, nor according to the Roman way, nor according to the Greek way. Then who invented the way for the first group of Christians to meet? The Holy Spirit invented the way. We can say this because on that day, the one hundred twenty were filled with the Holy Spirit economically. And no doubt, the three thousand new converts were also filled with the Holy Spirit. Therefore, whatever they did on that day was initiated by the Holy Spirit. The main thing they did was to begin to meet in the temple for big congregations and in the homes. I like the two phrases in Acts 2:46, *day by day* and *from house to house*. It is clear that the way they met had two sides. Perhaps at least three thousand met daily in the temple, a big meeting place. And at the same time they met day by day in the homes.

According to the Greek expression in Acts 2:46, they met from house to house. This indicates that they did not select some houses that would fit their purpose. They met from house to house. They included every house. Today we should have our home meetings entirely according to the Holy Spirit's created

and ordained way...You have to see that at the very beginning
the way created by the Holy Spirit and ordained by God was
to meet in two ways, in the congregational way and in the
home way, not in selected homes, but in all homes. If you are a
Christian, if you are a believer, you have to open up your
home for meeting. This is the first pattern at the initiation of
the church life.

Since the Lord has shown this, I have begun to see all the
benefits of this God-created-and-ordained way. If a new one
would believe in the Lord, be baptized, and right away begin
to open up his home for meetings, this opening up of his home
would encourage him and even uphold him. Therefore, we can
see that the home meetings are the top way, the super way,
and eventually the unique way to meet.

BUILDING THE CHURCH
THROUGH THE SMALL GROUPS

The way to build the church may be illustrated by the
building of this hall...[A] brother was directing every group.
At that time we had over eighty full-timers whom this
brother formed into groups. One group made the stairway,
and a group of sisters sanded the handrails on the stairway.
They were all grouped together to do a certain part for the
building and eventually to put all the pieces together. Now we
are enjoying the building.

In the early days of the church life, when the apostles
were first raised up by the Lord, they built the church in this
way. It was very quick. The church in Jerusalem was built up.
Acts 9:31 says, "So then the church throughout the whole of
Judea and Galilee and Samaria had peace, being built up." In
a short time they were all built up. Could we say that all the
churches in the U.S.A. have been built up? You cannot say that
we have been built up because we have never taken the building
way. What is the building way? Small groups! Home meetings! (*The Home Meetings—The Unique Way for the Increase
and the Building Up of the Church,* pp. 7-9, 10-11)

MEETING IN EVERY HOME

According to our study, experience, and observation, I would say that we have found that the home meetings are the unique way for the increase and building up of the church. There are many positive things that come out of the home meetings. In the home meetings, everyone becomes a seeking one, a serving one, a preaching one, a teaching one, and one that spontaneously witnesses for the Lord. We hope to encourage all the saints in the Lord's recovery to have meetings in their homes.

The Greek phrase [*from house to house*] in Acts 5:42 indicates that not one house was missed. They met from house to house. We should not take the way of selecting some promising homes and then having the meetings in those promising homes. This is wrong. Every home of the believers is promising. We need to open up our home. First we can meet with our folks. We do not need to meet with others first. We can initiate our home meeting by meeting with our family members. We who have wives and children all can have a home meeting. We just meet with our folks, with our wife, and with our little children. To set up a meeting will stir up our heart and will fan the flame in our heart and in our spirit. First of all, we will be burned, and then our family will be burned. To set up a home meeting will keep out many evil things from our homes. (*The Home Meetings—The Unique Way for the Increase and the Building Up of the Church,* pp. 19-20)

OUR LOCAL CHURCH

If we are clear about the revelation in the Bible, we shall realize that the proper place to enjoy God today is in the local churches. In particular, we need to be in a definite local church that we can say is our local church. Although I love all the churches, I must be honest and testify that no church is as dear and lovable to me as the church in Anaheim because the church in Anaheim is my local church. We should all feel this way about the church in our locality.

How pitiful is the situation of most Christians today! Because they are not in the church life, they are orphans without a home. This was our condition before we came into the church life in the Lord's recovery. Not only were we orphans— we were wanderers. Before we came into the local churches, we never had the sense that we had come home or that we had reached our destination. But the day we came into the church life, we knew that we had come home. After wandering for years, we had finally reached our destination. Something deep within said, "This is the place." Many seeking Christians today, on the contrary, are still travelers; they are traveling from one denomination or group to another. But the day we came into the church life, our wandering ceased. The local churches are what God desires today. This is the last station of His revelation. (*The Genuine Ground of Oneness,* pp. 125-126)

BRINGING THE MEETINGS TO THE HOMES

To bring the meetings to the homes is the very heart of the God-ordained way. It will be a great failure in the Lord's recovery if we cannot bring the meetings to the homes. For the past twenty years in the Lord's recovery, we have been bringing people to the meeting halls. The more we work in this way, the fewer people we have, and the worse the condition of the homes becomes. More and more our meetings have become a kind of Sunday morning service. In Christianity many people "go to church" to listen to the singing of hymns and to attend the "service," but their homes are deplorable; their tables may still be scattered with mah-jongg game pieces. In the morning the family attends the service, but in the afternoon the mah-jongg game goes on in the homes. In order to overturn this degraded situation, we must bring the meetings to the homes. I hope that every home will be mobilized, that everyone will become a soldier, and that together we will become an army of the Lord. (*Crucial Words of Leading in the Lord's Recovery, Book 1: The Vision and Definite Steps for the Practice of the New Way,* p. 216)

HAVING HOME MEETINGS

The practice of the saints in the early church was to meet in their homes (Acts 2:46; 5:42; 20:20). To gain the increase, we need to have the home meetings. The church has been dead, passive, and low in the rate of increase because we did not have the crucial way to gain people through the home meetings. We need to have meetings in the new believers' homes, in the homes of the ones we gain through our preaching of the gospel. If we can only gain people without setting up meetings in their homes, this will be a failure. The most successful way is to gain people's homes for home meetings. Meetings in the homes will work to the uttermost. (*Elders' Training, Book 9: The Eldership and the God-ordained Way (1),* p. 10)

* * *

The meetings in believers' homes can be a fruitful testimony to the neighbors around, and they provide an opportunity for witness and gospel preaching. Many who are not willing to go to a "church" will be glad to go to a private house. And the influence is most helpful for the families of the Christians. From early days the children will be surrounded by a spiritual atmosphere, and will have constant opportunity to see the reality of eternal things. (*The Normal Christian Church Life,* p. 170)

THE BENEFITS OF BUILDING UP THE CHURCH IN THE HOMES

We need to realize that the way the Lord is taking is to build up His church in the believers' homes. Once the church is built up in the homes, the homes will be transformed. The husbands and the wives might have been arguing couples, but once they have meetings in their homes, they will stop their arguing. The children will also be preserved from drifting with the current of the age. As a result, the family will become proper and normal. (*Crucial Words of Leading in the Lord's Recovery, Book 1: The Vision and Definite Steps for the Practice of the New Way,* p. 245)

THE SIX COMMISSIONS OF THE HOME MEETINGS

The first thing we must do is change our concept. The home meetings are not merely a method. From now on we will neither uplift the big meetings nor despise them. We will regard the big meetings and the home meetings equally. According to today's situation, you should not consider that to recover someone, you must bring that person to the big meetings in order to be successful. Of course that is very good, but you should not require this. As long as he can come to the home meetings every week, that will be very good. First, lay this foundation in him. Second, the home meetings should strive to recover those who have not been meeting for a long time. In Taipei, there are tens of thousands of brothers and sisters who have not been meeting. The three to five thousand of you who are meeting regularly must all be in the home meetings to recover those who have not been meeting for a long time. Third, preach the gospel widely. The home gospel must go out from the homes. Even the campus work can go out from the homes. The homes are the foundation. If the homes are not strong and even you yourself need shepherding, then who can shepherd? If the home meetings are not strong, even the children's work cannot be done. For a nation to be strong, the homes must be strong. For a church to be strong, the home meetings must be built up. The homes are the foundation, the base, of all activities. Fourth, keep the people. The home meetings must keep and uphold people and even cause people to want to come back. You have to work on the home meetings to such an extent that they have the power to attract and keep people. Fifth, you need to strengthen the riches in the home meetings. The content of the home meetings must be rich. Sixth, when the home meetings become so rich, the highest goal of expressing Christ will be attained. (*On Home Meetings,* p. 20)

*   *   *

According to the present situation, the first thing that the home meetings need to do is to restore those who have not been meeting for a long time. We hope that all the brothers and sisters will be mobilized to seek out, according to their addresses, those who have not been meeting for a long time and restore them to attend the home meetings. The second thing is to motivate every brother and sister, whether old or young, as long as he has a house, to open his house at least once every two weeks. You should have a gospel meeting in the home every other week. You need to gradually educate and enlighten people in the home meetings, providing them with the gospel materials and encouraging them to speak for the Lord and to open their homes. From house to house, every house should preach the gospel. The third thing is to do your best to keep people coming to the meetings. When a person comes, stick to that one; you must keep him. The responsibility for keeping people cannot rest on the elders, co-workers, or a few people. The responsibility for keeping the people must rest on the home meeting, that is, on all the brothers and sisters. This is a great responsibility for the home meeting. The fourth thing is to strengthen the home meetings. To have rich meetings, you must work the Lord's word richly into the home meetings. The fifth thing is to cause the home meetings to reach God's purpose for the church. The Lord desires to gain a living Body to express Him on the earth. (*On Home Meetings,* pp. 63-64)

ONLY THE HOME MEETINGS
BEING ABLE TO KEEP PEOPLE

When it comes to God's work, the beginning is always the best. After it is handed over to man, it begins to go downhill. The beginning of Acts was the best. There was the "skating rink" in the big meetings to skate people in. Many skated in. Then there were the meetings from house to house to bring people into the foundation of the church. Once a person joined the home meetings, he was kept. This is God's wisdom. (*On Home Meetings,* p. 16)

* * *

We need the young people to go to the campuses, especially those who are eighteen and nineteen years old. All the young people in the church life are useful. This is why we have to work with our high schoolers. After graduating from high school, they all will be on the campuses to effectively contact the freshmen. People over twenty-five have a more difficult time in contacting freshmen. They are not as useful and prevailing as the younger saints on the campus. There is an open door for the eighteen-year-old freshmen to contact other freshmen. A person is most effective when he contacts a person who is his same age. Someone who is eighteen may not easily talk with me because I am much older than he is, but it is so easy for an older man to talk with me. We can talk because we are birds of the same feather. Birds of the same feather can talk together.

The young people's preaching of the gospel on the campuses, however, should be in coordination with all the saints. Since we may not have that many young ones, we need many homes of the saints for coordination in the gospel work. Every young person who goes to the campus needs a home for his contacts. A young person who catches eighteen new ones should be able to bring all eighteen into the living rooms of the saints. We need living rooms to receive all these new contacts. All the ages can be used. No one is too old. The older saints can open up their homes to these new contacts. Even though the older saints have opened their homes, they can keep themselves in the background and invite some middle-aged saints to serve the new ones in the living room. This is coordination.

The younger you are, the more you should be in the front to take care of the new young ones. The older you are, the more you should be at the back. It would be good for the older ones to buy the groceries, cook the food, and wash the dishes to serve the young people and their contacts. The young ones should go to the campus and the middle-aged saints should serve the young people in the living room. Our living rooms should be filled with the enjoyment of Christ, especially through singing and psalming. Such an atmosphere of enjoyment and mutuality requires a great deal of coordination.

If all the churches practice preaching the gospel in the campus work in this way, we will have a prevailing church life. One of the best ways for the churches to get new contacts is to send our young people to the campus. The best fishing ponds for the Lord's recovery are the college campuses. We should send our fishermen to the fishing ponds. Then the older saints can stay home to prepare snacks, refreshments, and the best dinners to gather the new contacts at least once every four weeks. The living rooms will catch them.

We need a young army that can be sent to the campuses to bring in more young people, but all the older and middle-aged saints are also needed. We should not be discouraged that we may be too old to go to the campus. The church's gospel preaching needs all the saints. Because the local churches in the Lord's recovery are standing on the genuine ground of oneness, we can have a very good coordination. We all need to learn so that we can have the best coordination.

We should not preach the gospel in an individualistic way. We also should not invite people to our homes or serve them dinner in an individualistic way. We should do everything corporately in the Body. This needs much fellowship and coordination. If we have the faith to apply the truth in the Bible, we will have the power, and if we have the coordination in the Body, nothing will frustrate our preaching. Our preaching will be powerful and prevailing. Then we will gain many young people for the Lord's recovery in this generation. (*Preaching the Gospel on the College Campuses,* pp. 15-16)

* * *

The young people in the church can invite others to the homes of the middle-aged ones and of the young couples. All these homes need to be open and ready to receive the young people. When they come in, serve them something to eat and drink. This will touch their heart. In preaching the gospel we do not need any gimmicks. We should simply pray, preach the word, and open our homes. It is difficult for the young people both to go to the campuses and to prepare their homes to receive others. We need the youngest ones to go to the campuses, the oldest ones to pray, and the middle-aged ones to prepare their homes. Day and night the homes need to be ready. (*The Spirit and the Body,* p. 108)

* * *

We should endeavor to bring [the new ones in the small groups] into the practice of the church life. We can charge them to go and visit people in the same way that we reached out to them. We may go out with them and bring them one by one into the same practice. Eventually, this small group becomes our practical church life. It is a miniature of the church in which we are. Actually, the church life will be carried out practically in the group meeting.

In a larger meeting of, for example, two hundred, we can only do things in a general way and give a general word of fellowship. All of the detailed items of the church life, however, should be carried out in the group meetings. The fellowship, the intercession, the mutual care, the shepherding, and the teaching will all be realized in the group meeting. Then the entire church will be brought on through the small groups. In a church of two hundred saints, there may be twenty groups of ten or twelve who can even do a more thorough work than the elders. If a church desires a continual increase, they must make use of the groups.

THE NEED TO HAVE OUR OWN GROUP MEETING

My main burden is that all of us need to have our own group meeting. In Hebrews 10:25 the apostle Paul told the saints not to forsake the assembling of themselves together. We may forget everything, but we should not forget our own group meeting. All of the mothers know that they could never forget their own children. If we would take care of a group meeting in this way, the church where we are will be a great success.

In particular, the older sisters among us should pray in a definite way to become involved in their own group meeting. They can pray for this group as a whole and for each new member by name. The sisters must pray particularly for each group member a few times each day. Our prayer must lay the tracks for the locomotive to run on. So we must not pray in a general way but in a particular way.

Because we labored in a general way in the past, we do not have the adequate fruit. Today we must first concentrate our effort to bring a few new ones to be baptized. The second step is to have home meetings with them in order that they may be cherished and nourished. In a short while we can group them together to form a group meeting of two or three. As I have indicated previously, the most important thing today is to have our own group meeting. This can be considered as our own assembly (v. 25). (*Talks concerning the Church Services, Part 2*, pp. 62-63)

HOW TO BRING THE JUNIOR HIGH AND HIGH SCHOOL STUDENTS INTO THE CHURCH LIFE

We need to have a proper view of the church life. When we

arranged the specific services, we pointed out that the students should attend the meetings at the hall that is closest to their school. Therefore, when a student gets saved, we have to do our best to encourage him to do this. We should introduce him to the hall that is closest to his school. In this way he will become one of the saints belonging to that hall. This will also make it convenient for the students to come together for fellowship after school. Of course this matter will not be very easy to work out because the junior high students and the high school students have very tight study schedules. Most of them also live at home and must go home after school. It is also hard for them to go out during the weekends. Regarding this point, we must be flexible and know how to adjust according to the need of the situation.

For example, first we must bring them to the Lord's table meeting. It would be best if they could attend the Lord's table meeting on the Lord's Day. If they cannot do so (for example, if their parents would not allow them to come), then we can arrange to meet at an appropriate time during the week after school and lead them to break bread at a saint's home near the school. We have to learn to lead them to remember the Lord properly. Whether we do this or not will make a big difference. We need to lead them to come together to break bread and teach them to understand what the breaking of bread is and what its significance is. This is part of their church life.

Therefore, in order to adapt to their situations, we could have a meeting to remember the Lord on a weekday in the early evening at a saint's home near the school and lead ten or twenty of them to break the bread. By doing this, we will bring them into the church life and make that meeting a part of the church. This will give them a deep impression. (*Vessels Useful to the Lord,* pp. 43-44)

LESSON NINETEEN

THE YOUNG PEOPLE NEEDING
THE HUMANITY OF JESUS
FOR THE CHURCH LIFE

Scripture Reading: Exo. 25:10-11; 26:15, 19; 1 Tim. 3:15-16;
1 Thes. 4:3-4; Phil. 4:8; 2:5-8; 2 Tim. 2:22; 3:16; 1:7; 4:22

I. From the types in the Scriptures we can see the need
of a proper humanity for the church life—Exo. 25:10-11;
26:15, 19:

A. We have seen that the Ark and the tabernacle signify Christ and the church—the Ark is Christ and
the tabernacle is the enlargement of the Ark; just
as the tabernacle is the enlargement of the Ark,
so the church is the increase and enlargement of
Christ—25:10-11:

B. The boards of the tabernacle were also made with
the same material and in the same way as the
Ark—acacia wood overlaid with gold—26:15, 29:

1. The boards are to be standing up; gold is valuable, weighty, and shining, but gold is not
capable of standing by itself; in order for the
boards of the tabernacle to stand up, there is the
need for the acacia wood—v. 15.

2. We need humanity, and we also need divinity,
but it is the humanity in the church that causes
the church to stand up—1 Tim. 3:15-16.

3. The church is the church of the living God; the
church must have God living in it, and this
church of the living God is the pillar and base of
the reality.

II. Satan's main target today is the young people; he injects all his evil, satanic, devilish concepts and ideas into the young and fresh mentality of the young generation—Rom. 12:2; 2 Cor. 10:4-5; Eph. 4:17-24:

A. The young brothers and sisters in the church life must be clear that the source of all the damage in the mentality is Satan; the young people in the church must repudiate the concepts that they have held in the past.

B. The first issue of this kind of mental damage is fornication—1 Cor. 6:9-11:

1. Nothing damages our humanity like fornication; any act we commit is outside our body, but fornication damages our body—v. 18.

2. Because the church life is a meeting life, a communal life, we have considerable contact with one another—1 Thes. 4:3-5, 7; Heb. 13:4:

a. We must possess our vessel in sanctification and honor, not in the passion of lust; this is to be safeguarded against committing fornication—1 Thes. 4:3-5.

b. God's will is that His redeemed people, the believers in Christ, should live a life of holiness according to His holy nature, a life wholly separated unto Him from anything other than Him; for this He is sanctifying us thoroughly—5:23.

c. For the Lord's name, for the church's testimony, for your protection, and for the honor of your physical body, you must follow this principle of not being alone with a member of the opposite sex—Gen. 49:3-4; Heb. 12:16, footnote 1.

C. The second issue of the devilish concepts indoctrinated into the minds of the young people is to commit suicide:

1. Satan has indoctrinated the mentality of the young people with the concept of suicide; we all must pray and stand against such subtlety of the enemy.

2. Satan's whole purpose is to damage humanity so that man cannot be used for God's purpose.

D. The third issue of the indoctrination of devilish concepts is mental illness:

1. Paul says that God has given us a spirit of sober-mindedness; we must be exceedingly healthy in our thinking, concepts, and ideas, and we need to have a sound mind—2 Tim. 1:7.

2. Problems in the heart are often the cause of mental problems; if a person's mind is under attack by the enemy, this is an indication that his heart is wrong in some way—Col. 2:1-2.

III. We are in exactly the same kind of situation today as was the early church; at that time the church was degraded and society was ruined; it is clear that it is the same today—1 Thes. 4:3-4:

A. We must all realize that we are in a situation that requires the Lord's humanity for His recovery; there must be a group of people to stand against the tide of this age—2 Tim. 3:1-5.

B. The proper cure for this age, the proper dose for this generation, is the humanity that comes from the man Jesus; the proper humanity is the only healing power for today's generation—Matt. 5:13-16:

1. The Lord will use the church as a remedy for today's crooked and perverse generation; the remedy for such a generation is a church with the proper humanity—Acts 2:40; Phil. 2:15.

2. If the young people in the church take the humanity of Jesus, they will be the proper remedy for this generation.

C. Today in the church life the Lord is going to recover His humanity; we not only need His power; we need His humanity; we not only need what He can do; we need what He is.

D. The proper humanity shining forth through the young brothers and sisters will be a strong testimony and remedy to this present age; this humanity will also cause us to have the strongest church life.

E. It is abundantly clear that we need a strong, adequate, and proper humanity in order to have the Lord's recovery in such a degraded time—Phil. 4:8-9; 2:5-8:

1. We do not need divine power as much as we need the humanity of Jesus to stand up in such a degraded age; this is the standing power of the acacia wood.

2. If we follow the course of today's age, we are like the jellyfish, without any backbone; whatever way the tide goes, the jellyfish follow.

3. We need a strong backbone to stand against the current of today's age for the Lord's recovery, and this backbone can issue only from the humanity of Jesus.

IV. In 2 Timothy we are able to see the apostle Paul's concept concerning five ways to take the humanity of Jesus—2 Tim. 2:22; 3:16; 1:7; 4:22:

A. The first was to call on the name of the Lord from a pure heart; when we call on the name of the Lord, we are really taking His humanity into us—2:22.

B. We not only need to call on the Lord, but we must also breathe in every word of the Scriptures; this is simply to pray-read the Word—3:16.

C. The third item is the Body life; Paul did not say simply to call on the Lord by yourself but with "those"—this is a corporate life; we enjoy the Lord's humanity by being with those who call on the Lord out of a pure heart—2:22.

D. Fourth, Paul tells us that we have a spirit to exercise—1:7.

E. Fifth, we have a wonderful person in our spirit: "The Lord be with your spirit"—4:22.

F. "We must pray for the entire situation of the Lord's recovery, that all the brothers and sisters in the local churches may have a full enjoyment of the humanity of Jesus. Then we will be the acacia boards, standing steadfastly against the current of this evil age. This will be our strong testimony, and this will bring the recovery of the local church life to all the leading cities"—*Christ as the Reality*, p. 151.

Excerpts from the Ministry:

THE ARK OF ACACIA WOOD

From the types in the Scriptures we can see the need of a proper humanity for the church life. We have seen in the past what the Ark and the tabernacle signify: the Ark is Christ, and the tabernacle is the enlargement of the Ark. So the tabernacle signifies the enlargement of Christ. This enlargement of Christ is His Body, the church, which is His fullness. When Christ as the Ark is increased and enlarged, there is the tabernacle. Then we have the church. Just as the tabernacle is the enlargement of the Ark, so the church is the increase and enlargement of Christ.

This can be proved since the Ark was made of acacia wood overlaid within and without with gold. "And they shall make an ark of acacia wood…And you shall overlay it with pure gold; inside and outside you shall overlay it; and you shall make a rim of gold upon it" (Exo. 25:10a, 11). The gold was made into a type of crown all around the four sides of the top of the Ark. By the word *rim,* or *crown,* we realize that the gold was mainly for decoration. It is not called the Ark of gold, but the Ark of acacia wood. So the main and basic structure of the Ark is wood. Wood in typology always signifies humanity, and acacia wood typifies the humanity of Jesus. Gold, which in typology signifies the divine nature, overlays the wood, which is the human nature. So Christ as the Ark is the human nature overlaid with the divine nature.

THE BOARDS OF THE TABERNACLE

We must also consider the tabernacle. The tabernacle is mainly composed of forty-eight boards. These boards are made of the same material and in the same way as the Ark. "And you shall make the boards for the tabernacle of acacia wood, standing up…And you shall overlay the boards with gold" (26:15, 29a). The Ark was made with acacia wood overlaid with gold, and the boards of the tabernacle were also made with the same material and in the same way—acacia wood overlaid with gold.

However, we must note what Exodus 26:15 says concerning the boards of the tabernacle. In this verse God says that the boards are to be standing up. We all know that gold is valuable, weighty, and shining, but in a sense gold is not capable of standing by itself. In order for the boards of the tabernacle to stand up, there is the need of the acacia wood. Acacia wood is quite adequate for standing up.

So in the tabernacle, again the acacia wood is the main structure. This means that the enlargement of Christ, the church, is composed mainly of the humanity of Jesus overlaid with divinity. We need humanity, and we also need divinity, but it is the humanity in the church that causes the church to stand up. As we look at today's situation, we see that in so many places the so-called Christian churches are not standing up but rather falling down. Some have even fallen already. They may say they are spiritual, but they are spiritual lying down, not standing up. They are short of the acacia wood, the proper humanity of the man Jesus. Both the Ark and the tabernacle had the acacia wood as their main substance. Just as Christ stood by the proper humanity, so His humanity alone can cause the church to stand.

GOD MANIFEST IN THE FLESH

Now we need to read 1 Timothy 3:15-16. These two verses in the Scriptures are wonderful and far beyond our understanding. "But if I delay, I write that you may know how one ought to conduct himself in the house of God, which is the church of the living God, the pillar and base of the truth. And confessedly, great is the mystery of godliness: He who was manifested in the flesh, / Justified in the Spirit, / Seen by angels, / Preached among the nations, / Believed on in the world, / Taken up in glory." The church is the church of the living God. The church is not just the church of God in heaven or the church in doctrine. It is the church of the living God. The church must have God living in it, and this church of the living God is the pillar and base of the reality.

The architecture used during the time 1 Timothy was

written was mainly that of Greece. Greek architecture utilized columns or pillars, which supported the entire building. The church of the living God is just like such pillars with a base to hold Christ as the reality. The word *truth* in verse 15 can also be translated as "reality." For the church to be such a pillar to hold Christ as the reality, the proper humanity of Jesus is required. This is shown in the following verse, where we are told that God was manifested in the flesh. As we have seen, the flesh is simply humanity. This proves that for the church to be the proper pillar to support Christ as the reality, the humanity of Jesus is required. (*Christ as the Reality,* pp. 85-86, 86-87, 88)

* * *

God has drawn a boundary line to keep the human spirit for His purpose, but Satan has done and still is doing many things to damage both the soul and the body of man. All he can do to our spirit is to deaden it by means of the conscience. Praise the Lord that he can only do that much! However, according to the revelation of the Bible, Satan has liberty to do whatever he can to damage our mentality (the main part of the soul is the mind) and our body. This is the subtlety of the enemy.

We cannot tell how many mental cases there are in today's society; they are innumerable. This condition is not only a kind of mental illness, but it is also the subtle work of Satan. Experts will tell you that in the history of humanity, there have never been as many mental cases as today. According to our experience, it is easy to deal with demon possession, but it is really difficult for any Christian to deal with a mental case. Satan is so subtle today. He is doing whatever he can to damage the mentality of man.

SATAN'S TARGET

Satan's main target today is the young people. There are more mental cases among the young people than ever before. He does not care so much for the older generation, but he seeks to destroy the young people. Young people today have many kinds of concepts and movements. The source of all these concepts and movements is Satan. Satan has indoctrinated the mentality of the younger generation with all these things. We need to pray against this satanic tendency among today's young people. They do not know the risk they are running and the danger they are in. By considering how greatly they have changed from 1965 until today, we may realize how much the enemy is working. Satan is so subtle. He injects all his evil, satanic, devilish concepts and ideas into the young and fresh mentality of the young generation. This is his primary aim; he is out to damage the human mentality. This is why the Bible speaks so much of having a sound mind. Do you believe that the mentality of the younger generation today is sound? I would say that it is absolutely unhealthy. Their way of thinking is altogether dangerous. All the young brothers and sisters in the church life must be clear that the source of all this damage in the mentality is Satan. All the young people in the church must repudiate the concepts that they have held in the past. I do not care what kind of concept you had before you came into the church life; whatever you had, you must give it up. I am afraid that it may be something of Satan to damage your mentality.

THE FIRST ISSUE: FORNICATION

The issue of this kind of mental damage is of three categories. The first is fornication. In the past five or six years, I have heard much concerning this matter. Among today's young people, especially the so-called hippies, there are innumerable cases of fornication. They live just like animals. They do not even care for this word *fornication*. I believe that in their dictionary they do not have such a word. It is all done without shame. In the whole Bible, the greatest and most sinful act in God's eyes is idol worship. Fornication is second. Idol worship is an insult to God, and fornication is a damage to humanity. God created humanity for His divine purpose, but Satan damages this humanity by fornication.

On some occasions, the Lord Jesus tore down all of the rituals and ordinances of the Old Testament. But He did not tear down the law concerning fornication; rather He enforced it even the more. When the Pharisees spoke with Him about divorce, the Lord asserted that Moses had allowed them to divorce their wives because of the hardness of their hearts, but it was not so at the beginning (Matt. 19:3-9). The Lord enforced the commandment regarding fornication much more than it had been in the Old Testament times (5:27-28). This is because nothing damages our humanity like fornication. Paul says that any act we commit is outside our body, but fornication damages our body (1 Cor. 6:18). Oh, the enemy is so subtle! He first injects so many devilish concepts into the mentality of the young people, and the first issue of this is fornication.

I would like to say a word to the young people. I am not speaking my own idea, but something from the divine Word. You young brothers and sisters should not enter into marriage so quickly, so lightly, and so easily. You must realize that marriage is a very holy relationship (Heb. 13:4). No marriage should be broken (Matt. 19:6, 9). Anyone who breaks the marriage bond is exceedingly sinful to God. You must take the matter quite seriously to the Lord. Once you are married, you should never be divorced. Nothing offends the Lord so much as a wrong marriage, and nothing damages our humanity more than fornication. It is not just a moral matter; it is a matter of damaging the humanity that God created for His purpose.

I believe that many of you are acquainted with the cesspool of fornication existing among so many young people today. Three years ago when I was in San Francisco, I heard many detailed reports concerning this situation. I simply could not stand it. To me this is not human life, but animal life. (*Christ as the Reality*, pp. 123-126)

* * *

Eating, drinking, and marriage were originally ordained by God for man's existence. But due to man's lust, Satan utilizes these necessities of human life to occupy man and keep him from God's interests. Toward the end of this age, this situation will be intensified and will reach its climax during the days of the Son of Man.

The characteristics of the days of Noah were eating, drinking, marrying, and giving in marriage. The characteristics of the days of Lot were eating, drinking, buying, selling, planting, and building. These last four characteristics indicate business. Consider the characteristics of today's world. The characteristics of this generation are eating, drinking, marrying, giving in marriage, buying, selling, planting, and building.

THE APPEARING OF THE MAN-SAVIOR

The conditions of evil living that stupefied the generation of Noah before the deluge and the generation of Lot before the destruction of Sodom portray the perilous condition of man's living before the Lord's parousia (presence, coming) and the great tribulation (Matt. 24:3, 21). If we would participate in the overcomers' rapture to enjoy the Lord's parousia and escape the great tribulation, we must overcome the stupefying effect of man's living today. (*Life-study of Luke,* pp. 334-335)

FLEEING OUR TEMPER AND LUST

Our age is an age of fornication and adultery. Every country is filled with immorality. Concerning this matter, so many have been drugged by "garlic" and have lost their sense concerning this sin. May this word sober us! We must stay away from today's trend. Nothing insults God more than fornication, which damages the man created by God in His image. We all must flee our temper and our lust. Flee your temper! Flee your lust! It is not an insignificant thing to lose our temper or to give in to our lust. Indulging in these things may cause us to be burned. Thus, we need to heed this sober word, a word that will force us to stay close to Christ.

Temper, a problem to every Christian, is like a gopher: it is hidden, subtle, and prevailing. We all must be on guard concerning it. Lust is also a great problem. I am sorry to say that even among saints there have been a number of cases of fornication. What a shame! Nothing is more shameful than fornication or adultery among the saints. This damages the people created by God, the church life, and the testimony of the church. Again and again the apostle Paul warned us that no fornicator would share in God's kingdom (1 Cor. 6:9-10; Gal. 5:19-21; Eph. 5:5). Those believers who commit adultery or fornication are through with the kingdom of the heavens. The kingdom people must have the highest standard of righteousness. Do not lose your temper or look at a woman to lust after her. Be careful! You need to consider these matters seriously and deal with the motive at the very root. This word is not a threat; it is a warning that forces us to stay close to Christ. (*Life-study of Matthew,* pp. 233-234)

* * *

Fornication has its source in lust. People would never have a chance to indulge themselves in this lust if they did not have some form of social life. Social life is a hotbed of fornication. A person who does not have a social life is not in danger of falling into fornication. If you live alone and have little contact with others, it is very unlikely that you will commit fornication. But the church life is a meeting life, a communal life. In other words, the church life is a social life. In order to have the church life, we cannot avoid having a communal life, a social life, in which we have considerable contact with one another.

According to history, the problem of fornication has come up over and over again in one church after another. The facts prove that Christian workers in particular are often snared by fornication because they have so much contact with others. Furthermore, fornication has been the factor in damage caused to those in the Pentecostal movement. In certain places this movement has been limited because of the sin of fornication.

In 1 Thessalonians 4:3 Paul says, "For this is the will of God, your sanctification: that you abstain from fornication." God's will is that His redeemed people, the believers in Christ, should live a life of holiness according to His holy nature, a life wholly separated unto Him from anything other than Him. For this He is sanctifying us thoroughly (5:23).

At Paul's time, both in Corinth and Thessalonica sensuality and immorality were rife in the pagan religions and even fostered by their pagan worship. Man was made for expressing God (Gen. 1:26). Nothing ruins man for this purpose more than fornication. This prevents man from being holy, separated unto God, and contaminates man to the uttermost in the fulfilling of God's holy purpose. Hence, the apostle strongly charges the newly converted Gentile believers, by sanctification unto God, to abstain from the damage and contamination of fornication, the most gross sin in the eyes of God.

We also need this warning today. In the United States and Europe males and females have social contact with hardly any limitation. Because of this situation, it is easy for people to fall into fornication. In order for churches to exist in these regions, there is a need of a warning concerning fornication.

In verses 4 and 5 of 1 Thessalonians 4 Paul continues, "That each one of you know how to possess his own vessel in sanctification and honor, not in the passion of lust, like the Gentiles who do not know God." To possess one's vessel is to keep it, to preserve it...To keep or preserve man's vessel in sanctification and honor, not in the passion of lust, is the safeguard against committing fornication.

Sanctification refers more to a holy condition before God; honor, more to a respectable standing before man. Man was created for God's purpose with a high standing, and marriage was ordained by God for the propagation of man to fulfill God's purpose. Hence, marriage should be held in honor (Heb. 13:4). To abstain from fornication is not only to remain in a sanctified condition before God, but also to hold and keep a standing of honor before man. Whenever someone becomes involved in fornication, he is contaminated, and his sanctification is annulled. Moreover, he loses honor before man. Not even unbelievers honor those who commit fornication. Therefore, we must know how to possess, keep, preserve, our own body in sanctification toward God and in honor before man. We must be those who are sanctified unto God and those who have honor before man. In order to be such persons, we must absolutely abstain from fornication and not give ground for suspicion in this matter. (*Life-study of 1 Thessalonians*, pp. 130-131, 131-133)

* * *

At this point I need to say a strong word, especially to the young people. Do not think that defilement is an insignificant matter. We were made by God in His image. Because we have the image of God, we are honorable, even according to our natural make-up. Although other sins may not damage our body, fornication causes direct damage to our physical body, a vessel of honor (1 Cor. 6:18; 1 Thes. 4:4). Because we have been regenerated, our body is now the temple of the Holy Spirit (1 Cor. 6:19). Therefore, not only do we bear the image of God in our physical body, but after regeneration our body is the temple of God. Therefore, you must keep your body in an honorable way. Nothing damages your body as much as fornication. The practice of the world today is utterly hellish, devilish, and satanic. How devilish it is for young people to have contact with one another without any restriction! I wish to warn all the young people, even the young brothers and sisters in the church life, to exercise certain restrictions upon their contact with one another.

As a young brother coming into the ministry, I went to Shanghai to receive help from Brother Nee. During those days, Brother Nee had many long talks with me. The first instruction he gave me, as a brother in the Lord's ministry, was never to contact a member of the opposite sex alone, but, for my protection, to always have the presence of a third party. I have never forgotten this word; it has been a great help and protection to me. By the Lord's mercy, I have followed his word throughout the years.

Remember, you are still in the flesh. For a male and a female of the same age to be alone gives opportunity for the enemy to tempt them. Because your past experiences have already convinced you of this, there is no need for me to say too much. Never consider fornication as an unimportant matter. As we have seen, nothing damages your honorable physical body as much as fornication. What a shame it is that some of those in the government want to legalize homosexuality! To do this is to turn this country into a Sodom.

Again and again in the New Testament the apostle Paul issued the warning that no fornicator would have any inheritance in the kingdom of God (vv. 9-10; Gal. 5:19-21; Eph. 5:5). When we come to Matthew 5 in our life-study, we shall see how strict the Lord Jesus was regarding this matter. Never be loose in contacting members of the opposite sex. For the Lord's name, for the church's testimony, for your protection, and for the honor of your physical body, you must follow this

principle of not being alone with a member of the opposite
sex. If you follow this principle, you will be preserved. Remember, due to his defilement, Reuben's natural status, the status
derived from birth, was altogether changed. (*Life-study of Genesis,* pp. 1248-1249, 1250)

* * *

When the elders realize that some young saints are dating
in an improper way, they must render them some help. They
should tell the ones concerned that it is altogether not safe
for a young brother to be with a young sister in a loose way.
(*Elders' Training, Book 4: Other Crucial Matters concerning
the Practice of the Lord's Recovery,* p. 110)

THE SECOND ISSUE: SUICIDE

The second issue of the devilish concepts indoctrinated
into young people's minds is to commit suicide. If you study
the proper statistics, you will see that the number of suicides
is much larger than it was five years ago. In the earlier years
of my ministry I hardly ever heard someone tell me that he
wanted to end his life. But in these last few years, a number
of young believers have come to me and expressed such an
intention. Where did this kind of thinking originate? Undoubtedly, Satan has indoctrinated the mentality of the young
people with this concept. We all must pray and stand against
such subtlety of the enemy. Satan's whole purpose is to damage
humanity so that man cannot be used for God's purpose. (*Christ
as the Reality,* p. 126)

* * *

The work of Satan on man's body results not only in
illness but also in death. Satan was a murderer from the
beginning, in the same way that he was a liar from the beginning (John 8:44). We should withstand not only Satan's
sickness but also his murdering. All thought of death is from
Satan. Every notion of death as a means to escape from anything is from Satan. Satan made Job think of death. He did
this not only to Job but also to every child of God. All notions
of suicide, death wishes, and premature death are temptations

from Satan. He tempts man to sin, and he also tempts man to die. Even thoughts of danger during one's travels are Satan's attacks. We must reject these thoughts whenever they come and not allow them to remain in us. (*Messages for Building Up New Believers*, vol. 3, p. 726)

THE THIRD ISSUE: MENTAL ILLNESS

The third issue of the indoctrination of devilish concepts is mental illness. If you will check with today's younger generation, you will see that so many do not have a strong mind. Their way of thinking and their concepts are altogether unsound and unhealthy. Paul says in 2 Timothy 1:7 that God has given us a spirit of sobermindedness. We must be exceedingly healthy in our thinking, concepts, and ideas. We need to have a sound mind. (*Christ as the Reality*, p. 126)

* * *

Problems in the heart are often the cause of mental problems. If a person's mind is under attack by the enemy, this is an indication that his heart is wrong in some way. Whenever the heart is wrong, it is easy for the mind to be in darkness or subject to attack. This is an important principle. Most cases of mental illness have their source in problems that exist in the heart. More than forty years ago, the superintendent of a large mental hospital told me that, according to his experience and observation, mental problems are caused by problems related to greed for money and sex. These are problems of the heart. Greed for money causes problems in the hearts of some, whereas lust causes problems in the hearts of others. Such problems cause the mind to come under attack. Through years of experience, we have learned that mental illness can be traced to problems in the heart. The mind is attacked because the heart is wrong. Perhaps someone has a certain ambition or desire in his heart. If this ambition or desire is not fulfilled and is not dealt with, the mind may be attacked. (*Life-study of Colossians*, p. 140)

TODAY'S SITUATION

We are in exactly the same kind of situation today as was

the early church. At that time the church was degraded and society was ruined, and it is clear that it is the same today. Therefore, we must all realize that we are in a situation that requires the Lord's humanity for His recovery. There must be a group of people to stand against the tide of this age. But what is the way for us to stand? Is it by divine power? (*Christ as the Reality,* p. 145)

HUMAN VIRTUES FOR A DEGRADED AGE

When Paul wrote [1 and 2 Timothy and Titus], the church was degraded, and under that kind of degradation, the need was not mainly for teachings or gifts, but human virtues. I believe that the message of these three books just fits today's situation. We are under such a degradation. What is the proper cure for this age? What is the proper dose for this generation? The answer is the proper humanity that comes from the man Jesus. The proper humanity is the only healing power for today's generation. I have confidence that the Lord will use the church as a remedy for today's crooked and perverse generation. The remedy for such a generation is a church with the proper humanity. I have the full assurance that if the young people in the church take the humanity of Jesus, they will be the proper remedy for this generation.

I do believe that today in the church life the Lord is going to recover His humanity. We not only need His power; we need His humanity. We not only need what He can do; we need what He is. I cannot believe that the miraculous gifts are the remedy for today's generation. Rather, the proper humanity shining forth through the young brothers and sisters will be a strong testimony and remedy to this present age. And this humanity will also cause us to have the strongest church life. The fruit of the Spirit is just the expression of the humanity of Jesus. (*Christ as the Reality,* pp. 140-141, 142)

* * *

It is abundantly clear from [1 and 2 Timothy and Titus] that we need a strong, adequate, and proper humanity in order to have the Lord's recovery in such a degraded time. We do not need divine power as much as we need the humanity of

Jesus to stand up in such a degraded age. This is the standing power of the acacia wood. If we follow the course of today's age, we are like the jellyfish, without any backbone. Whatever way the tide goes, the jellyfish follow. We do need a strong backbone to stand against the current of today's age for the Lord's recovery, and this backbone can issue only from the humanity of Jesus.

THE PROPER WAY

Then what is the way to enjoy such a humanity? In [2 Timothy 3:16-17; 2:21-22; 1:7; and 4:22] we are able to see five main items. By these we can see the apostle Paul's concept concerning the way to take the humanity of Jesus. The first was to call on the name of the Lord from a pure heart. "Flee youthful lusts, and pursue righteousness, faith, love, peace with those who call on the Lord out of a pure heart" (2:22). When we call on the name of the Lord, we are really taking His humanity into us. Then Paul referred to the Scriptures: "All Scripture is God-breathed..." (3:16). All Scripture is breathed out by God to make us genuine and proper men of God. We not only need to call on the Lord, but we must also breathe in every word of the Scriptures. This is simply to pray-read the Word. How important are these two items for taking the Lord's humanity! We must call on the Lord, and we must breathe in His Word.

The third item is the Body life. Paul did not say simply to call on the Lord by yourself but with "those" (2:22). This is a corporate life. We enjoy the Lord's humanity by being with those who call on the Lord out of a pure heart. Fourth, Paul tells us that we have a spirit to exercise. "For God has not given us a spirit of cowardice, but of power and of love and of sobermindedness" (1:7). And fifth, we have a wonderful person in our spirit: "The Lord be with your spirit" (4:22).

We have these five matters to practice: calling on the Lord, breathing in the Scriptures, having the Body life, exercising our spirit, and realizing the Lord Jesus within our spirit. This reveals the concept of the apostle Paul. How can we enjoy the humanity of Jesus? Simply by these five things. We have to call on the Lord, we must breathe in the Word, and we must do these things in a Body way in the church life. For this we have such a strengthening factor in our spirit. The Lord Jesus, who is the real humanity, is in our spirit. By exercising our spirit to call on Him and to breathe in the Word in a corporate way, we simply enjoy His humanity.

We must pray for the entire situation of the Lord's recovery, that all the brothers and sisters in the local churches may have a full enjoyment of the humanity of Jesus. Then we will be the acacia boards, standing steadfastly against the current of this evil age. This will be our strong testimony, and this will bring the recovery of the local church life to all the leading cities. (*Christ as the Reality,* pp. 146, 149-150, 151)

HOW TO LEAD THE YOUNG PEOPLE
(1)

Scripture Reading: Luke 9:55; Matt. 18:10; Luke 15:20, 4; 24:15, 17-19

I. If you want to help the young people, you must have an interest in them:

A. Do not find their faults at first; if you do, you cannot help them—Luke 9:55; Matt. 18:10:

1. Some have a special liking for the young people whom they consider good, but they purse their mouths and shake their heads when they see those whom they think are not good; this is wrong.

2. Oftentimes God will prove to us that our evaluation of those whom we think are good is inaccurate; instead, those whom we consider not good may be greatly used by God.

B. Regardless of whether the young people are good or bad, we need to treat everyone the same, and we need to like them and be concerned for them:

1. Play a game with them, and then talk to them about the Lord Jesus when the game is over; this is genuine capability.

2. However, if you cannot talk to them about the Lord Jesus because He is gone after you play ball, then your spirituality is false.

C. If we want to help the young people, we need to be interested in them; do not be concerned first about their mistakes, and do not condemn them at all— cf. Luke 24:13-35.

D. We should give the young people the feeling that we are their good friend, that we sympathize with them, and that we are interested in them and in their affairs.

E. We all need to have the loving and forgiving heart of the Father God and the shepherding and seeking spirit of our Savior Christ—15:20, 4; 2 Tim. 1:7:
   1. Do not classify people, because no one can tell what they will become.
   2. The spirit that God has given us is a spirit of love—v. 7.
   3. The church is not a police station to arrest people or a law court to condemn people, but a loving home, a hospital and a school.

II. Learn to contact the young people; helping the young brothers and sisters depends not on our ability to give them messages but on our regular, frequent contacts with them; remember not to talk about spiritual things at the initial contact with them:

A. When you contact the young brothers and sisters, do not begin by asking, "How many chapters of the Bible have you read today? Have you prayed?"

B. Such questions should not be brought up until you have had many contacts with them, maybe even after eight or ten times.

C. If you do it prematurely, it is easy to cause a negative reaction; if you mess up the whole thing, he may not receive the Lord for his entire lifetime.

D. Do not stir up his negative feeling by talking to him right away about reading the Bible or praying.

E. You must wait until you have more contacts with him and he feels that he likes you and that you also like him.

F. Once you have touched his feeling and earned his trust, then you can begin to talk about spiritual things.

III. Emphasize practicality instead of stressing doctrines; when helping the young people, give them something practical:

A. We should not put too much emphasis on doctrines, not only when we have personal contact with them but also when we are preaching the gospel or giving messages to them:

   1. If we give them only some doctrines and they come only to listen, there will not be much effect.

   2. The more we speak doctrines, the more the young people become dead, cold, and backsliding.

B. Because young people have many practical problems, we need to sense their feelings, beginning with these problems:

   1. We need to spend some time to study the problems of the young people in their practical living, including problems both before and after their salvation.

   2. Based upon our studies, when we preach the gospel or speak a word of edification to them, what we speak is practical and is related to the practical matters that we have touched in their lives.

Excerpts from the Ministry:

HAVING AN INTEREST IN THE YOUNG PEOPLE

First of all, I have already said this earlier, but now I want to say it again: If you want to help the young people, you must have an interest in them. I was in a place where there was a group of brothers and sisters who were forty and fifty years of age. None of them had anything good to say about the young people. Some of them told me, "Brother Lee, look at the young people among us. Do they look proper? They don't know the difference between the elderly and the young, between seniors and juniors. They give us a cold shoulder when they see us on the street. They stare at us when they see us at the entrance of the meeting hall. Brother Lee, you have to give a message to render some help to these young people so that they will know the difference between seniors and juniors, between the elderly and the young." At another time a brother in his fifties came to see me and said, "Brother Lee, look at the young people among us. They are so improper. When they walk, their steps are flying and their eyes are wandering. They are really out of order." Some time later while I was with a group of elderly brothers, one of them asked me to give a message that would teach the young people to be obedient. He said, "Our young people simply do not obey the elderly ones." That day I felt it was a good opportunity to say a word to them. Therefore, I said, "Brothers, you have mentioned to me many times how wrong the young people are. I would like to ask you, if the young people are right, then what need is there for you, the older ones? No doubt they are wrong, but what kind of example have you given them?" I spoke at some length to them that day with the intention to incite them to help the young people and have an interest in them. Do not find their faults at first. If you do, you cannot help them.

Some have a special liking for the young people whom they consider good, but they purse their mouths and shake their heads when they see those whom they think are not good. This is wrong. Oftentimes God will prove to you that your evaluation of those whom you think are good is inaccurate. Instead, those whom you consider not good may be greatly used by God. Therefore, it is hard to say that those whom we feel are good now will be good in the future, and those whom we feel are bad today will be bad tomorrow. We should never trust in our own judgment. This applies even to our evaluation of ourselves. We may be good today, but that does not guarantee that we will be good to the end. We may be bad today, but the Lord may turn us to be good tomorrow. Likewise, regardless of whether the young people are good or bad, we need to treat everyone the same, and we need to like them and be concerned for them. Do they walk as if they are flying? Then you should fly with them. Are their eyes wandering? You should also let your eyes wander. Are they playing ball? Play a game with them, and then talk to them about the Lord Jesus when the game is over. This is genuine capability. However, if you cannot talk to them about the Lord Jesus because He is gone after you play ball, then your spirituality is false.

Let me give you another example. Suppose you run into a

young brother on the street. You ask him where he is going, and he says, "I am going to a movie because I am very bored." Never rebuke him with a long face, saying, "Why are you going to watch a movie? How can you do that?" If you do this, you will not be able to help this young man. It is better for you to have a little conversation with him. Ask him what movie and which theater he is going to. Then walk with him for a short distance or call a taxi and ride with him. While you are on the way to the theater, you can talk to him about some of the things that are on your heart. You may ask him, "Brother, did you enjoy reading the Word in the last couple of days?" In this way you can begin to talk to him about reading the Bible. You can also talk to him about prayer and ask him if he has prayed recently. When you get to the theater, you may tell him, "Brother, here we are. You go in, and I'll pay for the taxi. I have to go to a meeting. Ten minutes before the end of the movie I will come back and be here waiting for you." Instead of being impatient with him, you are fully interested in him. If you have some money with you, you may ask him, "Brother, do you have your cash ready? Is it enough to buy the ticket? If not, I can give you some." Brothers and sisters, if you can do this, see whether or not you can lead him! I am afraid that you may be like a "lawyer" with an expressionless face, teaching him sternly and even condemning him. After being condemned by you, he may not be able to be delivered from movies for the rest of his life—he will not be able to live without watching movies. His going to the movies for the rest of his life will be due to your provoking. Do not think that I am talking nonsense. I know what I am talking about.

This is what the Lord Jesus did that day on the way to Emmaus. The Lord asked the two disciples, saying, "What are these words which you are exchanging with one another while you are walking?" (Luke 24:17). One of them replied, "Do You alone dwell as a stranger in Jerusalem and not know the things which have taken place in it in these days?" (v. 18). Of course, the Lord Jesus was very clear, but He still asked them, "What things?" (v. 19). They talked a great deal, and the Lord Jesus just listened patiently. They were walking downhill, and the Lord Jesus just walked with them. In the end, however, the Lord opened their eyes, and they turned around. Brothers and sisters, I believe that you all know what I mean by these words. Do you want to help the young people? Then, first of all you need to be interested in them. Do not be concerned first about their mistakes; do not condemn them at all. You should give them a feeling that you are their good friend, that you sympathize with them, and that you are interested in them and in their affairs. This is the chief point. (*How to Lead the Young People,* pp. 15-21)

* * *

As I have said before, the spirit of not shepherding and seeking others and being without love and forgiveness is spreading in the recovery everywhere. I believe that not having the Father's loving and forgiving heart and not having the Savior's shepherding and seeking spirit is the reason for our barrenness. I realize that you all work hard, but there is almost no fruit. The Lord says, "By the fruit the tree is known" (Matt. 12:33), but we are a tree without any fruit. Everywhere among us barrenness is very prevailing. A good, gentle, pastor may not have a particular gift, such as the gift of speaking; he may simply visit people and welcome them when they come to his meeting, but according to statistics, he will have a ten-percent yearly increase. We, however, do not have even a ten-percent increase. Can you see how barren we are? Many of you are good speakers, knowing the higher truths. The truths we hold are much higher than those in Christianity. However, we do not have fruit because we are lacking in the Father's loving and forgiving heart and the Son's shepherding and seeking spirit. We condemn and regulate others rather than shepherd and seek them. We are short of love and shepherding. These are the vital factors for us to bear fruit, that is, to gain people. I am very concerned for our full-time training. Do we train the young ones to gain people or to regulate people? We have to reconsider our ways, as Haggai said (Hag. 1:5). Our way is not right; something is wrong. (*A Word of Love to the Co-workers, Elders, Lovers, and Seekers of the Lord,* pp. 40-41)

HAVING THE LOVING AND
FORGIVING HEART OF OUR FATHER GOD
AND THE SHEPHERDING AND SEEKING SPIRIT
OF OUR SAVIOR CHRIST

I love Luke 15. Verse 1 says, "Now all the tax collectors and sinners were drawing near to Him to hear Him." The gentlemen and righteous men were not joined to Him, but the tax collectors and sinners were. Therefore, the Pharisees murmured and complained again. Then the Lord spoke three parables. The first is concerning a shepherd seeking the one, unique, lost sheep. Of one hundred, this one was a lost one, so the shepherd came purposely for him. Why did the Lord go to a house full of sinners and tax collectors? It was because among them there was one lost sheep of His, whom He had come to seek. The second parable is concerning a woman who lit a lamp and swept the house to seek her lost coin. The third parable is about the prodigal son. The shepherd is the Son, the woman is the Spirit, and in the parable of the prodigal son there is the Father. As the prodigal son was returning, he was preparing and considering what to speak to his father. He prepared himself to say, "Father, I have sinned against heaven and before you. I am no longer worthy to be called your son; make me like one of your hired servants" (vv. 18-19). While he was walking and thinking like this, the father saw him. Verse 20 says, "But while he was still a long way off, his father saw him and was moved with compassion, and he ran and fell on his neck and kissed him affectionately." That the father saw the son a long way off was not an accident. From the time the son left home, the father must have gone out to look and wait for his coming back every day. We do not know how many days he watched and waited. When the father saw him, he ran to him. This is the Father's heart. The father interrupted the son while he was speaking his prepared word. The son wanted to speak the word he had prepared, but the father told his servants to bring the robe, the ring, and the sandals and to prepare the fattened calf. A teacher among the Brethren told me that in the whole Bible we can see God run only one time, in Luke 15, where the father sees the returning prodigal son. He ran; he could not wait. This is the Father's heart.

To speak truthfully, we have lost this spirit among the co-workers, elders, and vital groups. We do not have such a loving spirit that loves the world, the worst people. We classify people, choosing who are the good ones. Throughout my years I have seen many good ones. Eventually, very few of the good ones remain in the Lord's recovery. Rather, so many bad ones remain. In the beginning I also was one who classified them as bad, but today many bad ones are still here. If it were according to our concept, where would God's choosing be? Our choosing depends upon God, who chose His people before the foundation of the world...It is not up to our choosing, our selection. It is based upon God's eternal selection.

Do not classify people. Who can tell what they will be? When I was playing mah-jongg at the age of eighteen or nineteen, who would have thought that this mah-jongg player would sit in America many years later to talk to people about the Lord? Who brought me here? It was Christ as the heavenly ladder. He brought me up to God in the heavens, and He brought me down to the earth with Himself. The heavenly ladder has many steps, and God brought me up not in one year but over many years. When I arrived at the top, I met God, and He equipped me and sent me back down. I came down, first to Taiwan, then to the South Asian islands, and then to this country. Now I am here. The pastor in my hometown did not say of me, "I know this man. He is a gambler, a mah-jongg player. I do not like him, and I do not want to have such a member in my church." Rather, he visited me, and one day very mysteriously the seeking Spirit was seeking in me, like the woman in Luke 15.

Why would I spend so much time on this subject? I want to shepherd and disciple you from the Bible so you can see this matter and have a change. I am discipling you to change your concept. The God-man concept is that Christ came to save sinners, especially the top sinners. He saves the "gangsters," even the leader of the "gangsters," Saul of Tarsus. Paul said, "Faithful is the word and worthy of all acceptance, that Christ Jesus came into the world to save sinners, of whom I am foremost" (1 Tim. 1:15). Paul could say this because he was the top sinner opposing Christ. He rebelled against Christ, but while he was rebelling, Christ knocked him down, called him, and saved him. Jesus Himself said, "Those who are strong have no need of a physician, but those who are ill...I did not come to call the righteous, but sinners" (Matt. 9:12-13). That is why He was there among the sinners and tax collectors, eating and feasting with them, reclining at the table and enjoying with them.

lf we lose this spirit, whether we are elders, co-workers, or serving ones, we are finished. This is the main reason why we are so barren, bearing no fruit for so many years. Recently, a brother went to care for a couple, but he did not have this spirit. He visited them no more than ten times and became disappointed. Since the couple had no heart for this brother, he reported that it was useless to visit them further. When Pastor Yu visited me, I did not care for him, but he continued to come for three or four months, week after week. We need to have this spirit. We all have to change our concept. Therefore, we need discipling. We have too much of the natural thought. We need to be discipled to have the divine concept, the concept of the Father's heart and the heart of the Lord Jesus, who came to save sinners.

We like to rank people, saying that the co-workers are the first rank, while others are the subsequent ranks. This is absolutely wrong. There is no rank. We all are the people in the world and in the flesh...I do not even consider myself qualified to be a pastor. I am just the same as the other saints. Once we condemn anyone, we lose the position to take care of that one. Condemnation does not stir up our care for others. Who among the human race is lovable? In the eyes of God, everyone is not lovable in themselves, yet God still loves them; that is, He loves the world. I do not prefer to have this kind of fellowship with you, but I must speak in this way for your sake in order to shepherd you.

We all have to admit that we are on the same level, with only a little difference in degree. Regardless of how much higher one seems than another, we are still at the same level. We all need to see this; then our mouth will be shut. We should not talk about others; we are the same as they. If we are bothered by other people's criticizing, our spirit may tell us that we also criticize others. Then our mouth will be shut. We are the same as others. One may criticize ten percent, while another criticizes fifteen percent. We are the same; we are all criticizers.

We must humble ourselves. Pride is the biggest enemy of God. God resists the proud but gives grace to the humble (James 4:6; 1 Pet. 5:5). Whenever we criticize others, we miss grace and instead suffer God's resistance. We all must learn to shepherd one another. This does not mean that since I am shepherding you, I do not need your shepherding. I need your shepherding. We all have defects and shortcomings. Everyone has defects. Therefore, we have to humble ourselves to meet God's grace. This strengthens our spirit to visit people and to take care of people regardless of whether they are good or bad. Regardless of what they are, we must go to visit them and keep visiting.

We need to have this kind of love and go to tell all the dormant ones who think that the church condemns them that the church does not condemn anyone. Rather, the church wants to see all the dormant ones come back. If they all would come back, I would weep with tears of thanksgiving to the Lord. The Lord can testify for me that I do not condemn anyone. We have no qualification to condemn anyone. Without the Lord's mercy, we would be the same as the dormant ones. Therefore, we must love them. It all depends upon love, as the wise king Solomon said, "Love covers all transgressions" (Prov. 10:12). We love people. We love the opposers, and we love the top rebels. I really mean it. We love them and do not hate them. Who am I? I am not qualified to condemn or to hate. Am I perfect? Even the prophet Isaiah, when he saw the Lord, said, "Woe is me, for I am finished! / For I am a man of unclean lips, / And in the midst of a people of unclean lips I dwell" (Isa. 6:5). Who is clean today? If we criticize people and say something bad about them, we are not clean. (*A Word of Love to the Co-workers, Elders, Lovers, and Seekers of the Lord,* pp. 27-28, 29-30, 31, 31-32, 32-33)

THE SPIRIT THAT GOD GIVES US BEING OF LOVE

The spirit that God has given us is our human spirit regenerated and indwelt by the Holy Spirit. This spirit is a spirit of love; hence, it is of power and of sobermindedness (2 Tim. 1:7). We may think that we are very powerful and sober, but our spirit is not of love. We talk to people in a way that is full of power and sobermindedness, but our talk threatens them. Paul said that we need to fan our gift into flame (v. 6). The main gift that God has given us is our regenerated human spirit with His Spirit, His life, and His nature. We must fan this gift into flame. This means that we have to stir up our spirit so that our spirit will be burning. Romans 12:11 says that we should be burning in spirit. If our spirit is not a spirit of love, our fanning it into flame will burn the whole recovery in a negative way. We must have a burning spirit of love, not a burning spirit of authority, which damages. Whatever is mentioned in 2 Timothy is a requirement for us to face the degradation of the church. How can we overcome the degradation of the church? We must have a burning human spirit of love. Under today's degradation of the church, we all need a spirit of love fanned into flame to be burning in spirit. Love prevails in this way.

According to my observation throughout the years, most of the co-workers have a human spirit of "power" but not of love. We need a spirit of love to conquer the degradation of today's church. We should not say or do anything to threaten people. Instead we should always say and do things with a spirit of love, which has been fanned into flame. This is what the recovery needs.

The church is not a police station to arrest people or a law court to judge people, but a home to raise up the believers. Parents know that the worse their children are, the more they need their raising up. If our children were angels, they would not need our parenting to raise them up. The church is a loving home to raise up the children. The church is also a hospital to heal and to recover the sick ones. Finally, the church is a school to teach and edify the unlearned ones who do not have much understanding. Because the church is a home, a hospital, and a school, the co-workers and elders should be one with the Lord to raise up, to heal, to recover, and to teach others in love.

Some of the churches, however, are police stations to arrest the sinful ones and law courts to judge them. Paul's attitude was different. He said, "Who is weak, and I am not weak?"

(2 Cor. 11:29a). When the scribes and Pharisees brought an adulterous woman to the Lord, He said to them, "He who is without sin among you, let him be the first to throw a stone at her" (John 8:7). After all of them left, the Lord asked the sinful woman, "Woman, where are they? Has no one condemned you?" She said, "No one, Lord." Then Jesus said, "Neither do I condemn you" (vv. 10-11). Who is without sin? Who is perfect? Paul said, "To the weak I became weak that I might gain the weak" (1 Cor. 9:22). This is love. We should not consider that others are weak but we are not. This is not love. Love covers and builds up, so love is the most excellent way for us to be anything and to do anything for the building up of the Body of Christ. (*The Vital Groups,* pp. 73, 75)

DOING YOUR BEST TO CONTACT THE YOUNG PEOPLE

Second, learn to do your best to contact the young people. Helping the young brothers and sisters depends not on your ability to give them messages but on your regular, frequent contacts with them. When you contact the young brothers and sisters, do not begin by asking, "How many chapters of the Bible have you read today? Have you prayed?" Such questions should not be brought up until you have had many contacts with them, maybe even after eight or ten times. Remember not to talk about spiritual things at the initial contact with them. It is even more so in dealing with an unbeliever. Do not talk about the Lord Jesus when you first contact him. The reason you refrain from mentioning the Lord Jesus is that as you maintain contact with him, seemingly you are retreating, yet actually you are advancing. You need to sense his feeling until one day you can impart the gospel into him. Then you will be successful at once. However, if you do it prematurely, it is easy to cause a negative reaction. If you mess up the whole thing, he may not receive the Lord for his entire lifetime. It is the same in dealing with any young person. Do not stir up his negative feeling by talking to him right away about reading the Bible or praying. You must wait until you have more contacts with him and he feels that he likes you and that you also like him. Once you have touched his feeling and earned his trust, then you can begin to talk about spiritual things. This is like giving the right prescription for an illness. With the right medicine, the illness will be cured. Then you can expect to see a result.

EMPHASIZING PRACTICALITY
INSTEAD OF STRESSING DOCTRINES

Third, when you help the young people, do not give them a lot of doctrines; instead, give them something practical. You should not put too much emphasis on doctrines, not only when you have personal contact with them but also when you are preaching the gospel or giving messages to them. If you give them only some doctrines and they come only to listen, there will not be much effect. The more you speak doctrines, the more the young people become dead, cold, and backsliding. Because young people have many practical problems, you need to sense their feelings, beginning with these problems. Therefore, you need to spend some time to study the problems of the young people in their practical living, including problems both before and after their salvation. Based upon your studies, when you preach the gospel or speak a word of edification to them, what you speak is practical and is related to the practical matters that you have touched in their lives. (*How to Lead the Young People,* pp. 21-23)

HOW TO LEAD THE YOUNG PEOPLE
(2)

Scripture Reading: 1 Cor. 13:7; Matt. 19:26; 2 Cor. 5:7; 1 Cor. 9:19-23; 1 Thes. 2:11; 2 John 12; 3 John 14

IV. We must have a positive faith in every young person—
1 Cor. 13:7; Matt. 19:26; 2 Cor. 5:7:

A. Having a positive faith means that with the good ones you believe that they will get better, and with the ones who do not seem to be good, you believe that they will become good.

B. We are all Adam's descendants, a fallen race; even the children of godly people are fallen; you cannot judge a young person's future based on his situation today:

1. We cannot say that to be fallen is right, but please remember that all those who truly know God's salvation were once fallen people.

2. If a person has been preserved since his birth and has never lived in a fallen way, he cannot have a deep experience of God's salvation.

C. Whether the condition of the young people is good or bad, usually it is not trustworthy; all those who have some experience in the young people's work will not trust in the young people's condition but fully believe that God will gain them one day:

1. Today you may consider a certain young man very bad, but one day he may become very good, contrary to your view.

2. In the same way, today you may think that a

certain young man is very good, but some day he may become very bad.

D. This will deliver us so that we will not work only on the young people whom we consider good and put aside those whom we consider bad; do not believe either in their good condition or in their bad condition; believe only in God's work:

1. Actually, sometimes it is hard for those who are consistently good to have spiritual perception, and often their growth is slow.

2. If you spend time on those seemingly bad ones to turn them around, their spiritual understanding will be opened immediately after they have made a turn.

3. This shows that those of us who do the work among the young people should not trust in their present condition.

4. No matter how bad one may be, we still believe God's work can turn him; because we have such a positive faith, we pay attention to every young person.

V. Those who have a desire to do the young people's work need to learn how to match and adapt to the young people—1 Cor. 9:19-23:

A. Do not ask them to adapt to you; you need to adapt to them to such an extent that you are like glue:

1. We who do the young people's work should be like glue, so that it does not matter if a young person is soft or hard or if he is three-dimensional, flat, or a surface with bumps and dents; we still need to stick to him.

2. We have to go along with the young people and accommodate ourselves to them; we must bring people in not by our zeal but by our gentleness— learn to be as yielding as paste.

B. It seems very hard to do the young people's work because the young people are too busy to care about pursuing the Lord; if they are busy with entering a higher school, then we work on them by going along with them in their preparation for this matter:

1. If we are doing a real work, then even if a young person flies to the sky, we will follow him there to adapt to him.

2. The young people being too busy is not the problem; the real issue is their interest; if they are interested in something, no matter how busy they are, they will have time for it.

C. When you go to reach people, do not contact them according to your tradition, background, or disposition; look to the Lord that you will be able to enter into their condition and situation.

D. Learn to accommodate their character, age, disposition, and way of doing things, and contact people according to their situation and condition and not according to your disposition or tradition.

E. From the Bible we can realize that for others' profit, we must learn to accommodate their character, their age, their disposition, and even their ways of doing certain things.

VI. Paying attention to personal contact; the power and effect of doing a personal work with the young people are many times greater than the meetings:

A. The emphasis of a genuine work with young people is individual contact—1 Thes. 2:11; 2 John 12; 3 John 14:

1. Big meetings do not have much effect on young people; when you gather them together, usually all you can do is give them a message and at most a little work of revival.

2. It seems the way of personal contact is fragmentary and wastes a lot of time; seemingly, this way is less effective than holding big meetings where you can speak to hundreds of people at once.

3. If all you have is meetings, the young people's work will end up with something that is only on the surface, like loose sand without foundation; it will not be able to produce any solid ones.

B. We speak too much, preach too much, and teach too much with very little visiting; most people are gained by face-to-face contact, and most people are retained and built by such personal contact.

C. In the matter of personal contact, skills are needed; if you practice this matter seriously, gradually you will gain experience and insight:

1. You will know which one among so many young people should be contacted and gained first; after one has been gained, he will go to stir others up in the same way.

2. Even if there are no big meetings, many can still get saved and many can be raised up to love the Lord, and no matter what you speak, they will receive it; then the meetings will be one hundred percent effective, and you will be able to gain solid young people.

D. When you have personal contact with young people, on the one hand, you need to have broad contact with them, treating every one of them equally; on the other hand, you need to have specific contact:

1. Among so many young brothers and sisters, you need to feel and see which ones, once they are gained, will have impact on others.

2. Then you should spend your effort on them first and help them to love and pursue the Lord; once they are raised up, they will influence the other young brothers and sisters.

E. "Brothers, I say again, the Lord has a great need for the young people. This generation needs many young people to rise up in a strong way to receive the Lord's salvation and be led by the Lord to become useful vessels in His hands"—*How to Lead the Young People*, p. 37.

Excerpts from the Ministry:

HAVING A POSITIVE FAITH IN EVERY YOUNG PERSON

Fourth, you need to have positive faith in every young

person. This means that with the good ones you should believe that they will get better, and with the ones who do not seem to be good, you should also believe that they will become good. Moreover, you should have more faith in those who are seemingly not good and believe that they will become good and not have as much faith in those who are good.

I like to tell you, brothers and sisters, that we are all Adam's descendants, a fallen race. Even the children of godly people are fallen. We cannot say that to be fallen is right, but please remember that all those who truly know God's salvation were once fallen people. If a person has been preserved since his birth and has never lived in a fallen way, he cannot have a deep experience of God's salvation. One who has never lived in a fallen way cannot experience God's salvation. I am not encouraging people to be fallen. Neither am I encouraging them to be loose with their children. This is not what I mean. What I mean is that you should never think that it is all right to despise certain young ones simply because they are not good. This concept is wrong.

We know the story of George Müller, a spiritual man in the nineteenth century. He was clear about his salvation probably when he was twenty-one years old. He was born into a Christian family, and his father was a man who feared God. However, he was a very fallen young man before the age of twenty-one. He always stole money from his father to roam about from place to place. Once he stayed in a hotel, but because he was not able to pay the fee, he was even sent to prison by the owner of the hotel. At that time he was truly a dissipated and corrupt person. But one day the Lord found him. As a young man, after he was saved, he became one who greatly loved the Lord. If you look at George Müller before he was twenty-one, he was such an improper person. Who could ever have imagined that after he was twenty-one he would love the Lord so much and be so spiritual? Therefore, you cannot judge a young person's future based on his situation today.

Brothers and sisters, I can tell you that whether the condition of the young people is good or bad, usually it is not trustworthy. Today you may consider a certain young man very bad, but one day he may become very good, contrary to your view. In the same way, today you may think that a certain young man is very good, but some day he may become very bad. Therefore, all those who have some experience in the young people's work will say, "We don't trust in the young people's condition. On the positive side, however, we fully believe that God will gain them one day." This will deliver us so that we will not work only on the young people whom we consider good and put aside those whom we consider bad. Actually, sometimes it is hard for those who are consistently good to have spiritual perception, and often their growth is slow. However, if you spend time on those seemingly bad ones to turn them around, their spiritual understanding will be opened immediately after they have made a turn. This shows that those of us who do the work among the young people should not trust in their present condition. Do not believe either in their good condition or in their bad condition; believe only in God's work. No matter how bad one may be, we still believe God's work can turn him. No matter how poor one may be, we still believe God's work can carry him through. Because we have such a positive faith, we pay attention to every young person.

ADAPTING TO YOUNG PEOPLE

Fifth, all those who have a desire to do the young people's work need to learn how to match and adapt to the young people. Do not ask them to adapt to you. You need to adapt to them to such an extent that you are like glue. Glue adapts the best; there is not one place it cannot adapt to. It adapts to flat surfaces, rugged places, twisted places, and places with corners. Glue can be applied to any place. We who do the young people's work need to deal with our character to such an extent that we are just like glue. If anyone wants to serve God, he must have a character that is not only strong but also pliant; he must be one who tempers strength with pliancy to adapt to others like glue.

For example, young people are facing stiff competition for the entrance to a higher school, and there is a prevailing atmosphere to go abroad to study. After elementary school, they have to enter high school. Then after high school, they have to get into a university. After graduation from university, they have to go abroad to further their studies. Everyone is busy getting a higher education and going abroad. It seems very hard to do the young people's work because the young people are too busy to care about pursuing the Lord. But this perception is not accurate. We who do the young people's work should be like glue, so that it does not matter if a young person is soft or hard or if he is three-dimensional, flat, or a surface with bumps and dents; we still need to stick to him. We have to go along with the young people and accommodate ourselves to them. Are they busy with entering a higher school? Then we work on them by going along with them in their preparation for this matter. Are they going abroad to study? We still go along with them and adapt to them. Although we cannot go with any of them to a foreign country, our care and concern for him will go with him. We should work not only to the extent of gaining him but also to gain some people through him in that foreign country. We should work on him to such an extent that he will do the Lord's work in whatever university he goes to. Then as a result of his preaching of the gospel, he will gain some people there. Therefore, instead of regarding the prevailing trend of going abroad as a hindrance, we should consider it an outlet for our work. We need to correspond with the brothers and sisters who are studying abroad to continue communication with them. Before they leave, we need to lead each of them to have a normal spiritual life, so that after they go out they will not only study for themselves but also work for the Lord. You cannot, and must not, hope that everyone would give up entering a higher school or going abroad for further studies but would sit here waiting for you to work on them, just like a piece of tofu placed on a plate for you to eat. This is not called work. If we are doing a real work, then even if a young person flies to the sky, we will follow him there to adapt to him.

Many say that students today are too busy. However, if you really know the students' situation, you will know that with the young people, being busy is not a problem. Rather, the real issue is their interest. If they are interested in something, no matter how busy they are, they will have time for it.

They will find time for the things they are interested in even if they are busy.

At the apostles' time, the Roman Empire persecuted Christians. The Roman Caesar, the emperor, killed many Christians. However, the apostles were very effective. They were able to work to such an extent that even some who were in Caesar's household were saved. Philippians 4:22 says, "All the saints greet you, and especially those of Caesar's household." This proves that the apostles worked even into Caesar's home.

Therefore, we must remember that in doing the Lord's work we must not be rigid. We should not say that we can eat only tofu and not stones. A competent worker can eat not only tofu but also stones, and he can eat something even as hard as diamonds. Brothers and sisters, please believe me; learn to adapt to others. (*How to Lead the Young People,* pp. 23-30)

* * *

We must bring people in, not by our zeal but our gentleness. Everyone who wants to bring in others should learn to be as yielding as paste. The main characteristic of paste is that it is very accommodating. You can spread paste on anything, be it a flat surface, a sharp corner, or a crooked edge.

PREACHING THE GOSPEL BEGINNING WITH RELATIVES AND INTIMATE FRIENDS

Every lover of the Lord must be like paste; he must be able to be spread anywhere. Whoever touches us should get stuck to us. The lovers of the Lord cannot be like steel plates; they cannot have a hard and unyielding personality. If so, they will not bear fruit even if they love the Lord until they die. Every brother and sister who is like paste is able to catch men. (*Key Points on the Home Meetings,* p. 60)

CONTACTING PEOPLE BY ENTERING INTO THEIR SITUATION

When we contact people, we must be able to enter into their situation and condition. This is difficult. In his Gospel, John records at least nine cases of the Lord's contacting people. In each instance, the Lord reached people in a different way.

He never used only one way of reaching people. He reached
people with God's unique purpose, but He did not do so
according to His disposition. Rather, He contacted them
according to their situation and condition. In John 3 the Lord
knew that Nicodemus would come to Him. He did not visit
Nicodemus at his house because He knew that this would
have been inconvenient for him. He realized that Nicodemus
was timid, fearing that others might learn that Jesus had
come to see him. Thus, the Lord remained home, waiting for
that timid gentleman to come to Him. The case of the Samaritan woman was different. According to John 4, the Lord "had
to pass through Samaria" (v. 4). Having arrived at the well of
Sychar, He waited there for the Samaritan woman to come to
Him. This is a marvelous example of how the Lord Jesus
entered into someone's situation. This is the basic principle of
incarnation.

Incarnation means that God comes to man in man's condition, reaching people by entering into their situation. The Lord
did not stay in heaven and command people to contact Him.
No, He became a man and entered into our situation. Having
become a man, He conducted His outreach by constantly coming
into the condition of people. He did not just go to the people
themselves, but He entered into their situation. He knew that
the Samaritan woman would be thirsty; hence, He waited for
her at the well. When He met her, He did not say, "Have you
been saved? How long have you been a Christian? What church
do you go to?" The Lord did not ask any of these religious
questions. Rather, He said, "Give Me something to drink" (v. 7).
By this simple word, He touched her heart, for she was wholly
occupied with the matter of drinking water, even coming out
at noon, an extraordinary time for drawing water. When you
go to reach people, do not contact them according to your tradition, background, or disposition. Look to the Lord, that,
with His help, you will be able to enter into their condition
and situation.

Consider the example of the impotent man in John chapter 5. In chapter 3 Nicodemus came all the way to the Lord,
and in chapter 4 the Lord Jesus met the Samaritan woman
midway. But in chapter 5 the Lord went all the way to the

impotent man. Once again we see that the Lord reached people by getting into their situation. In John chapter 5 the Lord came to a man who had been impotent for thirty-eight years. The Lord did not ask him, "Do you read the Bible?" If He had said this, the sick man would have responded, "Get away from me! I don't care about the Bible." Without entering into a person's situation, you cannot touch his heart and feeling, and he will never respond to you. The Lord said to this man, "Do you want to get well?" (v. 6). The impotent man was, of course, very interested in this. (*Young People's Training,* pp. 51-52)

ACCOMMODATING ALL KINDS OF PERSONS

From the Bible we can realize that for others' profit, we must learn to accommodate their character, their age, their disposition, and even their ways of doing certain things. This need is especially obvious in America because it is such a melting pot of all kinds of people. We must not forget that in our going out to preach the gospel, we are going not only for individuals but for families. This requires us to learn to be human. (*The Exercise and Practice of the God-ordained Way,* p. 90)

PAYING ATTENTION TO PERSONAL CONTACT

Sixth, all those who care for the work among the young people must pay attention to doing a personal work. The power and effect of doing a personal work with the young people are many times greater than the meetings. Big meetings do not have much effect on young people; individual contact is most effective. When you gather them together, usually all you can do is give them a message and at most a little work of revival. The emphasis of a genuine work with young people is individual contact. If you ask me, "Brother Lee, how would you do the young people's work?" I would answer you by saying, "I can do it without holding any big meetings from the beginning to the end of the year but just absolutely working with them individually by personal contact." It seems this way is fragmentary and wastes a lot of time. You may be able to contact only one person in an hour, and sometimes you may not be able to contact even one person after half a day. It seems time is pitifully wasted. Seemingly, this way is less effective than holding big meetings where you can speak to hundreds of people at once. Rather, experience tells us that holding big meetings is useless. If you hold big meetings all year round, there may not be much result. All you gain will be some shallow ones. Please remember, however, if you pay attention to individual contact, although you may not gain one person in a month or may gain only one person in two months, each one who is gained through your personal contact counts. Moreover, like you, he will contact others. You have gained one, but eventually this one will become two, two will become four, four will become eight, and eight will become sixteen, and every one of them will be solid. After some time you will see a great number of people gained.

I hope that all the ones doing the young students' work, whether it is bringing them to salvation, helping them to be spiritual, or leading them to preach the gospel, will pay attention to individual contact. From 1946 to 1948, when we were in the regions of Shanghai and Nanking, we did not actually have any students' meetings or young people's meetings. Most of our work was carried out by individual contact, yet the result was quite good. If the brothers neglect individual contact and pay attention only to young people's meetings, I can say with certainty that after having so many meetings, the young people's work will end up with something that is only on the surface, like loose sand without foundation. It will not be able to produce any solid ones. If you want to produce solid ones, you must have personal contact. You must not be disappointed with anyone; rather, you would spend time to contact everyone individually.

Of course, in the matter of personal contact, skills are needed. But if you practice this matter seriously, gradually you will gain experience and insight. You will know which one among so many young people should be contacted and gained first. Later, after that one has been gained by the Lord, one thing is sure: Since you stirred him up in this way, he will go to stir others up in the same way. This is just like a machine with so many gear wheels; when one wheel turns, all the other wheels also turn. In this way, one by one will be affected, just like the unending multiplication of offspring. Therefore, you can see that even if there are no big meetings, many can still get saved and many can still be raised up to love the Lord. That is the time when you can begin to hold big meetings, and no matter what you speak, they will receive it. Then the meetings will be one hundred percent effective. You will be able to gain solid young people and do a deep work in them.

When you have personal contact with young people, on the one hand, you need to have broad contact with them, treating every one of them equally; on the other hand, you need to have specific contact. What I mean by specific contact is that you need to exercise your spiritual insight and follow the Spirit's leading to sense which ones, among so many young students, you should lead to the Lord first. Then you should spend your effort on them to help them receive the Lord's salvation. In the same way, among so many young brothers and sisters, you need to feel and see which ones, once they are gained, will have impact on others. Then you should spend your effort on them first and help them to love and pursue the Lord. Once they are raised up, they will influence the other young brothers and sisters.

Therefore, in doing the work among the young people, on the one hand, you need to have broad contact with them, dealing with them in a general way; on the other hand, you need to have specific contact, helping the ones who can take the lead and influence others. If you gain one, I repeat, he will go and help others without your teaching him. Because you have helped him in this way, he will go to help others in the same way. As a result, one will become two, two will become four, and so on. This is like the ripple effect achieved by throwing a stone in the center of the water. The ripple will eventually spread to cover the entire surface of the lake. Then you can hold big meetings, and they will be effective. If you hold big meetings from the outset, there will be only a twenty percent effect, and the other eighty percent will amount to zero. If you are willing to start from individual contact and then go on to big meetings, the messages you give will be practical and the work you do will produce a hundred percent result.

All the points above are some of the experiences I have

gained from touching the young people's work in the past years. Any matter has its own intricacy and requires experience. In particular, matters such as leading people to salvation, helping people to love the Lord, and bringing people to serve the Lord are very deep and very fine, consisting of many intricate points. Yes, it is the Spirit's work, but we all know that the Spirit needs the proper ones to coordinate with Him. Some can coordinate with the Spirit, but others cannot. Some are useful in the hands of the Spirit, but others are useless. We need to pay attention and study these matters when we start to do this work.

These six points which I have fellowshipped with you all are just an introduction. If you will take this fellowship and go on, you will learn more and make more progress. You will find better ways to lead the young people to the Lord to receive His salvation.

Brothers, I say again, the Lord has a great need for the young people. This generation needs many young people to rise up in a strong way to receive the Lord's salvation and be led by the Lord to become useful vessels in His hands. May the Lord be gracious to us that in His work and in the church we will treasure the souls of the young people. Not only will we not hinder them or damage them, but we will aggressively attract them, perfect them, lead them, and cultivate them so that they will experience the Lord's salvation and receive the Lord's building up to become useful ones in the Lord's hands. I truly hope that all the brothers and sisters will pray faithfully for this matter before the Lord for the future of the Lord's work. (*How to Lead the Young People,* pp. 31-37)

* * *

We speak too much, preach too much, and teach too much with very little visiting. Most people are gained by face-to-face contact, and most people are retained and built by such personal contact.

It seems difficult for us to gain new ones because we do not have the practice of visiting people. We all have to see this secret. If we do not pick up the practice of visiting people and talking to them face to face, the mere teaching of the new way, the biblical way, the God-ordained way, will not work. Only one thing works—visiting people and seeing them face to face.

All of us need to rise up to visit people, contacting them with Christ. As long as we pick up this practice, we have the secret. Just like in fighting with new weapons, we can win the battle for the increase of the church with the "new weapon" of visiting people.

When some of us visit people, we talk too much. We try to gain them by gaining their mind. This is wrong. We gain people by gaining an intimacy with them, by showing an intimate concern for them. If we merely teach them to help their understanding, they will not follow us. But if we visit them and become intimate with them in a proper way, we will gain them for the Lord. (*Elders' Training, Book 11: The Eldership and the God-ordained Way (3)*, pp. 82-83)

SHEPHERDING THE YOUNG PEOPLE ACCORDING TO THE LORD'S HEART

Scripture Reading: John 21:15-17; Acts 20:28; 1 Pet. 5:1-3; Luke 15:4-24, 32

I. In His heavenly ministry Christ is shepherding people, and we need to cooperate with Him by shepherding people; without shepherding, our work for the Lord cannot be effective—Heb. 13:20-21; John 21:15-17.

II. Shepherding is to take all-inclusive tender care of the flock; shepherding refers to taking care of all the needs of the sheep—vv. 15-17; Acts 20:28.

III. Peter charged the elders to shepherd the flock of God according to God; *according to God* means to live God— 1 Pet. 5:1-3:

A. To shepherd according to God is to shepherd according to what God is in His attributes—Rom. 9:15-16; 11:22, 33; Eph. 2:7; 1 Cor. 1:9; 2 Cor. 1:12.

B. To shepherd according to God is to shepherd according to God's nature, desire, way, and glory, not according to our preference, interest, purpose, and disposition.

C. In order to shepherd according to God, we need to become God in life, nature, expression, and function—John 1:12-13; 3:15; 2 Pet. 1:4:

1. We need to be the reproduction of Christ, the expression of God, so that in our shepherding we express God, not the self with its disposition and peculiarities—John 1:18; Heb. 1:3; 2:10; Rom. 8:29.

2. We need to become God in His function of shepherding the flock according to what He is and

according to His goal in His economy—Eph. 4:16; Rev. 21:2.

3. When we are one with God, we become God and are God in our shepherding of others.

IV. We need to shepherd the flock of God according to the Father's loving and forgiving heart and according to the Son's seeking, finding, and shepherding spirit— Luke 15:4-24, 32:

A. We should follow the steps of the processed Triune God in His seeking and gaining fallen people— vv. 4-6, 8-9, 18-24, 32.

B. Our natural tendency is not to shepherd others but to criticize them and regulate them:

1. Whenever we criticize someone, we lose the position to take care of that one.

2. Our natural tendency is to regulate others and place demands on them according to ourselves, not to cherish and nourish them according to God.

C. We need to have a change of concept through being discipled to have the divine concept, the concept that is according to the Father's loving heart and the Son's shepherding spirit.

D. Our shepherding should be according to God's love toward the fallen human race; the fallen human race is joined with Satan to be his world in his system, but God has a heart of love toward these people—John 3:16.

E. We need to be shepherds having the loving and forgiving heart of our Father God in His divinity and the seeking, finding, and shepherding spirit of our Savior Christ in His humanity.

F. "If this kind of fellowship is received by us, I believe there will be a big revival on the earth, not by a few spiritual giants but by the many members of Christ's Body being shepherds who follow the steps of the processed Triune God in seeking and gaining fallen people"—*The Vital Groups*, p. 40.

V. We need to stir up an atmosphere so that we would receive a burden to restore the dormant saints and to seek out our brothers and sisters who have not been meeting and those with whom we have lost contact— Gal. 6:1; cf. Luke 15:4-6, 8-9:

A. These saints are the harvest from our past labor and hard work; they were baptized, and they are our family members, but they have all disappeared; therefore, we must take this matter seriously—Matt. 18:11-13.

B. Now is the time to put the affairs of our household in order, and the first matter we should address is to find these saints in order to bring them back; if we would do this thoroughly by the Lord's grace, we could recover two-thirds of them within two to three years:

1. We need to begin by recovering the brothers and sisters who seldom attend meetings but whose whereabouts are known; this involves a work of visitation and restoration.

2. We also need to locate the saints whose whereabouts are unknown; this is very time consuming, and we are in the process of looking for a way that the churches can coordinate with each other in order to find these saints.

C. The key to recovering these saints is for the brothers and sisters who regularly meet in the small groups to receive a burden; without a burden, it will be difficult to move; with a burden, there will be grace—1 Cor. 15:10:

1. The saints who are wandering outside are scattered and not enjoying the riches of our family; they are truly like the prodigal son who could not find even carob pods to eat—Luke 15:13-16.

2. But in the Father's house, in God's house, which is the church, the food is plentiful; therefore, we must be compassionate toward them and bring them home to enjoy the riches in the Father's house with us—vv. 20-24.

D. Visiting dormant saints needs much consideration;

if we do not do it properly, we will drive them further away.

E. As we seek out the saints, we must rely on the work of the Holy Spirit; the work of the Spirit is likened in Luke 15 to a woman who lights a lamp to seek a lost coin; the Holy Spirit is able to shine upon the saints with the Lord's word and is willing to search for them until they are found—vv. 8-9.

F. Love is the most excellent way for us to be anything and to do anything for the building up of the Body of Christ—2 Tim. 1:7; 1 Cor. 8:1; 12:31b:

1. We must have the kind of love to go and tell the dormant ones who think that the church condemns them that the church does not condemn anyone; rather, the church wants to see all the dormant ones come back—Prov. 10:12b.

2. Because the church is a home, a hospital, and a school, we must be one with the Lord to raise up, to heal, to recover, and to teach others in love— 2 Cor. 11:28-29; 12:15; 1 Cor. 9:22; Matt. 12:20.

3. Love is not jealous, is not provoked, does not take account of evil, covers all things, endures all things, never falls away, and is the greatest— 1 Cor. 13:4-8, 13.

Excerpts from the Ministry:

I hope that there will be a genuine revival among us by our receiving this burden of shepherding. If all the churches receive this teaching to participate in Christ's wonderful shepherding, there will be a big revival in the recovery. In the past we did much speaking and teaching with very little shepherding. Shepherding and teaching should be like two feet for our move with the Lord. Our shepherding should always be with teaching, and our teaching should always be with shepherding.

We have seen from our crystallization-study of the Gospel of John that its last chapter, John 21, reveals the apostolic ministry in cooperation with Christ's heavenly ministry. In His heavenly ministry Christ is shepherding people, and we need to cooperate with Him by shepherding people. Without shepherding, our work for the Lord cannot be effective. We must learn all the truths so that we may have something to speak and go to contact people to shepherd them. (*The Vital Groups,* p. 40)

COMMISSIONING PETER TO FEED HIS LAMBS AND SHEPHERD HIS SHEEP

When the Lord stayed with His disciples after His resurrection and before His ascension, in one of His appearings, He commissioned Peter to feed His lambs and shepherd His sheep in His absence, while He is in the heavens (John 21:15-17). Shepherding implies feeding, but it includes much more than feeding. To shepherd is to take all-inclusive tender care of the flock. (*Crystallization-study of the Gospel of John,* p. 131)

* * *

In order to take care of the church properly, the elders have to receive this charge from the Lord. They must shepherd the saints conscientiously. The Lord asked Peter in John chapter 21, "Do you love Me more than these?" Peter answered the Lord, "Yes, Lord, You know that I love You." Then Jesus said to him, "Feed My lambs" (v. 15). To feed is to nourish others with the riches of the inner life. This is a mouth-to-mouth feeding. The second time, the Lord said to Peter, "Shepherd My sheep" (v. 16). To shepherd the sheep is to take care of all the needs of the sheep. The third time, the Lord said to him, "Feed My sheep" (v. 17). At the time the Lord said this to Peter, Peter had been following the Lord for over three years. After His resurrection, the Lord charged him especially with this matter of shepherding the sheep. This shows how important it is to shepherd the sheep. Later, when Peter wrote his first Epistle, he entreated the elders to shepherd the flock of God (1 Pet. 5:1-2).

Shepherding refers to caring for all of the needs of the sheep, whether the need is grass, water, or shelter. All the sheep are to be well provided for and well tended to. Of all the needs, the most important one is the feeding, that is, the mouth-to-mouth feeding. This is the duty of the elders. If all the elders in the various localities would do this, the saints would receive the suitable care. In the past, we baptized many but brought in few. The reason for this was the lack of feeding and care. Our messages were high and deep, but after the messages there was not much care. In the end, the flock was without shepherds. There was preaching without shepherding and teaching without feeding. This was our shortcoming in the past. Among us there is the begetting and the teaching, but there is a lack of feeding. As soon as a baby is born, what he needs most is feeding. A baby will not grow just by teaching him. (*A Timely Trumpeting and the Present Need,* pp. 52-53)

* * *

In his first Epistle, Peter spoke in 2:25 of Christ being the Shepherd and Overseer of our soul, our inner being and real person. Then in 5:1-2 he told the elders that their obligation is to shepherd God's flock according to God. *According to God* means that we must live God. We must have God on hand. We have God in our understanding, in our theology, and in our teaching, but we may not live God when we are shepherding people. When we are one with God, we become God. Then we have God and are God in our shepherding of others. To shepherd according to God is to shepherd according to what God is in His attributes. God is love, light, holiness, and righteousness. *According to God* is at least according to these four attributes of God. We must shepherd the young ones, the weak ones, and the backsliding ones according to these four attributes. Then we will be good shepherds.

CARRYING OUT
HIS SHEPHERDING OF HIS FLOCK

In addition to the shepherding by the main function of the gifted persons, Christ as the Head of the church also charged the apostles to appoint elders (overseers) in all the local churches to carry out His shepherding of His flock (1 Tim. 3:1-7; 5:17a). The Head of the church gave many gifted persons to function in shepherding for the building up of His Body, but the Body is manifested in the local churches. The Body is universal and abstract, but the churches are located and substantial. In the local churches, the elders as the local shepherds are needed. The local shepherds are more practical. Christ as the Head of the church charged the apostles, the universal shepherds, to appoint some local elders to take care of the located churches. (*The Vital Groups,* pp. 60-61, 63)

* * *

First Peter 5:2a says, "Shepherd the flock of God among you, overseeing not under compulsion but willingly, according to God." To shepherd according to God means according to God's nature, desire, way, and glory, not according to man's preference, interest, and purpose. The elders should not shepherd the flock according to their opinion, concepts, or likes or dislikes. Instead, they should shepherd according to God's choice, desire, intention, and preference. The elders must shepherd the saints as the flock of God altogether according to God's thought, feeling, will, and choice. They must shepherd according to God's likes and dislikes. (*The Conclusion of the New Testament,* pp. 1845-1846)

FOLLOWING THE STEPS
OF THE PROCESSED TRIUNE GOD
IN SEEKING AND GAINING THE FALLEN PEOPLE

My burden in this message is that we have to learn of the apostles, the elders, and even of the Triune God. We have to follow the steps of the processed Triune God in His seeking and gaining fallen people. Luke 15 records that the Pharisees and scribes criticized the Lord by saying, "This man welcomes sinners and eats with them" (v. 2). Then the Lord told three wonderful parables, which unveil the saving love of the Triune God toward sinners. (*The Vital Groups,* p. 39)

* * *

We often condemn others, exposing their failures and defects. We must admit that to speak well of ourselves and to expose others' defects is our natural disposition. Our disposition is like this by birth. There is no need for us to speak about others' defects, but we may simply like to do it. Many times the brothers come together and speak about others' weak points, defects, and failures. I have learned the lesson to be fearful and trembling about speaking of others' defects. In the world the legal term for this is *defamation*. Why do we need to speak in a defaming way? However, nearly all of us do this. Because by the Lord's mercy and grace I have learned the lesson, it is very hard for you to hear me speak of anyone's defects. Whenever I speak of others' shortages, I am condemned, saying to myself, "Do you not have shortages?" The Pharisees and scribes brought a sinful woman to the Lord and said, "Now in the law, Moses commanded us to stone such women. What then do You say?" (John 8:5). First, the Lord stooped down. This was to show them humility. He did not stand, saying, "What! Do you come to Me? Let Me tell you something!" The Lord stooped down to write on the ground. According to my study of the Bible, I believe that what the Lord wrote was, "Who is without sin?" It is as if He said, "There is no doubt that she is sinful, and she got caught. But are you without sin?" They charged the Lord to say something, so He said, "He who is without sin among you, let him be the first to throw a stone at her" (v. 7). Their conscience was caught. Everyone, beginning from the older ones, the experienced ones, was smitten. Who is without sin? When you speak of others' shortages, do you not have shortages? Yet according to our disposition by birth, to speak about others' defects is our "hobby." Do you like to expose your own shortages? You do not; you like to cover them. (*A Word of Love to the Co-workers, Elders, Lovers, and Seekers of the Lord,* pp. 41-42)

HAVING THE LOVING AND FORGIVING HEART OF OUR FATHER GOD AND THE SHEPHERDING AND SEEKING SPIRIT OF OUR SAVIOR CHRIST

I love Luke 15. Verse 1 says, "Now all the tax collectors and sinners were drawing near to Him to hear Him." The gentlemen and righteous men were not joined to Him, but the tax collectors and sinners were. Therefore, the Pharisees murmured and complained again. Then the Lord spoke three parables. The first is concerning a shepherd seeking the one, unique, lost sheep. Of one hundred, this one was a lost one, so the shepherd came purposely for him. Why did the Lord go to a house full of sinners and tax collectors? It was because among them there was one lost sheep of His, whom He had come to seek. The second parable is concerning a woman who lit a lamp and swept the house to seek her lost coin. The third parable is about the prodigal son. The shepherd is the Son, the woman is the Spirit, and in the parable of the prodigal son there is the Father. As the prodigal son was returning, he was preparing and considering what to speak to his father. He prepared himself to say, "Father, I have sinned against heaven and before you. I am no longer worthy to be called your son; make me like one of your hired servants" (vv. 18-19). While he was walking and thinking like this, the father saw him. Verse 20 says, "But while he was still a long way off, his father saw him and was moved with compassion, and he ran and fell on his neck and kissed him affectionately." That the father saw the son a long way off was not an accident. From the time the son left home, the father must have gone out to look and wait for his coming back every day. We do not know how many days he watched and waited. When the father saw him, he ran to him. This is the Father's heart. The father interrupted the son while he was speaking his prepared word. The son wanted to speak the word he had prepared, but the father told his servants to bring the robe, the ring, and the sandals and to prepare the fattened calf. A teacher among the Brethren told me that in the whole Bible we can see God run only one time, in Luke 15, where the father sees the returning prodigal son. He ran; he could not wait. This is the Father's heart.

To speak truthfully, we have lost this spirit among the co-workers, elders, and vital groups. We do not have such a loving spirit that loves the world, the worst people. We classify people, choosing who are the good ones. Throughout my years I have seen many good ones. Eventually, very few of the good ones remain in the Lord's recovery. Rather, so many bad ones remain. In the beginning I also was one who classified them as bad, but today many bad ones are still here. If it were according to our concept, where would God's choosing be? Our choosing depends upon God, who chose His people before the foundation of the world. The Bible says that God hated Esau and loved Jacob. If we were there, none of us would have selected Jacob. This man was too bad. We would have selected Esau, the gentleman. From his mother's womb, Jacob was fighting, and when he was born, he grabbed his brother's heel. Eventually, he did everything that caused Esau to want to kill him. His mother Rebecca knew this, so she sent him away to his uncle's house, but when he went there, he did the same thing; he cheated his uncle by getting four wives from him. This is to live like a gangster. None of us would have chosen Jacob. It is not up to our choosing, our selection. It is based upon God's eternal selection.

If we lose this spirit, whether we are elders, co-workers, or serving ones, we are finished. This is the main reason why we are so barren, bearing no fruit for so many years. Recently, a brother went to care for a couple, but he did not have this spirit. He visited them no more than ten times and became disappointed. Since the couple had no heart for this brother, he reported that it was useless to visit them further. When Pastor Yu visited me, I did not care for him, but he continued to come for three or four months, week after week. We need to have this spirit. We all have to change our concept. Therefore, we need discipling. We have too much of the natural thought. We need to be discipled to have the divine concept, the concept of the Father's heart and the heart of the Lord Jesus, who came to save sinners.

Once we condemn anyone, we lose the position to take care of that one. Condemnation does not stir up our care for others. Who among the human race is loveable? In the eyes of God, everyone is not loveable in themselves, yet God still loves them; that is, He loves the world. (*A Word of Love to the Co-workers, Elders, Lovers, and Seekers of the Lord,* pp. 27-29, 30, 31)

*   *   *

As I have said before, the spirit of not shepherding and seeking others and being without love and forgiveness is spreading in the recovery everywhere. I believe that not having the Father's loving and forgiving heart and not having the Savior's shepherding and seeking spirit is the reason for our barrenness. I realize that you all work hard, but there is almost no fruit. The Lord says, "By the fruit the tree is known" (Matt. 12:33), but we are a tree without any fruit. Everywhere among us barrenness is very prevailing. A good, gentle pastor may not have a particular gift, such as the gift of speaking; he may simply visit people and welcome them when they come to his meeting, but according to statistics, he will have a ten-percent yearly increase. We, however, do not have even a ten-percent increase. Can you see how barren we are? Many of you are good speakers, knowing the higher truths. The truths we hold are much higher than those in Christianity. However, we do not have fruit because we are lacking in the Father's loving and forgiving heart and the Son's shepherding and seeking spirit. We condemn and regulate others rather than shepherd and seek them. We are short of love and shepherding. These are the vital factors for us to bear fruit, that is, to gain people. I am very concerned for our full-time training. Do we train the young ones to gain people or to regulate people? We have to reconsider our ways, as Haggai said (Hag. 1:5). Our way is not right; something is wrong. (*A Word of Love to the Co-workers, Elders, Lovers, and Seekers of the Lord,* pp. 40-41)

ACCORDING TO GOD'S LOVE

Our shepherding should be according to God's love toward the fallen human race. The fallen human race is joined with Satan to be his world in his system, but God has a heart of love toward these people. (*The Vital Groups,* p. 38)

* * *

We must be shepherds with the loving and forgiving heart of our Father God in His divinity and the shepherding and finding spirit of our Savior Christ in His humanity. We also must have the heavenly vision of all the divine and mystical teachings of Christ. Shepherding and teaching are the obligation of the vital groups and the basic way ordained by God to build up the Body of Christ consummating in the New Jerusalem. (*The Vital Groups,* pp. 55-56)

* * *

If this kind of fellowship is received by us, I believe there will be a big revival on the earth, not by a few spiritual giants but by the many members of Christ's Body being shepherds who follow the steps of the processed Triune God in seeking and gaining fallen people. (*The Vital Groups,* p. 40)

STIRRING UP AN ATMOSPHERE
TO RESTORE THE DORMANT SAINTS

Although *Hymns,* #471 speaks of a saint returning to the Lord, we rarely sing this hymn because we have neglected the matter of restoring the dormant saints. I wrote this hymn at the start of the work in Taiwan because I felt a need to help the saints who were weak, backslidden, or cold. I used this hymn to stir up an atmosphere to help the weak ones and restore the backslidden ones. When we first arrived in Taiwan, we did not have an atmosphere of preaching the gospel, studying the truth, and pursuing the growth in life. We also did not have an atmosphere of taking care of people or serving the Lord. Hence, we felt that we needed to stir up such an atmosphere.

RECOVERING THE DORMANT SAINTS

The first move of the church must be to recover the saints who have not been meeting and those with whom we have lost contact. According to our records, this is not a small matter. The church in Taipei has more than fifty thousand information cards. If we subtract the ones who meet regularly, the ones who have gone abroad, and the small number who have passed away, there are still at least forty-five thousand. Since the church in Taipei typically accounts for about half of the saints on Taiwan, there should be more than ninety thousand dormant saints on the whole island.

These saints are the harvest from our past labor and hard work. They were baptized, and they filled out information cards. They are our family members, but they have all disappeared; therefore, we must take this matter seriously. Now is the time to put the affairs of our household in order, and the first matter we should address is to find these saints in order to bring them back. If we would do this thoroughly by the Lord's grace, we could recover two-thirds of them within two to three years. It would not be surprising to recover three to five thousand during the first half of this year, but recovering the majority will require a long-term effort by the saints who regularly meet in small groups. This is something that requires labor, but at least two-thirds will be recovered if we do it well. If thirty thousand saints are recovered, this will greatly strengthen the testimony and service of the church in Taipei.

THOROUGHLY EXAMINING THE INFORMATION CARDS

In order to recover these brothers and sisters, our initial plan is to thoroughly examine the existing information cards. Among the fifty thousand names in the church in Taipei, about ten thousand of the addresses are accurate. Of this number, there are approximately five to six thousand saints who participate in the church life regularly and about six thousand more who come to an occasional meeting. Thus, we have accurate address information for these saints. The information regarding these six thousand saints who occasionally meet has been distributed to each small group; this is a very good situation. We need to begin by recovering the brothers and sisters who seldom attend meetings but whose whereabouts are known. This involves a work of visitation and restoration.

We also need to locate the nearly forty thousand saints whose whereabouts are unknown. This is very time consuming, and we are in the process of looking for a way that the churches in Taiwan can coordinate with each other in order to find these saints. We have begun by distributing these information cards to each small group so that they can at least go to the addresses that are listed on the cards. This is a way for us to begin to restore these saints.

RECEIVING THE BURDEN TO GO OUT AND VISIT

The key to recovering these saints is for the brothers and sisters who regularly meet in the small groups to receive a burden. Without a burden, it will be difficult to move; with a burden, there will be grace. We need a burden to visit eight or nine, not just one or two. On average, each saint needs to be willing to contact at least eight. This is a great and difficult task. Nevertheless, I want to encourage you with one statistic: when the number of saints attending the meetings increases to forty thousand, approximately one out of every thirty people in Taipei will be one of our brothers and sisters. This will make it quite easy for us to penetrate every social level with the gospel. We will have brothers and sisters in every trade and profession, whether accountants, business owners, army generals, university professors, homemakers, or taxi drivers.

STRENGTHENING THE TESTIMONY AND PRAYING DESPERATELY

Our testimony needs to be strengthened. The saints who are wandering outside are scattered and not enjoying the riches of our family. They are truly like the prodigal son who could not find even carob pods to eat (Luke 15:13-16). But in the Father's house, in God's house, which is the church, the food is plentiful. Therefore, we must be compassionate toward them and bring them home to enjoy the riches in the Father's house with us.

Before going out, we need to pray thoroughly. I can absolutely testify to the effectiveness of prayer. In 1932, when the Lord raised up the church in Chefoo, I could see the effectiveness of our prayer every day. The Lord would bring people in ways that were quite wonderful. We have to believe that our concern matches the Lord's concern on the throne; in fact, His concern has touched us to be concerned for others. Thus, we must receive a burden to pray. In the beginning we may not know the names of the ones who need to be restored. We may only know that there are forty to fifty thousand who need our prayer. We can tell the Lord, "Remember these saints." I believe that if two to three thousand pray daily, the Lord will hear our prayer.

THE PRINCIPLE OF VISITING

Visiting dormant saints needs much consideration. If we do not do it properly, we will drive them further away. If our visiting will only drive them further away, it would be better not to visit them. When saints ask me what they should do when they visit, it is difficult to give a specific answer because I have found that my ways do not always work.

HAVING A PRAYING AND LEARNING SPIRIT

Consider the example of boxing. A teacher may teach boxing in the classroom in one way, but when it comes to the actual boxing match, the teacher's instructions may not work. In a boxing match, one has to make adjustments according to the actual situation. Consequently, the most important matter in visiting is to have a praying and learning spirit, saying, "O Lord, only You can restore this one." None of us can do this in ourselves. Those with no experience will certainly face difficulties, but even those with experience cannot rely on what they have learned in the past, because every person's situation is different. We must look to the Lord, praying, "Have mercy on me. I can do nothing. Give me the wisdom and the words I need to speak."

RELYING ON THE WORK OF THE HOLY SPIRIT

As we seek out the saints, we must rely on the work of the Holy Spirit. I truly believe that my return to the meetings was altogether the work of the Holy Spirit; it was the Holy Spirit who brought me back. The work of the Spirit is likened in Luke 15 to a woman who lights a lamp to seek a lost coin. The Holy Spirit is able to shine upon the saints with the Lord's word and is willing to search for them until they are found (vv. 8-9). (*Crucial Words of Leading in the Lord's Recovery, Book 4: The Increase and Spread of the Church,* pp. 162, 163-165, 165-166, 172)

LOVE BEING THE MOST EXCELLENT WAY

The end of 1 Corinthians 12 reveals that love is the most excellent way (v. 31b). How can one be an elder? Love is the most excellent way. How can one be a co-worker? Love is the most excellent way. How do we shepherd people? Love is the most excellent way. Love is the most excellent way for us to prophesy and to teach others. Love is the most excellent way for us to be anything or do anything.

The church is not a police station to arrest people or a law court to judge people, but a home to raise up the believers. Parents know that the worse their children are, the more they need their raising up. If our children were angels, they would not need our parenting to raise them up. The church is a loving home to raise up the children. The church is also a hospital to heal and to recover the sick ones. Finally, the church is a school to teach and edify the unlearned ones who do not have much understanding. Because the church is a home, a hospital, and a school, the co-workers and elders should be one with the Lord to raise up, to heal, to recover, and to teach others in love.

Some of the churches, however, are police stations to arrest the sinful ones and law courts to judge them. Paul's attitude was different. He said, "Who is weak, and I am not weak?" (2 Cor. 11:29a). When the scribes and Pharisees brought an adulterous woman to the Lord, He said to them, "He who is without sin among you, let him be the first to throw a stone at her" (John 8:7). After all of them left, the Lord asked the sinful woman, "Woman, where are they? Has no one condemned you?" She said, "No one, Lord." Then Jesus said, "Neither do I condemn you" (vv. 10-11). Who is without sin? Who is perfect? Paul said, "To the weak I became weak that I might gain the weak" (1 Cor. 9:22). This is love. We should not consider that others are weak but we are not. This is not love. Love covers and builds up, so love is the most excellent way for us to be anything and to do anything for the building up of the Body of Christ. (*The Vital Groups,* pp. 74, 75)

* * *

We need to have this kind of love and go to tell all the dormant ones who think that the church condemns them that the church does not condemn anyone. Rather, the church wants to see all the dormant ones come back. If they all would come back, I would weep with tears of thanksgiving to the Lord. The Lord can testify for me that I do not condemn anyone. We have no qualification to condemn anyone. Without the Lord's mercy, we would be the same as the dormant ones. Therefore, we must love them. It all depends upon love, as the wise king Solomon said, "Love covers all transgressions" (Prov. 10:12). We love people. We love the opposers, and we love the top rebels. I really mean it. We love them and do not hate them. Who am I? I am not qualified to condemn or to hate. Am I perfect? Even the prophet Isaiah, when he saw the Lord, said, "Woe is me, for I am finished! / For I am a man of unclean lips, / And in the midst of a people of unclean lips I dwell" (Isa. 6:5). Who is clean today? If we criticize people and say something bad about them, we are not clean. (*A Word of Love to the Co-workers, Elders, Lovers, and Seekers of the Lord,* pp. 32-33)

LOVE BEING THE GREATEST

Love is not jealous, is not provoked, does not take account of evil, covers all things, endures all things, never falls away, and is the greatest (1 Cor. 13:4-8, 13).

The elders need to realize that in their shepherding, they have to cover others' sins, not to take account of others' evils. Love covers all things, not only the good things but also the bad things. Whoever uncovers the defects, shortcomings, and sins of the members of the church is disqualified from the eldership. Our uncovering of the members under our eldership, our shepherding, annuls our qualification. Love also endures all things and never falls away. First Corinthians 13 concludes by saying, "Now there abide faith, hope, love, these three; and the greatest of these is love." (*The Vital Groups,* pp. 71, 72)

TEACHERS' TRAINING
(1)
THE PROPER UNDERSTANDING OF TEACHING, AND RECEIVING THE WORD AS THE BREATH OF GOD TO PRODUCE GOD-MEN

Scripture Reading: 2 Tim. 3:16-17; John 6:63; Matt. 4:4; Eph. 6:17-18; 1 Tim. 2:4

I. The Scriptures teach us the things of God and the things concerning God, even teaching us God Himself; there is a great difference between teaching about God and teaching God—2 Tim. 3:16-17; John 6:63; Eph. 6:17:

A. According to 2 Timothy 3:16, the Scriptures are God-breathed, indicating that the Scriptures are the breathing out of God and that our reading of the Scriptures should be our receiving of God's breath.

B. We need a clear understanding of the nature of our Summer School of Truth; we should not conduct the Summer School of Truth in a secular way; instead, our summer school is for the handling of the divine truth, which is the reality of the Triune God:

1. In a sense, our summer school is a kind of school, but actually it should be a "restaurant"; our intention is to serve, to minister, God as different "dishes" for eating; the nature of the Summer School of Truth is a matter of ministering, of serving, the Triune God to the young people.

2. Through our teaching, everyone in our class should be brought to God; we need to labor to

bring every young person in our class to the Triune God, so that by the time we have finished all the lessons, the students in our class will have gained the Triune God, not mere knowledge about God in letters.

II. Whereas all secular books are the same in nature, the Bible is different from other books; we need to see the uniqueness of the Bible:

A. The Bible is God's breath, and God's breath is the Spirit of God, for God is Spirit; we must be a person who is continually breathing the Lord, a person who is always inhaling God; our reading of the Bible should be a kind of inhaling, and our teaching of the Bible should be a kind of exhaling—2 Tim. 3:16; John 4:24; cf. 20:22.

B. The Lord's words are Spirit and life, the embodiment of the Spirit of life; when we receive His words by exercising our spirit, we get the Spirit, who gives life; when we read the Bible, we should receive life; and when we teach others concerning the Bible, they should receive life—6:63.

C. The Word of God is the sword of the Spirit; it is common for Christians to be enlightened, rebuked, corrected, and instructed by the Bible, but not many experience the word of the Bible as a sword that kills the enemy—Eph. 6:17-18:

1. Paul speaks of "the sword of the Spirit, which Spirit is the word of God" (v. 17); the sword is not the word directly; rather, the sword is the Spirit directly, and then the Spirit is the word:

   a. This indicates that if we would deal with the enemy Satan, the Bible must become the Spirit; if we would use the word of the Bible as a sword to kill the enemy, in our experience the word must be the Spirit.

   b. If we would take the word of the Bible as a sword for fighting the enemy, we must touch the Bible in a way that is full of the Spirit.

2. Ephesians reveals that our enemies are the evil

spirits, "the world-rulers of this darkness," "the spiritual forces of evil in the heavenlies"; experientially, the word we receive as the Spirit becomes the sword to slay these enemies—Eph. 6:12, 17:

   a. We need to realize that things such as our opinion, thought, temper, emotion, natural life, and point of view are often used by the powers of darkness in the air to damage the Body life.

   b. If the enemy is to be defeated, we must learn to receive the word as the Spirit, which becomes the sword to deal with the enemy.

 3. Without the word as the Spirit to be the killing sword, there would be no way for us to be kept in the church life over the years; we can be kept in the church life and in the ministry through the killing of the word as the Spirit.

 4. The word becoming the Spirit, which becomes a killing sword, may be compared to the effect of an antibiotic on the germs that cause illness in our body:

   a. In order for our body to be saved, the germs need to be killed by an antibiotic; the word that we receive in a living way as the Spirit is a spiritual antibiotic that kills the "germs" within us.

   b. When the germs are killed, the evil forces in the air have no way to take advantage of us; then we can live a healthy Body life, a healthy church life.

 D. The word that proceeds out of the mouth of God is our real food, indicating that the Bible is not only for life-imparting but also for nourishing; when we teach the Bible to others, we should nourish them— Matt. 4:4.

III. On God's side the Bible is God's breathing; on our side the Bible is for us to receive profit in four matters—

teaching, conviction or reproof, correction, and instruction—2 Tim. 3:16-17:

A. If we have the proper and adequate spiritual experience, we will realize that teaching equals revelation;
teaching is actually nothing less than a divine revelation:

1. A revelation is the opening of a veil; as we are
teaching the young people, we should be taking
away a veil so that they may see something of
the Triune God.

2. To teach is to roll away the veil; go to the summer
school for the purpose of rolling away the veil.

B. Whenever we see something of God, we realize our
mistakes, wrongdoings, shortcomings, and our sins;
the result is that we are reproved; this reproof
comes from the revelation we receive.

C. Conviction is followed by correction; correction is
a matter of setting right what is wrong, turning
someone to the right way, and restoring to an upright
state.

D. After we have been corrected, we will receive the
proper instruction—the instruction in righteousness; righteousness is a matter of being right.

E. The issue of teaching, reproof, correction, and instruction in righteousness is that the man of God
becomes complete; such a God-man, such a man of
God, is produced by God's breathing out of Himself; God's breathing produces God-men—v. 17.

IV. The purpose of the Summer School of Truth is to
bring our young people not only into God's salvation
but also into the full knowledge of the truth; we
should endeavor to bring the young people into the
experiential knowledge of the reality of the Triune
God—1 Tim. 2:4.

Excerpts from the Ministry:

THE PROPER UNDERSTANDING OF TEACHING

In this series of messages we will cover some important

matters related to training teachers to serve with the young people in the Summer School of Truth. What we will consider here will be helpful not only to those who teach in our summer school but to all those who speak for the Lord.

We need to have the proper understanding of the words *teacher, teaching,* and *school.* Regarding these words we all may have our own "lexicons." Let us drop the different lexicons and come to the Scriptures as the unique lexicon. The word *teaching* is found in 2 Timothy 3:16, where we are told that "all Scripture is God-breathed and profitable for teaching." The only time the word *school* is used in the New Testament is in Acts 19:9. This verse tells us that when "some were hardened and would not be persuaded, speaking evil of the Way before the multitude," Paul "withdrew from them and separated the disciples, reasoning daily in the school of Tyrannus." Tyrannus might have been a teacher, and Paul might have rented his school and used it as a meeting hall to preach and teach the word of the Lord to both Jews and Gentiles for two years (v. 10). Paul alluded to some kind of school when he told us that he was "trained at the feet of Gamaliel" (22:3), a teacher of the law (5:34).

THE SCRIPTURES TEACHING US GOD HIMSELF

The reason we need to set aside our personal lexicons and study the words of the Scriptures is that the Scriptures teach us the things of God and the things concerning God. We may even say that the Scriptures teach us God Himself. When some hear this they may ask, "Can we teach God? How can God be taught?" Today's seminaries do not teach God; they merely teach about God. The Scriptures, on the contrary, teach us God and also teach us the things of God. There is a great difference between teaching about God and teaching God.

THE SCRIPTURES BEING GOD-BREATHED

However, many Christians do not realize the significance of this difference. When they read the Bible, they read it in the same way as they read a secular book. This is absolutely wrong. The Bible, especially the New Testament, does not teach us to read the Scriptures in a common, secular way.

Rather, Ephesians 6:17 and 18 tell us to receive the word of God by means of all prayer and petition. The reason we need to receive the word of God by prayer is that, according to 2 Timothy 3:16, the Scriptures are God-breathed. This indicates that the Scriptures are the breathing out of God. God has breathed Himself out in the Scriptures, and thus our reading of the Scriptures should be our receiving of God's breath. When God breathes Himself out, He exhales Himself. When we read the Scriptures, or when we receive the Scriptures, we inhale God. Reading the Bible therefore involves both God's exhaling and our inhaling. This is altogether different from reading a book in a secular way. Unfortunately, many believers read the Bible in the same way as they read a textbook or a newspaper. This is a serious mistake, and we must avoid it as we are taking care of the young people in the Summer School of Truth.

We should not conduct the Summer School of Truth in a secular way. Actually, I do not like the word *school*. Using this word may cause others to think that we intend to teach in a common, secular manner. Some may even have the concept that the ones who take care of the Summer School of Truth should be school teachers by profession. This concept is mistaken. Being a school teacher does not qualify one for serving in our summer school. Do not think that having been a school teacher for many years qualifies someone to teach in our summer school. Those who serve in the Summer School of Truth should not serve according to their natural ability or professional training. Our summer school does not deal with any secular matters, such as mathematics, history, geography, and science. Instead, our summer school is for the handling of the divine truth, that is, the reality of the Triune God. What we intend to teach our young people is the reality of the Triune God. Concerning this, our natural teaching ability does not avail.

THE NATURE OF THE SUMMER SCHOOL OF TRUTH

My burden in this message is to point out what the nature of the Summer School of Truth is. Once we have a clear understanding of the nature of our summer school, we will know what to do and how to do it.

Not Teaching Theology but Ministering
the Triune God as Spiritual Food

The nature of the Summer School of Truth actually is not a matter of teaching but of ministering or serving. The purpose of our summer school is to minister something to the young people. We may use a restaurant as an illustration. A restaurant is not for teaching about food but for serving food. Those who serve in a restaurant do not merely give people a menu and then teach them about food. Instead, the serving ones supply others with different courses of food for eating. The principle should be the same with what we call the Summer School of Truth. In a sense, our summer school is a kind of school, but actually it should be a "restaurant." Our intention is not to give the young people a "menu" and then teach them about God. Our intention is to serve, to minister, God as different "dishes" for eating. Thus, the nature of the Summer School of Truth is a matter of ministering, of serving, the Triune God to the young people.

The situation of today's seminaries is very different from this. Seminary instructors pay very little attention, if any, to ministering spiritual food to the students. Instead of ministering God, these instructors mainly teach theology, the mere knowledge about God. They do not minister God Himself to the students. We do not want our summer school to resemble a theological school or seminary. Our school should actually be a "restaurant" serving the Triune God to the young saints.

Bringing the Young People
to the Triune God through the Lesson Books,
Which Are Based on the Bible

In the Summer School of Truth our textbook is the Bible, and all our lesson books are based on the Bible. Our goal is to bring the young people not to the lesson books but to bring them to the Triune God through the lesson books. Our lesson books should be a channel through which the young people are brought to the Triune God. If you realize this, then you will also realize that it is not sufficient merely to teach your class with the lesson book as if you were teaching in a secular school. Everyone in your class should gain the Triune God. Do not bring the young people to the lesson book—bring them to the Triune God through the lesson book. The lesson book is a channel for those whom you are serving to be brought to God and to gain God. This means that your aim is not to teach the lesson book but to bring the young people to God through the channel of the lesson book. This is the nature of the Summer School of Truth.

Through your teaching, your serving, in the Summer School of Truth, everyone in your class should be brought to God. You need to pray and endeavor concerning this. You need to labor to bring every young person in your class to the Triune God, so that by the time you have finished all the lessons, the students in your class will have gained the Triune God and will have been filled with God, not with mere knowledge about God in letters.

THE UNIQUENESS OF THE BIBLE

We have seen that our textbook is the Bible. Now we need to consider further what the Bible is. Apparently the Bible is the same as any other book—a composition of words. Whereas all secular books are the same in nature, the Bible is different from other books. The Bible is unique.

The Holy Breath

I would like to point out again that 2 Timothy 3:16 says, "All Scripture is God-breathed." The Scriptures are the breath of God, or the breathing out of God, God's breathing out of Himself. The Bible, therefore, is God's breath, and God's breath is the Spirit of God, for God is Spirit (John 4:24). The Greek word for *Spirit* is *pneuma,* which is also the word for *breath.* Thus, we may say that the Holy Spirit is the holy breath (cf. 20:22). God is Spirit, and the Spirit is the holy breath. To say that all Scripture is God-breathed is to say that the Bible is the breath, the breathing out, of the very God who is Spirit. God has breathed Himself out, and this breathing out of God is the Bible. This is what 2 Timothy 3:16 is saying when it tells us that the Scriptures are God-breathed.

Spirit and Life

In John 6:63 the Lord Jesus says, "It is the Spirit who gives life...the words which I have spoken to you are spirit and are life." The word that proceeds out of the mouth of the Lord Jesus is spirit, *pneuma*. His words are the embodiment of the Spirit, who gives life. This indicates that the word which comes out of the Lord's mouth is His breath, the breathing out of Himself. This is a further indication that the words of the Scriptures are God-breathed.

The Sword of the Spirit

In Ephesians 6:17 Paul charges us to receive "the sword of the Spirit, which Spirit is the word of God." The antecedent of *which* is *Spirit,* not *sword,* indicating that the Spirit is the word of God. When we read the Bible, we must touch the word of God as the Spirit. Along with 2 Timothy 3:16 and John 6:63, this verse reveals that the Bible is God's breathing out. Since God is Spirit, what He breathes out must also be Spirit. The words of the Bible, therefore, are the breathing out of God Himself as the Spirit.

PROFITABLE FOR TEACHING, CONVICTION, CORRECTION, AND INSTRUCTION IN RIGHTEOUSNESS

Second Timothy 3:16 says not only that the Scriptures are God-breathed but also that the Scriptures are "profitable for teaching, for conviction, for correction, for instruction in righteousness." On God's side the Bible is God's breathing. On our side the Bible is for us to receive profit in four matters— teaching, conviction or reproof, correction, and instruction. The order here is significant. Why does teaching and not instruction come first? Why does correction come before instruction and reproof before correction? And why does teaching come first? The order is first teaching and then reproof, correction, and instruction.

Teaching—the Rolling Away of the Veil

What is teaching? How do you understand the word *teaching?* We need to know the denotation of this word as it is used by Paul.

If we have the proper and adequate spiritual experience, we will realize that in verse 16 teaching equals revelation. Teaching is actually nothing less than a divine revelation. Since teaching equals revelation, as you are teaching the young people in your class in the Summer School of Truth, you must present a revelation to them.

A revelation is the opening of a veil. As you are teaching the young people, you should be taking away a veil so that they may see something of the Triune God. A certain matter may be hidden from view, but by your teaching you should gradually open the veil. This is teaching.

When you are serving in the Summer School of Truth, you should not allow the veil to remain over the eyes of the young people. Rather, as they are listening to you, the veil should be rolled away little by little. To teach is to roll away the veil. Go to the summer school for the purpose of rolling away the veil.

Now we can see that for the Bible to be profitable for teaching means that it is profitable for unveiling, for rolling away the veil. A veil cannot be taken away suddenly; it cannot be rolled away all at once. On the contrary, the veil is rolled away a little at a time. Time after time and in session after session, you need gradually to roll away the veil. If you do this, your way of teaching will be an unveiling. This kind of teaching always presents a revelation to others. Those who are under such teaching will be able to see something concerning the Triune God.

This understanding of teaching applies not only to those who teach in the Summer School of Truth but to all those who speak for the Lord. When you speak something in the church meeting, your speaking should be the rolling away of the veil. This means that your speaking should present a revelation.

Reproof Coming from the Revelation We Receive

It is significant that in verse 16 teaching is followed by conviction, or reproof. The reason for this is that no one can see something of God without being reproved by what he sees. Those who are under your teaching will see something, and what they see will convict, reprove, them.

Whenever we see something of God, we realize our mistakes, wrongdoings, shortcomings, and our sins. The result is that we are reproved; we are rebuked. This reproof comes from the revelation we receive. However, often in our reading of the Scriptures, we read without receiving any revelation, and thus there is no reproof. But when in our reading of the Scriptures we receive a revelation, the revelation will reprove us and rebuke us.

Correction

Reproof is followed by correction. Teaching, or revelation, brings us reproof, and reproof produces correction. Correction is a matter of setting right what is wrong, turning someone to the right way, and restoring to an upright state.

Instruction in Righteousness

After we have been corrected, we will receive the proper instruction—the instruction in righteousness. Whereas Paul here does not use any modifiers for teaching, reproof, and correction, he does use a modifier for instruction and speaks of the instruction in righteousness. Righteousness is a matter of being right. Hence, the instruction here is for us to be right.

The reason we are reproved and rebuked is that we are wrong in many different ways and aspects. We may be wrong with God, with Christ, and with the Spirit. We may be wrong with the church, with the brothers and sisters, with our husband or wife, with our parents, with our children, with our neighbors, and even with ourselves. We may be wrong in the way we spend our money, in the way we spend our time, in the way we dress, or in the way we style our hair. Because we may be wrong in so many different things, we are rebuked by the revelation we receive when we read the Scriptures.

From our experience we know that often we are rebuked immediately after receiving a revelation. I can testify that time after time I have been rebuked by a revelation that came from reading the Bible or from a teaching. Have you not had such an experience? Because we are sinful and unrighteous, we need the rebuking that comes through teaching.

We may memorize Bible verses and recite them without

experiencing any rebuking. But when we receive a revelation from the Word, that revelation exposes our sinfulness and rebukes us. We are not rebuked by man nor are we rebuked directly by God—we are rebuked by the teaching of the Word. When we are rebuked in this way, we are spontaneously corrected, and when we are corrected we have the instruction in righteousness. The result is that we are adjusted.

We may be adjusted in a particular matter and become right in this matter. However, we may not be right in this matter once for all. For example, suppose a brother is wrong with his wife. Under the revelation from the Word, he is rebuked and adjusted. He repents and then apologizes to his wife, and as a result he is now right with her. But a few days later he may be wrong with her again, and once again he will need to be rebuked, corrected, and adjusted.

THE MAN OF GOD BECOMING COMPLETE

In verse 17 Paul goes on to say, "That the man of God may be complete, fully equipped for every good work." A man of God is a God-man, one who partakes of God's life and nature (John 1:13; 2 Pet. 1:4), thus being one with God in His life and nature (1 Cor. 6:17) and thereby expressing Him. Such a God-man, such a man of God, is produced by God's breathing out of Himself. God's breathing produces God-men.

Not a Good Man but a God-man

You may be a good man but not a God-man. This means that with you there is an extra *o*. You should have only one *o*, but instead of one you have two. The more you receive teaching, revelation, the more this extra *o* will be cut off. However, it is hard to get rid of the second *o* once for all, for it is like a man's beard that appears again after it has been shaved or like the grass that grows again after the lawn has been mowed. From experience we know that the second *o* always comes back. Perhaps with you this extra *o* has only partially been cut off, and the part that has been shaved keeps coming back again. If this is our situation, then we are a man of God—a God-man— with an extra *o*. We need the teaching from the Scriptures to shave away this *o* again and again.

The Issue of Teaching, Reproof, Correction, and Instruction in Righteousness

The word *that* at the beginning of 2 Timothy 3:17 indicates that this verse is an issue of the preceding verse. The issue of teaching, reproof, correction, and instruction in righteousness is that the man of God becomes complete.

In the Summer School of Truth you should present a teaching that is an unveiling, the rolling away of the veil. Then the young people in your class will see something of God, and what they see will rebuke them, correct them, and afford them the proper instruction in righteousness to make them right both with God and with man. The issue, the outcome, will be that the man of God becomes complete and equipped for every good work.

The purpose of the Summer School of Truth is not to give mental knowledge to the young people. The goal of our summer school is to present teaching after teaching, revelation after revelation, so that the young ones may see God, see themselves, and be reproved, corrected, and instructed to be right with God and man that the man of God may be complete, fully equipped for every good work. Such a person will be a true man of God, a real God-man, continually inhaling the Triune God and thereby receiving revelation, reproof, correction, and instruction in righteousness.

RECEIVING THE WORD AS THE LIVING SPIRIT AND COMING TO THE FULL KNOWLEDGE OF THE TRUTH

We have seen that in nature the Scripture, the holy Word, is God's breath. The function of the Scripture is to unveil, to roll away the veil. Proper teaching is always a kind of unveiling. After the unveiling, we have reproof, correction, and instruction in righteousness "that the man of God may be complete, fully equipped for every good work" (v. 17).

THE LORD'S WORDS BEING SPIRIT AND LIFE

Let us now go on to consider further another important verse related to the nature of the Bible—John 6:63. Here the Lord Jesus says, "It is the Spirit who gives life...the words which I have spoken to you are spirit and are life." This indicates that the Lord's words are the embodiment of the Spirit of life. When we receive His words by exercising our spirit, we get the Spirit, who gives life.

When we read the Bible, we should receive life; and when we teach others concerning the Bible, they should receive life. If we do not receive life when we read the Bible, something is wrong. In our reading of the Bible, there may be no spirit; and in our teaching of the Bible to others, there also may be no spirit. For there to be no spirit means that there is no life. We may read a portion of the Bible, several verses or a few chapters, without receiving the life supply. The reason for this lack of supply is that in our reading of the Word there is no spirit. If we do not sense the Spirit as we are reading the Bible, we should realize that something is wrong, and then we should adjust ourselves.

In the same principle, as we are teaching the young people in the Summer School of Truth, we need to check whether there is any spirit in our teaching. If there is no spirit, we should change our way of teaching. Teaching a class in the Summer School of Truth should not be the same as teaching a class in a secular school. In a secular school there is no need of spirit, but in our summer school there is the need of much spirit.

INHALING AND EXHALING GOD

From experience we know that in order for there to be much spirit in our reading and teaching of the Bible, we need much prayer. We must be a person of prayer. In other words, we must be a person who is continually breathing the Lord, a person who is always inhaling God. Our reading of the Bible should be a kind of inhaling, and our teaching of the Bible should be a kind of exhaling. As you are teaching a class in the Summer School of Truth, you should be exhaling God into your students.

The Bible is God's breath; this breath is the Spirit; and the Spirit gives life. When you breathe the Spirit you receive not only unveiling, rebuking, correcting, and instructing—you receive life. Whenever you touch the Spirit as you are reading

the Bible, you receive life. Likewise, as you are teaching in the
Summer School of Truth, you need to touch the Spirit. You
should have the sense that you are touching not only the
Spirit but also the spirits of your students. You should have
the sense that you are exhaling God and that they are inhaling God. This means that there is a communication between
your exhaling and their inhaling. This indicates that your
way of teaching is right, for you are exercising to minister life
to the young people.

In teaching the Bible to others, you must be very strict
with yourself, adjusting yourself again and again. During
one class session you may need to adjust yourself a number
of times. If you experience failure the first few times you
teach, you should go back to the Lord with much prayer. Pray
yourself into the Lord, breathing God into you. Then, having
become a praying person, a person who inhales God, go back
to your class and exhale what you have received of God.

NOURISHING OTHERS
WITH THE WORD THAT PROCEEDS OUT
THROUGH THE MOUTH OF GOD

In Matthew 4:4 the Lord Jesus said, "Man shall not live on
bread alone, but on every word that proceeds out through the
mouth of God." Here we see that the word that proceeds out
through the mouth of God is our real food. This indicates that
the Bible is not only for life-imparting but also for nourishing.
When you teach the Bible to others, you should nourish them.
I hope that all the young ones in your class will have the
sense that they are not only being taught but also being nourished. Whether or not they are nourished through your teaching
depends on you.

The instructors in today's seminaries may claim that they
are teaching the Bible to their students. Yet most seminary
students are being starved to death. They receive no nourishment, because their instructors teach the Bible in a wrong way.
They teach the Bible in the same way as instructors in secular schools teach subjects such as geography, history, science,
and mathematics. Thus, there is no nourishment. Our way of
teaching must be different. When we teach the Scriptures to

the young people in the Summer School of Truth, we must nourish the students with the life supply, with words that proceed out of God's mouth.

We all need to be living persons, those who are living channels with the words of God proceeding out through us. God's word proceeds out through God's mouth, and we should let it proceed also out through us as a channel. When in the meetings a certain brother reads the Bible or teaches from the Bible, we do not receive any nourishment, but when another brother does the same thing, we are nourished. The reason for the difference is that the first brother read or spoke without any spirit, but the second brother read or spoke with much spirit. The principle is the same in your teaching a class in the Summer School of Truth. Your teaching must be in spirit and must be with spirit. As you are teaching, you need to be a living channel out through which the word of God is proceeding. If you are such a living channel, then the students in your class will receive spiritual food for their nourishment.

THE SWORD OF THE SPIRIT KILLING THE ENEMY

Let us now turn to Ephesians 6:17. Here Paul charges us to receive "the sword of the Spirit, which Spirit is the word of God." When I was a young Christian, I did not understand how the word of God could be a sword. I understood what it means to be enlightened by the Bible, for by reading the Bible I was enlightened. To some extent, by the Bible I was also rebuked, corrected, and instructed to be right with God and man. But I did not know how the Bible could become a sword, an offensive weapon to deal with the enemy. To understand this requires spiritual experience.

It is common for Christians to be enlightened, rebuked, corrected, and instructed by the Bible, but not many experience the word of the Bible as a sword that kills the enemy. The reason for this lack of experience is that we may receive the word of the Bible for teaching, rebuke, correction, and instruction without touching the Spirit. Even unbelievers may be enlightened by what they read in the Scriptures. Also, they may be rebuked, corrected, and instructed by what the Bible says concerning honor, love, humility, and honesty.

However, in their reading of the Scriptures there is nothing of the Spirit. However, if we would take the word of the Bible as a sword for fighting the enemy, we must touch the Bible in a way that is full of the Spirit.

The Word of God Being the Sword Indirectly

According to Paul's word in Ephesians 6:17, the word of God is the sword not directly but indirectly. Paul speaks of "the sword of the Spirit, which Spirit is the word of God." Here we have indirectness. The sword is not the word directly. Rather, the sword is the Spirit directly, and then the Spirit is the word. This indicates that if we would deal with the enemy Satan, the Bible must become the Spirit. Without the Spirit it may be possible for us to teach from the Bible that the young people should honor their parents and ask for forgiveness for what they have done wrong. But if we would use the word of the Bible as a sword to kill the enemy, in our experience the word must be the Spirit.

Understanding Ephesians 6:17 Experientially

At this juncture I would ask you to consider how, in a practical way, the word of the Bible can become the sword of the Spirit for fighting against the enemy. Can you give an illustration of this or a testimony concerning it? Ephesians 6:12 reveals that our enemies are the evil spirits, "the world-rulers of this darkness," "the spiritual forces of evil in the heavenlies." Can you testify from your experience how you have slain these enemies by taking the word as the sword? In order to give such a testimony, we need to understand Ephesians 6:17 experientially by handling the Bible in the way of the Spirit and not merely in a mental way. I am concerned that in the Summer School of Truth you will teach the young people merely in a mental way, as if you were teaching in a secular school. We all have to learn to teach the Bible in the way of the Spirit.

Ephesians, a book on the church as the Body of Christ, talks about the Body life, the oneness of the Body (4:4), and the Body being the fullness of the One who fills all in all (1:23). We need to realize that things such as our opinion,

thought, temper, emotion, natural life, and point of view are
often used by the powers of darkness in the air to damage
the Body life. As brothers and sisters in the church, we all
have our emotion, thought, opinion, and natural life, and we
all have our own point of view. Quite often we are offended,
not due to the wrongdoings of others but simply due to our
emotion or opinion. A chair cannot be offended, because it
does not have feelings. No matter how you treat a chair, it will
not be offended. However, it is easy for brothers and sisters in
the church to be offended.

Due to their emotion, sisters are easily offended. Suppose
an older brother speaks a word to a particular sister and she
is offended because of her emotion. Then the evil power in the
air comes in to take advantage of her emotion, and she determines not to forget that she has been offended. Apparently
the problem is her emotion. Actually the problem is that her
emotion has been taken over by the evil force in the air. This
means that the real enemy is not this sister's emotion but the
evil spirit in the air that takes advantage of her emotion in
order to damage the church life. Because of the enemy's use
of her emotion, this sister first has a negative effect on her
husband, and then she goes on to have a negative effect on
several others. As a result, part of the Body is poisoned. If the
enemy is to be defeated in this situation, the sister must
learn to receive the word as the Spirit, which becomes the
sword to deal with the enemy.

Being Preserved in the Church Life
and in the Ministry by Receiving
the Word as the Spirit

This is something I have learned through many years of
experience. I am not a "marble" person who cannot be offended.
I have often been offended by others in the church life or in
my family life. How have I been able to get through all the
offenses? I get through by receiving the word as the Spirit.
The word I receive as the Spirit then becomes the sword to slay
the enemy. Apparently the sword of the Spirit kills my emotion;
actually it kills the evil spirit in the air who takes advantage
of my emotion. Whereas my emotion is killed directly, the evil

spirit is killed indirectly. In this way I have been able to get through the offenses.

When some hear this they might say, "Brother Lee, show me a verse that can kill your emotion directly and kill the evil power in the air indirectly." This is not a matter of a particular verse that touches our emotion but a matter of applying Ephesians 6:17 in an experiential way. Suppose in the evening I am offended by one of the elders. Because I fear the Lord, I do not dare to talk about this with others. The next morning I rise up to contact the Lord in the Word. I do not read any verses that touch the matter of my emotion. Instead, I simply begin to read the Bible with the exercise of the spirit. I may read Genesis 1:1: "In the beginning God created the heaven and the earth." As I read this verse, I receive the word in a living way as the Spirit, and the Spirit, which is the word, becomes the sword that kills my emotion directly and kills the evil force indirectly. Spontaneously, the offense is gone, and no damage is done to the church. However, if the offense were allowed to remain, it would cause serious damage to the church life. I believe that many of us have experienced receiving the word of God in this way.

Without the word as the Spirit to be the killing sword, there would be no way for us to be kept in the church life over the years. For more than half a century, I have been traveling, visiting the churches, and contacting thousands of saints. Without the word as the Spirit to kill all the enemies, I would not still be here ministering. If I had allowed myself to remain offended with a certain church or saint, I would have been finished with the ministry. I have been kept in the church life and in the ministry through the killing of the word as the Spirit.

A Spiritual Antibiotic

Suppose a particular brother is not happy with the church in his locality. He moves to another city, supposing that he will like the church there. However, after a short period of time, he becomes unhappy with this local church, so he moves to another place. But soon he is offended by something or someone in this church and he moves to yet another locality. Such a person cannot participate in the building up of the church. On the contrary, because there is no killing of the enemy within him, he causes the church to suffer damage.

According to Paul's word toward the end of Ephesians, a book concerning the church, we need to receive the word of God in a living way, that is, receive the word as the Spirit. The Spirit will then become the killing sword. This sword first kills us directly and then kills the power of darkness in the air indirectly. We may compare this kind of killing to the effect of an antibiotic on the germs that cause illness in our body. In order for our body to be saved, the germs need to be killed by an antibiotic. The word that we receive in a living way as the Spirit is a spiritual antibiotic that kills the "germs" within us. When the germs are killed, the evil forces in the air have no way to take advantage of us. Then we can live a healthy Body life, a healthy church life.

This is the way I have been preserved in the church life and in my ministry for so many years. Apart from the killing through the word as the Spirit, my ministry would have been terminated. Once again I would emphasize that we need to receive the word of God in a living way, so that in our experience the Spirit becomes the killing sword. When the word becomes the Spirit, the Spirit becomes the sword—the sword of the Spirit that kills the germs in us and the evil spirits in the air. In this way the Body, the church life, and our ministry are saved. This will enable our ministry to have a long life. However, the ministry of certain brothers has not lasted long. In their situation it was their ministry and not the enemy that was killed.

Let us all receive the word of God in a living way! As long as in our experience the word becomes the Spirit, the word will not only heal us but also kill the enemy.

All those who teach in the Summer School of Truth should help the young ones not merely to receive the word for the learning of certain biblical truths but to receive the word as the living Spirit. When they receive the word as the living Spirit, in their experience the Spirit will become the sword. Receiving the word in this way requires much prayer. This is why we need to have the proper pray-reading. Through pray-reading the Bible, we receive the word in a living way as the Spirit.

THE FULL KNOWLEDGE OF THE TRUTH

In 1 Timothy 2:4 Paul tells us that God "desires all men to be saved and to come to the full knowledge of the truth." Today it seems that most Christians bring others only into God's salvation; they do not go further to bring them into the full knowledge of the truth. The purpose of the Summer School of Truth is to bring our young people not only into God's salvation but also into the full knowledge of the truth. In this verse *truth* does not mean doctrine; it means reality and denotes all the real things revealed in God's Word, which are mainly Christ as the embodiment of God and the church as the Body of Christ. Every saved person should have a full knowledge, a complete realization, of these things. In our summer school, we should endeavor to bring the young people into the experiential knowledge of the reality of the Triune God. In order to do this, we ourselves need to be persons who are in this reality. (*Teachers' Training*, pp. 7-25)

LESSON TWENTY-FOUR

TEACHERS' TRAINING
(2)
LEARNING TO TEACH GOD'S ECONOMY
IN AN EXPERIENTIAL WAY, AND
CONVERTING DOCTRINE INTO EXPERIENCE

Scripture Reading: 1 Tim. 1:3-4; 2:4; 3:15; 2 Tim. 1:6-7; 2:2,
15, 22, 25

I. When you help the young people, do not give them a
   lot of doctrines; instead, give them something practical:

   A. We should not put too much emphasis on doctrines,
      not only when we have personal contact with them
      but also when we are preaching the gospel or giving
      messages to them.

   B. Because young people have many practical prob-
      lems, we need to spend some time to study the
      problems of the young people in their practical
      living; then what you speak is practical and related
      to the practical matters that you have touched in
      their lives.

II. In teaching the truth to the young people, we need to
    learn how to teach God's economy in an experiential
    way—1 Tim. 1:3-4; 2 Tim. 1:6-7; 2:2, 22:

    A. The teaching in the New Testament is focused on
       God's economy; however through the centuries there
       have been many teachings that have not been on
       God's economy; we must learn from history not to
       teach anything other than God's economy—1 Tim.
       1:3-4:

       1. The Greek word for *economy* means "household

law" and implies distribution; this word denotes a household management, a household administration, a household government, and, derivatively, a dispensation, a plan, or an economy for administration (distribution); hence, it is a household economy—v. 4; Eph. 1:10; 3:9.

2. There are many other matters in the Bible, such as the law, history and the prophecies, which can become distractions to us; some are distracted from God's economy through their readings of the Psalms or Proverbs.

3. As we teach in the Summer School of Truth, we should not have any burden, any view, or any vision other than God's economy; in our teaching we should know only one thing—God's economy.

B. In order for us to be those who are competent to teach God's economy and fulfill our commission, we have to be on fire; this is the reason Paul reminded Timothy to "fan into flame the gift of God," which was in him—2 Tim. 1:6; 2:2:

1. God has given us two precious things—His divine life and His divine Spirit; now we need to fan the gift of God into flame:

a. The first step in fanning the gift is not to exercise; the first step is to open all the "doors" and "windows"; we need to open our entire being—our mind, emotion, and will, our entire soul, our heart, and even our spirit.

b. Those who teach in the Summer School of Truth must open their entire being so that the "draft" may come in; the Spirit is in us already, but we need to fan the fire, the Spirit, into flame.

2. If our being is closed, we need to call on the name of the Lord Jesus; as we call on the Lord, we open not only our mouth but also our spirit and our heart; then the draft will come in, and that will fan into flame the eternal life and the eternal Spirit within us—v. 22.

C. If we would go to our class in the Summer School of Truth with a flame, we must be a person of prayer; if we are such a person, we will bring a spirit of prayer, an atmosphere of prayer, to our class.

III. Once we have an atmosphere of prayer, we are now ready to teach, not in a doctrinal way but in an experiential way; by doing this we will turn our teaching from doctrine to experience; this experiential fellowship will deeply impress the young people:

A. We should not ask our students merely to remember and recite all the points related to the lesson; that would be to teach in a doctrinal way:

1. If we would teach in an experiential way, we should help the young people to realize their situation and condition.

2. We must learn in our teaching to touch others experientially; we must apply every point of our teaching to their personal, practical situation.

B. When we teach a class in the Summer School of Truth, we should not take the way of giving messages or lectures; instead, we need to have personal talks with the young people, teaching every point experientially:

1. Every point of the lesson should be presented in a way that will create an experiential impression; apply every point to their actual situation.

2. As we are talking with them, we should be watchful over each one, paying particular attention to their expressions; this will help us to know the needs of our students.

C. If you want to stir up a praying spirit in the person with whom you are speaking, you yourself must be a person who is full of the praying spirit; adequate prayer will accomplish at least three things: it will impress the young people in an experiential way with the points of the lesson, stir up the praying spirit within them, and cause them to become living.

IV. In order to teach in an experiential way, we must convert every point in the lesson from doctrine into experience; after making such a conversion during our time of preparation, we should then speak to the young people about each point in the way of experience:

A. The more we speak in this way, the more they will be unveiled; they will see a vision that will expose them, and spontaneously they will be ushered into the experience of the very matter we have been presenting.

B. If we teach in the way of merely imparting doctrines from the printed materials, we will do nothing more than impart some knowledge to the minds of our students; as a result, they will gain nothing in an experiential way:

　1. The knowledge they gain may damage them; later, on another occasion, when they hear that word, they might say, "I know this already; I heard all about it in the Summer School of Truth."

　2. We must not damage the young people by giving them mere knowledge; in order to profit them with the truth, we must always teach them in an experiential way.

V. Before we begin to teach the young people in the Summer School of Truth, we ourselves need to receive Paul's inoculation and be filled, soaked, and saturated with the truth—1 Tim. 2:4; 3:15; 2 Tim. 2:15, 25:

A. The word *truth* has been wrongly understood by many readers of the Bible because they regard truth as a matter of doctrine; in the New Testament *truth* refers not to doctrine but to the real things revealed in the New Testament concerning Christ and the church according to God's New Testament economy—1 Tim. 2:4; cf. 1 John 1:6.

B. The element of the inoculation against the decline is the structure of the divine truth; the structure of the divine truth is the Triune God plus His redemption, which becomes our salvation.

C. The general subject of the first series of lessons in the Summer School of Truth is God's full salvation;

the full salvation of God is actually equal to the truth, because the Triune God with His all-inclusive redemption is the structure of the truth.

D. As we prepare ourselves to teach, we should not merely put our trust in the lesson book; we need to immerse ourselves in the truth concerning God's full salvation.

Excerpts from the Ministry:

EMPHASIZING PRACTICALITY INSTEAD OF STRESSING DOCTRINES

When you help the young people, do not give them a lot of doctrines; instead, give them something practical. You should not put too much emphasis on doctrines, not only when you have personal contact with them but also when you are preaching the gospel or giving messages to them. If you give them only some doctrines and they come only to listen, there will not be much effect. The more you speak doctrines, the more the young people become dead, cold, and backsliding. Because young people have many practical problems, you need to sense their feelings beginning with these problems. Therefore, you need to spend some time to study the problems of the young people in their practical living, including problems both before and after their salvation. Based upon your studies, when you preach the gospel or speak a word of edification to them, what you speak is practical and is related to the practical matters that you have touched in their lives. (*How to Lead the Young People*, pp. 22-23)

LEARNING TO TEACH GOD'S ECONOMY IN AN EXPERIENTIAL WAY

In the books of 1 and 2 Timothy we can see the way we should teach others. Regarding teaching, Paul charged Timothy, saying, "The things which you have heard from me through many witnesses, these commit to faithful men, who will be competent to teach others also" (2 Tim. 2:2). Let us consider what these two books tell us about teaching in an experiential way.

NOT TEACHING DIFFERENTLY
FROM GOD'S ECONOMY

In 1 Timothy 1:3-4 Paul spoke to Timothy, one of his closest co-workers, saying, "Even as I exhorted you, when I was going into Macedonia, to remain in Ephesus in order that you might charge certain ones not to teach different things nor to give heed to myths and unending genealogies, which produce questionings rather than God's economy, which is in faith." This indicates that some were teaching differently from God's economy, God's dispensation.

God's Household Administration

The Greek word for *economy* means "household law" and implies distribution. This word denotes a household management, a household administration, a household government, and, derivatively, a dispensation, a plan, or an economy for administration (distribution); hence, it is also a household economy. God's economy in faith is His household economy, His household administration, which is to dispense Himself in Christ into His chosen people that He may have a house to express Himself, which house is the church (3:15), the Body of Christ. Paul's ministry was centered on this economy of God (Col. 1:25; 1 Cor. 9:17), whereas the different teachings of the dissenting ones were used by God's enemy to distract His people from this economy.

Not Distracted by Other Biblical Things

The teaching in the New Testament is focused on God's economy, His dispensation. However, during the centuries following the completion of the Bible, there have been many teachings that have not been on God's economy. This should be a warning to us. We need to learn from history not to teach anything other than God's dispensation.

In 1 Timothy 1 Paul presents God's economy in opposition to different teachings. According to Paul's word here, some were teaching the law and genealogies rather than God's economy. In the Bible the law is a major subject. Judaism was built upon the law, and the Judaizers were zealous for the law and were wholly given to it. The Bible also contains many

genealogies, such as the genealogy of Abraham and the genealogy of David. In verse 4 the word *genealogies* probably refers
to Old Testament genealogies adorned with fables (Titus
3:9).

There are many other matters in the Bible, such as the
history and the prophecies, which can become distractions to
us. Some are distracted from God's economy through their
readings of the Psalms or Proverbs. If as we read the Bible we
are not under the control of a clear vision of God's economy,
we may be distracted not by heresies but by various things
found in the Bible. When you hear this you may question
whether biblical things can become distractions. It is a fact of
history that throughout the centuries nearly all Christians
have been distracted from God's economy by different biblical
things.

We must take heed to Paul's charge not to teach differently
from God's economy. We believe that since the time of the
apostles God's economy has not been stressed as much as it
has been stressed in the Lord's recovery, especially in the past
twenty years. God has a great plan—to dispense Himself in
His Trinity into His chosen people. This is God's economy. Our
teaching must be governed by a clear view of God's economy.
Whatever we teach should be related to God's economy.

God's Economy Being
Our Unique Burden, View, and Vision

As you teach in the Summer School of Truth, you should
not have any burden, any view, or any vision other than God's
economy. You need to be not only burdened with God's economy
but also soaked and saturated with God's economy. In your
teaching you should know only one thing—God's economy.
You should be able to declare, "God's economy is my burden,
my view, and my vision. My entire being has been soaked
in God's economy, and I know nothing else." To be sure, you
will teach many different lessons, but every lesson will be
structured with God's economy. Only when you are clear concerning this basic matter will you know what we intend to do
in the Summer School of Truth.

FANNING INTO FLAME THE GIFT OF GOD

We have pointed out that in 2 Timothy 2:2 Paul charged Timothy to commit to faithful men the things which he had heard from Paul. These faithful men should be those who are competent to teach others. In order to fulfill this commission, Timothy himself had to be on fire. This is the reason Paul reminded him to "fan into flame the gift of God," which was in him (1:6).

The Divine Life and the Divine Spirit

At this juncture we need to ask a question: What was the gift of God that Timothy was charged to fan into flame? The Pentecostal people might say that this was the gift of speaking in tongues, but this is doubtful, especially in view of the fact that in Paul's latest writings the miraculous things are rarely mentioned. I believe that, first, the gift in verse 6 is the gift of eternal life. A gift, of course, must be given by someone. God surely has given us something, and the first thing that He has given us is the divine life. We all have received eternal life, the divine life. I also believe that, second, the gift here is the gift of the divine Spirit. The eternal life and the divine Spirit, or the eternal Spirit, are both God Himself.

Bringing In the Draft
by Opening Our Entire Being

This understanding of the gift in verse 6 raises another question: How is it possible for us to fan the Holy Spirit? Christians usually think that the Holy Spirit fans us, that the Holy Spirit fans our spirit. Do we fan the Spirit, or does the Spirit fan us? Concerning this matter of fanning into flame the gift of God, we may still be under the influence of traditional Christian teaching. According to traditional teaching, the believers are told to ask for the Spirit, not to fan the Spirit. To ask for something implies that we do not have that thing. Hence, to ask for the Spirit implies that we do not have the Spirit. To fan the Spirit, on the contrary, implies that we have the Spirit already. The "fire" of the Spirit is in us as the "stove," but in order for the fire to burn, there is the need of a "draft." To fan the flame is to bring in the needed draft. This illustration may give you an idea about what it means to fan the Spirit as the gift of God within us.

God has given us two precious things—His divine life and His divine Spirit. Now we need to fan the gift of God into flame. The first step in fanning the gift is not to exercise; the first step is to open all the "doors" and "windows." We need to open our entire being. Open your mind, emotion, and will. Open your entire soul, open your heart, and open your spirit. Every morning we need to go to the Lord and open ourselves to Him. However, often we may spend time with the Lord without opening our being to Him. In such a situation the fire does not burn.

Those who teach in the Summer School of Truth must open their entire being—spirit, heart, soul, mind, emotion and will—so that the "draft" may come in. The Spirit is in you already, but you need to fan the fire, the Spirit, into flame. I am somewhat concerned that when you go to teach a class in our summer school, you will be a shut-up person, a person whose being is closed to the draft. You have the Spirit and eternal life within you, but because you are closed the draft cannot come in. If you are this kind of person, you will teach the young people merely according to your knowledge or according to what is printed in the lesson book. That kind of teaching is deadening. Before you go to teach, you must first fan the gift into flame. The more you open, the more the fire will burn. The draft from your fanning may cause the fire to burn for hours or even for the whole day.

Calling on the Name of the Lord Jesus and Exercising Our Spirit

In 2 Timothy 2:22 Paul told Timothy to "pursue righteousness, faith, love, peace with those who call on the Lord out of a pure heart." If your being is closed, you need to call on the name of the Lord Jesus. As you call on the Lord, open not only your mouth but also your spirit and your heart. Then the draft will come in, and that will fan into flame the eternal life and the eternal Spirit within you. Fan into flame the gift that you have received from God. Let the gift become a flame. Then go to teach the young people not with an "ice-cold" mind but with a flame. If you are too sober in your mind, you will be cold ice when you go to teach. Do not be cold! Be "boiling hot" with the gift that has been fanned into flame!

Thus far, we have seen that we should teach God's economy and that we should fan into flame the gift of God, opening our whole being and calling on the name of the Lord Jesus. In addition, we surely need to exercise our spirit. After charging Timothy to fan into flame the gift of God, Paul went on to say, "For God has not given us a spirit of cowardice, but of power and of love and of sobermindedness" (1:7). The spirit here denotes our spirit, regenerated and indwelt by the Holy Spirit (John 3:6; Rom. 8:16). To fan into flame the gift of God is thus related to our regenerated spirit. *Of power* refers to our will; *of love,* to our emotion; and *of sobermindedness,* to our mind. This indicates that having a strong will, a loving emotion, and a sober mind has very much to do with having a strong spirit for the exercise of the gift of God that is in us.

BRINGING IN A SPIRIT OF PRAYER

We all should be those who teach God's economy, who fan the gift of God into flame, who call on the name of the Lord Jesus, and who exercise our spirit. At this point we need to consider another crucial matter—being persons of prayer.

I have no doubt that, as believers in Christ, you have received the eternal life and the divine Spirit, but I am concerned that you will go to your class with "ice water" instead of a flame. We have emphasized the fact that to have a flame you need to let the draft come in through opening up to the Lord. Every morning you need to bring in the draft by fanning the gift of God into flame. However, suppose that you have just had a most unpleasant situation with your spouse, and now it seems impossible for you to fan the flame. It may take several days for you to be able once again to fan the flame by yourself, but this will be much easier to do if you pray with a small group of saints. If you pray by yourself, you may keep thinking about the situation with your spouse and thus have no way to fan the flame. However, if you pray with others, they will fan the flame within you. Eventually you also will be able to pray and you will fan them. Then the draft will come in, and you will have a flame.

If you would go to your class in the Summer School of Truth with a flame, you must be a person of prayer. If you are such a person, you will bring a spirit of prayer to your class. You will then be able to stir up the praying spirit of the young people in your class. Everyone must be stirred up to pray. This means that you need to create an atmosphere of prayer. Do not teach unless there is such an atmosphere in your class. To have an atmosphere of prayer, you should allow an adequate time in every class session for prayer.

Do you know what a living meeting is? A living meeting is a meeting that has an atmosphere of prayer. All those who speak for the Lord know that it is easy to speak in a meeting where there is an atmosphere of prayer. Otherwise, it will be very difficult to speak, for you may feel as if you are speaking in a cemetery.

I would remind you that teaching in the Summer School of Truth is absolutely different from teaching in a secular school. There is no need to fan the gift of God into flame in order to teach a class in a secular school. But to teach in our summer school, you must be a person of prayer, a person with a flame who brings in an atmosphere of prayer.

TEACHING NOT IN A DOCTRINAL WAY BUT IN AN EXPERIENTIAL WAY

Once you have fanned the gift of God into flame, stirred up the praying spirit, and created an atmosphere of prayer, you are now ready to teach. You should teach not in a doctrinal way but in an experiential way.

Applying All the Points of the Teaching to Practical, Personal Experience

Suppose you are teaching a lesson on man's fallen condition and man's need of salvation. You should not ask your students merely to remember and recite all the points related to man's fallen condition. That would be to teach in a doctrinal way. If you would teach in an experiential way, you should help the young people to realize that they themselves are fallen. You may ask them to paint a picture of their own fallen condition, not just to remember a number of doctrinal points. Take, for example, the matter of lying. Concerning this, those in your class should come to realize that, because they were born in sin, there is no need for them to learn how to lie; they lie spontaneously. To teach in this way is to teach not according to doctrine but according to experience.

One of the points in the lesson on man's need of salvation is that man is under God's condemnation. Man has sinned by disobeying God's commandment and thus has come under God's condemnation. If you teach in a doctrinal way, you will ask questions such as the following: What is God's commandment? What does it mean to be condemned? What is the significance of being under God's condemnation? If you would teach in an experiential way, you must help your students to realize that they have sinned by disobeying particular commandments. Furthermore, you should point out to them that often they have disobeyed the demands of their conscience. You may ask them, "Can you say that you have never disobeyed your conscience? If you have disobeyed your conscience, then surely you have sinned." By speaking to them in this way, you will help them to realize experientially what it means to be under God's judgment.

Learn in your teaching to touch others experientially. Apply every point of your teaching to their personal, practical situation.

Not Giving Lectures but Talking in a Personal Way

As you are teaching the young people in your class, you should frequently talk to them in a personal and practical way. For instance, you might say, "Are you not unhappy when your brother or sister has something that you do not have? Do you not hate that? Also, have you not offended your parents many times? Do you not have a sense deep within that it is wrong to offend your parents? Do you not realize that you should honor, respect, regard, and love your parents?" Instead of only covering the points in the lesson book, talk to the young people in a very personal way. Every point of the lesson should be presented in a way that will create an experiential impression. Apply every point to their actual situation.

When you teach a class in the Summer School of Truth, do not take the way of giving messages or lectures. Instead, you need to have personal talks with the young people, teaching every point experientially. As you are talking with them, you should be watchful over each one, paying particular attention to their expressions. This will help you to know the needs of your students. Then in the next class session you should endeavor to meet these needs. As the Lord leads you, you may speak to certain ones in particular and then ask them to pray with you. In this way you will help them to open up, you will strengthen their praying spirit, and you will bring them into the experience of the truths that you are presenting.

The principle is the same with preaching the gospel. When we preach the gospel, we should not just gather people together and give them a message. We should have direct, personal contact with people. We may give a message, but afterward, according to the condition of the attendants, we need to talk with them in a personal way about their need. Then we should pray with them. We all need to learn to do this.

Stirring Up a Praying Spirit

The hardest thing for us to do in teaching in an experiential way is to get people to pray with us. You may be able to give a message and talk with others, but when you come to the point where it is necessary to pray, you may be void of the praying spirit. If you are void of the praying spirit, you cannot stir up a praying spirit in someone else. If you want to stir up a praying spirit in the person with whom you are speaking, you yourself must be a person who is full of the praying spirit.

I hope that there will be much prayer in your class in the Summer School of Truth. Adequate prayer will accomplish at least three things. It will impress the young people in an experiential way with the points of the lesson; it will stir up the praying spirit within them; and it will cause them to become living. Those who attend such a summer school will surely become very living.

Let us not merely train the young people in our summer school with the knowledge of truth. Mere doctrinal knowledge is vain, and I have no confidence in it. Rather, let us impress the young ones with truth as the reality of God's economy. This is the truth that we are burdened to impart to our young people. In order to carry out this burden, you need to put into practice all the points we have covered in this message. Be governed by a clear view of God's economy; fan into flame the gift of God, which is within you; and be a person of prayer with an atmosphere of prayer who can stir up a praying spirit in others. As a teacher in the Summer School of Truth, you should be ready to pray at any time. Then you will be able to teach.

KNOWING THE STRUCTURE OF THE TRUTH, BEING SATURATED WITH THE TRUTH, AND CONVERTING DOCTRINE INTO EXPERIENCE

The books of 1 and 2 Timothy were written to deal with the church's decline and to inoculate the believers against this decline. This is true especially of 2 Timothy, which was written at a time when the churches established through Paul's ministry in the Gentile world were in a trend of degradation. That situation was a prefigure of the situation of decline in today's Christianity. Because of the influence of this decline, we need to train our young people with everything that Paul taught Timothy. This kind of teaching will be a strong inoculation against the decline and degradation of the church. The fact that Paul wrote concerning "the last days" (3:1) indicates his writing applied not only to his time but applies also to the times in which we live. We all need to be inoculated against the decline by knowing the truth revealed in these two books.

THE FULL KNOWLEDGE OF THE TRUTH

The matter of truth is emphasized strongly in 1 and 2 Timothy. Paul tells us that God "desires all men to be saved and to come to the full knowledge of the truth" (1 Tim. 2:4). The church's decline was due to the lack of the adequate knowledge of the truth. In 1 Timothy the decline crept in subtly through different teachings (1:3), and in 2 Timothy it developed openly and even worsened through heresies (2:16-18). To deal with such a decline, the truth must be maintained. First Timothy emphasizes that God desires all His saved ones to have the full knowledge of the truth and that the church is the pillar and base of the truth (3:15). Second Timothy stresses that the word of the truth should be unfolded rightly and straightly without distortion (2:15) and that the ones who have deviated should return to the truth (v. 25).

Unfortunately, the word *truth* has been wrongly understood. Many readers of the Bible regard truth as a matter of doctrine. In the New Testament, especially in 1 Timothy and 2 Timothy, *truth* refers not to doctrine but to the real things revealed in the New Testament concerning Christ and the church according to God's New Testament economy. If we would have the proper understanding of the word *truth* in the New Testament, we need to realize that it denotes all the realities of the divine economy as the content of the divine revelation, conveyed and disclosed by the holy Word (see footnote 6 on 1 John 1:6).

THE STRUCTURE OF THE TRUTH
BEING THE TRIUNE GOD
WITH HIS ALL-INCLUSIVE REDEMPTION

Before you begin to teach the young people in the Summer School of Truth, you yourself need to receive Paul's inoculation and be filled, soaked, and saturated with the truth. If you study 1 and 2 Timothy carefully, you will see that the structure of these two books is actually the structure of the truth and that the structure of the truth is the element of Paul's inoculation.

What is the element of this inoculation? What is the structure of the truth? Through a careful reading of 1 and 2 Timothy, we can realize that the structure of the truth is the Triune God with His all-inclusive redemption. God's redemption implies, or includes, salvation. Redemption has been accomplished by God. When God's accomplished redemption is applied to us, it becomes salvation. Thus, salvation is our experience of God's redemption. The structure of the divine truth is nothing less than the Triune God plus His redemption, which becomes our salvation.

In order to teach the young people in a living way, you need to learn all the aspects of the truth in the Scriptures concerning the Triune God—the Father, the Son, and the Spirit. This means that you need to become saturated with the truth, the reality, of the Divine Trinity. Furthermore, you need to dive into the truth regarding the divine redemption—how it was planned by the Father, how it was accomplished by the Son, and how it is applied by the Spirit. Then you need to have a clear view of how the redemption accomplished by the Triune God becomes our full salvation.

GOD'S FULL SALVATION

The general subject of the first series of lessons in the Summer School of Truth is God's full salvation. The full salvation of God is actually equal to the truth, because the Triune God with His all-inclusive redemption is the structure of the truth. Through Paul's writings this truth has become an inoculation against the decline of Christianity. On the one hand, we may speak of the structure of the truth; on the other hand, we may speak of the element of the inoculation. This inoculation is like a dose of medicine containing various elements. The elements in the "dose" ministered by Paul as an inoculation are the Triune God—the Father, the Son, and the Spirit—and His all-inclusive redemption.

In helping the young people to experience God's full salvation, you have to unveil to them their fallen condition, which involves sin, Satan, and the world, the satanic system. These negative things are related to the actual condition of the saved ones. If we would experience and enjoy God's full salvation, we should consider our condition and its involvement, with sin, Satan, the world, and many other negative things.

PREPARING YOURSELF TO TEACH BY BEING SATURATED WITH THE TRUTH OF GOD'S ECONOMY

As you prepare yourself to teach, you should not merely put your trust in the lesson book or in the compendium. You need to immerse yourself in the truth concerning God's full salvation. This means that you need to be saturated with a thorough knowledge, realization, and experience of the Triune

God with His all-inclusive redemption in relation to all the aspects of man's fallen condition. To prepare yourself to teach, it is not adequate simply to read the lesson book. As a teacher in the Summer School of Truth, you need to be soaked and saturated with the truth. I hope that you will be impressed with your need to dive into the divine truth, which is the reality of the Father, the Son, and the Spirit and of His all-inclusive redemption understood in relation to the condition of fallen man.

When you hear this, you may be troubled and feel that you are not qualified to teach the young people. I would urge you not to feel this way. Your experience may be limited, but the amount of experience you have qualifies you.

In your teaching do not speak peculiar things to arouse people's curiosity. Also, do not make a display of your knowledge about other subjects, such as history or science. It is shameful to make a display. You must be focused on God's economy and be restricted by God's economy. All of the class time, which is actually quite limited, should be used for presenting the truth of God's economy.

Once again I wish to point out that you need to be fully soaked and saturated with the divine truth. The summer school should be a school not only to the students but also to all the teachers. I hope that you yourself will be the first one to learn the truth. You cannot teach others without first being taught yourself. Likewise, you cannot minister a certain thing to others without first experiencing and enjoying that matter yourself. You can minister to others only what you yourself have enjoyed. Otherwise, your teaching will be merely doctrinal and thus will be in vain.

**TEACHING IN
AN EXPERIENTIAL WAY
RATHER THAN IN A DOCTRINAL WAY**

Let us now go on to consider the practical matter of teaching in an experiential way rather than in a doctrinal way. Suppose you are teaching lesson 17, which is on transformation. The lesson book says, "Transformation is the result of sanctification and is related to man's soul." To ask the students merely to understand and remember the facts is to teach in a doctrinal way. If you would teach in an experiential way, you should fellowship with the young people regarding why transformation is the result of sanctification. By doing this you will turn your teaching from doctrine to experience. This experiential fellowship will deeply impress them.

As you speak in this way about why transformation is the result of sanctification, one of the students might offer an explanation. He might say that sanctification separates us, changes us, and causes us to become holy with God's holy nature and that the result is a metabolic change, which is transformation. If someone speaks in this way, you should immediately ask him certain questions: "How about you? Have you been changed with God's holy nature? Has your being been made holy by the divine nature?" This way of teaching is experiential.

However, if you have not been soaked in the truth concerning sanctification and if you have not had any experience of sanctification, you have no choice other than to teach people doctrinally. You will be able to do nothing more than simply repeat what you have read in the lesson book. Having been "educated" with doctrine in letters, you will then teach the doctrine that transformation is the result of sanctification and is related to man's soul. But neither you nor the students will know the truth, the reality, of sanctification and transformation. Since you do not have any experience, you cannot minister life to the young people in your class. Rather, you will pass on mere knowledge, as if you were teaching in a theological school. If you teach in this way, you will ruin the summer school and even damage your students.

CONVERTING DOCTRINE INTO EXPERIENCE

In order to teach in an experiential way, you must convert every point in the lesson from doctrine into experience. Suppose a particular lesson has five points. In your preparation, you should try to convert every point of doctrine into experience. This requires practice. After making such a conversion during your time of preparation, you should then speak to the young people about each point in the way of experience. The more you speak in this way, the more they will be unveiled. They will see a vision that will expose them, and spontaneously they will be ushered into the experience of the very matter you have been presenting.

However, if you teach in the way of merely imparting doctrines from the printed materials, you will do nothing more than impart some knowledge to the minds of your students. As a result, they will gain nothing in an experiential way. Moreover, the knowledge they gain may damage them. Later, on another occasion, when they hear a word about transformation, they might say, "I know this already. I heard all about it in the Summer School of Truth. I know that transformation is the result of sanctification and is related to man's soul. I also know that transformation means that a certain substance changes in nature and in form." We must not damage the young people by giving them mere knowledge. In order to profit them with the truth, we must always teach them in an experiential way. This is a very basic matter.

We should also speak in an experiential way in the church life. In the meetings, in fellowship, in shepherding the saints, and in visiting others for gospel preaching, we need to learn to speak not in a doctrinal way but in an experiential way. By speaking in this way, we will "hit two birds with one stone"— the "bird" of experience and the "bird" of doctrine. Then the one to whom you are speaking will get the doctrine along with the experience. I hope that you all will endeavor to practice this from now on.

In the ministry in the Lord's recovery, we present our teachings not in the way of doctrine but in the way of life. For this reason our study of the Bible is called a life-study. However, although we do not stress doctrine, our way of teaching conveys a great deal of doctrine. Every message of our life-study of the Scriptures conveys a certain amount of doctrine, yet the impression made upon the reader is not the impression of doctrine but the impression of the experience and enjoyment of God, Christ, and the Spirit. Eventually, one does learn some doctrine, but it is experiential doctrine, doctrine that is learned through experience.

I believe that teaching in the Summer School of Truth will

be a good opportunity for you to learn something. If you try to convert every point in the lessons into experience, you yourself will be helped. You may realize that you do not know how to convert doctrine into experience, because you are lacking in experience. This will expose you, and then you will know where you are. You will see that you may know many things as doctrines, but you do not know them in experience. Then as you are preparing a lesson, you may begin to check yourself regarding your experience. Point by point you may ask yourself, "Do I have the experience of this matter? Is my experience of this point adequate? Am I able to teach others about this point in an experiential way?" You may conclude that your experience is not even adequate for a testimony, much less for teaching a class of young people. This may cause you to pray, "Lord, have mercy upon me. I need some experience of this matter." This is the way to prepare yourself to teach every lesson.

I would encourage you to prepare not only by yourself but also with others who will be teaching the young people. Come together with several others and check every point of every lesson according to experience. In addition, practice converting the doctrinal points into experience. This will be a good preparation for teaching in an experiential way. If you do this, the summer school will be a great benefit not only to the young people but to the entire church. Let us take this way to teach the young people in the Summer School of Truth. (*Teachers' Training*, pp. 27-43)

PART SIX:
CONCLUSION

SERVING IN COORDINATION AND
IN A BLENDED WAY TO MINISTER LIFE

Scripture Reading: Col. 1:28; 1 Thes. 2:7, 11; 2 Cor. 12:15; 1 Cor.
12:24; 10:17; Acts 1:14

I. Church service is mainly for the saints to minister life
to others; the best opportunity for us to minister life to
others is in the service groups; we must help the saints
not primarily to carry out the service; rather, we should
fellowship with them and minister life to them so that
they may grow—Eph. 4:15; Col. 1:28:

A. We need a life and work that flows out from the
love of the Lord in order to maintain our victory; if
we do not have a revived living or a labor in shepherding, we will not be overcoming for long; there
will be no way for us to maintain our victory; what
maintains us in the victory is a life and work of
love toward the Lord—1 John 5:16a; John 21:15-17:

1. Every day we need renewal, and this renewal
has to be refreshed day by day; every morning
we should allow the Lord Jesus, our Sun, to rise
up in us so that we can be renewed—Lev. 6:12-13;
Mal. 4:2; Psa. 119:147-148; Prov. 4:18.

2. After we have a thorough dealing with the Lord
and pick up a burden, we must learn to be interested in people and involved with people; then
we can pick up a burden for specific persons.

3. In our care for the young saints, we should consider ourselves as a nursing mother and an
exhorting, consoling father—1 Thes. 2:7, 11.

B. The apostle Paul was a person who always spent

and was spent; because his disposition was fully dealt with by the Lord, it was soft, bendable, flexible, and applicable to any situation; he was on earth for nothing else but to gain people—2 Cor. 12:15:

1. On the one hand, we need to be strong, but on the other hand, we should not be hard; we need to be soft, flexible, and applicable, good for any situation we are placed in, able to fit into every bend and corner.

2. To care for little children requires much flexibility; therefore, we first need a thorough dealing with the Lord, and then we need to become available, flexible, and fully dealt with in our disposition.

II. In our service to God, we must be brought by God to the point where we have the consciousness of the Body and do not serve individually but in coordination with the brothers and sisters—Acts 1:14; 2:46; 5:12; 15:25:

A. We must realize that there are two kinds of coordination: one kind is the coordination involved in outward arrangements, and the other kind of coordination is a coordination that grows out of the life within and is spiritual:

1. Coordination requires that our natural being, the world, our disposition, and our flesh all be dealt with so that the Lord can grow out of us; when He grows out of you and me, we are spontaneously in coordination.

2. Many have had the experience that as soon as they were put in the coordination, their condition was exposed; once they began to serve, their self immediately became manifest, particularly in their opinions.

3. The most important thing in the church service is not that we perform our tasks successfully; rather, the important matter in our serving together in coordination is how much our flesh,

our disposition, and our individualism are being dealt with.

B. The greatest indication that we see the Body is that we cannot be independent; we feel that we need the Body, that we need the brothers and sisters— cf. 1 Cor. 1:1:

1. Coordination means that we cannot do anything without one another; there is a sense that we need others and that others need us; those who work with young people should be like this.

2. Those who truly coordinate in spirit should have a strong feeling that they cannot do anything without the help and coordination of others and have the spirit of a learner and the spirit of needing help.

3. To feel that we do not need one another and that we do not need to fellowship is the greatest form of pride; it is the most offensive thing to the Lord and to the Body.

4. If we lack coordination with others, we will always criticize what they do; because we lack coordination in our service and do not rely and mutually depend on one another, we often step on others.

III. We must learn to serve in a blended way; without the blending, the Lord has no way to go on with us; blending is the Body, blending is the oneness, and blending is the one accord—1 Cor. 12:24; 10:17:

A. God has blended the Body together; the word *blended* means adjusted, harmonized, tempered, and mingled; God has blended the Body, adjusted the Body, harmonized the Body, tempered the Body, and mingled the Body; the Greek word for *blended* implies the losing of distinctions—12:24:

1. In order to be harmonized, blended, adjusted, mingled, and tempered in the Body life, we have to go through the cross and be by the Spirit, dispensing Christ to others for the sake of the Body of Christ.

2. If we would practice the blending, we should not

forget the matter of fellowship; fellowship is the basis for blending; by practicing fellowship we will lay the foundation for the blending.

3. Fellowship tempers us; fellowship adjusts us; fellowship harmonizes us; and fellowship mingles us; we should not do anything without fellowshipping with the other saints who are coordinating with us.

4. Fellowship requires us to stop when we are about to do something; in our coordination in the church life, in the Lord's work, we all have to learn not to do anything without fellowship.

B. When we blend together, we have the cross and the Spirit; without the cross and the Spirit, all that we have is the flesh with division; blending requires us to be crossed out; blending requires us to be by the Spirit to dispense Christ and to do everything for the sake of His Body.

C. The way to be blended is by much and thorough prayer, as fine flour of the wheat, with all the members of our group, with the Spirit as the oil, through the death of Christ as the salt, and in the resurrection of Christ as the frankincense—John 12:24; 1 Cor. 10:17.

Excerpts from the Ministry:

THE PURPOSE OF OUR SERVICE
BEING TO MINISTER LIFE TO OTHERS

The first point for our training is to realize that in the church service we do not do anything in the way of organization. The church is an organism, and what an organism needs is life. Therefore, our church service is mainly for ministering life to others. Even the arranging of chairs and the cleaning of restrooms are not for themselves; they are for ministering life. In ushering, clerical work, and any aspect of the church service, we must do everything to minister life to others. Of course, it is good for us to do things in a proper way. Not doing things well can be a frustration, but this does not mean that merely doing a good job is to have the proper service. In worldly religious organizations it is sufficient to do the jobs well, but in the church the main thing we need is the ministry of life. Even if we cannot do things very well, but by His mercy we minister life to others, the service is still successful. The main matter is to minister life to others.

The best opportunity for us to minister life to others is in the service groups. Many saints who have a heart for the Lord have been placed into these groups under the care of the responsible ones. The leading ones in the service should not care merely for doing things properly. The main thing they must do is care in life for all the ones who serve in the groups. They must help the saints not primarily to carry out the service; rather, they should fellowship with them and minister life to them so that they may grow. If the leading ones do this, spontaneously all the saints will do the same for others. Then the entire church will be under the care of the proper ministry of life. (*The Normal Way of Fruit-bearing and Shepherding for the Building Up of the Church,* pp. 12, 13)

A REVIVAL OF THE INNER LIFE

The revival that I am talking about is not the kind of revival commonly known in Christianity. It is not something sudden, brought about by days of prayer and fasting and accompanied by extraordinary events, resulting in a general excitement. The revival that I am talking about is the renewing described in the New Testament. Second Corinthians 4:16 says, "...though our outer man is decaying, yet our inner man is being renewed day by day." The renewal here is a revival. Every day we need a renewal, and this renewal has to be refreshed day by day. What we need today is this kind of renewal in the inner life as opposed to a renewal in outward actions or expression. God has set up a natural law that the rising of the sun affords a new beginning and a fresh renewal every day for everything, whether plant, animal, or human being. The same is true with our Christian life. Every morning we should allow the Lord Jesus, our Sun, to rise up in us so that we can be renewed. This is the revival that I am talking about.

If we are daily revived spiritually, there will be no need for a big revival. Actually, none of the so-called big revivals are long lasting. For example, the great Welsh revival at the beginning of this century was over by 1933. All the revivals brought in by various spiritual movements in the past were transient. After a while, they all cooled down. This kind of sporadic revival is not reliable. The reliable revival is the kind that comes from a daily renewal.

I hope that the elders and co-workers would take this word of fellowship and exhortation to give their all and their time to contact and shepherd people. This was our shortage in the past. Now we must recover this matter. Only by this will the organic building up of the Body of Christ in Ephesians 4:12-16 and the meetings of mutuality in 1 Corinthians 14:26 be realized and practiced among us. For this we need a daily revival and a daily overcoming as the base. We also need a life and work that flows out from the love of the Lord in order to maintain our victory. If we do not have a revived living or a labor in shepherding, we will not be overcoming for long; there will be no way for us to maintain our victory. What maintains us in the victory is a life and work of love toward the Lord. We need both these aspects. (*A Timely Trumpeting and the Present Need*, pp. 50, 51, 57)

LEARNING TO BE INTERESTED IN PEOPLE

After we have a thorough dealing with the Lord and pick up a burden, we must learn to be interested in people. Because of the fall, many of us are not interested in others. We consider that whether others go to heaven or to hell is their own business. We do not care whether others grow in life, and we feel that it is sufficient for us to care for our own spiritual welfare. However, the church service requires every one of us to be involved with others. We need an interest in the Lord's people. We may illustrate this interest by the taste for certain foods. Many Chinese people are interested in Chinese cooking and have the taste to go to Chinatown. We, however, need to be interested in the Lord's people. Every day the Lord's people must be our "food" (John 4:31-34). Some older teenage sisters should say, "All the young girls between ten and fifteen years old in the church life are my food. I am interested in the young people to this extent."

Then we can pick up the burden for some specific persons. We should make a list of their names, always keep it in front of us, and pray for them one by one. A teenage sister may pray, "Lord, this one is still not saved. Lord, I will never be at peace until I see her saved. Lord, even for my sake You must save her." We may be too spiritual and say, "Lord, this is not for my sake." However, the Lord may say, "Because you have a genuine burden for this one, I will save her for your sake." Eventually the sister will see the little one be saved. After this she may say, "Lord, this little one is now saved, but she does not love You. I can never be satisfied with this. Do something in her so that she will love You, Lord, as I love You." Again, the sister will see the Lord answer her prayer. Likewise, the older generation must be burdened and pray in the same way. We need to be interested in people and involved with people. Then we can pick up a burden. Many in the church need our shoulders to bear them and our breast to embrace them (Exo. 28:9-12, 15-21, 29). We must love them. When they fall, we should weep, and when they rise up, we should be joyful. We must bear them as our burden. Our service is not to arrange the chairs, do the cleaning, usher, or do clerical work. These are temporary matters as the means, instruments, and channels for us to take care of people. We must all go to the Lord, pray, and pick up this burden. (*The Normal Way of Fruit-bearing and Shepherding for the Building Up of the Church,* pp. 16-17, 17-18)

* * *

First Thessalonians 2:7 says, "We were gentle in your midst, as a nursing mother would cherish her own children." To cherish is not merely to do a job or to carry out a business; it is to care for a living person. Verse 11 says, "Just as you know how we were to each one of you, as a father to his own children, exhorting you and consoling you and testifying." Paul nourished the Thessalonians as a mother and exhorted them as a father. The apostle was not a businessman or a schoolmaster. He was a nourishing mother and an exhorting father. He had an interest in people. If we do not have an interest in people, we are finished with the church service; we are not qualified to serve. We should not say that only the apostle Paul could be like this. What the apostle did is an example for all the believers. We are not apostles, but we should still be nursing mothers. Even the brothers must nourish others as a mother, and the sisters should exhort others as a father. This does not depend on our being male or a female; it depends on the kind of heart we have. A sister can have the heart of a father, and a brother can have the heart of a mother.

Strictly speaking, we do not care for keeping the chairs. We care for keeping the persons. The keeping of chairs will not enter into the New Jerusalem, but the keeping of persons will go on forever.

I am afraid that too many of us in the church service care only for the practical service, not for the persons. We need the Lord's mercy to properly exercise our heart. This is a great test to us. Some of us were born in such a way that we do not care for anyone. This is according to our natural disposition. Hallelujah, we have been reborn in another way! We have been reborn, not into a natural family but into the church. This is another birth with another disposition that is absolutely different. The disposition of our new birth is one that sacrifices our self, our soul, and even our lives for the care of others. (*The Normal Way of Fruit-bearing and Shepherding for the Building up of the Church*, pp. 22-23)

* * *

Paul was this kind of person. He always spent and was spent. He meant business with the Lord. He was on earth for nothing else but to gain people. Therefore, he also said, "To the weak I became weak that I might gain the weak. To all men I have become all things that I might by all means save some" (1 Cor. 9:22). Some in the church life are too strong in their disposition to be touchable in this way; it seems that no one can cause them to be shaped. Paul, however, seemed to have no disposition of his own. He was simply like a piece of wood that could be cut into any shape. Because his disposition was fully dealt with by the Lord, it was soft, bendable, flexible, and applicable to any situation. In my training in Taiwan in 1954, I told the serving ones that they should have a character and a disposition like paste, that can be applied to any kind of surface. On the contrary, some of the brothers and sisters are like pieces of hard rock that cannot be applied to any situation. This kind of "rock" is good only for beating others. Some may even feel good about this and say that a hard piece of rock was useful to the Lord to kill the Philistine giant (1 Sam. 17:49), but it is pitiful to think in this way. On the one hand, we need to be strong, but on the other hand, we should not be hard. We need to be soft, flexible, and applicable, good for any situation we are placed in, able to fit into every bend and corner. (*The Normal Way of Fruit-bearing and Shepherding for the Building up of the Church,* pp. 40-41)

DEALING WITH OUR NATURAL DISPOSITION TO BECOME FLEXIBLE IN CARING FOR PEOPLE

We must all be tested by the church life, by fruit-bearing, and by lamb-feeding because these are the three matters that kill our natural disposition. The church life is a killing, not of the good things but mostly of our disposition. Likewise, fruit-bearing and lamb-feeding are a killing. All these are killing "knives" for our disposition. Passing through these three tests causes us to become right, because after passing through them we become persons who have dealt with our natural disposition. Then we will be flexible. To care for little children requires much flexibility. Any mother who is not flexible should not expect to have good children. Her children will all be damaged by her inflexibility. To bear fruit among our in-laws, cousins, and schoolmates requires us to be flexible. We should not speak of inconvenience or say that we do not have time. Whether we have time depends on our desire. We may illustrate this by the need to answer correspondence. In the early years of my work, I would often apologize for not answering people sooner, telling them that I had been too busy. However, something within condemned me, saying, "It is not because you were too busy; it is because you did not have the desire." Everyone is busy. Even a sister with no husband, children, job, or school can stay busy every day. She can tell people she does not have the time for this or that. This is absolutely due to our dispositional inflexibility.

If we are not flexible, we cannot bear fruit. In order to bear fruit, we need to be flexible, available at any time, and never claiming to be too busy. We should always have time to talk to people. If we wait until we have time to help people to be saved, we may wait forever. We have all been cheated in this regard. We have said, "This week I am very busy; let me see how next week will be," but the next week we are busier and have even more things to do. Then the following week is worse, and we are never free. Being busy or available is a matter of our disposition. Therefore, we first need a thorough dealing with the Lord, and then we need to become available, flexible, and fully dealt with in our disposition. (*The Normal Way of Fruit-bearing and Shepherding for the Building Up of the Church,* pp. 63-64)

HAVING THE CONSCIOUSNESS OF THE BODY IN OUR SERVICE IN COORDINATION

In our service to God, we must be brought by God to the point where we have the consciousness of the Body and do not serve individually but in coordination with the brothers and sisters. We must be brought to a point where the brothers' move is our move, and our move is the brothers' move. Regardless of the circumstance we are in, our feeling should always be that what the brothers are doing is no different from what we are doing. The two should be the same.

Not only so, whenever there is a problem in our coordination with the Body, we should sense it immediately. When our coordination with all the members is normal, we may not have much feeling that we are in coordination. This is similar to the coordination in our body. In a normal situation the members of our body do not have much feeling about each other's existence. However, when a certain member has a problem, then there is a consciousness. Therefore, if we sense the existence of a certain member, then that member must have a problem. When we are particularly conscious of our eyes, something must be wrong with our eyes.

LIFE ISSUING IN
SPONTANEOUS COORDINATION

We must realize that there are two kinds of coordination. One kind is the coordination involved in outward arrangements such as sweeping the floor, cleaning the chairs, and dusting the windows. This kind of coordination is not very deep. The other kind of coordination is a coordination that grows out of the life within and is spiritual. This coordination is deeper and more real. This kind of coordination requires that our natural being, the world, our disposition, and our flesh all be dealt with so that the Lord can grow out of us. When He grows out of you and me, we are spontaneously in coordination.

COORDINATION MAKING
OUR SELF MANIFEST

While learning to serve the Lord, many have had the experience that as soon as they were put in the coordination, their condition was exposed. When they were at home praying, reading the Word, or pursuing the Lord, they did not sense their own condition very much. When they went out by themselves to preach the gospel and distribute gospel tracts, they also were not very conscious of their condition. However, once they began to serve together with the saints, their self immediately became manifest, particularly in their opinions, because opinions are the best representative of a person's self.

COORDINATION BEING MAINLY NOT FOR
RIGHT OR WRONG BUT FOR DEALING WITH
OUR SELF AND INDIVIDUALISM

Suppose five of us are serving in coordination to dust the chairs, and suddenly I suggest that we turn the chairs over with the legs pointing upward. How would you react? This would be a test to you. Immediately opinions and thoughts would rise up from within you. You must realize that the most important thing in the church service is not that we perform our tasks successfully. Rather, the important matter in our serving together in coordination is how much our flesh, our disposition, and our individualism are being dealt with. When we who serve the Lord are coordinating together, the main thing is that our flesh and our disposition are dealt with. The emphasis of our service in coordination is not on whether a certain matter is right or wrong nor on whether the reason behind a matter is right or wrong. Rather, the emphasis is on whether or not our person is right and on whether or not the life is right.

The biggest reason the church service is not strong and does not have much blessing is that the reality of coordination is missing. Our coordination in service has to be so real that it surpasses human organization and is as organic as the human body. (*Being Apt to Teach and Holding the Mystery of the Faith*, pp. 44, 45-46, 47)

LACKING A FEELING FOR COORDINATION

Another problem among us is that although the serving ones are capable, they do not have a feeling for coordination in their spirit when they come together to serve. It seems as if everyone is able to serve without others. Consequently, few among us have the spirit of a learner and the spirit of needing help. Those who truly coordinate in spirit should have a strong feeling that they cannot do anything without the help and coordination of others. Our present coordination is one of formality. They do their part without needing anyone else. We may not argue, but there is not much interdependence in spirit. This shows that our spirit of service is improper.

This is the situation of those who work with the young people and the children. The coordination is formal; everyone does what he should do when it is his turn. This is cooperation, not coordination. Coordination means that we cannot do anything without one another. There is a sense that we need others and that others need us. Those who work with young people should be like this; all the service of the church should also be like this. It is normal when the deacons and elders mutually need one another, and the saints feel that they cannot do anything without the elders and deacons.

Today we have rules and arrangements. The elders do things pertaining to elders, and the deacons do things pertaining to deacons. Everyone works when it is his turn. However, we do not have a deep feeling that we cannot go on without the elders and deacons in our service. Some brothers not only lack a sense of the need for the elders and deacons, but they even think that elders and deacons are unnecessary. This is dangerous.

HAVING THE GREATEST FORM OF PRIDE

Those who live in the workers' home are bright and capable. They seem to be independent and do not need others. This is very dangerous because it is the greatest form of pride. If four brothers are living in the workers' home, they should depend on one another, and others should sense their dependence on one another. Sadly, this is not the atmosphere among us. For example, if it is my turn to preach the gospel, I will either do everything or do nothing. From the human perspective, this may be considered to be coordination, but this coordination is according to regulation and arrangement. There is no sense of needing others in spirit. Some may think that coordination is unnecessary and troublesome and that it is better to not coordinate.

Those who do not need to coordinate are dry, lack blessing, and are useless. The fact that we are clever, capable, and do not need one another's help is a great danger. This is a sad and pitiful situation. The fearful thing is that this situation is hidden and not very apparent. This situation can be compared to leprosy. If it is manifested, it is easier to deal with it.

This shows that we lack the fellowship of the Body. When we come together, we seldom have thorough fellowship. For example, when saints from other cities visit Taipei, we sit together for a meeting. After the meeting, however, we all go our separate ways without fellowshipping. This was not our situation during our first six years in Taiwan. In those years, whenever we had a conference, we came together and had much fellowship. Now we are all capable, brilliant, and knowledgeable. We do not need one another; we do not need to fellowship. This is the greatest form of pride. It is the most offensive thing to the Lord and to the Body. We should humbly minister to others and restrict our cleverness through coordination.

NEEDING FELLOWSHIP AND COORDINATION
IN THE BODY AND IN LIFE

If we lose the principle of coordination and dependence in the Body, we will not be strong in our administration of the church and ministry of the word. Once we lose this principle, we will not have much blessing. Our coordination should not become mechanical, and we should not work only when it is our turn. We should have the feeling that we cannot do anything without others, that we truly need one another. If we come together and assign work, with each doing only his own work, our situation is similar to the division of labor in a civic organization or a large institution. This lack of the flavor of coordination among the members of the Body must be dealt with.

What does it mean to see the Body? The greatest indication that we see the Body is that we cannot be independent. We feel that we need the Body, that we need the brothers and sisters. Presently, however, our coordination can be compared to work in an organization. It seems that we are moving like a machine and that we lack the sense of the fellowship of life.

THE LACK OF COORDINATION PRODUCING CRITICISM

If we lack coordination with others, we will always criticize what they do. Even if we do not express it, we are filled with criticism, and we disapprove of what others do. Such people are narrow and pitiful. In our service we should not expect others to be like us, nor should we expect to be like others. However, because we lack coordination in our service and do not rely and mutually depend on one another, we often step on others. We either do not walk, or we step on others when we do walk. We either do not work, or we do the job of others. We either are not concerned, or we criticize the work of others. When a certain matter is in others' hands, we are not able to do anything, but when an opportunity comes to us, we do it according to our way and discard the help of others. Although this condition is not apparent among us, it will be in our future, because we are not willing to submit to others. This is a foolish way. (*The Administration of the Church and the Ministry of the Word,* pp. 25-27)

GOD HAVING BLENDED THE BODY TOGETHER

God has blended the Body together (1 Cor. 12:24). The word *blended* also means adjusted, harmonized, tempered, and mingled. God has blended the Body, adjusted the Body, harmonized the Body, tempered the Body, and mingled the Body. The Greek word for *blended* implies the losing of distinctions. One brother's distinction may be quickness, and another's may be slowness. But in the Body life the slowness disappears and the quickness is taken away. All such distinctions are gone. God has blended all the believers of all different races and colors. Who can make the blacks and the whites lose their distinctions? Only God can do this. A husband and a wife can have the harmony in their marriage life only by losing their distinctions.

In order to be harmonized, blended, adjusted, mingled, and tempered in the Body life, we have to go through the cross and be by the Spirit, dispensing Christ to others for the sake of the Body of Christ. The co-workers and elders must learn to be crossed out. Whatever we do should be by the Spirit to dispense Christ. Also, what we do should not be for our interest and according to our taste but for the church. As long as we practice these points, we will have the blending.

All of these points mean that we should fellowship. When a co-worker does anything, he should fellowship with the other co-workers. An elder should fellowship with the other elders. Fellowship tempers us; fellowship adjusts us; fellowship harmonizes us; and fellowship mingles us. We should forget about whether we are slow or quick and just fellowship with others. We should not do anything without fellowshipping with the other saints who are coordinating with us. Fellowship requires us to stop when we are about to do something. In our coordination in the church life, in the Lord's work, we all have to learn not to do anything without fellowship.

Among us we should have the blending of all the individual members of the Body of Christ, the blending of all the churches in certain districts, the blending of all the co-workers, and the blending of all the elders. Blending means that we should always stop to fellowship with others. Then we will receive many benefits. If we isolate and seclude ourselves, we will lose much spiritual profit. Learn to fellowship. Learn to be blended. From now on, the churches should come together frequently to be blended. We may not be used to it, but after we begin to practice blending a few times, we will acquire the taste for it. This is the most helpful thing in the keeping of the oneness of the universal Body of Christ. Today it is very convenient for us to blend with one another because of this modern age with its modern conveniences.

When we blend together, we have the cross and the Spirit. Without the cross and the Spirit, all that we have is the flesh with division. It is not easy to be crucified and to do all things by the Spirit in ourselves. This is why we must learn to be blended. Blending requires us to be crossed out. Blending requires us to be by the Spirit to dispense Christ and to do everything for the sake of His Body.

We may come together without much blending because everyone stays in themselves. They are afraid to offend others and make mistakes, so they keep quiet. This is the manner of man according to the flesh. When we come together, we should experience the terminating of the cross. Then we should learn how to follow the Spirit, how to dispense Christ, and how to say and do something for the benefit of the Body. That will change the entire atmosphere of the meeting and will temper the atmosphere. Blending is not a matter of being quiet or talkative but a matter of being tempered. We can be in harmony, because we have been tempered. Eventually, the distinctions will all be gone. Blending means to lose the distinctions. We all have to pay some price to practice the blending.

A group of elders may meet together often without being blended. To be blended means that you are touched by others and that you are touching others. But you should touch others in a blending way. Go through the cross, do things by the Spirit, and do everything to dispense Christ for His Body's sake. We should not come to a blending meeting to be silent. We have to prepare ourselves to say something for the Lord. The Lord may use you, but you need to be tempered and crossed out, and you need to learn how to follow the Spirit to dispense Christ for His Body's sake.

THE BLENDING NOT BEING SOCIAL

Such a blending is not social but the blending of the very Christ whom the individual members, the district churches, the co-workers, and the elders enjoy, experience, and partake of. (*The Divine and Mystical Realm,* pp. 86-88)

The New Testament tells us, first, that we are grains of wheat. In John 12:24 the Lord Jesus was the unique grain. Through His death and resurrection He released His life into us, making us the many grains. This is very good. However, the New Testament goes on to tell us that as grains, eventually we need to become a lump (1 Cor. 5:6-7a). This means that we need to become dough. The making of dough requires the blending of grains of wheat; but before being blended, the grains need to be ground into fine flour.

The New Testament also tells us that eventually we all become a loaf (10:17). In a sense, the grains, the fine flour, the lump, and the dough are nothing until they become a loaf. After we become a loaf, we mean something and we are something in the hand of the Lord. The loaf is the group. At the Lord's table, we often praise the Lord for the loaf, the bread, yet in actuality we may not be a loaf. A number of saints among us may never have been ground or broken. Although we are grains, it is possible that we have never been broken and ground into fine flour. On the other hand, we may be broken, yet we may never have been blended together. Thus, we are far from being a loaf. The way to become a loaf is to be blended together in the groups. The loaf is the group.

The way to be blended is by much and thorough prayer, as fine flour of the wheat, with all the members of our group, with the Spirit as the oil, through the death of Christ as the salt, and in the resurrection of Christ as the frankincense. We need to pray over all these points with much and thorough prayer. We need to be blended into a dough for the Lord. Our becoming dough implies our being broken, our being ground, and our being blended. According to the type of the meal offering in Leviticus 2:1-13, to be blended requires the adding of oil so that the flour will not be dry. It is impossible to blend fine flour that is dry; oil is needed to make the flour moist. In the same way, we need the Spirit as the oil to "moisten" us so that we can be blended together.

To be blended together, we also need the salt, that is, the death of Christ, to kill all the germs within us. We need to realize that we have many germs in our being. All these germs need to be killed by the death of Christ. Then, we also need to be in the resurrection of Christ. In the blending we need to experience the Spirit as the oil, and we also need to pass through the experiences of the death of Christ and the resurrection of Christ. If by the Lord's mercy we are able to experience such a blending, we will be absolutely different from what we are today. It is not enough just to put people together and call them a group. That can be done very quickly. The proper grouping with the blending of the members will take time.

PRACTICING THE FELLOWSHIP
TO LAY THE FOUNDATION FOR THE BLENDING

If we would practice the blending, we should not forget the matter of fellowship. Fellowship is the basis for blending. Thus, we must practice the fellowship. By so doing we will lay the foundation for the blending. However, instead of practicing the fellowship, we have practiced hypocrisy for years; we have all been hiding ourselves under a mask. Without the foundation of intimate and thorough fellowship, there can be no blending.

We should not be afraid of being known by others. The more we are known in a proper way, the better. This will put down our pride, take away our boasting, annul our superiority complex, and even put aside our inferiority complex. However, most of us are not willing to expose ourselves. Instead, we prefer to cover ourselves by pretending to one another. Because of this, it is difficult for us to have an intimate and thorough fellowship that results in our being blended together.

Without the blending, the Lord has no way to go on with us. Blending is the Body, blending is the oneness, and blending is the one accord—it is all these things. But we prefer to remain untouched and unknown by others. Because we do not like people to know us, we have become very sensitive, and our being sensitive causes us to be very touchy. Such a condition has forced us to be very cautious in our speaking, for fear of offending one another.

Among us there is a great need for a breakthrough to allow the Lord to carry out the grouping. From the very beginning in the four Gospels, when the Lord Jesus sent out His disciples, He did not send them one by one; rather, He always sent them two by two, grouping them together. From the time the recovery came to the United States the Lord has not been able to carry out the grouping among us. A number of saints came into the recovery in a very strong way and remained with us, but at a certain point they left. That indicated that they were not willing to be grouped together in the recovery. We who have remained in the recovery all have the problems of our disposition and character that keep us separate from one another. Although by the Lord's mercy we are still together, among us there has been very little grouping. Because of this, we do not have the impact. The impact is with the one accord, and the one accord actually is the blending.

If we do not have the one accord, God cannot answer our prayer, because we do not practice the Body. Our not being in one accord means that we do not practice the Body. According to the proper interpretation of the New Testament, the one accord is the one Body. We must practice the principle of the Body; then we will have the one accord. Although we may not fight with one another, we still may not have the one accord. Because we have remained together, we have seen the Lord's blessing, but only in a limited way. Therefore, we need to have the one accord to practice the Body.

It is difficult for us to open ourselves to one another, but it is even more difficult, after listening to one another's fellowship, to speak something in response in a way that is frank and full of love. After coming together in our groups, we should be free to tell the others concerning our inward situation with the Lord. Likewise, the others should be free to respond. Because we are afraid to expose ourselves and are afraid of offending others, we pretend with one another and are unwilling to let people know our real situation. We need the intimate and thorough fellowship. Of course, we need to be careful concerning what we open to one another in public. In certain cases the public confession of sins has caused serious trouble in the past. I do not mean that we should open ourselves in a careless way. Nevertheless, we need to find a way to be blended. Otherwise, the Lord has no way out of our present situation. We need to be blended until we have an intimate love for the members of our group. If we continue to hide ourselves and keep a distance from one another, when we go out to visit people, we will not have the impact. The people whom we visit will sense that we are not one.

Our situation today is very different from that of Peter, James, and John. When they were together following the Lord as His believers, they were genuine, as seen in the fact that they fought with one another. In Matthew 20, while the Lord Jesus was unveiling His death and resurrection to them (vv. 17-19), it seems that they did not hear what He was speaking. After the Lord Jesus finished His speaking, they had a contention among themselves (vv. 20-24). This indicates that they were very genuine.

If we do not practice the points in this message, there will be no way for us to be grouped. Grouping is an urgent need among us. We are trying to break through in this vital matter. (*Fellowship Concerning the Urgent Need of the Vital Groups,* pp. 81-82, 87-90)

**EXPECTING THE LORD'S BLESSING,
AND DOING THE UNIQUE WORK
OF THE BODY IN ONENESS TO PRODUCE
BEINGS OF THE NEW JERUSALEM**

Scripture Reading: Psa. 133; Rev. 21:2

I. We need to treasure God's blessing and realize that in God's work everything depends on His blessing; if we see this, it will bring about a basic change in our labor for God—Matt. 14:19-21:

A. In serving the Lord, we should believe in and expect the Lord's blessing; to be under the Lord's blessing means that in our service the Lord gives us unexpected results, results that are not in proportion to the cause and that are far beyond our expectation.

B. We need to learn to live in a way that does not hinder the Lord's blessing; the future of our service does not depend on our being right—it depends on the Lord's blessing.

C. Whatever we bring to the Lord must be broken for it to become a blessing to others; the broken bread became the satisfaction to all the hungry people, and there was great blessing—vv. 19-21.

II. The oneness of the Triune God, which is the oneness of the Body of Christ, includes all that Christ is to us in and for God's economy; the practice of this oneness, the one accord, is the master key to every blessing in the New Testament—Psa. 133; Eph. 4:1-6; Acts 1:14; 1 Cor. 1:9-10; Phil. 1:27; 2:2:

A. The Holy Spirit is the power, the means, and the

factor for God's move on this earth, but that is just on one side; there is the need of another side, the human side; there is the need of another factor—the one accord—Acts 1:14; 2:46.

B. If there were no Spirit on the Lord's side, it would be impossible for the Lord to move on this earth; in the same principle, without the one accord on our side, God cannot move; but if we offer to the Lord this one accord, then we will match God, and anything can be done—Rom. 15:6; 1 Cor. 1:10; Phil. 1:27; 2:2; 4:2.

C. God will only grace and bless the one accord, that is, the practice of the oneness; in order to receive God's blessing we must practice the oneness by the one accord—Psa. 133; Acts 1:14.

D. Day by day we have to move out of ourselves with the evil of division and into the divine "Us," the Triune God as the blessing of oneness, and we have to remain in Him for His corporate expression; if we continually touch the Word and allow the Spirit to touch us day by day, we shall be sanctified by moving out of ourselves, our old lodging place, and into the Triune God, our new lodging place—John 17:15, 17, 21; 15:5; Eph. 5:26:

1. Oneness is the full mingling of the Triune God with the saints; oneness nullifies all of our old creation and the natural man, sanctifies us from the Satan-ensnared world, and frees us from the world and Satan—John 17:2, 6, 11, 14, 17, 21-22; Eph. 4:4-6; Rom. 16:20.

2. Under the anointing oil and the watering dew, we experience the commanded blessing of life on the ground of oneness—Psa. 133:3b.

III. Our work in the Lord's recovery is the work of God's economy, the work of the Body of Christ—1 Cor. 15:58; 16:10; Col. 4:11:

A. The Body of Christ is organic and does not allow anything of human work, and the Body is not built up by using man's natural methods or the organization of human work—Eph. 4:16; Col. 2:19.

B. Most of the work in today's Christianity is human work, is natural, and has nothing to do with the building up of the Body of Christ—1 Cor. 3:12-16.

C. In the recovery we should not have the thought that we can do a particular work according to our way; rather, we need to realize that in the Lord's recovery there is only one work—the work of the Body of Christ consummating in the New Jerusalem—Col. 2:19.

IV. According to the entire revelation of the New Testament, the unique goal of the Christian work should be the New Jerusalem, which is the ultimate goal of God's eternal economy—Matt. 7:21-24; 1 Cor. 3:10; Heb. 12:22; Rev. 21:2:

A. The co-workers must see that we should do only one work, which is to make God's chosen people regenerated ones, sanctified ones, renewed ones— the new man—transformed ones, conformed ones— those conformed to the image of the firstborn Son of God—and glorified ones; all those who will be in the New Jerusalem are this kind of people.

B. In this way, we go up level by level until we reach the highest point, where we become the same; there is no more flesh and no more natural being; all are in the spirit; all are the kingdom of the heavens, and all are beings of the New Jerusalem; this is the highest point.

Excerpts from the Ministry:

I would like to bring out the matter of multiplying the five loaves (Mark 6:35-44; 8:1-9) with respect to God's blessing. It is not a matter of how many loaves we have in our hands, but whether or not God has blessed them. Even if we had more than five loaves, this would not be enough to feed four or five thousand people. Even if we had ten times or even one hundred times more, we still would not have enough to feed four or five thousand people. It is not a matter of how much we have. Sooner or later, we must be brought to the point of seeing that it is not a matter of what we can pull out of our storage shed, nor is it a matter of how great our gift is or how much power we have. The day must come in which we say to the Lord, "Everything depends on Your blessing." This is a basic matter. How much blessing has the Lord really given us? It does not really matter how many loaves there are. The Lord's blessing nourishes people and gives them life.

One matter is troubling my heart: Do we truly treasure God's blessing? This is a basic question concerning the work. Perhaps we do not even have five loaves today, but our need is greater than four thousand or five thousand people. I am afraid that we have less in our storehouse than the apostles, but our need is greater than the need at the time of the apostles. Our own store, source, power, labor, and faithfulness will be manifest one day that they are useless to us. Brothers, our future holds great disappointment for us because we will see that we can do nothing.

Brothers, if God brings us to the point of seeing that everything in God's work depends upon His blessing, it will bring about a basic change in our labor for God. We would not consider how many people, how much money, or how much bread we have. We would say we do not have enough, but the blessing is sufficient. The blessing meets the need that we cannot meet. Although we cannot measure up to the size of the need, the blessing is greater than our lack. When we see this, the work will have a basic change. In every matter we must look at the blessing more than we consider the situation. Methods, considerations, human wisdom, and clever words are all useless. In God's work we should believe in and expect His blessing. Many times we are careless and damage the work, but this is not a problem. If the Lord gives us a small blessing, we can get through any problem.

We truly hope that we would not make mistakes or speak and act loosely in the work. When we have the Lord's blessing, however, it seems that we cannot err even when we are wrong. Sometimes it seems that we have made a serious mistake, but with God's blessing the result is not really an error.

I once said to Brother Witness that if we had the Lord's blessing, the things we did right would be right and the things we did wrong would be right as well. Nothing could damage the blessing.

The basic concern today is that we must learn to live in a way that does not hinder God's blessing. Some habits force God to withhold His blessing, and these must be eliminated. Some temperaments keep God from blessing, and these must be done away with. We must learn to believe in God's blessing, rely on it, and eliminate the barriers that prevent us from receiving it.

We must see that the Lord withholds no good thing from us. If the work is not going well, if the brothers and sisters are in a poor condition, or if the number of saved ones is not increasing, we should not use the environment or certain people as an excuse. We cannot blame the brothers. I am afraid that the real reason lies with our harboring of some frustrations to the blessing. If the Lord can get through in us, the Lord's blessing will be greater than our capacity. Once God said to the Israelites, "Prove Me, if you will, by this,...whether I will open to you the windows of heaven and pour out blessing for you until there is no room for it" (Mal. 3:10). God is still saying this today. The normal life of a Christian is a life of blessing, and the normal work of a Christian is a work of blessing. If we do not receive blessing, we should say, "Lord, perhaps I am the problem."

What is blessing? Blessing is God working without any cause. Logically speaking, one penny should buy one penny's worth of goods. But sometimes, without spending a cent, God gives us ten thousand pennies' worth of goods. This means that what we have received is beyond reckoning. God's blessing is any work He performs without cause. This work surpasses what we should receive. Five loaves fed five thousand people, and there were still twelve full baskets left over! This is blessing. Some people should not get a certain kind of result. They should only have a little, but surprisingly they have much. Our entire work is built upon God's blessing. The blessing is the result of receiving what we do not deserve, that is, the result of receiving beyond what our gift warrants us to receive. The result that we get, which is beyond what our strength earns, is the blessing. Putting it more strongly, we do not deserve any results because of our weaknesses and failures, but astoundingly we obtain something, and what we obtain is the blessing. If we look for God's blessing, He will give us unexpected results. In our service do we hope for God to give us great results? Many brothers and sisters only look for results that can be expected from themselves alone. Blessing means that the result is not in proportion to the cause.

If we only look for results based on what we are, if we only look for a little fruit, and if we do not hope for great results, we run the risk of losing God's blessing. Since we only pay attention to the fact that we are laboring night and day, God cannot do anything beyond our expectation. We must put ourselves in a position in which God can bless us. We must say to the Lord, "Based on what we are, we should not obtain any results, but, Lord, for the sake of Your name, Your church, and Your way, we hope You will give something to us." Having faith in the work is believing and expecting God's blessing. In God's work, having faith means having the conviction that the result will not be in proportion to us. When we practice this, I believe God will bless our way. I hope that as the brothers discuss the matter of the migrations, the Lord's blessing will exceed our expectation.

The entire future of the work depends on God's blessing, not on being right. If God blesses, then many sinners will be saved. If God blesses, we will be able to send people out to the remote regions. If there is no blessing, people will not get saved. If there is no blessing, workers will not be produced. If there is no blessing, no one will offer anything. If there is no blessing, no one will migrate. When the blessing is here, even things that seem wrong are right. When God blesses, we cannot go wrong even if we try. One time there was a meeting in which it seemed that we sang the wrong hymn, but we had a good result because we had God's blessing. Sometimes when we preach, it seems that we are speaking the wrong word to the wrong audience, but God still blesses some in the audience. When we speak again, we still may speak the wrong word, but God blesses another group of people. I am not saying that we can be loose intentionally. I am saying that we cannot go wrong when we have God's blessing. It seems that our mistakes should be a frustration, but He cannot be hindered. God said, "Jacob have I loved, but Esau have I hated" (Rom. 9:13). God blesses whom He likes. This is a very serious matter. We should not think that the blessing is a small thing. The blessing is souls and consecrated people. Behind the word *blessing* perhaps there are fifty souls or one hundred consecrations. The words, attitudes, and opinions of certain people can stop the Lord's blessing. We must ask the Lord to prick us inwardly until we obtain His blessing. If we do not do this, our sin of losing the Lord's blessing will be greater than any other sin. The blessing could be hundreds or thousands of souls. We must look to God for the blessing and not let it escape. We must beg God to give us grace. (*Expecting the Lord's Blessing,* pp. 1-3, 5-7, 7-8, 13-15, 16-18)

FEEDING THE PEOPLE

Matthew 14:19 says, "And after commanding the crowds to recline on the grass, He took the five loaves and the two fish, and looking up to heaven, He blessed and broke the loaves and gave them to the disciples, and the disciples to the crowds." The Lord fed the people; He ministered the life supply to them. By having the crowds recline on the grass, He put the people into good order. This shows the Lord's wisdom and orderliness. By looking up to heaven the heavenly King indicated that His source was His Father in the heavens. Then He blessed the loaves and fish and broke them. This indicates that whatever we bring to the Lord must be broken for it to become a blessing to others.

After the Lord broke the loaves, He gave them to the disciples. The loaves were from the disciples, and they brought them to the Lord. After being blessed and broken by the Lord, they were given back to the disciples for distribution to the crowds, to whom the loaves became a great satisfaction. This indicates that the disciples were not the source of blessing; they were only the channels used by the Lord, who was the source of the people's satisfaction. The broken bread was passed on to the disciples, and the disciples distributed it to

the crowds. This broken bread became the satisfaction to all
the hungry people, and there was great blessing. The principle is the same today. No doubt there has been great blessing
in the Lord's recovery in this country. Nevertheless, we must
realize that some dear ones have offered themselves to the
Lord. In the Lord's hand, they all have been broken, and those
broken pieces have brought in the blessing. (*Life-study of Matthew,* pp. 517, 518)

PRACTICING THE ONENESS OF THE DIVINE TRINITY

The believers need to practice the oneness of the Divine
Trinity in the Divine Trinity as the Divine Trinity does (John
17:21-23). We need to ask ourselves what kind of oneness we
are practicing. Some claim to be practicing the oneness of the
Body, but they are actually practicing a sectarian, factious
oneness. The oneness of the Body is the oneness of the Triune
God. We practice the oneness of the Divine Trinity not in ourselves but in the Divine Trinity. The three of the Divine
Trinity—the Father, the Son, and the Spirit—are continually
practicing the divine oneness. For example, the Lord Jesus
said, "I and the Father are one" (10:30). The oneness of the
Father and the Son includes the Spirit, who is the consumma-
tion and totality of the Triune God. The Spirit is also the
Triune God reaching us. When Christ came into us, He came
as the Spirit. Wherever the Father and the Son are, there the
Spirit is also. (*The Secret of God's Organic Salvation: "The
Spirit Himself with Our Spirit,"* p. 53)

*   *   *

We must realize that the practices in the Lord's recovery
are not matters for others to copy. You must have the life. To
do anything you need the life. You have to see what the landmark was of the one hundred twenty in the book of Acts. The
landmark that divides the Gospels and the Acts was not the
baptism in the Holy Spirit. The landmark was the one accord
of the one hundred twenty. If you want to experience the baptism in the Spirit, you must have the one accord. If all the
members of a local church have the one accord, the baptism
in the Spirit will be there. If you really want to practice the

proper way to preach the gospel, you need the one accord.
Without this key, no door can be opened. The one accord is the
"master key to all the rooms," the master key to every blessing in the New Testament. This is why Paul told Euodias and
Syntyche that they needed this one accord (Phil. 4:2). Paul
knew that these sisters loved the Lord, but that they had lost
the one accord.

What we need is to recover this one accord. If we mean
business to go along with the Lord's present-day move, we
need this one accord. Who is right does not mean anything;
we need this one accord. We need to have the same mind and
the same will for the same purpose with the same soul and
the same heart. Philippians tells us that this matter starts
from our spirit (1:27), yet we must realize we are not persons
of spirit only. We are persons also of the mind, will, purpose,
soul, and heart. For us to be in the same one spirit with the
same one soul, one mind, and one will is to have the one
accord, which is the key to all the New Testament blessings
and bequests. Otherwise, we will repeat the pitiful history
of Christianity by being another group of Christians repeat-
ing the same kind of disaccord. (*Elders' Training, Book 7: One
Accord for the Lord's Move,* pp. 18-19)

*   *   *

On one side, God's move depends upon Himself as the consummated Spirit. He needs us as the other side so there could
be the possibility of accomplishment. If we do not render Him
any kind of cooperation or give Him any kind of response,
nothing can happen, regardless of how powerful, dynamic,
and mighty the Holy Spirit of the Triune God can be. God can
do the work of creation by Himself but not the work of the
new creation. The new creation work must be carried out in
the principle of incarnation, the principle of God being one
with man, making one entity out of two elements with no
third element produced. The Holy Spirit is the power, the
means, and the factor for God's move on this earth, but that is
just on one side. There is the need of another side, the human
side. There is the need of another factor—the one accord.

The matter of one accord controls the entire revelation

concerning the Lord's move on one side. If there were no Spirit on the Lord's side, it would be impossible for the Lord to move on this earth at all. In the same principle, without the one accord on our side, God cannot move. We have to match God. He is now the consummated Spirit, and we have to say, "Lord, we are ready here as the very one accord. We want to not only render but we are also ready to offer to You this one accord." Immediately there is a kind of marriage, and a couple comes out. Then anything can be done. (*Elders' Training, Book 7: One Accord for the Lord's Move*, pp. 99, 100)

PRACTICING THE ONENESS
TO BRING IN GOD'S BLESSING

All who are sitting here today are elders and co-workers. We must be in one accord to maintain the oneness Christ seeks. Since we are bearing the responsibility of the church, we should see the way for the church to receive grace and blessing. We must all realize that the blessing and grace of God can only come upon a situation of one accord. This situation is the practice of oneness. In the Old Testament, Psalm 133 says, "Behold, how good and how pleasant it is / For brothers to dwell in unity! / It is like the fine oil upon the head / That ran down upon the beard, / Upon Aaron's beard, / That ran down upon the hem of his garments; / Like the dew of Hermon / That came down upon the mountains of Zion. / For there Jehovah commanded the blessing: / Life forever." God will only grace and bless the one accord, that is, the practice of oneness.

Hence, we have to be on the alert. If we would first consider and think a little before we speak and would ask if it is Christ or not, there would be no problem. If we love the saints, we should ask ourselves if our love has different classes, degrees, or depths, and should be adjusted by the Lord accordingly. The same is true with our speaking. We should only speak if our speaking is Christ; otherwise, we should not speak. I have a heavy burden within me. We all want the church here to receive grace and blessing. But do not forget Psalm 133. The commanded blessing of the Lord, which is life forever, is upon the brothers dwelling together in oneness. It is like the ointment that flows through the whole body and like the dew that descends on Zion. Tonight we have seen that the oneness of the believers prayed for by the Lord is neither a oneness like the world speaks of nor a oneness according to what we formerly understood. Rather, it is a perfected oneness by all of us being in the Father's name and life, in His word of reality, and in His divinely expressed glory. Only by this is there the blessing of God. Of course, we should labor and work for the Lord, but if our situation is not in oneness and if we do not practice the one accord, I am afraid our result will not be abundant. Therefore, in order for us to receive God's blessing, we must practice the oneness, and the way to practice the oneness is by the one accord. (*The Oneness and the One Accord according to the Lord's Aspiration and the Body Life and Service according to His Pleasure,* pp. 18-19)

* * *

Only by our being sanctified can we abide in Christ and can Christ live in us. Again I say, to be sanctified is to move out of ourselves and into the Triune God and to allow Christ to live in us. According to chapters 14 through 17 of John, this is the proper concept of sanctification. The more we are sanctified, the more we are out of ourselves and in the Triune God.

SANCTIFICATION BY THE WORD AND THE SPIRIT

This sanctification takes place by the Word, which is truth, and by the Spirit, which is the Spirit of truth. In these four chapters of John the Word and the Spirit are mentioned again and again. Actually, the Word and the Spirit are one. I thank the Lord that so many of us have come back to the Word and are getting into the Word every day. As we come to the Word every morning, outwardly we touch the Word, but inwardly the Spirit touches us. By the Word and by the Spirit, both of which are the reality, we are sanctified.

To be sanctified is not merely to be separated from the world; it is to move out of ourselves and into the Triune God. If you check with your experience, you will see that the more you touch the Word and the more the Spirit touches you, the more you move out of yourself. You move from one dwelling place, the self, to another dwelling place, the Triune God. Every day we need to make this move. If we do not move out of ourselves, we are wrong; for in the self there is worldliness, ambition, self-exaltation, and opinion. (*Truth Messages,* p. 58)

THE EVIL OF DIVISION

The major symptom of the sickness in the satanic system is division. In the world today there is no oneness. On the contrary, there is division everywhere, among the nations, in the family, in the schools, in business, and in politics. Every society is filled with division. The whole world is ill with the disease of division. This divisiveness is the evil in the world. According to Genesis 11, at Babel division and confusion came in. We see the same on earth today. Every nation and every people are divided. This is the evil in Satan's system.

We need to move out of ourselves and into the Triune God and remain in Him for the expression of the Father's glory. We need to allow this glory to swallow up our self-exaltation so that Christ can live in us. When Christ lives in us, all our concepts will be put to death. Then, instead of evil, we shall have the genuine oneness.

This oneness is what the Lord desires; it is the well-pleasing will of God (Rom. 12:2). It is also the real building. The building is possible only in the Triune God, and it is prevailing only when Christ lives in us. Hallelujah, now we are in the Triune God, and we are allowing Christ to live in us! Now we can express the glory of the Father and experience the genuine oneness. May we all bring this word to the Lord in prayer. (*Truth Messages,* pp. 67, 71-72)

* * *

The oneness revealed in the New Testament is not a oneness where we come together, give up our prejudices, and convince each other to agree to be together. This is a oneness produced by the world. The oneness we are talking about is the full mingling of the Triune God with us. If we do not see this matter to such an extent, I am afraid that the oneness we are talking about is only human-manufactured oneness; it is not the oneness of the Body.

ONENESS NULLIFYING THE NATURAL MAN,
THE WORLD, SATAN, AND THE SELF

This mingling of the Triune God is in you, in me, and in every saint. Moreover, the common and unique life which is in all the millions of believers has mingled us all into one. This is the oneness of the Body. This oneness has nullified all of our old creation and the natural man. This is accomplished by the Father's name and the Father's life. This oneness has also sanctified us from the Satan-ensnared world and has freed us from the world and Satan. This is the effect of the Father's word of reality. Finally, this oneness will deliver us from the self so that there will be only God, and the splendid glory of divinity will be expressed. (*The Oneness and the One Accord according to the Lord's Aspiration and the Body Life and Service according to His Pleasure,* pp. 25-26)

* * *

If we would be under the Lord's commanded blessing of life, we must be on the ground of oneness. Dissenting ones may claim to have the commanded blessing, but actually they do not have it. (*The Genuine Ground of Oneness,* pp. 24-25)

EXPERIENCING TRUE ONENESS
AND PRESERVING IT

The oneness about which we have been speaking is the precious ointment upon Christ the Head and the refreshing dew that descends upon the mountains of Zion. It makes a tremendous difference whether we remain in this oneness or forsake it. Christians today feel free to come and go because they do not see this genuine oneness. They do not have the preserving and keeping element the oneness affords. In His recovery the Lord has shown us that real oneness is the mingling of the processed Triune God with His chosen people. On the one hand, the processed God is the compound, all-inclusive Spirit that anoints us and "paints" us day by day. On the other hand, the processed God is the life supply for our enjoyment. Under this anointing oil and watering dew we experience true oneness. As long as we remain in the experience of the ointment and the dew, it is not possible for us to be divided.

Rather, we are preserved in oneness. This is the meaning of Paul's word in Ephesians 4:3 about endeavoring to keep the oneness of the Spirit. Actually, this oneness is simply the all-inclusive, life-giving Spirit Himself. We guard and preserve this oneness by remaining under the anointing oil and the watering dew. (*The Genuine Ground of Oneness*, p. 96)

TO BUILD UP SUCH A BODY OF CHRIST

Our work must be a work that builds up such a Body of Christ (Eph. 4:12, 16). This will change our idea. This will change our view. If you have such a view, you cannot carry out any piece of work that is not a part of the Body of Christ. (*The Practical Way to Live a Life according to the High Peak of the Divine Revelation in the Holy Scriptures*, p. 63)

THE BUILDING UP OF THE BODY OF CHRIST IS NOT OF HUMAN WORK, NOR IS IT THE FORMING TOGETHER OF A GROUP OF PEOPLE BY MAN'S NATURAL WAY

According to Ephesians chapter 4, the issue of the union of the Spirit of God and the spirit of the believers is the building up of the Body of Christ. This building is not of human work, nor is it a forming together of a group of people by man's natural way. Hence, it has nothing to do with man's work, effort, ways, ideas, moral teachings, philosophy, or any religious system or activities. God's eternal economy is to obtain the Body of Christ. Any work outside of this is not on the central lane of God's eternal economy.

Most of the work in today's Christianity is human work, is natural, and has nothing to do with the building up of the Body of Christ. Some people may say that Christianity also preaches the gospel and saves sinners. However, preaching the gospel and saving sinners are not simple matters; they involve many important matters. Christianity preaches the gospel by human work, human effort, human doing; but Paul preached the gospel by supplying the person being saved by him with the Spirit of God, so that within him he might have God, the life of God, and also Christ. (*The Issue of the Union of*

the Consummated Spirit of the Triune God and the Regener-
ated Spirit of the Believers, p. 49)

* * *

Such a building up of the Body of Christ is formed by
organic growth, not organized by human work. All those who
are not in life, not walking according to the union of the two
spirits, are not in the building up of the Body of Christ. We
need to see this vision clearly. The Body of Christ is absolutely
not built up by using man's natural methods or the organization of human work. The building up of the Body of Christ can
be attained only through the co-living and co-walking of the
Spirit of God with the spirit of man in the believers in their
experience of the co-death and co-resurrection with Christ
and their growing up into the Head, Christ, in all things. The
Body of Christ, which is altogether organic, does not allow
anything of human work. We need to see this vision clearly so
that we can build up the Body of Christ organically. (*The
Issue of the Union of the Consummated Spirit of the Triune
God and the Regenerated Spirit of the Believers,* p. 69)

* * *

We should not have the thought that we can do a particular work according to our way in the recovery. We may be very
gifted and have a large capacity to work out something. But
what we work out may be the same as worldly people carrying
out a certain enterprise. We have to realize that in the Lord's
recovery there is only one work. (*Elders' Training, Book 10:
The Eldership and the God-ordained Way (2),* p. 118)

THE UNIQUE GOAL OF THE CHRISTIAN WORK

According to the entire revelation of the New Testament,
the unique goal of the Christian work should be the New
Jerusalem, which is the ultimate goal of God's eternal economy.

THE MAIN CAUSE OF THE CHURCH'S DEGRADATION

The degradation of the church is mainly due to the fact

that nearly all the Christian workers are distracted to take many things other than the New Jerusalem as their goal.

OVERCOMING EVERYTHING THAT REPLACES THE NEW JERUSALEM AS OUR GOAL

Hence, under the degradation of the church, to be an overcomer answering the Lord's call needs us to overcome not only the negative things but even more the positive things that replace the New Jerusalem as the goal.

AN OVERCOMER'S GOAL

An overcomer's goal should be uniquely and ultimately the goal of God's eternal economy, that is, the New Jerusalem. (*The Vital Groups,* p. 131)

BROTHER LEE'S FELLOWSHIP ON APRIL 6, 1997

The following is Brother Lee's fellowship given on April 6, 1997:

The co-workers must see that we should do only one work, which is to make God's chosen people regenerated ones, sanctified ones, renewed ones—the new man—transformed ones, conformed ones—those conformed to the image of the firstborn Son of God—and glorified ones. All those who will be in the New Jerusalem are this kind of people.

Specifically, God proceeds step by step to make a chosen one of God a person who is regenerated, sanctified, renewed, transformed, conformed to the image of the firstborn Son of God, and even glorified by God. In this way, we go up level by level until we reach the highest point, where we become the same. There is no more flesh and no more natural being. All are in the spirit. All are the kingdom of the heavens, and all are beings of the New Jerusalem. This is the highest point. If you understand this, you can explain it to the brothers and sisters, and you can ask them to speak the same. (*The Ministry,* vol. 1, no. 1, October 1997, p. 49)

ABOUT THE AUTHOR

Witness Lee was born in 1905 in northern China and raised in a Christian family. At age 19 he was fully captured for Christ and immediately consecrated himself to preach the gospel for the rest of his life. Early in his service, he met Watchman Nee, a renowned preacher, teacher, and writer. Witness Lee labored together with Watchman Nee under his direction. In 1934 Watchman Nee entrusted Witness Lee with the responsibility for his publication operation, called the Shanghai Gospel Bookroom.

Prior to the Communist takeover in 1949, Witness Lee was sent by Watchman Nee and his other co-workers to Taiwan to ensure that the things delivered to them by the Lord would not be lost. Watchman Nee instructed Witness Lee to continue the former's publishing operation abroad as the Taiwan Gospel Bookroom, which has been publicly recognized as the publisher of Watchman Nee's works outside China. Witness Lee's work in Taiwan manifested the Lord's abundant blessing. From a mere 350 believers, newly fled from the mainland, the churches in Taiwan grew to 20,000 in five years.

In 1962 Witness Lee felt led of the Lord to come to the United States, settling in California. During his 35 years of service in the U.S., he ministered in weekly meetings and weekend conferences, delivering several thousand spoken messages. Much of his speaking has since been published as over 400 titles. Many of these have been translated into over fourteen languages. He gave his last public conference in February 1997 at the age of 91.

He leaves behind a prolific presentation of the truth in the Bible. His major work, *Life-study of the Bible,* comprises over 25,000 pages of commentary on every book of the Bible from the perspective of the believers' enjoyment and experience of God's divine life in Christ through the Holy Spirit. Witness Lee was the chief editor of a new translation of the New Testament into Chinese called the Recovery Version and directed the translation of the same into English. The Recovery Version also appears in a number of other languages. He provided an extensive body of footnotes, outlines, and spiritual cross references. A radio broadcast of his messages can be heard on Christian radio stations in the United States. In 1965 Witness Lee founded Living Stream Ministry, a non-profit corporation, located in Anaheim, California, which officially presents his and Watchman Nee's ministry.

Witness Lee's ministry emphasizes the experience of Christ as life and the practical oneness of the believers as the Body of Christ. Stressing the importance of attending to both these matters, he led the churches under his care to grow in Christian life and function. He was unbending in his conviction that God's goal is not narrow sectarianism but the Body of Christ. In time, believers began to meet simply as the church in their localities in response to this conviction. In recent years a number of new churches have been raised up in Russia and in many eastern European countries.

OTHER BOOKS PUBLISHED BY
Living Stream Ministry

Titles by Witness Lee:

Abraham—Called by God	978-0-7363-0359-0
The Experience of Life	978-0-87083-417-2
The Knowledge of Life	978-0-87083-419-6
The Tree of Life	978-0-87083-300-7
The Economy of God	978-0-87083-415-8
The Divine Economy	978-0-87083-268-0
God's New Testament Economy	978-0-87083-199-7
The World Situation and God's Move	978-0-87083-092-1
Christ vs. Religion	978-0-87083-010-5
The All-inclusive Christ	978-0-87083-020-4
Gospel Outlines	978-0-87083-039-6
Character	978-0-87083-322-9
The Secret of Experiencing Christ	978-0-87083-227-7
The Life and Way for the Practice of the Church Life	978-0-87083-785-2
The Basic Revelation in the Holy Scriptures	978-0-87083-105-8
The Crucial Revelation of Life in the Scriptures	978-0-87083-372-4
The Spirit with Our Spirit	978-0-87083-798-2
Christ as the Reality	978-0-87083-047-1
The Central Line of the Divine Revelation	978-0-87083-960-3
The Full Knowledge of the Word of God	978-0-87083-289-5
Watchman Nee—A Seer of the Divine Revelation ...	978-0-87083-625-1

Titles by Watchman Nee:

How to Study the Bible	978-0-7363-0407-8
God's Overcomers	978-0-7363-0433-7
The New Covenant	978-0-7363-0088-9
The Spiritual Man • 3 volumes	978-0-7363-0269-2
Authority and Submission	978-0-7363-0185-5
The Overcoming Life	978-1-57593-817-2
The Glorious Church	978-0-87083-745-6
The Prayer Ministry of the Church	978-0-87083-860-6
The Breaking of the Outer Man and the Release ...	978-1-57593-955-1
The Mystery of Christ	978-1-57593-954-4
The God of Abraham, Isaac, and Jacob	978-0-87083-932-0
The Song of Songs	978-0-87083-872-9
The Gospel of God • 2 volumes	978-1-57593-953-7
The Normal Christian Church Life	978-0-87083-027-3
The Character of the Lord's Worker	978-1-57593-322-1
The Normal Christian Faith	978-0-87083-748-7
Watchman Nee's Testimony	978-0-87083-051-8

Available at
Christian bookstores, or contact Living Stream Ministry
2431 W. La Palma Ave. • Anaheim, CA 92801
1-800-549-5164 • www.livingstream.com